THE SHADOW OF
CHRIST
IN THE LAW OF
MOSES

THE SHADOW OF
CHRIST
IN THE LAW OF
MOSES

VERN S. POYTHRESS

P&R
PUBLISHING
P.O. BOX 817 • PHILLIPSBURG • NEW JERSEY 08865

Unless otherwise indicated, Scripture quotations are from the HOLY BIBLE, NEW INTERNATIONAL VERSION. Copyright © 1973, 1978, 1984 International Bible Society. Used by permission of Zondervan Bible Publishers.

Printed in the United States of America

Library of Congress Cataloging-in-Publication Data

Poythress, Vern S.
    The shadow of Christ in the law of Moses / Vern Sheridan Poythress.
        p.   cm.
    Originally published: Brentwood, Tenn. : Wolgemuth & Hyatt, c1991.
    Includes bibliographical references and index.
    ISBN 0-87552-375-7 (trade pbk.)
    1. Typology (Theology) 2. Law (Theology)—Biblical teaching. 3. Jewish law.
I. Title.
[BS478.P69 1995]
221.6'4—dc20   95-11897

This book is dedicated to the Jews

and

to my children, Ransom and Justin,
to whom God has given through Moses a
most wonderful story in pictures.

CONTENTS

Part II: Understanding Specific Penalties of the Law

PREFACE

To Jews who read my book I would like to give a special message: I love you. Through your ancestors and through your people I received the most beautiful book in the world, the Bible. Through that book I came to know the true God, the God of your ancestors Abraham, Isaac, and Jacob. I am one of those people who believe that Jesus is the Messiah who was promised in the Torah and the Prophets. Through Jesus I have come to know about the Torah that God gave to Moses and to submit to it. I am deeply sorry for the harm that has come to your people through Christians who thought that they were serving Jesus. I am convinced that they were doing the very opposite of what He commanded.

In this book I tell part of my story. Doubtless you will not agree with some of the things that I say. I am sorry if anything offends you; I do not intend it. I would kindly ask you to keep reading. I think that you will find a good deal of interest to you, because I am writing about the most precious heritage of the Jews, the Torah. I am writing primarily to those who accept the New Testament as part of God's word, and so I sometimes appeal to portions of the New Testament. Nevertheless, the essential parts of my argument do not depend on the New Testament but only on the Old Testament, the Bible of the Jews. It will help if you keep in mind that the Bible of the Jews contains many promises looking forward to a great future time of salvation for Israel (see Isaiah 9:6–7; 11:1–16; Ezekiel 34:17–31; 36:1–38; Isaiah 40–66). At that time the Messiah, the Son of David, will come, and the majesty and glory of God will be openly revealed (Isaiah 40:5; Habakkuk 2:14; Zechariah

14:9). The law and the prophets were never intended to be the whole of God's communication to the world, but only the first half of it. If I am right in thinking that the New Testament completes the story that God began in the Old Testament, it is quite proper for me to look back now in the light of the full story and see what more I can learn from its first half. If you do not accept my view of the New Testament, you must still ask yourself what that first half points forward to.

My thanks are due to my friends Edmund P. Clowney, John M. Frame, Richard B. Gaffin, Jr., Meredith G. Kline, Greg L. Bahnsen, James B. Jordan, Steven M. Schlei, and Gary North for helping me to love God's law. I would like to indicate also my appreciation for the late Geerhardus Vos and for Rousas J. Rushdoony, whom I have not met personally, but who introduced some of the ideas that led to the present discussion. My apologies are extended to all these men for any way in which I may have underestimated the insights of their positions in the past or even in the present book. The more I have worked on these issues, the more I have appreciated their depth. I have not always found it easy to interpret what people are saying on these issues within the context in which they intended it and above all in the context of the unsearchable divine wisdom of God's word.

PART ONE

UNDERSTANDING THE DIFFERENT ASPECTS OF THE LAW

ONE

THE CHALLENGE
OF THE LAW OF MOSES:
INTERPRETING MOSES
IN THE LIGHT OF CHRIST

W hen I was a teenager, an older Christian woman learned that I had read the entire Bible during the preceding year. She came up to me and asked, "How did you get through the Book of Leviticus?" I didn't really know what to say to her in return. I knew what she meant. Parts of the Old Testament were difficult for me too. Somehow the Lord had given me sufficient motivation and interest to read the whole Bible. But how was I to help her? And how could I learn to appreciate the difficult parts better myself? What were she and I supposed to be learning from Leviticus, Numbers, and Deuteronomy?

I did not learn the answer until years later. The answer came to me through another story, not the story of my life, but the story of two other people with struggles like my own.

The Challenge of the Old Testament

Long ago in Palestine two disciples of Jesus were walking along the road from Jerusalem to Emmaus (Luke 24:13–35). A stranger joined them. He asked them about the things they had been through, and they began to explain. They were heartbroken because the master and friend in whom they had put all their hopes was dead. But the stranger said some strange things to comfort them. Instead of sympathizing, He said, "How foolish you are, and how slow of heart to believe all that the prophets have spoken!" (Luke 24:25). The disciples' real problem was not with a dead master but with themselves. They did not understand the Old Testament. And so the stranger helped them to understand. "Beginning with Moses and all the Prophets, he explained to them what was said in all the Scriptures concerning himself" (Luke 24:27). The stranger, of course, was Jesus Christ, the master Teacher of the Old Testament. What did Jesus tell those two disciples? We do not know the details. But we do know the heart of His teaching: "Did not the Christ have to suffer these things and then enter his glory?" (Luke 24:26).

Even before Jesus was finished, and even before He revealed who He was, a remarkable transformation began to take place in the hearts of the disciples. They said, "Were not our hearts burning within us while he talked to us on the road and opened the Scriptures to us?" (Luke 24:32). The Old Testament Scriptures began to open up to them, and they were awed, amazed, and overwhelmed all at once.

Later on Jesus appeared to a larger group of His disciples. He continued teaching along the same line:

> Then he opened their minds so they could understand the Scriptures. He told them, "This is what is written: The Christ will suffer and rise from the dead on the third day, and repentance and forgiveness of sins will be preached in his name to all nations, beginning at Jerusalem. You are witnesses of these things. I am going to send you what my Father has promised; but stay in the city until you have been clothed with power from on high." (Luke 24:45–49)

Christ enabled the disciples to understand not merely the implications of a few passages of the Old Testament, but "the Scriptures"—the whole Old Testament. What do these Scriptures really say? Christ introduces His explanation with the words, "This is what is written" (Luke 24:46). That is, He promises to give them the substance and heart of what is written in the Old Testament. What He says next contains His answer: "The Christ will suffer and rise from the dead on the third day, and repentance and forgiveness of sins will be preached in his name to all nations, beginning at Jerusalem" (Luke 24:46–47).[1]

The whole Old Testament finds its focus in Jesus Christ, His death, and His resurrection. The Apostle Paul says the same thing in different words: "For no matter how many promises God has made, they are 'Yes' in Christ. And so through him the 'Amen' is spoken by us to the glory of God" (2 Corinthians 1:20). "These things [in the Old Testament] happened to them as examples and were written down as warnings for us, on whom the fulfillment of the ages has come" (1 Corinthians 10:11). Jesus says, "Do not think that I have come to abolish the Law or the Prophets; I have not come to abolish them but to fulfill them. I tell you the truth, until heaven and earth disappear, not the smallest letter, not the least stroke of a pen, will by any means disappear from the Law until everything is accomplished" (Matthew 5:17–18).

Basic Principles for Interpreting the Old Testament

A great heritage awaits us in the Old Testament. But how do we unlock it? Christ Himself is the key that unlocks the riches of the Old Testament. Let us see how.

First of all, Christ is the all-glorious Lord, the only Son of the Father, who from all eternity beholds the Father face to face, who is with God and who is God (John 1:1). Every word of the Old Testament is the word of God Himself (2 Timothy 3:16–17), and God is the trinitarian God—Father, Son, and Holy Spirit. Thus all of the Old Testament is Christ's word to us, as well as God the Father's word to us.

Second, the Old Testament teaches us about Christ. Such is one main implication of the story in Luke 24. Christ is the focus of the message of the Old Testament. He is the One to whom it points forward, about whom it speaks, and whom it prefigures in symbols.

Third, Christ not only instructs us but establishes communion with us through His word. We abide in Christ as His word abides in us (John 15:7). As the Holy Spirit works in our hearts, we find that we are meeting Christ, and He talks to us very personally through the Bible, including the Old Testament.

Fourth, Christ changes us and transforms us through His word. As we meet with Christ and experience His glory, we are transformed into His image. The Bible says that we start out with a lack of understanding of the Old Testament, due to hard hearts (Luke 24:25; 2 Corinthians 4:4). This lack is like a veil over our hearts, keeping us from seeing it correctly (2 Corinthians 3:14–15). When we turn to the Lord, the Holy Spirit works in us and the veil over our hearts is removed (2 Corinthians 3:16–17). Then we see the true glory of Christ. "And we, who with unveiled faces all reflect the Lord's glory, are being transformed into his likeness with ever-increasing glory, which comes from the Lord, who is the Spirit" (2 Corinthians 3:18).

Fifth, as our hearts are changed we begin to respond to Christ in adoration, thankfulness, and obedience. Christ is our Lord, our master, and that means that we must obey Him. But Christ is also our beloved, and that means that we come to love to please Him and obey Him (John 14:15, 23). Our response ought not to be a reluctant, grumbling obedience, but joyful, enthusiastic obedience. And so it will be more and more, if we belong to Him and have fellowship with Him, because Christ writes His own law on our hearts (2 Corinthians 3:3, 6; Hebrews 10:16).

Thus when we read the Old Testament we should pray that Christ will both enlighten us and transform us. Because the Old Testament as well as the New is Christ's word, we should believe what God teaches there, obey what He commands, and give thanks for the blessings and communion that He gives. Above all, we should endeavor to search out how the Old Testament speaks of Christ.

We need to keep in mind two final key elements: humility and love. We are beset by sin and our understanding will be imperfect as long as we are in this life (1 Corinthians 13:12). We must be humble enough not to overestimate our abilities. We must realize that God's thoughts are above our thoughts (Isaiah 55:9), and that we will never come to the bottom of their unsearchable depths (Romans 11:33–36). In Christ "are hidden all the treasures of wisdom and knowledge" (Colossians 2:3). We should come to Christ for all enlightenment. But when we do so, we also acknowledge "how wide and long and high and deep is the love of Christ" (Ephesians 3:18). Paul prays for us "to know this love that surpasses knowledge—that you may be filled to the measure of all the fullness of God" (Ephesians 3:19). Truly Christ's love surpasses knowledge, and we adore Him in awe rather than come to a complete mastery of what we study.

Because of our limitations we must also be deeply grateful for insights that God provides through other human beings who study the Bible. When we differ with others in our understanding of Scripture, we must be willing to defend its precious central truths, but we must also be willing to listen to others in love (Ephesians 4:12–16). We may not always be right, and even when we are right, we may have something to learn from other people who have seen some other aspect of the infinite depth of God's truth.

In particular, we must be ready to learn something from the Israelites of long ago. God did not begin to exercise His wisdom or care with us today. He started long ago, even at creation. Through many generations He dealt patiently with people in circumstances very different from ours, and He proved Himself faithful. Again and again He spoke to them about Christ in symbols and shadows that were appropriate to them and their circumstances rather than immediately to our circumstances. That is why the Old Testament is so remarkably unlike the New Testament in some ways. Yet because the same God and the same Christ are proclaimed in both, they are also remarkably alike in their overall thrust.

If we have humility about ourselves and enough love to look beyond ourselves to other people's situations, we can begin to appreciate how God dealt with the Israelites in the Old Testament, and how things looked from their point of view. Then we gain understanding of what God really said in the Old Testament, as opposed to ideas that we might fancifully impose on the Old Testament out of our own imaginations.

Thus we have a threefold task. First, we must try to understand the law of Moses on its own terms, within its own historical environment. God intended it to be heard and understood by Israelites who had recently been redeemed from Egypt. Second, we must try to understand how the New Testament completes God's story and God's word that He began to speak in the Old Testament. Third, we must obey and apply God's word to ourselves and our own circumstances. Often Biblical scholars stop with the first step. But it is legitimate to read the first part of the story again in the light of the end. By doing so we may understand more clearly how the beginning already introduced the teachings and the tensions that are completed and resolved at the end. Jesus Christ Himself is the center of New Testament revelation. Since the New Testament completes the story begun in the Old, Christ is also the center about which the Old Testament begins to speak in its preliminary way, and to which the Old Testament points forward.

In addition, it is spiritually vital for us to obey and apply God's word. Jesus Christ is still our Lord today, and we acknowledge Him as Lord not only by receiving His blessings with thanksgiving but by wholeheartedly obeying Him.[2]

So let us take a journey, back, back, in time and space to the Near East, to the days when Moses led the people of Israel out of Egypt and taught them in the wilderness. These people were like all people in their hearts, but some of their experiences were very different from our own. They lived in tents. They herded cattle and sheep. They lived in the open air a lot. The sun, the moon, the stars, the clouds, the trees, and the land were their companions. Above all, they had experienced a miraculous visit from God Himself, who had brought them out of miserable bondage and slavery in Egypt through their deliverer, Moses. Let us go back and hear what God said to them.

TWO

THE TABERNACLE OF MOSES: PREFIGURING GOD'S PRESENCE THROUGH CHRIST

N ear Lancaster, Pennsylvania, the Mennonites own and maintain a strange-looking building. It is a full-scale replica of the tabernacle of God, a special tent-like building described in Exodus 25–30. God commanded the Israelites to make just such a building as His dwelling place among them. The modern Mennonite replica also has within it a mannequin wearing robes like the garments of the high priest of Israel. People come to tour the Mennonites' building, and as they do so, tour guides explain the significance of the various furnishings. People who have read the Bible and go on the tour almost always come away excited. They say, "I never understood those Old Testament passages about the tabernacle and the priests. But now that I have seen how it all fits together, and now that I have had some things explained to me, I want to go back to read the passages in the Bible and see how they symbolize who Christ was and what He did."

I wish that I could take all my readers on that tour. The Israelites long ago did not have to visualize the tabernacle; they could see it. The priests were allowed to enter the rooms at certain times and could explain to everyone else what was there. The people could watch the priests sacrifice the animals. Messages came home to the Israelites that tend to pass us by unless we make a conscious effort to understand. But we also have an advantage over them. We can read the New Testament and see the completion of what those Old Testament images pointed forward to.

The Tabernacle as a Symbol of the Messiah

The Old Testament tabernacle is full of meaning because it is a symbol of the Messiah and His salvation. The book of Hebrews gives much instruction concerning the tabernacle.

> But only the high priest entered the inner room [of the tabernacle], and that only once a year, and never without blood, which he offered for himself and for the sins the people had committed in ignorance. The Holy Spirit was showing by this that the way into the Most Holy Place had not yet been disclosed as long as the first tabernacle was still standing. This is an illustration for the present time, indicating that the gifts and sacrifices being offered were not able to clear the conscience of the worshiper. They are only a matter of food and drink and various ceremonial washings—external regulations applying until the time of the new order.
>
> When Christ came as high priest of the good things that are already here, he went through the greater and more perfect tabernacle that is not man-made, that is to say, not a part of this creation. He did not enter by means of the blood of goats and calves; but he entered the Most Holy Place once for all by his own blood, having obtained eternal redemption. The blood of goats and bulls and the ashes of a heifer sprinkled on those who are ceremonially unclean sanctify them so that they are outwardly clean. How much more, then, will the blood of Christ, who through the eternal Spirit offered himself unblemished to God, cleanse our consciences from acts that lead to death, so that we may serve the living God! (Hebrews 9:7–14)

The earthly tabernacle was a copy or a shadow of the true dwelling place of God in heaven (Hebrews 8:5; 9:24). It showed what God was like and what was needed to deal with sin. In this way it symbolized what the Messiah was to do for our salvation. We may say that it "foreshadowed" the Messiah and His work. It was like a shadow of the Messiah cast backward in time into the Old Testament period. The shadow was always inferior to the reality. The earthly tabernacle was made of earthly things, and could never equal the splendor or holiness of God in heaven. The earthly sacrifices of bulls and goats could never equal the blood of Christ, who cleansed us from sin forever. The shadow was not itself the reality, but a pointer to Christ who was the reality. Yet the shadow was also like the reality. And the shadow even brought the reality to bear on people in the Old Testament. As they looked ahead through the shadows, longing for something better, they took hold on the promises of God that He would send the Messiah. The promises were given not only verbally but symbolically, through the very organization of the tabernacle and its sacrifices. In pictorial form God was saying, as it were, "Look at My provisions for you. This is how I redeem you and bring you to My presence. But look again, and you will see that it is all an earthly symbol of something better. Do not rely on it as if it were the end. Trust Me to save you fully when I fully accomplish My plans."

Israelites had genuine communion with God when they responded to what He was saying in the tabernacle. They trusted in the Messiah, without knowing all the details of how fulfillment would finally come. And so they were saved, and they received forgiveness, even before the Messiah came. The animal sacrifices in themselves did not bring forgiveness (Hebrews 10:1–4), but Christ did as He met with them through the symbolism of the sacrifices.

The Tabernacle
As a Symbol of God's Dwelling with Israel

What did Israelites see when they looked at the tabernacle so long ago? They saw a tent with two inner rooms and a yard outside. In the yard was the Israelite equivalent of a stove, namely, a place where meat could be roasted on a fire.

A tent means very little to us, but Israelites knew all about tents because they were living in tents themselves. Then God told them to make a tent for Him, a tent where God Himself would dwell and meet with them (Exodus 25:8, 22). His tent had rooms and a yard and a fireplace like their own. Yet it was also unlike their own. It was majestic, covered with gold and blue. It was beautiful, because of the symmetry of its dimensions and the artistry of its construction. Do you see?

God was saying that He was majestic and beautiful. But He would not simply remain in heaven and let Israel go its way. He would come right down among them. They were living in tents. He too would be in a tent, side by side with their own tents. They were going to the promised land. He too would travel to the promised land, as His tent was packed up by the Levites and moved to the next encampment. The special cloud of fire symbolizing God's presence was a more intensive, miraculous form of the same reality. God would be among them, right with them, "Immanuel" (see Matthew 1:23). A bright cloud of glory symbolizing God's presence accompanied the Israelites and came over the tabernacle after it was constructed (Exodus 40:34–38; Numbers 9:15–23).

The theme that God dwells with His people was fulfilled with the coming of Jesus Christ. In fact, the tabernacle foreshadowed the fact that Christ would become incarnate and dwell among us. "The Word became flesh and lived for a while [tabernacled] among us. We have seen his glory, the glory of the one and only Son, who came from the Father, full of grace and truth" (John 1:14). Christ's glory superseded the bright cloud of glory. Now Christ sends His Holy Spirit like a cloud of fire to make His church and His people into a tabernacle of God (Acts 2:2–4; 1 Corinthians 3:10–17; 6:19).

The tabernacle expresses another side to the character of God, namely, that He is holy and inaccessible. The altar, several coverings, and two sets of curtains bar the way into His presence. No one can enter into the inner room (the Most Holy Place) except the high priest, and even then he does so only once a year in a special ceremony, during which he is protected from his sin and from the accusation of the law by the blood that he sprinkles on the mercy seat (Leviticus 16). Death is threatened to transgressors of God's holiness (Exodus 19:12–13, 21–25). Even the priests may suffer death if they do not honor God (Numbers 10:1–2; Leviticus 22:9; 16:2; Exodus 30:21). They are especially in danger of death as they approach the inner rooms of the tabernacle. The high priest must take special care not even to see the atonement cover when he performs his actions in the Most Holy Place (Leviticus 16:13).

By these means the Lord shows the preciousness of the love between the Father and the Son. The tabernacle symbolism points to Christ. Defilement of this symbolism constitutes an attack on Christ, and so rouses God's indignation in intense form. The same truths also embody a lesson concerning Christ's sacrificial death. God's holiness is so great that faults against Him deserve death. Christ Himself was perfectly holy. But when He bore our sins and "became sin for us" (2 Corinthians 5:21), the Father had to put Him to death. To this death He consented willingly, and went like a sheep to slaughter, because of His love for us and His hatred of sin's rule over us (1 Peter 2:24; John 10:18).

Christ had to die. There was no other way by which we might enter into the true tabernacle in heaven and enjoy the blessing of God's presence forever. But now, because Christ has died, the animal sacrifices are ended, and we have access to God with freedom (Romans 5:1-2). The veil barring the way to God's presence is taken away, or rather fulfilled in the body of Christ. Christ does not bar us out, as the veil did, but provides the way in. "We have confidence to enter the Most Holy Place by the blood of Jesus, by a new and living way opened for us through the curtain, that is, his body" (Hebrews 10:19-20). The veil has become the gate into the security of the sheepfold (John 10:7-9).

For those outside of Christ, the death penalty for violations of God's holiness says something else. When Christ returns to judge the world, God's holiness will appear in intense form. Just as at Mount Sinai the mount was covered with the glory of God's holiness, so at the Second Coming the world as a whole will be covered with His glory (2 Thessalonians 1:7-10). The wicked must experience eternal death, because they are violators of the holiness of Christ. God's love for Christ also implies His hatred for Christ's enemies and His zeal to vindicate Christ's honor. "Those who honor me I will honor" (1 Samuel 2:30) is true also at the last day. When Christ receives the full honor due to Him (Philippians 2:10-11), all rebellion is utterly crushed.

The Tabernacle as a Symbol of Heaven

What happened to the tabernacle? After the years in the wilderness, the Israelites entered the Promised Land and settled down. Instead of living in tents, they built houses for themselves. Fittingly, King Solomon was commissioned by God to build a permanent house for God, the temple, which replaced the mobile tent-like tabernacle. The temple had the same basic arrangements as the tabernacle, two rooms and an outside yard, but each of the horizontal dimensions was doubled.

What does Solomon foreshadow? Why, the work of Christ, of course. Solomon was the son in David's line, the line leading to the Messiah. He built a dwelling place for God, foreshadowing Christ who builds His church (Matthew 16:18) and who is Himself the chief cornerstone (Ephesians 2:20) or foundation (1 Corinthians 3:11). Christ builds not on the earthly Mount Zion but on a heavenly site: "But you [Christians] have come to Mount Zion, to the heavenly Jerusalem, the city of the living God" (Hebrews 12:22).

Solomon himself recognized that the true dwelling of God is in heaven. As he dedicated the temple he spoke of the earthly temple as a place where God had put His name (1 Kings 8:29). Heaven is the true dwelling place of God (1 Kings 8:30, 43) and the place from which God hears. Thus Solomon recognized what we have learned from Hebrews, that the tabernacle and temple were shadows of heavenly things.

God dwells in a special sense in heaven. Of course in the broadest sense, as Solomon reminds us, "The heavens, even the highest heaven, cannot contain you" (1 Kings 8:27). Yet in a particular way the visible sky represents God's own majesty and inaccessibility. Even more inaccessible than the visible sky is God's special throne room as we find it described by prophets like Isaiah (Isaiah 6:1–13), Daniel (Daniel 7:9–10), and John (Revelation 4:1–5:14). From God's throne angels issue to perform His commands.

When God came down in a cloud at Mount Sinai, the cloud symbolized both God's heavenly character and His inaccessibility to human eye. Moses went up to meet God, foreshadowing Jesus' function as a mediator between God and man. On the mount Moses received a pattern for the tabernacle. What else would it be than a heavenly pattern, since he received it by symbolically going up to heaven? Thus the book of Hebrews appeals to the fact that God instructed Moses to "make everything according to the pattern shown you on the mountain" (Hebrews 8:5).

When we look at the tabernacle again, we see unmistakable signs of symbolism of heaven. The two cherubim by the ark are replicas of angelic heavenly beings guarding the throne of God (cf., Ezekiel 1; Genesis 3:24). More figures of cherubim are woven into the veil that guards the way into the Most Holy Place (Exodus 26:31). Still more cherubim are woven into the ten curtains that constitute the main material of the tent, enclosing the two rooms (Exodus 26:1). The curtains are woven with blue, symbolizing the royal blue of heaven. The Ten Commandments are the very words of God, heavenly words in the fullest sense. They are written on tablets that Moses received from the mount, that is, from a symbolic replica of heaven. They are placed in the ark of the testimony (Exodus 25:21), the most holy object in the entire tent. The ark itself is a box with the approximate shape of an ancient king's footstool.[1] Thus the ark represents part of God's throne room in heaven. Fittingly, the space above the ark is empty, because God may not be seen and no images of Him are permitted (Exodus 33:20; 20:4–5; Deuteronomy 4:15–19). Thus the tabernacle as a whole is a replica of heaven. When God comes to dwell with the Israelites, He brings down to them in His wonderful condescension a little replica of heaven.

Let us look at the arrangements in greater detail (see figure 1). The tabernacle has two rooms. The inner room, measuring 10 cubits by 10 cubits by 10 cubits high (about 15 feet on a side), is called the Most Holy Place. The outer room, measuring 10 cubits by 20 cubits by 10 cubits high, is called the Holy Place. The two rooms are separated from one another by the special curtain or veil barring the way, the curtain to which Hebrews refers (Hebrews 10:20). Another curtain made of similar material separates the Holy Place from the yard outside ("the courtyard"). The courtyard measures 50 cubits by 100 cubits. If one takes into account the curtains forming the fence around the courtyard, which are 5 cubits high, the total dimensions are 50 by 100 by 5 (Exodus 27:9–19). The dimensions clearly become less perfect as one moves outward. The inner room is a perfect cube. The outer room is not, but deviates from perfection simply by multiplying one dimension by two. The courtyard is still less perfect, inasmuch as all three dimensions are different. But the dimensions still have simple ratios to one another, expressing a kind of limited balance and perfection. Thus each of the three areas is a kind of lesser image of the preceding one.

As a priest proceeded inward, he came first to the courtyard. Then he crossed the courtyard to the altar of burnt offering in the middle of it. Then he came to a "laver" or washing basin, then to the first curtain, then to the Holy Place. In the middle of the Holy Place were a lampstand on one side and a table with bread on the other. At the far end of the Holy Place the priest came to an altar of incense, then to the second curtain, and finally to the Most Holy Place with its ark (a gold covered box), the cherubim, and the special cover for the ark called the "mercy seat" or atonement cover. Inside the ark were the tablets of the law (Exodus 25:21).

All these aspects of the tabernacle may be expected to say something to Israel about the meaning of communion with God and dwelling with God. They picture the nature of God's dwelling and the manner in which He is approached. But before we enter into any detail, let us try to understand the overall structure. The inner and outer rooms are both covered with blue curtains and interwoven cherubim, signifying heaven. All the furnishings in the rooms are covered with gold, signifying the royal splendor of heaven. Outside in the courtyard, the altar is made of bronze, a less expensive metal, and common Israelite worshipers may enter. The courtyard is much more earthy in character. The relations between the two would doubtless suggest to Israelites their own earthiness in contrast with God's heavenly character. Israelites are on earth and God is in heaven. God's throne in heaven is, as it were, concealed by clouds and the visible sky, which correspond to the curtains barring the way into the two rooms.

Why are there two rooms rather than one? Doubtless two rooms are needed to show some of the variety of aspects belonging to communion with God. The use of two rooms also emphasizes the remoteness of God's presence, since there is more than one layer separating the Israelites from the inner room. The imagery of heaven suggests something more, namely, that the outer room corresponds more directly to the visible heavens, with sun, moon, stars, and clouds, while the inner room corresponds more directly to the very throne room of God Himself, which is distinct from the visible sky.

The same Hebrew and Greek words are used for "heaven" in both of these senses. No special distinct terminology is needed, because Biblical writers were not making scientific astronomical distinctions but

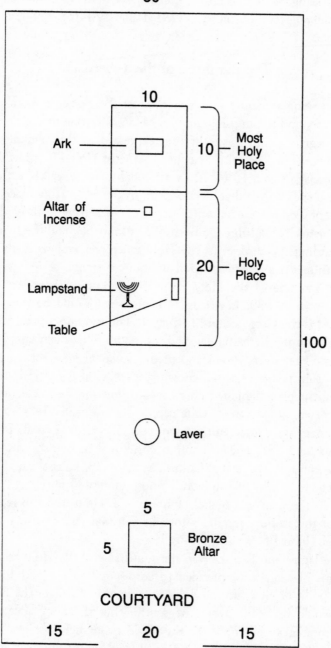

Figure 1: Physical Arrangement of the Tabernacle

were dwelling on the fact that the majesty and inaccessibility of the visible sky reflects the majesty of God (Psalm 19:1–6).

The Furniture of the Tabernacle

Thus, in some ways the visible heaven of the sky corresponds to the Holy Place, and the invisible heaven of God's throne to the Most Holy Place. Degrees of inaccessibility are expressed in this symbolism. Degrees of perfection are also evident. The Most Holy Place has the perfect dimensions of a 10 by 10 by 10 cube, as we saw, while the Holy Place and the courtyard are less perfect. In the Most Holy Place are the symbols of God's immediate presence: the law setting forth God's standards, the ark symbolizing God's throne or footstool, and the two cherubim guarding the throne. In the Holy Place are symbols easily associated with mediation between God and human beings.

On one side of the Holy Place the lampstand provides light all night (Exodus 27:30; Leviticus 24:1–4). Israel would be reminded of how God is the Creator and Light-giver. The sun, moon, and stars provide light during both the day and the night. The seven lamps on the lampstand may even correspond to the seven major lights of heaven, namely, sun, moon, and five known planets. God is not only the Creator who supplies light by natural means, but the Redeemer who supplied redeeming light to lead the people out of Egypt. The cloud of fire guided them and protected them from the Egyptians (Exodus 14:19–20; Numbers 9:15–23). This symbolism is fulfilled in Christ, who is both our Creator and Redeemer (Colossians 1:15–20). Christ was the original uncreated Light of the world, whose glory and purity is dimly reflected in the heavenly bodies (John 1:3–5). He is also the redeeming Light of the world: He comes into its spiritual darkness to make the blind see (John 1:5, 9; 8:12; 9:3–6).

The lampstand is placed on the south side of the Holy Place. Perhaps this placement is intended to correspond to the fact that from Israel's point of view, north of the equator, the circuit of the heavenly lights would be primarily to the south. That there are seven of the lamps correlates not only with the seven major lights of heaven, as I have mentioned, but with the general symbolism for time within Israel.

The heavenly bodies were made in order to "serve as signs to mark seasons and days and years" (Genesis 1:14). The whole cycle of time marked by the sun and moon and stars is divided up into sevens: the seventh day in the week is the Sabbath day; the seventh month is the month of atonement (Leviticus 16:29); the seventh year is the year of release from debts and slavery (Deuteronomy 15); the seventh of the seven-year cycles is the year of jubilee (Leviticus 25). Fittingly, the lampstand contains the same sevenfold division, symbolizing the cycle of time provided by the heavenly lights.

The lampstand is also in the shape of a tree, with branches, buds, blossom, and almond flowers (Exodus 25:31–39). What message is conveyed by this shape? Once more it is a message about time, the familiar cycle of growth of plants, springtime, summer, and harvest. Indeed elsewhere in Scripture the almond is a symbol of a time of watching or waiting (Jeremiah 1:11–12), because of a play on the Hebrew word for almond. "Almond," shāqēd, is related to the Hebrew word for "watch," shāqad. If we follow this symbolism through, we see that the lamps themselves symbolize the fruit of the tree. This strange tree has buds, blossoms, almond flowers, and fruit all at once, because it must be a static picture of the whole cycle of time that God has created and sustains. The tree symbolizes the growth of life. It issues new light in the form of fruit that in turn will give birth to new trees. The tree is truly both a tree of light and a tree of life. The reproductive living power of the tree is in its fruit, that is, the light, which shines on the earth and sustains its growth. As John says of Jesus, "Through him all things were made; without him nothing was made that has been made. In him was life, and that life was the light of men" (John 1:3–4).

In addition, the tree reminds us of the Garden of Eden with its original tree of life. But now the true life of creation has been lost through sin. It is restored through God coming to be "God with us." The tabernacle is a renewed version of the Garden of Eden. But curtains with cherubim on them still bar the way into God's presence, just as cherubim barred the way into the original Garden of Eden after the Fall (Genesis 3:24).

On the other side of the Holy Place is the table with "the bread of the Presence" on it (Exodus 25:23–30). The "Presence" spoken of is clearly the presence of God. In the ancient Near East sharing a special meal together was an act of friendship and personal communion (see Genesis 18:1–8; Exodus 24:9–11). The host undertook solemn responsibility to serve and protect his guest while they enjoyed the meal. Thus God invites Israel to share a meal with Him and enjoy His protection. But only the priests can eat the special holy food (Leviticus 22:10–16), and the restriction to the priests signifies the special restrictions on fellowship, due to God's holiness. In this way God symbolizes His provision of food to the Israelites.

The Israelites had a common experience to which to relate this symbolism. Day after day they ate manna, the "bread from heaven" (Exodus 16:4), miraculously provided by God. The Israelites complained about its taste (Numbers 11:6), but actually it was sweet tasting (Exodus 16:31), reminding them of the sweet goodness of God the Provider (cf., Psalm 19:10). It came with the dew and looked like frost (Exodus 16:14), reminding them of the fact that God provides rain and dew to water crops, which in turn provide food. It looked like coriander seed (Exodus 16:31), again reminding them of the association with crops. Thus God by His supernatural provision indirectly pointed to the fact that He provides food to us every day by natural means (Matthew 6:11). He is the Creator and Sustainer of agriculture. The descent of rain from heaven is a continual reminder of His provision. Once the people entered the land of promise, the bread of the Presence itself would have been made from grain growing in the Promised Land.

Thus the bread of the Presence was a continual pointer to the fact that God provides food to human beings every day through the processes of reproduction, growth, and harvesting. But in addition, God provided to His people, Israel, the manna, a special supernatural food, redemptive food, food from heaven, when He brought the people from bondage into the Promised Land (Exodus 16:32). A portion of manna was permanently kept in the Most Holy Place to signify its holy character and to encourage the Israelites to remember its lessons (Exodus 16:32–35).

When Jesus came, He fulfilled this symbolism. Not only did He supernaturally provide a meal for five thousand people (John 6:1–13), but explained its significance: "I tell you the truth, it is not Moses who has given you the bread from heaven, but it is my Father who gives you the true bread from heaven. For the bread of God is he who comes down from heaven and gives life to the world. . . . I am the bread of life. He who comes to me will never go hungry, and he who believes in me will never be thirsty" (John 6:32–33, 35).

The details of the bread of the Presence may also be significant. The table has the same rectangular shape as the Holy Place and as the courtyard, twice as long as it is wide. This proportionality suggests that it is a little replica of the larger land. The twelve loaves correspond to the twelve months, the cycle of seedtime and harvest by which God provides foods. The twelve tribes of Israel come to share in the inheritance when they enter the Promised Land and receive plots of the land themselves. Fittingly, the manna stops coming when they enter the land and eat its fruit (Joshua 5:10–12). But remember that the table is in the Holy Place, a representation of heaven. It therefore stands for the heavenly origin of food. It represents the patterns of the seasons and of the heavenly lights, which are then replicated in the shape of the courtyard representing the earth. The land of Palestine is in turn a replica of the courtyard. When Jesus says that He is the bread of life, He shows that He is the heavenly original of which these things are copies, both in creation and in redemption.

One more item stands in the Holy Place, namely, the altar of incense (Exodus 30:1–10). The altar of incense was a special small altar covered with gold that was placed at the far end of the Holy Place, just in front of the curtain leading to the Most Holy Place. Unlike the bronze altar outside in the courtyard, it burned no animal sacrifices, but only incense (Exodus 30:8–9). It was "most holy," and in this respect logically belonged with the Most Holy Place (Hebrews 9:4), even though it stood physically outside the curtain.

The outstanding function of the altar was to burn sweet smelling incense. The smoke and fragrance from the incense would have filled the entire tabernacle, both inner and outer rooms. What picture does this process present to Israelites? For one thing, it would have suggested the lavish and thoughtful hospitality of a host. The life of the average Israelite was accompanied by the strong and not-always-pleasant smells associated with animals and physical labor. The fragrance of burning incense was used by hosts to add to the pleasant atmosphere of a special social occasion. God as the Supreme Host made sure that such items of pleasant hospitality were associated with His house.

Once we take into account the theme of replication, involving the inner and outer spaces replicating heaven, the incense also suggests another set of associations. The smoke from the animal sacrifices offered on the bronze altar outside would have gone up into heaven. The altar of incense signifies what happens to the smoke when, figuratively speaking, it rises to the very top of the visible heavens. It becomes a sweet smelling fragrance that enters even into the Most Holy Place, God's throne room. God smells and is pleased. He receives the offering. The offerings themselves are a sort of nonverbal prayer—prayer for forgiveness of sin, prayer of adoration, prayer of thanksgiving, prayer of intercession by the priest for those whom he represents. Appropriately the New Testament clearly identifies the rising incense with the prayers of the saints (Revelation 5:8; 8:3). But first of all we must think of the prayers of Jesus Christ as He prayed on earth (Hebrews 5:7) and as He now intercedes for us in heaven (Hebrews 7:25).

The altar of incense has the dimensions 1 cubit by 1 cubit by 2 cubits high (Exodus 30:1–6). The dimensions of 1 cubit by 1 cubit in horizontal space make it square, a replica of the square shape of the Most Holy Place. Its vertical dimension, 2 cubits, makes it the same in overall shape as the Holy Place, but one-tenth the size. The ark has dimensions of 1½ cubits high, 1½ cubits wide, and 2½ cubits long (Exodus 25:10). The two equal dimensions make the ark into a square, replicating the square shape of the Most Holy Place. They are also equal to the vertical dimension of the table. The bronze altar has a vertical dimension of 3 cubits, twice the size of the vertical dimension of the ark, and two dimensions of 5 cubits, twice the size of the length of the ark. As we have already observed, the two equal dimensions of 5 cubits make the bronze altar into a square, replicating the shape of the Most Holy Place and the cross section of the ark.

What does all this symmetry and replication suggest? Perfect craftsmanship. Inside the ark is the law, symbolizing the blueprint for the whole pattern of the tabernacle. The tabernacle itself is nothing else than a replica of the law, God's word, which described the pattern to

Moses in the first place. This building is truly beautiful, the work of a master hand, the Creator Himself!

The courtyard outside corresponds to the earth. The altar there is made of bronze, a less expensive metal, in contrast to the gold that covers everything in the two rooms. The altar measures 5 cubits by 5 cubits, a perfect square, showing its perfection. But the figure of 5 has already been associated with the courtyard as a whole, which measures 50 cubits by 100 cubits by 5 cubits. Thus the very measurements of the altar suggest its association with the whole of the court. But again its dimensions are not completely symmetric. It is 3 cubits rather than 5 cubits high, breaking the perfect symmetry in order to allow the priests to work on it without too much onerous effort. To this altar the ordinary earthly people of Israel are allowed to approach, at least to the entrance of the courtyard, and to present their earthly, animal sacrifices. In addition, the vertical dimension of three corresponds to the threefoldness in the total length of the two rooms of the tabernacle.

In between the bronze altar and the rooms is a washing basin or "laver." It is also made of bronze, suggesting the same association with earth. In fact, here we have a little replica of the earth. The laver represents the waters of the earth, while the space around the laver represents the dry land. The altar itself replicates the whole tabernacle, since it is the special place rising up from the earth where sacrifices may be offered. Thus the altar is suggestive of a little replica of Mount Zion, the later resting place of the temple, or Mount Sinai where God meets with Moses. The three-cubit height of the altar might perhaps even suggest the three tiers or stories of the world, the highest invisible heavens, visible heaven, and earth.

Another little pattern is suggested by the function of the washing basin and its relation to the priests. The washing basin supplies the priests with water for their ceremonial washings. It is a basin for cleansing. Water descending from heaven through the seasonal pattern of rains represented in the Holy Place comes to the earth, with its life-giving power, and renews it. It is the cleansing, life-giving water of life.

Note also the sequence of actions that a priest would go through. The altar stands closest to the entrance to the courtyard. After that comes the washing basin, then comes the tabernacle itself with its two rooms. The Israelites' own experience in the immediate past portrayed the same sequence. First they are in bondage, in Egypt, then they are delivered through the sacrifice of the passover lamb, symbolized by the altar. Then they pass through the Red Sea and still live, whereas their enemies are destroyed. The waters of the Red Sea stand for a kind of ceremonial cleansing from their enemies, as Paul points out: "For I do not want you to be ignorant of the fact, brothers, that our forefathers were all under the cloud and that they all passed through the sea. They were all baptized into Moses in the cloud and in the sea" (1 Corinthians 10:1–2). Then they enjoy the manna in the wilderness, symbolized by the table of the bread of the Presence (Exodus 16:1–36). They come to Mount Sinai, the special holy mountain, symbolized by the whole tabernacle.

Characteristically, God delivers His people by stages. The same basic elements of salvation are repeated in different forms, again and again, as the Israelites see God's salvation progressively manifested. Hence, the same sequence of symbols can be used again and again to stand for the steps in God's deliverance. For example, we may see the bronze altar as corresponding to Mount Sinai, the washing basin as corresponding to the crossing of the Jordan, and the rooms of the tabernacle as corresponding to entrance into the Promised Land, a new Eden, flowing with milk and honey, a holy land.

Once the people are in the Promised Land, the same pattern can be seen again. The bronze altar stands for Mount Zion with the temple on top, the rooms of the tabernacle stand for heaven, and the washing basin symbolizes the clouds or heavenly water separating the people from the pure holiness of heaven.

In this situation things remain for a long time. Then, when Jesus dies, the soldier pierces His side, "bringing a sudden flow of blood and water" (John 19:34). John is amazingly emphatic in his testimony: "The man who saw it has given testimony, and his testimony is true. He knows that he tells the truth, and he testifies so that you also may believe" (John 19:35). Then John shows other connections with the Old Testament (John 19:36–37). Perhaps John intends us to understand, among other things, that the blood corresponds to the blood of the altar and the water to the water of the washing basin. Shortly after

Zechariah has given the prophecy of the piercing quoted by John 19:37 (Zechariah 12:10), he says in Zechariah 13:1, "On that day a fountain will be opened to the house of David and the inhabitants of Jerusalem, to cleanse them from sin and impurity." That is, they will receive not a static basin but a fountain bubbling up with running water. Such a source of cleansing is symbolically represented by the water flowing from Jesus' side.

Jesus also says, "Everyone who drinks this water [ordinary water] will be thirsty again, but whoever drinks the water I give him will never thirst. Indeed, the water I give him will become in him a spring of water welling up to eternal life" (John 4:13–14). The priests "thirst" again and again, that is, they need to be washed again and again. But Christ's cleansing cleanses forever. Later Jesus identifies the water with the Holy Spirit:

> Jesus stood and said in a loud voice, "If a man is thirsty, let him come to me and drink. Whoever believes in me, as the Scripture has said, streams of living water will flow from within him." By this he meant the Spirit, whom those who believed in him were later to receive. Up to that time the Spirit had not been given, since Jesus had not yet been glorified. (John 7:37–39)

The coming of the Spirit is now signified by baptism, a cleansing ceremony with water.

> For John baptized with water, but in a few days you will be baptized with the Holy Spirit. (Acts 1:5)

> Repent and be baptized, every one of you, in the name of Jesus Christ for the forgiveness of your sins. And you will receive the gift of the Holy Spirit. (Acts 2:38)

> Can anyone keep these people from being baptized with water? They have received the Holy Spirit just as we have. (Acts 10:47)

Jesus' discussion with Nicodemus about being born of water and the Spirit (John 3:5) builds on the picture of cleansing in Ezekiel 36:25–27 and points to these same truths.

The Separations of the Tabernacle

The interfaces between the various spaces of the tabernacle are carefully designed to separate the places, to isolate them so that the unholiness of Israel cannot come in contact with the holiness of God. One curtain or "veil" separates the inner room, the Most Holy Place, from the outer room, the Holy Place. As we have argued, it signifies the inaccessibility of God generally, but more particularly the fact that the highest heaven, the immediate throne room of God, is distinct from the visible sky and cannot be seen.

A second curtain separates the Holy Place from the courtyard. From an Israelite point of view it signifies the inaccessibility even of the visible heaven. Human beings cannot climb to heaven. But the curtains are both separations and doorways, inasmuch as the high priest can pass through even the first curtain once a year. The second curtain is an imperfect replica of the first.

Remember now that the courtyard represents the earth. The tabernacle, i.e., the two rooms taken together, is filled with the gold of heavenly royalty, while the courtyard has only bronze furnishings. But does not the tabernacle touch the courtyard by resting on the earth of the courtyard? It does not. Sockets or bases made of silver hold up the entire tabernacle so that no part of its sides touches the courtyard. The silver sockets or bases function like a solid form of curtain to separate heaven from earth, or to separate God from human beings.

On the outside of the courtyard is a fence made of curtains. The curtains separate the common people of Israel from the courtyard. As such, they are a less exalted replica of the curtains of the tabernacle. Bases of bronze, corresponding to the bronze of the altar and the washing basin, separate them from direct contact with the earth. The posts have silver bands and hooks, corresponding to the silver bases of the tabernacle.

The symbolism seems to picture a situation in which the bottom tip of the tabernacle, i.e., the silver bases, fit into the top tip of the courtyard, i.e., the silver bands and hooks. The tabernacle proper is a kind of upper story to the courtyard. Such is a fitting symbolism for a replica of heaven placed in the middle of the courtyard, which in turn is a replica of earth. The tent pegs are all of bronze because they go directly into the ground of the courtyard (Exodus 27:19).

The dimensions of the courtyard also signify the perfection of architectural plan that we have already seen elsewhere. Each curtain is 5 cubits by 5 cubits, replicating the square shape of the 10 by 10 curtains that separate the tabernacle rooms. The courtyard as a whole is 50 cubits by 100 cubits by 5 cubits high, replicating the horizontal shape of the Holy Place. The starting dimension of five is the same as the horizontal dimensions of the bronze altar, thus indicating that the courtyard is a replica of the altar, which in turn replicates elements of the tabernacle proper. But five also suggests a half value, half of ten, a kind of incompleteness in relation to the complete spatial dimension of ten. This incompleteness is remedied in the temple, when all the dimensions are doubled. These things symbolize the fact that Israel and its communion with God is incomplete until they rest in the Promised Land. In the temple the washing basin is transformed into a "sea," confirming our guess about the significance of the washing basin.

The eastern side of the courtyard is composed of three parts (cf., Exodus 27:13–16). In the center is an entrance 20 cubits wide. To the two sides are two fences each 15 cubits long. Even these dimensions are distantly related to other dimensions used at other places. The 20 cubits is the same as the length of the Holy Place, while the 15 cubit dimension is half the amount of the 30-cubit-long tabernacle, and ten times the width of the ark. The entrance to the courtyard on the east has a curtain of material similar to the two main curtains of the tabernacle, thus replicating them.

The remaining separation is the separation of the vertical sides of the tabernacle from the surrounding courtyard. Not merely a curtain but several layers are added, signifying that there is only one way into the presence of God, the way God Himself has provided. "Salvation is found in no one else, for there is no other name under heaven given to men by which we must be saved" (Acts 4:12). Likewise Jesus says, "I am the way and the truth and the life. No one comes to the Father except through me" (John 14:6).

The tabernacle is supported by frames overlaid with gold, each 10 cubits by 1½ cubits. The 10-cubit dimension matches the dimensions of the Most Holy Place, while the 1-cubit dimension matches the width of the ark. The frames taken together form a complete layer, suggesting to the person inside them not a tent but a house of gold. Thus the nature of the structure points forward to the permanency of the temple, the solid house that Solomon will build. It also pictures the stability of the larger "house" or dwelling place of God, the created universe itself. Several passages in the Bible liken God to a workman who, in creating the universe, builds a house. Amos speaks of Him "who builds his lofty palace in the heavens and sets its foundation on the earth" (Amos 9:6). Proverbs says concerning wisdom,

> I was there when he set the heavens in place,
>   when he marked out the horizon
>   on the face of the deep,
>   when he established the clouds above
>   and fixed securely the fountains of the deep. . . .
> Then I was the craftsman at his side
>   [like Bezalel who crafted the tabernacle,
>   Exodus 31:2–5].
> I was filled with delight day after day,
>   rejoicing always in his presence,
> rejoicing in his whole world
>   and delighting in mankind.
>   (Proverbs 8:27–28, 30–31)

Outside the frames is the curtain of blue material. Actually the curtain is composed of ten distinct curtains, ten being the perfect spatial number of the Most Holy Place (Exodus 26:1–6). Clasps of gold—gold corresponding to the royal majesty of the tabernacle—hold together two sets of five curtains each. The introduction of the number five begins to point outwards to the fundamental number five that occurs over and over again in the courtyard. Each curtain is 28 cubits by 4 cubits, a little short in both dimensions, so that the curtains do not hang down low enough to touch the courtyard on either side of the tabernacle. Five curtains are sewn together, and the other five sewn together. Fifty loops and clasps of gold hold the two parts together, suggesting the dimension of 50 cubits in the courtyard. Thus certain minor elements in the curtains begin to suggest a transition to the outside courtyard. In addition, there is no denying that the total covering has two parts, carefully held together but with the potential of being separated. Of course, this technique would have made it much more convenient for the Levites to carry the covering from place to place, since they would not have had to carry the total weight of the covering in one operation. But it also creates the barest suggestion of a possibility of an entranceway being created. This possibility is more fully realized in the two main curtains separating the courtyard from the Holy Place and the Holy Place from the Most Holy Place. Symbolically, all this arrangement anticipates the rending of the veil at the death of Christ (Matthew 27:51). At the same time, the firm manner in which the two parts are held together suggests the manner in which God constructs the world and His way to salvation as one whole, all parts being held together in Christ (Colossians 1:17).

All these associations are of a vague, suggestive, allusive kind. Each detail of the tabernacle, in my opinion, is not simply a code-word signifying one thing exclusively. Rather, it is one part of a tantalizing visual poem suggesting a multitude of relationships, all tied together in a single structure. It is fitting that the symbolism of the tabernacle should be multifaceted. After all, such is the character of the physical universe: it is created by God as one whole, one universe, and also with a fascinating, overwhelming multitude of inner relations of the parts. Such also is the character of Christ, who as one person contains in Himself "all the fullness of the Deity," a manifold richness of wisdom and love.

Let us continue to look at the details. A second covering of goat hair is placed over the blue curtain (Exodus 26:7–13). The pattern is basically the same as for the inner blue curtain, again suggesting the all-pervasiveness of replication. But certain imperfections are introduced. The material of the curtain is not royal blue of heaven, but goatskins, suggesting associations with the earthly sacrifices of the altar and the covering of the nakedness of sin by the skins of dead animals (Genesis 3:21). The covering is composed of eleven curtains, not ten, suggesting its imperfection. The additional curtain also makes it possible for the total covering to hang down an additional 2 cubits at the two ends, completely concealing the inside curtain from view. The manner of overlap between the curtains also prevents anyone outside from seeing the gold loops connecting the two parts of the inner covering of blue. The individual curtains are each 30 cubits long, so that an extra cubit of length on each side assures that the inner covering of blue will not be seen from the outside courtyard. Thus, in several ways the goatskin curtain not only separates the rooms from the outside but also separates the inner, heavenly curtain from the outside.

A third and fourth covering are briefly mentioned in Exodus 26:14. It is clear from the terminology and from the comparatively few references to them that these coverings do not constitute part of the tabernacle proper. Over the covering of goatskin was one of "ram skins dyed red" (Exodus 26:14). In view of the intense amount of replication in the tabernacle as a whole, it is clear that this red covering must signify the covering of animal blood separating the tabernacle from the contamination of the outside world.

We cannot be certain of the character of the outermost covering, because there is an unusual key word. The covering is made of "hides of sea cows" (NIV) or "porpoise skins" (NASB) or "badgers' skins" (KJV). The animal was clearly known to the Israelites, but we do not have enough information nowadays to be certain what animal it was. But the material was probably waterproof to keep off the rain. Either porpoises or sea cows would serve adequately. Keeping off the rain and dust was a very practical function. Yet it also suggests once again the intense separation of the tabernacle from the outer world. Even the rain and dust must not be allowed to penetrate.

The Multifaceted Character of Tabernacle Symbolism

The symbolism that we have uncovered so far may seem to be bewildering in its variety. Can the items and the measurements in the tabernacle really suggest so many different things? Are we in danger of being carried away or beguiled by our imaginations?

The tabernacle is first of all the dwelling place of God, as God Himself says in Exodus 25:8. This much cannot be denied. Hence, we can expect it to reveal certain things about the character of God and the nature of His fellowship with His people. We at least know the most general area in which to look for clues to the meaning of the symbols. Yet the history of interpretation of tabernacle symbolism shows a great deal of variety and apparent arbitrariness in just how individual items have been interpreted. The danger of letting imagination go wild is a real one.

In my opinion, one major guideline is to be found in the general Biblical teaching with respect to God and His dwelling place. God dwells in a special sense in heaven, as we have seen. Yet in a wider sense God is present everywhere. His character is displayed in the whole of His creation (Romans 1:18–21). We may therefore proceed to categorize dwelling places of particular types.

1. God dwells in heaven in the midst of His holy courtroom of angels and ministering spirits. (See, e.g., 1 Kings 8:30; Isaiah 6:1–2; Psalm 89:7; Job 1:6; Revelation 4:1–11.)

2. The whole universe has been created in a manner like constructing a house (Psalm 104:2–3; Amos 9:6; Proverbs 8:22–31; Isaiah 40:22). God fills it all (Jeremiah 23:24) and in this sense it is His dwelling place.

3. The tabernacle and later Solomon's temple are special dwellings of God. After their construction and dedication, the cloud of glory descends on them to signify God taking up His abode (Exodus 40:34–38; 1 Kings 8:10).

4. The Garden of Eden was a special dwelling of God where God met with Adam and Eve (cf. Genesis 2:15–3:8). Some of the symbolism of the tabernacle and the temple undoubtedly looks backward toward the lost communion with God that Adam had enjoyed in the Garden of Eden. The cherubim in the tabernacle are reminiscent of the cherubim guarding the way to the tree of life in Genesis 3:24.

5. The people of God corporately become a dwelling place of God. Teaching of this kind becomes most explicit in the New Testament, where the church is called God's temple: "Don't you know that you yourselves are God's temple and that God's Spirit lives in you?" (1 Corinthians 3:16; cf. 1 Peter 2:5). But it is implicit in the Old Testament when the people of Israel are called a holy people by virtue of the fact that God dwells in their midst.

6. The body of each individual saint is a dwelling place of God, according to 1 Corinthians 6:15, 19. This teaching is fully revealed only in the New Testament. Beginning at Pentecost the Holy Spirit is sent to dwell within God's people in a special way, and only this coming of the Spirit makes people temples in a full sense. But the same truths are foreshadowed in the fact that in Israel the high priest's clothing is analogous to the tabernacle (see chapter 4). Thus the high priest is a kind of mini-tabernacle. Since the whole of Israel is a nation of priests (Exodus 19:5–6), each Israelite reflects the pattern of the high priest at a subordinate level. Moreover, Israelites were told to wear tassels on their clothes as a reminder of "all the commandments of the LORD" (Numbers 15:37–40). These tassels are naturally associated not only with the holiness of the commandments but also with the blue of the tassel-like pomegranates attached to the hem of the high priest's robe (Exodus 28:33–34). Thus each Israelite is depicted as a subordinate priest.

7. The new Jerusalem of Revelation 21–22 is the final dwelling of God with human beings (Revelation 21:3, 22). The new Jerusalem as a city primarily represents the people of God corporately. Hence, it is the fulfillment of the principle that the people of God corporately are a dwelling of God (point 5 above). But the new Jerusalem is also a *heavenly* city (Revelation 21:2, 10), suggesting that it is also the fulfillment of God's dwelling in heaven (point 1 above). It has an exact cubical shape, the same shape as the Most Holy Place of the tabernacle, suggesting that it is the final tabernacle or temple (Revelation 21:16, 22). The mention of the river, the tree of life, and the removal of all curse in Revelation 22:1–3 suggest that it is also the new Eden, the final garden where God meets human beings. Thus many of the motifs concerning God's dwelling place are united and woven together in this final vision, just as we might expect to happen in a vision relating to the consummation or summing up of all things.

8. Christ Himself is the ultimate dwelling of God with human beings. Matthew 1:23 says that Christ is called "Immanuel," which

means "God with us." In John 2:19–22 Jesus says, "Destroy this temple, and I will raise it again in three days." And John comments, "But the temple he had spoken of was his body." John 1:14 says that the "Word was made flesh and dwelt among us" (KJV), deliberately using a word for "dwelling" that alludes to the Old Testament tabernacle. Finally, John 14:11 says, "I am in the Father and the Father is in me." This and similar language in John about the mutual indwelling of the Father and the Son presents us with the ultimate form of indwelling, namely, the original indwelling of the Persons of the Trinity. This original uncreated indwelling must be the model for all instances of God dwelling with human beings who are made in the image of God.

We can arrive at the same results by paying close attention to the Old Testament language of holiness. In a supreme sense, God Himself is holy (Isaiah 6:3). But other things can be called holy when they are dedicated to Him and are associated with His presence. Thus heaven is holy according to Psalm 20:6. The tabernacle and the temple are holy, and the Most Holy Place ("Holy of Holies") is called such because it is closest to the immediate presence of God. Likewise, Eden is the mountain of God from which profane things are cast out, implying that it is holy (Ezekiel 28:13, 16). The priests are holy and as such representative of the holiness of the tabernacle (Leviticus 21:6). The people of God corporately are a "kingdom of priests and a holy nation" (Exodus 19:6). The new Jerusalem is the "holy city" (Revelation 21:2). Christ is supremely "the Holy One of God" (John 6:69; cf. Acts 3:14). Thus all these instances are dwelling places of God and reflections of his supreme holiness.

Because God is always the same and because sin is always the obstacle to communion with God's holiness, we may naturally expect that the same principles will be expressed again and again in each form of God's dwelling. In fact, since Christ is the supreme archetype for all of God's dwellings, all of them must be modeled on Him. Hence, there are bound to be connections between the tabernacle and other forms of God's dwelling. The tabernacle will naturally point us in several directions at once. Within the Old Testament, no one of these directions by itself reveals everything. That is, because the tabernacle ultimately points upward to God Himself, and forward to the revelation of God in Christ, no one set of connections within the Old Testament ought to be viewed as a kind of exclusive clue to its significance. But when Christ appears, He Himself sums up all the dimensions of significance, because "in Christ all the fullness of the Deity lives in bodily form" (Colossians 2:9). Yet because of the infinite, divine depths of Christ's wisdom, we can never master or comprehend Him in His fullness. Because He is Lord of all, He is Himself the ultimate basis for unity in all the diverse connections.

Thus we must also realize that the tabernacle in itself cannot tell us everything. Its insufficiencies and its mysteries indicate that in its own time and place it did not exhaust the revelation of God but was only a stage on the way to fullness. In fact, the pattern of the tabernacle includes within itself notice of its temporary character. On the most elementary level, it is a portable, tent-like dwelling place. It therefore has to be succeeded by the temple, a permanent, fixed dwelling place, once the people have settled in the land. But in addition, the pattern of replication found in the tabernacle speaks of the dynamic character of God's revelation and of his program for history. The tabernacle is a replica of heaven, while the Holy Place is a replica of the Most Holy Place, the courtyard is a replica of the Holy Place, and even the people's tent dwellings are replicas of the tabernacle in a more distant way. These replicas move outward from a centerpoint in heaven to the prosaic everyday life of the people. The outward movement shows that there is yet more to be revealed—the tabernacle is only a copy of heavenly things (Hebrews 8:5; 9:23; 10:1). The greater revelation of the future goes hand in hand with the accomplishment of God's program for history, namely, to fill the whole world with His heavenly glory (Revelation 21:22–23). Then His will shall be done on earth as it is in heaven (Matthew 6:10).

Practical Lessons from the Tabernacle

In its own time, though the tabernacle did not say everything, it still said a great deal. It had some very practical lessons for the Israelites. To a large extent, they can still be lessons for us today as well.

First, because of its symbolic connection with heaven, the tabernacle reminded the Israelites that God was the true God, the exalted Lord of the whole universe, not simply a god confined to a local spot. God is the exalted, universal Ruler, the King of kings and Lord of lords. Likewise, we should recognize now that God our Father and Christ our Redeemer is the heavenly Lord, the Lord of all (Matthew 28:20; 1 Corinthians 8:6). We must obey Him and not be intimidated by human claims to wisdom and power (1 Peter 3:14–17).

Second, because the whole universe was God's house, the tabernacle depicted for the Israelites the way in which God's care was demonstrated in their day-to-day circumstances. Food, life, and light all derived from God who had made the whole universe as His dwelling place and their home. Likewise, we today are to see our circumstances and our daily blessings not as the product of some chance, impersonal process, but as the provision of our God and our Savior Jesus Christ. We are to pray to God to give us our daily bread (Matthew 6:11). We are to seek first His kingdom and His righteousness, with the confidence that all earthly needs will be ours as well (Matthew 6:33).

Third, the tabernacle as a unique structure reminded Israel that they had unique privileges. Out of all the nations of the world God chose them to be His people, and condescended to live among them in a special way (Exodus 19:5–6; Deuteronomy 7:7–8). Likewise, in New Testament times God dwells in a unique way in the church (1 Corinthians 3:16) and in individual Christians (1 Corinthians 6:19; Romans 8:9–17). This indwelling distinguishes us from the world at large. We are not to become proud, because God's favor is a gift to undeserving sinners (Romans 5:6–10; 2 Timothy 1:9–10). But we are to be thankful for our special status: we are children of the great King! We are to remember that as people chosen out of the world we are spiritually separate and are not to follow the ways of the world (John 15:19; 17:15–19; Ephesians 2:1–10; 5:1–6:9; 1 Peter 1:13–3:12).

Fourth, the tabernacle symbolized Eden, and thereby reminded the Israelites of their sinful, lost, separated condition as descendents of Adam. Entrance into Eden was barred to them. And yet they could enter in a sense, when the priest entered as their representative. Hence, the tabernacle spoke both of being lost and also of the promise of overcoming sin through a representative man, ultimately through Jesus

Christ our final high priest (Hebrews 7:27–28). Like the Israelites, we need to be reminded of the misery of our sinfulness deriving from Adam and of the hope—and now present reality[2]—of redemption, restoration, and adoption into God's family and house through Jesus Christ.

Fifth, the tabernacle symbolized the people of God corporately. Israel as a collective body was called upon to imitate the beauty, order, holiness, and purity of the tabernacle itself. It was to embody beauty, order, holiness, and purity in its own communal living. This principle was most evident in the case of Israelite families. The families lived in tents just as God lived in His tent. Their own work in constructing and repairing their tents, caring for their animals, cooking and eating their food, distinguishing clean and unclean, separating right from wrong, and instructing their children was to be modeled after the work of God who was their heavenly Father (Deuteronomy 8:5), and who was the exalted Head of their spiritual household. For example, a humble task like washing the cookware was an echo of that exalted work of God the Savior in which He cleanses the tabernacle and ultimately cleanses the whole universe through the work of Jesus Christ. Mending clothing was an act by which Israelite clothing was restored to being a reflection of the exalted clothing of the high priest and the curtains of the tabernacle, which in turn pointed forward to the perfection of righteousness, beauty, order, and spiritual "mending" in Jesus Christ and His "robe of righteousness" (Isaiah 61:10).

Likewise, the church in our day is to be holy. The church is not a voluntary association to be governed as its members see fit, but a dwelling place of God. It ought to be structured according to the orders of its commander, the Lord Jesus Christ. Our families and our homes are to reflect the spiritual purity, beauty, and orderliness that was temporarily pictured through the tabernacle and is now supremely set forth in Jesus Christ Himself. Christ's work of cleansing the universe was definitively accomplished in His death and resurrection. But when we wash dishes in His name we do our little work of cleansing, which humbly reflects His great work.

Sixth, the tabernacle symbolized the people of God individually. The Israelites were commanded to keep their bodies pure, pure first of all from sin but also from ceremonial defilements that symbolized sin. In the New Testament the bodies of Christians are temples of the Holy Spirit (1 Corinthians 6:19). We are "to purify ourselves from everything that contaminates body and spirit, perfecting holiness out of reverence for God" (2 Corinthians 7:1). Sexual sins as sins directly against the body are strongly forbidden (1 Corinthians 6:18–20).

Seventh, the tabernacle pointed forward to the new Jerusalem, the final dwelling of God with human beings. The Israelites were supposed to look forward to God's salvation in the future and to pray for His coming. By doing so they were to stir themselves up to be faithful to God and to trust Him in their own time. We have now received the down-payment of our salvation through the gift of the Holy Spirit (Ephesians 1:13–14; 2 Corinthians 1:22). But we must stir ourselves up to long for the second coming of Christ when we will receive fully what God has promised.

Eighth, the tabernacle symbolized God Himself. The teaching of the Old Testament did not reveal the mysteries of the trinitarian nature of God as fully as they have now been revealed. But the Israelites were being instructed by the veils and the not-fully-analyzable symbols to realize that God's character and His purposes were unfathomably deep, and that their salvation rested in God's own character and wisdom. We now know, in the light of fuller revelation, that the God of Israel is our trinitarian God, the one God revealed through the work of Christ as He obeyed the Father through the power of the Holy Spirit. The tabernacle points forward to Christ the final dwelling of God with human beings, but also to the Father and the Spirit who in Christ reveal the fullness of the Deity to us (Colossians 2:9). For us as well as for the Israelites, the tabernacle is a revelation of God Himself: His holiness, His beauty, His majesty, His purposes of salvation. The law of Moses is intended above all to draw us into communion with this wonderful God, to adore Him, to worship Him, and to enjoy His presence forever. We are members of His household, adopted sons of a heavenly Father, and brothers of Jesus Christ our elder brother (Romans 8:17, 28–30).

Guidelines for Interpreting
The Revelation of the Tabernacle

Now let us stand back and ask how we have gone about interpreting the significance of the tabernacle.

As I mentioned in chapter 1, we have a threefold task of interpretation. On the one hand, we must try to understand the law of Moses within its original historical context, as God gave it to the Israelites. On the other hand, we must understand it in relation to the rest of the Bible, the complete communication from God. And we must endeavor to see its implications for our lives and our circumstances. For my own benefit, as well as for the benefit of convincing others, I endeavor most of the time to start with the original historical context. We ought to place ourselves in the position of an Israelite in the time of Moses, or in the position of Moses himself. What would they think about the tabernacle? What could they have legitimately discerned about its significance? Moses and the Israelites would have known about the background of God's dealing with their ancestors, as recorded in Genesis. They would have experienced the mighty acts of deliverance by which God brought them out of Egypt and sustained them in the wilderness. In addition, it would have been obvious to them that the tabernacle contained symbols.

How then would they have interpreted a symbol? We in the West are not very much at ease with symbolism ourselves. We live in an industrialized society dominated by scientific and technological forms of knowledge. Such knowledge minimizes the play of metaphors and the personal depth dimensions of human living. For many people "real" truth means technological truth, that is, truth swept free of metaphor and symbolism. We meet symbolism mostly in advertising, and such use of symbolism rouses our suspicions and often ends by producing indifference.

I am convinced that God does not share our general cultural aversion to metaphors and symbols. He wrote the Old Testament, which contains a good deal of poetry and many uses of metaphor. Jesus spoke in parables, which are a kind of extended metaphor. Godly Israelites of Old Testament times were able to appreciate His language, whereas we have a hard time with it. We must adapt to the fact that symbols and metaphors can speak truly and powerfully without speaking with pedantic scientific precision. A symbol may suggest a deep truth or even a cluster of related truths without blurting everything out in plain talk and making everything crystal clear. An element of mystery may remain, because a symbol may suggest a whole host of connections. We do not know for certain exactly how far we are supposed to carry the implications when we analyze the symbol in a more scientific way. For example, Psalm 23:1 says, "The LORD is my shepherd." In what ways is the Lord like a human shepherd? We can receive personal comfort and true meaning from the psalm even without being able to analyze precisely in an academic way all the respects in which God is like a shepherd and precisely where we are to stop drawing more implications.

I believe, then, that we treat God's word with the greatest reverence and fairness when we recognize that God may use symbol. We ought not to impose our own modern biases. To appreciate a symbol, we must let our imaginations play a little, and ask what the symbol suggests. What does it bring to mind? What is it like? What does it remind me of in my own past experience? What does it allude to in other writings by the same author? We must explore all these questions, but endeavor to do so like an Israelite, not like a twentieth-century Westerner. Then the associations of the tabernacle with sky, earth, and creation come to mind, as well as associations with Israel's past deliverance and presence experience. The correspondences of the parts of the tabernacle with one another and the simple ratios between its dimensions express a beautiful craftsmanship and the principle of replicating a pattern on different levels. Then we are on our way to appreciating the tabernacle as an Israelite might potentially have done. We must of course recognize that some associations and connections are more obvious than others, and that we may possibly be wrong about some details. But the overall picture emerges clearly.[3]

Having obtained a picture from the original historical circumstances, we are ready to extend the picture and fill it out by seeing how God continues His story and His revelation in the later prophets and in the New Testament. These further reflections may also help us to discriminate better between what is incidental and what is most central in our earlier reflection. We may sometimes correct earlier impressions when we hear more of the story.

The two stages, involving the original historical context and involving use of the whole Bible, are not rigidly separable from one another. They each help to correct and enhance the other. But errors can arise if we concentrate wholly on one stage. First, people who concentrate only on the original historical context have frequently not done justice to that context because they have underestimated the power and richness of the symbolic significance of the tabernacle. Knowing that the tabernacle points to heavenly things that are fulfilled in Christ can encourage us to study the original context more diligently.

Second, people who concentrate only on the whole Bible frequently do become fanciful because they are occupied too much with their own ideas, not with what God communicated to the Israelites. For example, some have thought that every mention of wood in the Old Testament somehow points to the cross of Christ. Since almost all the tabernacle furniture and the beams supporting the tabernacle are made of acacia wood, all these items must somehow prefigure the cross. But such a move is really very superficial. It never asks what the tabernacle items really meant within their own context and how they really functioned, but simply imposes a meaning from outside. We do not really learn anything from the Bible when we proceed in this way, because what we hear is only what we already knew, namely, New Testament teaching about the work of Christ. Thus we need to proceed in a way that utilizes the full resources of the Bible and respects the way in which God has actually communicated to people over a long period of history.

It is time now to proceed forward with our examination of the law of Moses. Many other questions about interpretive principles could be raised, and we could explore more deeply the questions that I have already raised. But such questions are best left to other books besides this one.[4]

In some respects interpretive principles are validated by the increase that they bring to our understanding, just as the proof of the pudding is in the eating. If this book helps you to understand the Old Testament, its interpretive concerns are fulfilled.

THREE

THE SACRIFICES: PREFIGURING THE FINAL SACRIFICE OF CHRIST

W hat is the meaning and purpose of the sacrifices described particularly in Leviticus 1–7? We understand best if we pay attention to the way in which Leviticus 1–7 fits together with what comes before it in Exodus and what goes after it in the rest of Leviticus.

The Necessity of Holiness

When Moses was on Mount Sinai he received instructions about the construction of the tabernacle (Exodus 24:15–18; 25:9; 26:30; Hebrews 8:5). But even before he reached the bottom of the mountain the people had committed open idolatry with the golden calf (Exodus 32). Sin on the part of the Israelites threatened to abort God's purpose of dwelling with them. But Moses interceded and even proposed to offer himself as a substitute for their sin (Exodus 32:31–32). God did not accept his substitutionary offer. But the sacrifices indicate that the general principle of substitution is valid. In fact, it points forward to the substitutionary work of Christ who bore our sins.

The tabernacle was finally constructed and the cloud symbolizing God's presence settled on the tabernacle (Exodus 35–40). Yet sinfulness on the part of the people clearly remained a continuing problem. The entire contents of Leviticus deal in one way or another with this problem. Now that the tabernacle was there among the people, sacrifices had to be instituted to provide access to the presence of God and to remove the defilements arising from Israel's sin (Leviticus 1–5). Priests had to be given instructions on their role in presenting the sacrifices (Leviticus 6–7). They had to be installed and provided with a special holiness in order to present the sacrifices to God (Leviticus 8–10). The people as a whole had to keep separate from uncleanness in order to approach the tabernacle (Leviticus 11–16). Gross defilements could be expected to receive severe penalties (Leviticus 17–20). The priests had to observe even more rigorous standards for cleanness and separation than did the common people (Leviticus 21–22). In addition, special care had be taken for holy days and seasons and for holy things (Leviticus 23–27).

In short, the entire contents of Leviticus are in principle related to the tabernacle and to the obligations of purity that derive from it. Leviticus sums up the matter in the words, "Be holy because I, the LORD your God, am holy" (Leviticus 19:2; cf. 1 Peter 1:16). The people could not survive alongside the tabernacle unless they respected the holiness of God and maintained holiness among themselves. Or, to put it another way, now that the people themselves had in some sense become a dwelling place of God through the erection and consecration of the tabernacle, they had to maintain practices exhibiting the principles of God's dwelling. Such principles are all fulfilled in Christ as the final dwelling place of God.

Redemption from Sin

But how do sacrifices fit into this general principle? They are the means for cleansing and removing defilement of the people and of the tabernacle itself. Thus they are a central means for maintaining the holiness of the people and the tabernacle, and thus ensuring that the earthly things continue to reflect the holiness of God. Special sacrifices must be presented when individual Israelites have sinned, even unknowingly, and when the priest or the whole community has sinned (Leviticus 4). The animals must be without blemish or defect, signifying that God requires perfection.[1] The worshiper places his hand on the animal, signifying his identification with the animal, and then the animal dies in his place (note the parallel with Genesis 22:13–14). The blood represents the life of the animal (Leviticus 17:14). Blood is placed on the horns of the altar, and once a year on the atonement cover in the Most Holy Place (Leviticus 16). The blood has power to cleanse the tabernacle from defilement. Since the blood signifies the life of the slain animal, it testifies that the animal has been slain and that the value of the death is applied to the designated object. The fat of the animal, representing the sweetest and best part, is burned on the altar to signify its being given to the Lord. The rest of the animal may be burned or eaten by the priests or partially eaten by the worshiper, as the case may be.

But animal sacrifices are ultimately inadequate. Israel goes on sinning year by year, and new animals must be presented year after year in the same repetitious ceremonies (Hebrews 10:1–4). Are you bored by the repetitious descriptions in Leviticus 1–9 of how each animal is sacrificed or the descriptions in Numbers 7 of the offerings of the tribes? There is more food for thought in these passages than we suspect, but in a sense we are meant to be bored. It goes on and on. The process never suffices. Animals could never be an adequate substitute for human beings made in the image of God. The very inadequacy of these sacrifices confirms the inadequacy associated with the tabernacle structure. They are only copies of the heavenly realities.

Their inadequacies have only one remedy. God must provide the ultimate sacrifice (Genesis 22:8). The guilt of the whole land will be removed in one day by the Branch, the son of David, who is simultaneously high priest (Zechariah 3:8–9; cf. Isaiah 11:1). A fountain—a permanent supply of water welling up—will be opened to cleanse them from sin and iniquity (Zechariah 13:1). A Man will die like a sheep, as a guilt offering for the iniquity of the people (Isaiah 53:4–8, 10). But afterwards He will be satisfied with new life (Isaiah 53:10–12).

The Old Testament thus reaches out in longing for Christ who brings an end to its frustrations and brings to accomplishment its promises. Christ is the final offering to which all the animal sacrifices look forward. As the Bible puts it, you were redeemed "with the precious blood of Christ, a lamb without blemish or defect. He was chosen before the creation of the world, but was revealed in these last times for your sake" (1 Peter 1:20). "He himself bore our sins in his body on the tree, so that we might die to sins and live for righteousness; by his wounds you have been healed. For you were like sheep going astray, but now you have returned to the Shepherd and Overseer of your souls" (1 Peter 2:24–25).

The Sequence of Events in Sacrifice

The sequence of events in sacrifice is also instructive to Israelites. In a typical case the process begins with the worshiper who brings an animal without defect to the priest. The worshiper has raised the animal himself or paid for it with his earnings, so that the animal represents a "sacrifice" in the modern sense of the word. It costs something to the worshiper, and a portion of the worshiper's own life is identified with it. The worshiper lays his hand on the head of the animal, signifying his identification with it. He then kills the animal at the entranceway into the courtyard, signifying that the animal dies as a substitute for the worshiper.[2]

From that point onward the priest takes over in performing the sacrificial actions. The intervention of the priest indicates that a specially holy person must perform the actions necessary to present the worshiper before God, even after the death of the animal. The priest takes some of the blood and sprinkles it on the sides of the bronze altar or on the horns of the altar or on the horns of the altar of incense, depending on the particular type of sacrifice. All of these actions constitute the permanent marking of the altar as testimony to the fact that the animal has died. For the most important sin offerings, blood is brought into the Holy Place to the altar of incense. For the day of atonement, once a year, the high priest brings blood into the Most Holy Place and sprinkles the atonement cover, to make atonement for the people. All these actions with blood recleanse the tabernacle and its furnishings when they are polluted by sins and uncleanness in Israel.

The symbolism with respect to whole burnt offerings and sin offerings is reasonable clear. For a whole burnt offering, blood is sprinkled on the sides of the bronze altar, signifying a recleansing of the altar

(Leviticus 1). This procedure suggests that the altar threatens to be defiled by the mere presence of imperfect people in the courtyard. The altar is then ready to receive the animal that has been killed.

A sin offering is presented when an individual or the community has committed some sin, even if unwittingly (Leviticus 4). A portion of the blood is put on the horns of the altar, signifying its cleansing as before. The rest of the blood is poured out at the base of the altar, signifying a recleansing of the interface between the altar and the land on which it stands. The land in general is cleansed from pollution by the shedding of sacrificial blood on it (see Deuteronomy 21:6–7; Numbers 35:33–34). We have already seen that the outer courtyard, in which the bronze altar stands, represents the earth. Thus the poured out blood symbolizes general cleansing of the earth, while the blood sprinkled on the altar signifies cleansing of the altar itself as the special holy focal point within the land. Significantly, the blood is placed on the horns of the altar, not merely sprinkled on its sides. The horns are its extremities, its highest points, its projections toward heaven. Thus the whole procedure suggests that a specific sin, as opposed to the general sinfulness associated with the whole burnt offering, defiles the altar up to a higher point, closer to heaven.

When a priest or the whole community sins, the tabernacle itself is defiled, not merely the bronze altar, because the priest functions in the tabernacle and the tabernacle stands in the midst of the community as a whole. Thus the blood of the sin offering is placed not on the horns of the bronze altar, as is usual with a sin offering, but on the horns of the altar of incense (Leviticus 4). The blood is also sprinkled on the curtain separating the inner and outer rooms. Such a procedure shows that defilement from the priest or community reaches up to heaven itself, to the very entrance of God's throne room, signified by the act of sprinkling the curtain. It defiles the highest point of the ascending smoke of the offerings into the sky, signified by the horns of the altar of incense in the Holy Place.

In addition to all these procedures, once a year the high priest enters the Most Holy Place with blood from the sin offerings for himself and for the people (Leviticus 16). He sprinkles the atonement cover with blood in order to cleanse it from the defilements of Israel.

Thus the whole procedure of pouring out blood and sprinkling blood constitutes repeated testimony to the repeated defilements of Israel and the necessity of continual cleansing by the value of life sacrificed to God. It shows moreover that as sin intensifies and spreads to the whole community or to its specially holy priests, the sin threatens to defile the whole sacrificial system and break off communion with God completely.

We may return to the same conclusion that we reached before: the sacrifice of animals is inadequate to achieve final cleansing, and it cannot cleanse anything more than the copies of heavenly things. Then who will bring the definitive sacrifice? A man must do it. A similar point is made indirectly in Numbers 35:33–34: "Do not pollute the land where you are. Bloodshed pollutes the land, and atonement cannot be made for the land on which blood has been shed, except by the blood of the one who shed it. Do not defile the land where you live and where I dwell, for I, the LORD, dwell among the Israelites." When a man had shed blood, the man must die. But there is one exception, when the blood of the death of the high priest releases a manslaughterer to return home (Numbers 35:25–28). The blood of the high priest has special value. In agreement with this principle, Zechariah 3 uses all the symbolism of a defiled human high priest, Joshua, and then speaks mysteriously of the Branch in connection with which "I [the LORD Almighty] will remove the sin of this land in a single day" (Zechariah 3:9).

The final atonement must be simultaneously like a sheep who dies and like the high priest who presents the sacrifice. This final high priest is described in Isaiah 53 as the Servant of the Lord. He presents His own body as a guilt offering (Isaiah 53:10) and dies (Isaiah 53:9). Like a sin offering where the body of the animal is carried outside the camp, He dies outside the camp (Hebrews 13:11–14). Then He will "see his offspring and prolong his days, and the will of the Lord will prosper in his hand" (Isaiah 53:10). He will live again. As the high priest now living, He goes through the rest of the steps in the sacrificial system. That is, He presents the blood of the sacrifice, His own blood (Hebrews 9:12). The blood has already been poured out on the earth as He died, cleansing the ground itself. If we follow the images of Leviticus 16 exactly, we would say that the blood is put first on the atonement cover, not this time in the earthly tabernacle but in the real one in heaven, the throne of God. Heaven itself is propitiated. Then blood is used to cleanse the whole "Tent of Meeting" (Leviticus 16:16), standing for the whole of the visible heavens. Then the bronze altar is cleansed, standing for the earth (Leviticus 16:18). Each cleansing is complete, signified by sevenfold sprinkling (16:14, 19). The whole universe is cleansed by the blood of His sacrifice (Romans 8:20–21; Colossians 1:20), but in stages: first heaven, then earth. Satan has been thrown out of heaven (Revelation 12:9–12). The full cleansing of earth yet awaits the time of Christ's coming out of the Most Holy Place in heaven and appearing bodily on earth.

The Types of Sacrifices

So far we have considered what is common to all the types of sacrifices. It is safe to say that all the sacrifices speak in some way of sin, atonement, and communion with God. Yet we can still say that different types of sacrifices emphasize various elements in the process of communion. In Leviticus 1–5 we have a description of five basic types of sacrifice, the burnt offering (Leviticus 1), the grain offering (Leviticus 2), the fellowship offering (Leviticus 3), the sin offering (Leviticus 4), and the guilt offering (Leviticus 5). In some versions of the Bible the grain offering is called a "cereal offering" and the fellowship offering a "peace offering."

The sin offering is presented to make atonement for sin (Leviticus 4:35). The emphasis here is clearly on the necessity of punishment in payment for sin. The punishment is borne by the animal instead of the worshiper. The guilt offering of Leviticus 5 seems to be a variation of the sin offering, and thus has a similar emphasis.

In the fellowship offering the worshiper himself is allowed to eat most of the parts of the animal that has been offered (Leviticus 7:15–18). To an Israelite this procedure would signify that the worshiper enjoys a meal in the presence of God and with the special blessing of God. Fellowship with God and enjoyment of God's blessings would seem to be the principal emphasis.

The grain offering is eaten by the priests, not by the worshiper (Leviticus 6:14–18). Since no death of an animal and no shedding of blood is involved, the principal idea suggested is that of giving back to God a portion of what one has produced through God's strength and blessing. This idea is confirmed by the fact that when the priests offer a grain offering on their own behalf rather than on behalf of someone else, the entire offering is to be burned (Leviticus 6:23). Thus the offering is never eaten by those who give it, but is presented to God.

The burnt offering described in Leviticus 1 is the most difficult to interpret. Leviticus 1:4 and 14:20 indicate that the burnt offering like the sin offering is used to "make atonement" for the worshiper.[3] The sin offering seems to focus on atonement for specific sins, whereas the burnt offering focuses on atonement for sinfulness generally.[4] But still, the two offerings have a great deal of similarity in their function. Can we find any other differences? Of all the animal sacrifices, this one alone is to be entirely burned. What does this complete burning signify? Many interpreters have suggested that the idea of entire dedication and consecration to God is uppermost. The burning of the whole animals might certainly suggest this meaning to an Israelite, but the meaning might just as likely be entire destruction. Nothing of the original animal is left; all is destroyed by fire. Actually, the two possible meanings are complementary. If we focus on what happens to the animal, entire destruction is the most obvious meaning. The animal represents the worshiper, so we may infer that entire destruction of the worshiper is signified. But the worshiper is not destroyed but preserved. Because of the substitutionary value of the animal, the worshiper and the priest can remain alive—we might say that they can enjoy new life. Hence, what happens to them does suggests entire dedication to God. But this entire dedication is accomplished by an entire destruction of the substitute, superimposed on an entire preservation or even resurrection of the worshiper.

These guesses about the burnt offering are confirmed by the statement in Deuteronomy 13:16. That passage speaks of a special situation in which a whole city is turned into a burnt offering and utterly destroyed. Utter destruction is clearly the significance of the burnt offering in this instance. But since the burnt offering is offered by those who are still faithful to God, it also results in their preservation (Deuteronomy 13:17–18).

The differences between the types of sacrifices are largely a matter of degree, and so we must be careful not to distinguish the types too sharply. In particular, the sin offering and the burnt offering serve quite similar purposes. But the different types do seem to emphasize different aspects in the process of communion with God. The sin offering and guilt offering emphasize punishment or retribution for sin. The burnt offering emphasizes consecration to God, which includes utter destruction of sin and uncleanness. The grain offering emphasizes payment of what is due in thanksgiving to God. Fellowship offerings emphasize enjoyment of God's presence and blessing. Since the food of the sacrifice is special, holy food (Leviticus 22:15–16), symbolizing the holiness of God, we might even venture to say that eating this food suggests sharing in God's holiness. The Israelites are commanded to "be holy, for I the LORD your God am holy" (Leviticus 19:2). The partaking in sacrificial food suggests being transformed into holiness as one enjoys God's presence.

All these aspects are combined fully in the sacrifice of Jesus Christ on the cross. Christ bore the punishment for our sins (1 Peter 2:24; Isaiah 53:5). Thus He is the final sin offering. Christ was wholly consecrated to God. He suffered death and destruction for sin, and also brings about our death to sin (Romans 6:2–7). Thus He is the final burnt offering. Christ in His perfect obedience gave to God the honor and thanks that are due to Him. Thus He is the final grain offering. Christ now offers us His flesh to eat (John 6:54–58). By partaking of His flesh and blood we have eternal life, we have communion with the Father, and we are transformed into Christ's image (2 Corinthians 3:18). Thus Christ is the final fellowship offering.

FOUR

THE PRIESTS AND THE PEOPLE: PREFIGURING CHRIST'S RELATION TO HIS PEOPLE

The priests of the Old Testament serve as mediators between God and human beings. Because of human sin, people cannot come into the presence of God in his holiness. Instead, the priests represent the people and approach God on behalf of the people. For example, on the Day of Atonement Aaron is instructed to offer a sin offering first of all for himself (Leviticus 16:6, 11). Then he performs services dealing with the sins of the people (Leviticus 16:15–16, 19–22). The priest "makes atonement for himself and for the people" (Leviticus 9:7, 16:24). The story of Numbers 15–18 confirms that the descendants of Aaron alone are to represent the people. Similarly, we find statements about the priest "bearing guilt" on behalf of the people. "He will bear the guilt involved in the sacred gifts the Israelites consecrate, whatever their gifts may be" (Exodus 28:38). "It [the priest's portion of the sin offering] was given to you to take away the guilt of the community by making atonement for them before the LORD" (Leviticus 10:17). "You, your sons and your father's family are to bear the responsibility for offenses against the sanctuary, and you and your sons alone are to bear the responsibility for offenses against the priesthood" (Numbers 18:1). "The Levites . . . are to do the work of the Tent of Meeting and bear the responsibility for offenses against it" (Numbers 18:23).

The priests thus present the sins of the people to God for cleansing. They also convey the blessing of God to the people.

Tell Aaron and his sons, "This is how you are to bless the Israelites. Say to them: 'The LORD bless you and keep you; the LORD make his face shine upon you and be gracious to you; the LORD turn his face toward you and give you peace.' So they will put my name on the Israelites, and I will bless them." (Numbers 6:23–27)

In all these respects the priests serve as figures mediating between God and the people. They prefigure a final mediatorial figure who will have no need to offer sacrifices for His own sins, because He is the perfect Mediator.

Such a high priest meets our need—one who is holy, blameless, pure, set apart from sinners, exalted above the heavens. Unlike the other high priests, he does not need to offer sacrifices day after day, first for his own sins, and then for the sins of the people. He sacrificed for their sins once for all when he offered himself. For the law appoints as high priests men who are weak; but the oath, which came after the law, appointed the Son, who has been made perfect forever. (Hebrews 7:26–28)

Even in the Old Testament we see many hints of the inadequacy of the priests descended from Aaron. Aaron himself got involved in the grievous sin of making the golden calf (Exodus 32). Two of his sons died because of their presumption in offering "unholy fire" to the Lord (Leviticus 10). At the end of the period of the judges, Eli's sons became corrupt, and the Lord had to replace them with Samuel (1 Samuel 2). The sins of the priests became one of the causes of the exile (Micah 3:11; Jeremiah 1:18; Ezekiel 22:26). The Lord explicitly pronounced that a new priest would have to arise "in the order of Melchizedek" instead of being a descendant of Aaron (Psalm 110:4). Like Melchizedek, He is both a priest and a king (Psalm 110:2). Unlike the descendants of Aaron, who die and have to be succeeded by new priests, He is a "priest forever" (Psalm 110:4). Hebrews comments concerning the way in which these passages point out the incompleteness and ultimately the inadequacy of the Old Testament priests:

If perfection could have been attained through the Levitical priesthood (for on the basis of it the law was given to the people), why was
there still need for another priest to come—one in the order of
Melchizedek, not in the order of Aaron? For when there is a change
of the priesthood, there must also be a change of the law. . . . Now
there were many of those priests, since death prevented them from
continuing in office; but because Jesus lives forever, he has a permanent priesthood. Therefore he is able to save completely those who
come to God through him, because he always lives to intercede for
them. (Hebrews 7:11–12, 23–25)

Similarities of Priests to the Tabernacle

The priests themselves are cleansed in a procedure reminiscent of the
cleansing of the tabernacle. The priests must be cleansed by blood. On
the day of the consecration of the priests, a sin offering and a whole
burnt offering are first presented on their behalf (Leviticus 8). They are
cleansed from sin and symbolically dedicated wholly to the Lord. Then
a special ram is slaughtered. The blood of the ram is placed on their
extremities, the lobe of the right ear, the thumb of the right hand, and
the big toe of the right foot (Leviticus 8:22–24). Since most people are
right-handed, the right side is chosen as the principal, representative,
"orderly" side. The ear, the upper extremity, is touched first because it is
the extremity nearest heaven. Then those extremities are touched that
are involved in manipulating the sacrifices and walking on the ground
of the tabernacle. Thus the priests' relations to all the holy things
around them are cleansed from defilement.

They are also given garments woven of material similar to the tabernacle material, of gold and blue and scarlet. The high priest is
crowned with a turban with a gold plate inscribed, "Holy to the LORD"
(Exodus 28:36). The high priest himself is in fact a kind of vertical
replica of the tabernacle. His garments correspond to the curtains of the
tabernacle. His head band with the inscription "Holy to the LORD" corresponds to the Most Holy Place, the representation of heaven. His
hands manipulate the blood that mediates between heaven and earth.
His feet remain planted on the earth. Ears, hands, and feet are all consecrated with blood, corresponding to the consecration of all parts of

the tabernacle. Thus he is not only a human being, sinful like ourselves, but a human being clothed with the majesty of heaven.

Majestic as he is, he is not majestic enough. In the development of Old Testament history, the priesthood itself fails to be truly consecrated (1 Samuel 2:30–36). Even Aaron himself fails in the incident of the golden calf (Exodus 32:2–6). The priests die and must be succeeded by others in a process of endless repetition. These priests are really only a shadow and copy of reality, just as the tabernacle itself is a shadow and copy of heaven. The real priest must be heavenly. That is, He must be a man from heaven, true God and true man (Hebrews 1:1–5). He is Himself the final union of heaven and earth, a Man who is the "radiance of God's glory and the exact representation of his being" (Hebrews 1:3). He is the original of which cloud, fire, tabernacle, throne, and animals' blood are the copies.

Pagan Counterfeit Worship

The priesthood and the tabernacle in Israel present us with proper images of heavenly things. But paganism always attempts to produce idolatrous substitutes for the true God. We can see this counterfeiting procedure of paganism at work in Nebuchadnezzar's dream in Daniel 2. Nebuchadnezzar's dream is given to him by God (Daniel 2:28, 30, 45). But the details of its imagery contrast strikingly with the imagery given to Daniel himself in a later dream in Daniel 7. Daniel sees four earthly kingdoms in their true dimensions, as four rapacious beasts. The pagan Nebuchadnezzar sees the same four kingdoms as a pagan would see them, in a much more attractive and man-like form. In fact, Nebuchadnezzar sees what is undoubtedly an idol image. All the four kingdoms that the image represents are at root idolatrous kingdoms, aspiring to have godlike powers and therefore trampling God's people under foot. The dream that Nebuchadnezzar saw in Daniel 2 may or may not have motivated him to set up the idol image described in Daniel 3. But no one should miss the fact that this image of gold has a striking resemblance to the head of gold in Daniel 2 that is identified with Nebuchadnezzar himself (Daniel 2:38).

Thus Nebuchadnezzar's dream reveals a false priesthood and a false worship that earthly kingdoms would set up. These earthly kingdoms are to be destroyed and superseded by God's kingdom. Nebuchadnezzar as a pagan is given no inner insight into the constitution of God's kingdom, but sees only the contrast with earthly kingdoms. God's kingdom is a "rock cut out of a mountain, but not by human hands" (Daniel 2:45). Daniel in his dream sees the true dimensions of the new heavenly kingdom. He sees a heavenly man in contrast to the bestial character of the four kingdoms (Daniel 7:13–14).

Thus the representation of the final heavenly kingdom in the form of "one like a son of man" (Daniel 7:13) is no accident. This Son of Man figure combines in Himself the features of much previous revelation. He is man, the antithesis of the bestial character of the four earthly kingdoms. He is also heavenly in origin, "coming with the clouds of heaven," (Daniel 7:13), the symbolism of the coming of God Himself. He is also, I would suggest, a priest, the mediator of God's presence and blessing to His people (cf. Daniel 7:27). One can see connections between this figure in Daniel and both the heavenly man-like figure in Ezekiel 1:26–28 and Ezekiel the prophet, who is a priest repeatedly called "son of man." In Ezekiel, the heavenly picture of God in Ezekiel 1:26–28 and the human priesthood of Ezekiel himself are still held apart. In Daniel they are subtly combined using the fluid imagery available in visionary depiction.

The People of Israel

The people of Israel as a whole are to be "a kingdom of priests and a holy nation" (Exodus 19:6). The Aaronic priests, as we have seen, are imitators of God and His divine order. The people in turn are imitators of the Aaronic priests. Moreover, the fundamental command, "Be holy because I, the LORD your God, am holy" (Leviticus 19:2) is directed to everyone. Each person individually is to imitate God in holiness, and the nation as a whole is to be "a holy nation" imitating God corporately.

The holiness of which the Old Testament speaks is not merely a matter of mysterious inward attitudes or scrupulosities with respect to certain minor matters. It is first of all theological in character. God has acted in the Exodus to redeem Israel, and has called them to be in fellowship with Him. Through the Red Sea, the tabernacle, the cloud, the manna, and the other elements in the Mosaic era, He has blessed them and distinguished them from all other peoples (Deuteronomy 7:7–11). Therefore they are to live in conformity with the status they have been given as the special people of God. Every aspect of their lives is transformed: their relation to God's special presence among them (approach to the tabernacle), their expectation for the future (possession of the land), their attitudes of pride or coveting (Deuteronomy 8:10–20; 5:21), their use of the land (Leviticus 25:23), their sexual relations (Leviticus 18:1–30), their diet (Deuteronomy 11), their farming practices (Deuteronomy 24:19–22), their use of money (Deuteronomy 24:17–18; 23:19–20), their social relations to one another (Leviticus 19:13–18).

In these respects Israel was intended to model the character of God and thus be a witness to surrounding nations. "Observe them [the laws] carefully, for this will show your wisdom and understanding to the nations, who will hear about all these decrees and say, 'Surely this great nation is a wise and understanding people.' What other nation is so great as to have their gods near them the way the LORD our God is near to us?" (Deuteronomy 4:6–7). As "priests" in a broad sense, they would be mediators of the presence of God to the other nations. God had promised to Abraham that "all people on earth will be blessed through you" (Genesis 12:3). Zechariah pictures the fulfillment of this purpose in saying, "In those days ten men from all languages and nations will take firm hold of one Jew by the edge of his robe and say, 'Let us go with you, because we have heard that God is with you'" (Zechariah 8:23).

Israel was not only a nation of priests, but God's "firstborn son" (Exodus 4:22; cf. Deuteronomy 8:5). Israel failed, however, to live in obedience to God. She was corrupted by injustice (Isaiah 1:21). Her very failure testified to the need for a final, obedient Son who would come from the line of David and would establish justice (Isaiah 11:1–5; 9:6–7). In Isaiah God promises to raise up His Servant, whom He names "Israel" (Isaiah 49:3), but who will also "bring Jacob back to him" (Isaiah 49:5). Injustice and impurity are cleansed (Isaiah 4:4) by the Servant's death as a sacrificial lamb (Isaiah 53). Isaiah is speaking, of course, about the work of Jesus Christ. Christ is the final, definitive seed of Abraham (Galatians 3:16). And when Christ comes, Matthew notes that His life is patterned after the life of Israel the son (Matthew 1:15). Or rather, he notes that the Old Testament history of Israel was patterned after the true and final Son.

The church in turn is patterned after the fullness of Christ (Ephesians 4:7–16). The experience of Christians is thus in a multifaceted way analogous to that of Israel (1 Corinthians 10:1–13; Hebrews 12:14–29; Galatians 4:21–31). We are the first fruits of a new humanity in a new heaven and new earth (James 1:18; Revelation 14:4; 21:1). Christopher J. H. Wright sums up these matters by saying that Israel as a people is related "paradigmatically" to fallen mankind, "eschatologically" to the whole of redeemed humanity, and "typologically" to the church.[1] He could have added to these observations the fact that Israel is a type pointing to Christ first of all, and only through Christ to the church and to the new humanity. These rich connections indicate the multidimensional significance of the Old Testament for us.

FIVE

GENERAL PRINCIPLES FOR GOD'S DWELLING WITH HUMAN BEINGS: PREFIGURING UNION WITH CHRIST

W hat general principles may we see illustrated by the joint operation of the tabernacle, the sacrifices, and the priests?

The Interaction of Tabernacle, Sacrifices, and Priests

In many ways the tabernacle, the sacrifices, and the priesthood go together. None of them is really workable or even intelligible apart from
the rest. The tabernacle must have sacrifices and priesthood to provide
cleansing and access for sinful people. To be of any value, the sacrifices
must be presented in the presence of God by priests whose special holiness qualifies them to approach God. The priests must themselves be
consecrated and cleansed by sacrifices and must have a space and equipment with which to accomplish their work.

On a more fundamental level the priesthood, the tabernacle, and
the sacrifices together express three aspects of God's dwelling with

human beings. God's relation to human beings always involves His personal presence, His order, and His power exerted to bless or to curse.

The priesthood represents the fact that God's relation to human beings is a personal one. Sinful human beings cannot enter God's presence on their own; hence, they must be represented by others who are themselves persons.

The tabernacle structure itself represents the divinely imposed order. God's holiness involves beautiful regularity, an architectural order imposed by God's own commands or law. The Ten Commandments are another form of God's order. They specifically articulate the order for the life of human beings, whereas the instructions for constructing the tabernacle articulate an order for God's own dwelling and the elements involved in communion with Him.

Moreover, the tabernacle contains many instances of replication or copying. The tabernacle as a whole is a copy of a heavenly pattern (Hebrews 8:5). The Holy Place is a less exalted replica of the Most Holy Place. The courtyard is in some respects a replica of the Holy Place (for one thing, it has similar shape). The priest is a replica of the tabernacle. Since Israel is a "kingdom of priests" (Exodus 19:6), they are all to imitate their Father in heaven, to "be holy as I, the LORD your God, am holy" (Leviticus 19:2). Thus the tabernacle expresses in a visible way the fact that the order of God Himself is to be imposed and replicated in Israel as a whole and in every Israelite dwelling place (for they dwell in tents after the pattern of God's dwelling).

The sacrifices embody preeminently the aspect of God's power exerted for people's benefit. Sacrificial animals, by acting as a symbol for atoning substitution, take away curse and result in blessing to the people for whom they are presented.

However, we cannot rigidly separate these aspects of God's communion with human beings. For example, the theme of God's order is manifested not only in the tabernacle with its orderly structure and arrangements, but also by the sacrifices and the priesthood. The sacrifices and the priestly actions must be performed exactly as God's law-order prescribes them. The priests must be clothed in special, heavenly garments, thereby indicating that they must have God's order and righteousness imposed on them or represented in them rather than simply appearing in their own innate imperfection.

Similarly, the power of God to bless or curse is visible in each area. The sacrifices, as we have seen, manifest God's power to cleanse from sin and defilement. But the priests demonstrate the same operations of power because they are involved in priestly actions manipulating the sacrifices in order to accomplish the blessing. In addition, they are given authority to pronounce a verbal blessing on the people (Numbers 6:22–27).

The personal character of God's presence is shown most vividly by the priests who are themselves persons. But the whole symbolism of the tabernacle is also a reminder of God's personal character because it is a tent-house, a dwelling place for persons. The sacrifices, however, admittedly show the personal character of communion with God only in indirect ways. They are presented by worshipers who are persons and manipulated by priests who are persons. Moreover, by placing a hand on the animal the worshiper signifies a kind of personal identification with the animal. The blood of the slain animal represents the animal's life— not personal life, but at least the life of an animate creature. As we have observed, the deficiency in animal sacrifice is remedied only when Christ becomes not only the priest but the offering as well.

These three themes or aspects of God's dwelling are manifested in each of the three spatial areas of the tabernacle. Let us begin with the Most Holy Place. The personal presence of God is symbolized most vividly by the ark. The ark is the container for the "testimony" or covenant, the two tablets with the Ten Commandments, in which God speaks to His people (Exodus 25:21; 40:20; Deuteronomy 10:5). It is closely associated with God's presence throughout the Old Testament.[1] God is represented as most immediately present in the space between the cherubim: "There, above the cover between the two cherubim that are over the ark of the Testimony, I will meet with you and give you all my commands for the Israelites" (Exodus 25:22). The power of God to bless or curse is represented most vividly by the atonement cover. Its very name reminds us of the need for atonement and the provision that God Himself makes to satisfy violation of His law. The orderliness of God's dwelling is represented most vividly by the tablets of the law contained inside the ark. These tablets specify the order that the people of God must follow as they dwell in His presence.

The Holy Place contains furnishings suggesting the same truths. The personal presence of God is suggested by the bread of the Presence, not only because it is named after the "Presence" of God, but because it suggests the privilege of having a meal in communion with God. The power of cursing, blessing, and atonement is suggested most immediately by the altar of incense, because its smoke conceals the wrath of God and because it receives blood from some of the sacrifices offered on the bronze altar. The order of God is suggested by all the carefully constructed furnishings of the Holy Place, but perhaps most of all by the lampstand because it lights the Holy Place and thereby reveals the order. In the darkness human beings feel lost and in disorder, but when the light comes, it gives them order. Since the lampstand also has a symbolic relation to the lights of heaven, it suggests the most fundamental orderings of the universe and of time, such as God has ordained them.

Finally, the courtyard contains suggestions of the same truths. The personal presence of God is suggested most by the contact between layperson and priest. The power of blessing, cursing, and atonement is symbolized by the use of sacrificial animals in order to make atonement and thereby bring blessing to the people. The order of God is suggested by prescribed rituals for each kind of sacrifice, as well as by the fixed presence of the bronze altar and the laver.

In each of the main spatial areas of the tabernacle precincts, the fundamental aspects of God dwelling with human beings are symbolized. In each case the three aspects are not ultimately separable from one another, but the various features of the tabernacle precincts represent one or the other of the aspects more prominently. In this respect also, each precinct of the tabernacle is a replica of the more holy precincts, and the Most Holy Place is a replica of the intimate dwelling of God in heaven.

In addition, we might perhaps discern within each major precinct of the tabernacle a distinct emphasis. For instance, God is most immediately present in the Most Holy Place, and so this place most vividly represents the personal presence of God. The courtyard with its sacrifices and sacrificial procedures speaks of the power of God to make atonement. The Holy Place is a place of intense order, where each item of furniture has a distinct shape and function, and where the items together symbolize the order that God imposes on the universe at large (order of lights of heaven, seasons, agriculture, etc.). But since all three of our aspects are really manifested in all three precincts of the tabernacle, perhaps it is best not to attribute much significance to the possibility of these distinct emphases.

Interestingly, Moses himself, at least to a degree, embodies all three of these aspects in his own person. First, consider the theme of personal presence. Moses as a person mediates between God and the Israelites. Moses went up to Mount Sinai, symbolically representing an ascent into God's heavenly presence, while the people stayed at the foot of the mountain (Exodus 19). After hearing the terrifying voice of God, the people asked that Moses be the regular mediator of God's words (Exodus 20:18–22; Deuteronomy 5:23–33). Next, consider the theme of blessing and cursing. Moses is the mediator of God's judgments. When Israel apostatized from God in the wilderness, Moses pronounced judgment on them and called them back to God. In the great sin of the golden calf, Moses even proposed to offer himself as a substitute, and thus functioned in a manner parallel to the regular function of animal sacrifices (Exodus 32:31–32). Finally, consider the theme of order. Moses is the ultimate human authority and leader of the Israelites, and serves to mediate God's order to them in the form of commandments.

Covenant: The Way of God with His People

The tabernacle arrangements and the priesthood are closely related to the covenantal form of God's dealings with Israel. According to Exodus 19:5 and other texts, God's relation to Israel had the form of a covenant, i.e., a formalized pact with sanctions (see Exodus 24:7–8; 34:10–28; Deuteronomy 29:1, 9, 14, 21). When such pacts were made between human beings, the parties expressed loyalty to one another and spelled out their mutual obligations (e.g., Genesis 21:26–31; 26:28–30; 31:44–54). They also took an oath calling down curses on themselves if they did not keep the terms of the covenant. Thus all covenants necessarily had three parts: (1) an identification of the parties involved ("identification"); (2) specification of their mutual obligations ("stipulations"); and (3) an oath indicating how God (or, in polytheistic contexts, gods) would reward obedience and punish disobedience to the stipulations ("sanctions"). When God uses the covenantal form to establish and express his relation to Israel, these three elements of the covenant express, respectively, the principles of (1) personal presence, (2) divine order, and (3) God's power to bless or curse and to make atonement through substitution.

Covenantal loyalty and communion can be expressed in a multiplicity of ways. Symbolic actions and signs can be said to sum up God's covenantal relation to Israel (Genesis 17:10–11; Exodus 31:16). The tabernacle itself is a kind of sign of God's covenant, because through its symbolism God indicates that He undertakes to dwell with Israel and bless them as they remain faithful to His law-order. But though it is symbolized in a variety of ways, a covenant is by nature a formalized verbal pact. The pact generally includes all three major elements, namely, identification of the parties, stipulations, and sanctions. These three major elements usually appear in fixed, 1–2–3 order because this order represents a smooth logical and literary development. A covenant first identifies the parties, then specifies their obligations, and then tells about the future consequences of their behavior.

At this point we must compare our own analysis with other discussions of covenantal forms. Meredith G. Kline's analysis of covenant, building on previous work by George Mendenhall and others, sees major Old Testament covenants as falling into five distinct literary parts, parallel to the distinct parts of so-called suzerainty treaties made by Hittite kings in the second millennium B.C.[2] Powerful Hittite kings or "suzerains" made treaties with subordinate rulers or "vassals." The vassal promised loyalty, obedience, and support to the suzerain in return for the suzerain's blessing and protection. Since even pagan Hittite kings derived their authority from God, their practices inevitably imitated the authority of God in certain respects. God providentially controlled the whole situation in the Ancient Near East in such a way that these Hittite treaties became a suitable analogy for the Israelites to understand better God's dealings with them.

The Hittite treaties customarily had six distinct parts: (1) a preamble identifying the suzerain; (2) a historical prologue, recounting previous relations with the vassal; (3) stipulations, specifying the duties of the vassal; (4) provision for deposit of the treaty in the temple of the vassal and for periodic public reading; (5) list of gods as witnesses; (6) curses and blessings for violation or loyalty to the treaty.[3] In the monotheistic context of God's revelation to Israel, God is Himself the sole Divine Witness; hence, we ought not to expect anything corresponding exactly to part 5 of the Hittite treaties.[4] After eliminating part 5, Kline finds that the Book of Deuteronomy can be analyzed as a treaty with five parts, a preamble (1:1–5), historical prologue (1:6–4:49), stipulations (5:1–26:49), sanctions (27:1–30:20), and a final section that he entitles "dynastic disposition: covenant continuity" (31:1–34:12).

But there are some notable differences between the Hittite treaties and the book of Deuteronomy. For example, the final section of Deuteronomy in 31:1–34:12 contains provisions for continuation of the song of Moses (Deuteronomy 32) in the memory of the people and for deposit of the document in the ark (31:19–21, 24–27). Thus it corresponds in some ways to section 4 of the Hittite treaties. But it contains other material as well that connects to section 4 only in a distant fashion. In addition, sections 4 and 6 of the Hittite treaties occur in the book of Deuteronomy in the reverse of their normal order. Finally, the preamble in Deuteronomy 1:1–5 introduces Moses in the key role, by using "These are the words which Moses spoke . . . ," in a manner analogous to the preambles of Hittite treaties, "These are the words of the Sun Mursilis, the great king, the king of the Hatti, the valiant . . ."[5] But God rather than Moses is the great King who makes a treaty with His people; hence, the preamble of Deuteronomy does not correspond exactly to anything in the Hittite treaties.

Altogether, it appears that the formal literary structure to the book of Deuteronomy does indeed correspond to the structure of Hittite treaties. But the correspondence arises from a loose and free adaptation of a treaty form rather than the use of an exact replica of the form. The number and the arrangement of distinct literary sections of the treaties is not quite preserved in Deuteronomy.

According to Mendenhall and Kline, the same treaty form is also visible in the Exodus 20 account of the Ten Commandments. We have a preamble ("I am the LORD your God," 20:2), a historical prologue ("who brought you out of Egypt, out of the land of slavery," 20:2), stipulations (the Ten Commandments themselves, 20:3–17), sanctions (20:5–6, 7, 12), and provisions for deposit (25:16). But here the correspondence with Hittite treaties is even looser. The preamble and the prologue are compressed into a single sentence so that they no longer form two distinct literary sections. The sanctions are interwoven with the stipulations rather than being arranged in a separate section. The provisions for deposit and reading of the treaty are not included at all in Exodus 20, but are discussed only at later points in the Mosaic narrative. Thus the Hittite treaty forms of the Ancient Near East are used with considerable freedom within Exodus and Deuteronomy.

Even apart from the comparisons with Hittite forms, it is clear that Exodus 20 with its Ten Commandments constitutes a covenant between God and His people Israel (Exodus 34:8; Deuteronomy 4:13, 23; 5:2; 9:9). To these central words are added supplements and explanations, such as we find in Exodus 21–23 and 34:10–26, and such supplements also are said to belong to the covenant (24:7; 34:27). After the people broke God's covenant in the incident of the golden calf, it was renewed in Exodus 34:10–28. The book of Deuteronomy as a whole constituted a second renewal, appropriate to the situation where the people were on the point of entering the Promised Land (Deuteronomy 29:1, 9).

In a rough way the five sections of a treaty correspond to the three themes that we have already discerned in the tabernacle and its ministry. The preamble and historical prologue preeminently express the theme of God's personal presence; the stipulations express His order; and the sanctions and provisions for deposit express God's power to bless and curse, and therefore the importance of preserving the words for the future. Thus the same basic principles concerning God's relations to Israel are expressed in both the tabernacle and the covenant documents.

There are nevertheless some differences between themes expressed in the tabernacle and in the covenant documents. The tabernacle is a fixed, static symbol. As such, it is suited for representing the constancy of God's communion with His people Israel. The covenantal documents, on the other hand, can directly speak of the past and future of God's dealings with Israel. The historical prologue narrates past acts of deliverance. The sections on sanctions and on deposit of the documents can be expanded to speak of the future. Even in this respect, however, we must not underestimate the significance of the tabernacle. The setting up of the tabernacle announces God's victory and celebrates the glory of God; as an act of worship it forms the climactic event in the exodus from Egypt. God delivers the people from slavery under false gods and oppressive masters in order to bring them into allegiance to the true God and true Master of a new household of faith. Thus the tabernacle has natural connections backward in history to the events of the Exodus. In addition, the sacrifices are reminiscent of the passover lamb and more distantly of Abraham's sacrifice of Isaac. The tabernacle also includes forward-pointing elements, since it is only a copy and shadow of the real sanctuary in heaven, and since its sacrifices can never remove sins for all time. Access to God and communion with Him is still barred by veils. The tabernacle is thus a symbolic form of the promise of a future coming of the new Jerusalem.

The themes of God's dwelling with human beings are all fulfilled in Christ. First, Christ expresses the personal presence of God. "For in Christ all the fullness of the Deity lives in bodily form" (Colossians 2:9). "Anyone who has seen me has seen the Father. How can you say, 'Show us the Father'? Don't you believe that I am in the Father, and that the Father is in me?" (John 14:9–10). God comes uniquely to meet us and even to dwell within us through Christ: "On that day you will realize that I am in my Father, and you are in me, and I am in you" (14:20). "My Father will love him, and we will come to him and make our home with him" (14:23).

Second, Christ expresses the order of God, in that His character is the perfect pattern of righteousness: "you are in Christ Jesus, who has become for us wisdom from God—that is our righteousness, holiness and redemption" (1 Corinthians 1:30). "Rather, clothe yourselves with the Lord Jesus Christ, and do not think about how to gratify the desires of the sinful nature" (Romans 13:14).

Third, Christ expresses the power of God to atone for sin, since He has died as the final sacrifice for sins: "Christ was sacrificed once to take away the sins of many people" (Hebrews 9:28). "He is the atoning sacrifice for our sins, and not only for ours but also for the sins of the whole world" (1 John 2:2).

Since Christ is the fulfillment of the whole of Mosaic revelation, we may expect to find these three themes throughout the books of Moses. Whether we subdivide them into three emphases or five or some other number matters little.

SIX

THE LAND OF PALESTINE, THE PROMISED LAND: PREFIGURING CHRIST'S RENEWAL OF AND DOMINION OVER THE EARTH

The land of Palestine also plays a special role in the books of Moses and even in the whole Old Testament. One of the main aspects of the promise made to Abraham is the promise that he and his offspring will inherit the land (Genesis 12:1, 7; 13:14–17; 15:18–21; 17:8).

God's Promise of the Land

Much of the story of the Old Testament can be plotted around this center. Genesis recounts how Abraham's offspring waited several generations looking for fulfillment of the promise. Exodus tells how they were delivered from Egypt as an aspect of the promise. Numbers tells how a whole generation failed to enter the land. Deuteronomy largely contains instructions for the people's conduct in the land and concludes with the people standing on its borders about to enter. Joshua through 2 Samuel tells of the vicissitudes of conquest, completed only with the reign of Solomon (1 Kings 4:20–21). After Solomon the story concerns the pattern of Deuteronomy 29:1–30:10, where the disobedience of the people leads to exile from the land, and then restoration.

The land is so important not only because it is an important part of God's foundational promise, but also because it sustains symbolical connections in several directions. The land is granted to Abraham and his descendants as part of the covenantal relation between God and His people: the land is a covenantal grant or gift, a benefit of the royal charter between God and His people.[1] Thus it shares in the complex connections of Biblical covenants.

The land is God's own land; the people are only tenants (Leviticus 25:23–24). Because the land is particularly associated with God, it is in a broad sense *holy* and will be defiled by gross sins (Leviticus 18:24–28). The land is the land "where I dwell, for I, the LORD, dwell among the Israelites" (Numbers 35:34). The land as the dwelling of God is analogous to the tabernacle and the temple, which are the dwelling of God in a more intensive sense. The small piece of land occupied by the temple is replicated on a large scale by the land as a whole. Thus we should not be surprised that the land is a large-scale embodiment of the principles of the tabernacle. Defilement of the land corresponds to defilement of the tabernacle, and cleansing of the land, as in Numbers 35:33–34, corresponds to cleansing the tabernacle. The people as a whole, who live on the land, are analogous to the priests who offer special service in the tabernacle.

The Holiness of the Land and Its Symbolic Associations

In light of this framework of correspondences, we should ask ourselves whether the land shares in the multiple symbolic relations of the tabernacle, as listed earlier in chapter 2. It must share in such relations at least indirectly, since it is symbolically related to the tabernacle and the tabernacle in turn is related to the entire list. Are there also direct indications of such relations in the Bible? We ought not necessarily to expect the same quantity of material, since the land shares in holiness only at a reduced level of intensity. Let us go through the list in chapter 2, item by item, to confirm our analysis.

1. Heaven is the dwelling of God. Is the land analogous to heaven? Hebrews 11:14–16 says that the promise of land to Abraham

caused him and his descendants to be "looking for a country of their own. If they had been thinking of the country they had left, they would have had opportunity to return. Instead, they were longing for a better country—a heavenly one." Thus Abraham himself discerned that the land of Palestine was a shadow of a final heavenly dwelling place.

2. The whole universe is the dwelling of God. The land of Palestine is to be a paradigmatic land, a representative sample standing for the whole earth. What happens there is intended to be paradigmatic for all nations (Deuteronomy 4:5–8; 29:22–28).

3. The tabernacle is a dwelling of God. We have just seen above that the treatment of land and tabernacle is analogous. Moreover, the exile of the land goes together with the destruction of the temple, while the return from exile goes together with the rebuilding of the temple.

4. The Garden of Eden was a dwelling of God. The land of Palestine is described as a rich, garden-like land reminiscent of Eden (Deuteronomy 8:7–9; 7:13–15; Joel 2:3; Isaiah 51:3; Ezekiel 36:35).

5. The people of God are the dwelling place of God. The books of Moses connect the people and the land not mainly by symbolic analogies but by showing that the prosperity or adversity of the two go together. Prosperity in the land is conditioned on the fundamental spiritual prosperity of loyalty to God (Deuteronomy 28).

6. The body of an individual saint is a dwelling of God. This theme is comparatively rare in the background in the Old Testament. There do not seem to be prominent instances of the use of the land as analogous to a human body (but note the language of vomiting in Leviticus 18:24–28).

7. The new Jerusalem is the final dwelling of God with human beings. The inheritance of the land is a shadow of this final inheritance (Hebrews 11:16; 12:22).

8. Christ is the ultimate dwelling of God. The language concerning holy places and spaces is now replaced by the language of being

in Christ. As W. D. Davies says, "for the holiness of place, Christianity has . . . substituted the holiness of the Person: it has Christified holy space."[2]

Christopher J. H. Wright aptly analyzes the main symbolic connections of the land in parallel with the connections of the Israelite people. The people are simultaneously related to (a) all humankind; (b) eschatological new humanity; and (c) the church as the new people of God (see chapter 4). Likewise the land is related "paradigmatically" to the whole earth (point 2 above); "eschatologically" to the new heavens and new earth (point 7 above); and "typologically" to participation in blessing in the church (point 5 above).[3] If we add to these relations that of Christ Himself as the ultimate holy space, we shall have noted the main elements necessary for understanding the significance of the land in the Old Testament.

The land then was God's gift to Israel, and therefore a tangible sign of His goodness, favor, and blessing. Like all the other important institutions in Israel, it was a means of communion with God. It showed His goodness and beauty. By dispossessing the wicked Canaanites and giving the land to Israel, God also showed His righteousness and His salvific power (Deuteronomy 7). The land spoke of God's faithfulness and the truthfulness of His promises, because its possession was a fulfillment of God's ancient promise to Abraham (Deuteronomy 6:10).

But the land was simultaneously a trust and a responsibility. Israel, as a kind of corporate Adam, was to guard the land from defilement. They were to tend and till the land in order to obtain and enjoy its increase. The fact that the land belonged first of all to God meant that it could not be permanently sold (Leviticus 25:23–24). Poor people were to be protected from land-grabbers, and were to be given access to some of the yield of the land (Leviticus 23:25–28; 19:9–10; Deuteronomy 23:25–25; 24:19–22; 26:11–15).

Prosperity in the land was to be an index of Israel's faithfulness (Deuteronomy 28:1–14). Exile and loss of the land would result from continued disobedience (Deuteronomy 28:15–29:28). These arrangements prefigured the inheritance of the new heaven and new earth, which we receive now on the basis of Christ's obedience, not our own (1 Peter 1:4). Our own obedience still matters, because as imitators of

Christ we are meant to reflect His generosity to us (2 Corinthians 8:9). Whatever gifts we receive, whether tangible or intangible in character, are not only a blessing but a trust to be used responsibly in His service (1 Peter 4:10; 1 Timothy 6:17–19).

SEVEN

THE LAW AND
ITS ORDER: PREFIGURING
THE RIGHTEOUSNESS OF CHRIST

T he law of God plays an important role in God's communion with Israel in Mosaic times. To begin with, in terms of sheer quantity law-like material dominates: it makes up a considerable portion of the five books of Moses. Moreover, the Ten Commandments as a heart of the law receive special attention. God spoke the Ten Commandments directly to all Israel from the top of Mount Sinai, in contrast to the rest of the material that the people received through Moses (Exodus 20:1–21; Deuteronomy 4:10–13). The Ten Commandments alone were written directly by the finger of God on the two stone tablets that Moses received on Mount Sinai (Deuteronomy 4:13; 10:4). In the beginning these tablets alone were deposited in the ark (Deuteronomy 10:1–5; Exodus 25:16; 40:20). The many other instructions that God gave through Moses were also later written down and put not inside the ark but *beside* it (Deuteronomy 31:24–26). The ark itself, the most central and most holy item associated with the tabernacle, is specifically designated "the ark of the testimony" (e.g., Exodus 25:22; 26:33, 34; 30:6, 26; 31:7) or "the ark of the covenant" (e.g., Numbers 10:33; 14:44). In these designations it is understood that the "testimony" or "covenant" refers to the Ten Commandments (cf. Exodus 25:21 with Deuteronomy 10:1–5).

Thus the main function of the ark is to contain the tablets of the covenant with the Ten Commandments written on them.

The Law as the Sovereign Treaty of the Great King

To an Israelite the basic function of God's law was clear. God's law was the treaty of God the great King. In it He promised care and benefits for His people, and they pledged their loyalty and obedience to Him. As we have seen (chapter 5), the law had some notable formal parallels with treaties and laws of Ancient Near Eastern kings.

When the ancient Hittites made treaties, they produced two copies, one for the suzerain and the other for the vassal. Corresponding to this practice, God wrote the Ten Commandments on two tablets—almost certainly two copies of the same Ten Commandments rather than one copy in two parts. Both copies were deposited in the tabernacle since in the case of Israel the central residence of God the Suzerain was simultaneously the central point for Israel the vassal.[1]

Thus the law was the instrument and expression for God's kingly rule over Israel. Such a perspective is quite compatible with what we have seen from the tabernacle. The tabernacle, by imaging heavenly realities, emphasizes the exalted, heavenly character of God's presence within Israel, whereas the treaty pattern emphasizes the analogy between the rule of God and the rule of human kings. But these two emphases are two sides of the same coin. The tabernacle, heavenly as it is, constantly uses analogies, both analogies with the visible heavens and analogies from the Israelites' experiences of deliverance. The presence of analogy and the fact that the tabernacle is itself a copy, not the original, bring its message down to earth. Conversely, when we start with the analogy with Hittite treaties, we must simultaneously recognize that God's kingship is the origin and pattern for all earthly kings. Hence, His treaty is exalted and unique, not like that of a merely human king.

The tabernacle itself suggests a harmony between the two viewpoints because it is a replica of the heavenly palace of the great King of the universe. The ark resembles in shape the footstool of a king. The two copies of the treaty, as we have seen, are deposited in the ark. The two cherubim attached to the ark and the cherubim woven into the pattern of the curtains represent guards of God's throne room. Hence, the basic imagery of the tabernacle affirms the kingship of God and puts the law in its rightful position as the treaty-deposit of the great King.

Moreover, the insight that God is the great King of the whole universe is powerfully expressed in the tabernacle by the use of imagery from creation. The symbolism of the tabernacle combines imagery from creation and redemption. The lampstand simultaneously has a connection in two directions, with the supernatural redemptive light that God provides in the fiery cloud, and the natural creational light from the heavenly bodies. The bread of the Presence simultaneously has a connection with the supernatural redemptive manna from heaven and the natural creational supply of food that God brings about through ordinary agricultural processes. The tabernacle as a whole is simultaneously an image of the creational structure of heaven and earth and the redemptive structure of the animal sacrifices and the priesthood. All these relations are no accident. The same God is both Creator and Redeemer. More than that, redemption is itself a kind of new creation or re-creation. The fall damaged the whole of the lower creation. Effects flowed out from Adam who was the key representative. Appropriately, redemption repairs and overcomes this damage. Effects flow out from Christ, the representative to the whole of creation (cf. Romans 8:22). The idea of a representative standing for a larger group runs through the entire plan. Adam as the creational son represented all his descendants. He was placed in the Garden of Eden, a plot of land representative of all the earth. Similarly, Christ as the Redeemer Son represents all those who are united to Him (Romans 8:29–34). Israel in the Old Testament typified Christ. As a redemptive son, Israel was to be placed in the new garden land of Palestine, flowing with milk and honey.

The same insights are reexpressed when we look at God as the great King. At creation, the King originated His dominion by speaking words of power and order that called the world into being and gave it structure. The same King in the Exodus originated a re-creative dominion over Israel (a kingdom of priests) by speaking and acting through

Moses. He redeemed Israel out of Egypt and then gave the law. The law as His word of order formed Israel into a structured nation under God.

The law expresses God's rule in at least three complementary ways. First, it publishes and imposes an order, a system of regularity, righteousness, and fitness. It specifies the way life is to be lived within God's dominion, and the distinctions and orders that are to be preserved. Second, it expresses the character of God and opens to Israel a personal communion with God the speaker. God's communication to Israel embodies an intimacy with Israel unlike His relation to other nations (cf. Psalm 147:19–20). Third, it expresses the awesomeness of punishments and judgments that fall on people who are disobedient and unholy, and the rewards for the obedient.

The tabernacle expresses God's rule in visible form in these same three ways, as we saw in the preceding chapter. Thus the law and the tabernacle are complementary expressions of the same basic realities about the character of God, His dominion and His fellowship with Israel. Law and tabernacle are each to be used to appreciate more deeply the meaning of the other. Each is a guide to properly understanding the other. In fact, in certain respects each is the origin of the other.

First, consider the tabernacle. The tabernacle is built according to specific law-like instructions. Law in the general sense of instruction from God makes up the key chapters Exodus 25–30 describing the design of the tabernacle. The order of the tabernacle itself is thus a replica of the order given in the designs or law set forth in Exodus 25–30. The chapters Exodus 36–39 repeat Exodus 25–30 almost exactly, in order to stress that Bezalel in constructing the tabernacle carried out God's designs exactly. In addition to all these facts, one might almost claim that the tabernacle as a whole is designed to house the law, since the copies of the law are the main things deposited in the Most Holy Place. The holiness of the tabernacle is thus in one respect a replica of the holiness of the law.

Second, consider the law. Though the Ten Commandments were spoken to Israel with the direct voice of God (Deuteronomy 4:12–13), this direct communication was an exceptional procedure used to validate the mediation of Moses (Deuteronomy 4:14; 5:28–30; Exodus 20:18–19). God indicated that as a general rule He would speak to

Moses from "above the cover between the two cherubim" (Exodus 25:22; see Exodus 33:7–11). That is, God communicated the bulk of the law through the means of His symbolic presence represented in the tabernacle system. Moses heard the law spoken from the presence of God in the Most Holy Place of the tabernacle. From this point of view, the law of Moses as a whole embodies the verbal side of God's communion with Israel through the tabernacle.

This point becomes still clearer if we go beyond the tabernacle itself to consider what the tabernacle symbolizes. The tabernacle symbolizes the heavenly presence of God, the throne room of God in heaven where God sits as King (cf. Isaiah 6:1–4). From God's throne come all His utterances. Hence, the tabernacle symbolizes and depicts the majestic divine origin of all God's speech to human beings.

We have already seen that the tabernacle foreshadows the coming of Christ as "Immanuel," God with us. The tabernacle signifies the reconciliation and communion with God that we enjoy through Christ. The close connection between the law and the tabernacle suggests that the law must fundamentally foreshadow and signify the same realities. The law is the treaty of the great King. This great King came to reign in fullness when Christ came. Christ's own message on earth is summarized in the words, "Repent, for the kingdom of heaven is at hand" (Matthew 4:17). The kingdom of heaven or the kingdom of God is the saving rule of God, exercised in fulfillment of all the promises of salvation in the Old Testament. Thus the Old Testament proclamations of God the King foreshadow this final proclamation through Christ. "In the past God spoke to our forefathers through the prophets at many times and in various ways, but in these last days he has spoken to us by his son, whom he appointed heir of all things, and through whom he made the universe" (Hebrews 1:1–2). The Old Testament treaties or covenants made by God anticipate the great new covenant later made through Christ (2 Corinthians 3:1–18).

Christ brought to fulfillment the three sides of God's rule that we have already seen. He brought to expression the order of God's life by His example, His teaching, and the teaching of the apostles sent by Him. He also opened the way to a new depth of communion and personal fellowship with God as He revealed to us the very character of

God. He is "the radiance of God's glory and the exact representation of his being" (Hebrews 1:3). And He made the definitive atoning sacrifice for sins when He died on the cross, thus satisfying the law's penalties for disobedience.

The Law Articulating God's Order

The law of Moses sets forth a detailed order for Israel's existence and life. Orderliness is a characteristic of God, since He is in fact the Source and Creator of all the order of the universe. Any people who live in His presence as Israel did must submit to His order and reflect in their own lives the order and righteousness of God. They must be imitators of God. Their moral behavior must conform to the purity and righteousness of God. Thus the Ten Commandments set forth the basic features of God's moral order, an order required as part of our submission to God.

We also see the order of God reflected in a striking way in those more puzzling aspects of Mosaic law, namely, the laws for diet and for cleanness and uncleanness. Many people have seen nothing but arbitrary commands in the distinctions between clean and unclean foods and in the instructions for cleansing from ceremonial defilements. But a closer look at these commands shows their inner rationale.

To begin to understand the special distinctions between clean and unclean, we must keep clearly before us two basic facts. First, God as the Creator of the universe is the origin, standard, and life-giving Creator of all order in the universe. God by creating the separations between heaven and earth, sea and dry land, divided the universe into "rooms," analogous to the separations within the tabernacle. God also populated the universe with plants and animals that reproduce "according to their various kinds" (Genesis 1:11–12). Thus He produced an order among living things and gave to those living things a limited ability to spawn further production of order as they reproduce other living things having the same orderly pattern. Human beings as the crown of creation embody the order of God in a most special way. Of course, like the animals, they have capability of reproducing further order according to their kind. But in addition they are made "in the image of God" (Genesis 1:26). In a special way they replicate on earth the order of

God, their Designer. They are the unique representatives of God on earth. The unique ability of human beings to know God, to respond actively to Him, to use language, to think, to exercise dominion over the lower creation—all these things imitate God's original knowledge, language, thought, and dominion, and contribute to human ability actively to represent God's presence on earth.

Second, the original created order of God described in Genesis 1–2 has been disrupted by the fall. In God's acts of salvation He undertakes to restore and advance His order. Salvation thus takes the form of renewal or re-creation. We see hints of this language in the Old Testament (e.g., Isaiah 65:17), but the fuller realization comes in the New Testament. "Therefore, if anyone is in Christ, he is a new creation; the old has gone, the new has come!" (2 Corinthians 5:17). The Old Testament naturally represents this renewal, not in its final form but by way of foreshadowing. The land of Palestine is a kind of new Eden; but, of course, in many respects it remains a land like all other lands and becomes subject to curse when the people of Israel disobey God. The people of Israel themselves are a kind of small-scale version of a renewed humanity; but their disobedience shows how they fall short.

The laws for cleanness and uncleanness fit into this picture in a natural way. They signify and foreshadow the way in which God cleanses sin. They show that a renewed or recreated people are characterized by renewed behavior, behavior conforming to God's order and separating them from sin. A close look at the classification of things into categories of holy, clean, and unclean shows a pattern of order.[2] God, the ultimate Creator of order, is supremely holy. He is the origin of life with its order-producing potential. By contrast, death is associated with sin and disorder. Hence, things associated with death or producing disorder are unclean. Created things that are closely associated to God or the initiation of life are counted holy. Thus the tabernacle as the center of order is holy. The firstborn human being or animal is holy and belongs to God in a special way.

Dead bodies are unclean both because of the immediate connection with death and because they degrade the order of living things back to the relative disorder of the nonliving earth. Birds that feed on carrion (dead bodies) are unclean. Things that are somehow defective or deviate from a paradigmatic order are also unclean. Fish with scales are the paradigmatic form of water creature; hence, all water creatures without scales or fins are deviant and unclean. Animals with "real" legs functioning in a familiar way are normal; but all kinds of crawling animals and insects are unclean. Grasshoppers and other hopping insects with "normal" legs are clean. Defective animals, with disease or an injured part, are not acceptable for sacrifice, even though they are not literally unclean. Animals that chew the cud and have parted hoofs are regarded as normal, possibly because these are the most common herd animals; but animals that do not have these two key features deviate from the norm and are reckoned as unclean.

It may be that the classifications are also related to the curse in Genesis 3.[3] In Genesis 3 the snake and the ground are cursed because of sin. Hence, all the things that creep on the ground like a snake are unclean (Leviticus 11:41–45). Animals that have no hooves but walk in direct contact with the ground are also unclean (Leviticus 11:27). Animals that part the hoof and chew their cud are clean (Leviticus 11:3). Possibly chewing the cud suggests a greater separation in taking in the food that comes from the ground, and the cloven hoof suggests a greater separation with respect to contact with the ground.

We do not know for certain which kind of connection may have been uppermost in the mind of an Israelite. But in a sense it does not matter. The two themes—the theme of order and the theme of separation from death and the curse—are in fact complementary, since death and the curse bring disorder and frustration.

Mixtures are usually regarded as deviant, though in some cases (e.g., the special fragrant incense and the priestly garments) they are holy. Thus Israelites are told not to mix two kinds of seed in sowing a field, and not to mix two kinds of cloth in a garment (Leviticus 19:19).

A spreading skin disease makes a person unclean because it is producing disorder.[4] When the disease has covered the whole body, it is no longer producing more disorder and the person can be pronounced clean (Leviticus 13:12–13). Spreading mildew in a house is creating disorder in the house and makes the house unclean (Leviticus 14:33–53). Any abnormal bodily discharge is creating disorder and makes the person unclean (Leviticus 15:1–33).

In the light of modern medical knowledge we can appreciate the hygienic value of some of these laws. The instructions concerning infectious skin disease are similar to modern quarantine procedures, while the prohibitions with respect to dead bodies, carrion birds, and pigs guard the people from sicknesses transmitted through contaminated food. God promised to deliver the people from "every disease," especially "the horrible diseases you knew in Egypt" (Deuteronomy 7:15). Doubtless God fulfilled His promises partly through the natural means involved in the dietary and quarantine procedures, though He was also free to employ special supernatural protection when appropriate. When the people disobeyed, they would experience the diseases of Egypt as part of God's curse (Deuteronomy 28:60–61).

Yet our modern medical knowledge must not become the most basic framework through which we read the Old Testament laws. Their own context says nothing about hygiene but stresses the need of Israel to "be holy, because I, the LORD your God, am holy" (Leviticus 19:2). The entire system is a pervasive expression of the orderliness and separation required of a people who have fellowship with God the Holy One, the Creator of all order. As Gordon Wenham says, "Theology, not hygiene, is the reason for this provision."[5]

The Law Expressing the Way of Life

The theme of order is closely related to the theme of life. God is the source of both order and life. In creation God not only brings order out of chaos but life out of nonlife. The world is created not only to express the order and beauty of God, but to serve as a suitable arena for human life. The disorderly watery chaos of Genesis 1:2 cannot sustain life, and a return to watery chaos in Noah's flood extinguishes life. Moreover, the life of both plants and animals manifests itself preeminently in their powers of reproduction, which enable them to replicate order "according to their kind."

The fall exhibits the stark contrast between life and death. God is the source of life, and disobedience to Him fittingly results in death (Genesis 2:17). Life means first of all spiritual life, real life in communion with God. On the day when Adam and Eve ate the forbidden fruit, they died in a real and spiritual sense. But physical death is a fitting concomitant to this deeper spiritual death. Because human beings have renounced and destroyed their true life with God, their own physical life is in turn destroyed. Physical death is thus simultaneously a punishment and a symbol of deeper spiritual loss.

In the Exodus God gives Israel new life. They are redeemed not only from the physical oppression of Egyptian slavery, but from the spiritual bondage and deceit involved in worship of the Egyptian gods. God commands them to worship Himself alone as their true life (Exodus 20:2–3). Accordingly, the law in its total scope sets forth the way of life. True life comes from God and involves fellowship with Him. If the Israelites obey the commandments, they will live (Leviticus 18:5; Deuteronomy 28:1–14), and if they disobey they will die (Exodus 19:21–22; 32:9–10; Deuteronomy 6:15; 28:15–68). The Ten Commandments embody the core of this life. They express what true life is like in our relations directly to God (primarily commandments 1–4) and in our relations to fellow human beings (primarily commandments 5–10).

The laws concerning clean and unclean also embody the themes of life and death, often on an indirect, symbolic plane. Contact with the dead body of a human being is of course direct contact with human death, the primary curse of the fall. It creates maximum defilement, requiring seven days for cleansing (Numbers 19:11–19). An animal that has died by itself is a more distant mirror of the curse of death; accordingly, it requires only part of one day to become clean again (Leviticus 11:24–40). Creatures that crawl on the ground are indirectly associated with the curse on the ground and the curse on the serpent. Hence, they are unclean and unsuitable for food (Leviticus 11:41–45).

All the things described in Leviticus 11 and Deuteronomy 14 are unclean *for Israel.* But Deuteronomy 14:21 explicitly allows Israelites to sell carcasses to aliens and foreigners. What is prohibited to Israel is not prohibited to others. Rather, the prohibition rests on the fact that "you [Israelites] are a holy people to the LORD your God" (Deuteronomy 14:21). The world has been contaminated with curse and uncleanness originating in the fall. The Gentile nations participate in this uncleanness through their contact with unclean animals. But such uncleanness is not in itself sin. It is merely *symbolic* of sin. And separation from uncleanness accompanies *symbolic* holiness. Israel alone is required to observe a special ceremonial cleanness, because they are the holy people. Their special access to God makes it necessary for them to maintain special distance from the fall and its curse. At the same time, all these special observances serve to reinforce their consciousness of being a unique nation. They are thereby reminded not to participate in the idolatry and moral corruption of the surrounding nations.

New Testament Application
Of Laws of Cleanliness

In the light of the New Testament we know that the distinctions between clean and unclean were temporary in nature. Jesus' teaching while He was on earth already pointed to the fact that all foods were to be reckoned clean (Mark 7:19). The Apostle Paul explicitly confirms this teaching (Colossians 2:20–23; 1 Timothy 4:3–5). Thus on the level of literal observance the Old Testament food laws are obsolete.

But such laws still have their symbolic value. The general principle of separation from what is unclean is still valid. For example, Paul counsels us not to compromise with unbelief or commit ourselves to unnatural alliances with unbelievers:

> Do not be yoked together with unbelievers. For what do righteousness and wickedness have in common? Or what fellowship can light have with darkness? . . . As God has said: "I will live with them and walk among them, and I will be their God, and they will be my people." "Therefore come out from them and be separate, says the Lord. Touch no unclean thing, and I will receive you." (2 Corinthians 6:14, 16b–17)

In verse 17 Paul invokes the Old Testament prohibition against touching unclean things in order to reinforce the general principle of separation from sinfulness.

Paul's use of the Old Testament here is quite in line with its real meaning. The disorders of unclean things in the Old Testament symbolically indicate the disorders of sin itself, which is the root of uncleanness. Israel's separation from unclean foods also proclaims its obligation to be a uniquely holy nation, a kingdom of priests. In the Old Testament the principles of holiness and separation were temporarily expressed on a symbolic, physical level in the distinction between clean and unclean foods. Such a symbolic distinction was appropriate during the time when salvation as a whole was expressed in a symbolic and shadowy form. Salvation had not yet come in its definitive and final form, namely, Christ Himself and His sacrifice on the cross. The sacrifices of the Old Testament cleansed copies and shadows of heavenly things, but they did not permanently cleanse the heart. The earth itself and all its creatures had not been cleansed definitively through the power of Christ's blood.

Hence, it was appropriate that the need for cleansing the heart be expressed in external ways through food distinctions. It was appropriate also that these distinctions be related to separation from the curse of Genesis 3. Thus these distinctions foreshadow the need for a re-creative work of God that will affect the curse on the lower creation.

The orderliness of the distinction between clean and unclean, and the rejection of the disorder of unclean things, signify beforehand the comprehensive character of the order of Jesus Christ, King of kings and Lord of lords, who rules all things (Hebrews 1:3) and to whom all authorities in heaven and on earth are subject (Ephesians 1:21). All order in the original creation derives from Him who is the Word of God and the wisdom of God (John 1:1; Colossians 2:3). The distinction between life and death in Old Testament cleanliness laws signifies that Jesus Christ is the Originator of life and the Overcomer of death.

Now in the time of fulfillment in the New Testament we see clearly the meaning to which these distinctions pointed. Sin and righteousness are shown forth fully in the cross. Life and death are shown fully in Christ's death and resurrection. All foods are cleansed by the Word of God and by prayer now offered in the name and power of Christ (1 Timothy 4:1–5).

Order in Personal Relationships: The Ten Commandments

How do the Ten Commandments more specifically embody God's order and God's life? The Ten Commandments make up the heart of the Mosaic law. Fittingly, they focus on permanent obligations for personal relationships rather than on temporary obligations concerning the distinction between clean and unclean. But they reflect the same pervasive themes of divine order and divine life.

The first three commandments deal focally with responsibilities in the relationship between God and human beings. The holiness and order of God must be properly reflected in the very character of our relations to Him. True life is expressed only in service to Him. First and foremost, as the first commandment insists (Exodus 20:3), God must be acknowledged as the sole Lord, the sole Creator and Originator of order. Any competition with another supposed source introduces a most fundamental confusion and disorder and leads to spiritual death. In the first sin Adam and Eve listened to a competitive source, the deceit of the serpent. They ended by virtually setting themselves up as judges of right and wrong. They aspired to be prime sources rather than grateful receivers of God's order. Every sin has this same character at its root. Sin is always a kind of idolatry and destructive confusing of order at the most fundamental level, namely, confusing who God is as the standard of all earthly order.

With Reformed and Orthodox interpreters I maintain that the second commandment begins with Exodus 20:4 and discusses the question of making images for worship.[6] It goes beyond the first commandment by forbidding not only the worship of false gods but the pretended worship of the true God through making an image of Him. Not only is the attempt to make an image of God principally inappropriate, but it misses the fundamental character of the revelation at Mount Sinai, a revelation where no image appeared (Deuteronomy 4:15-20). Worship of God must conform to the order of God's own revelation, not only in the general sense that it follows the way that God commands, but more particularly in the sense that it harmonizes with the character of God. The character of God is expressed in the fact that He reveals Himself apart from any permanent, reproducible image. So His worshipers must not make an image for themselves.

The third commandment, Exodus 20:7, enjoins us to protect the holiness that marks God's name, i.e., the revelation of His character. This commandment is one instance of the preservation of distinctions between holy and unholy.

The fourth commandment, Exodus 20:8–11, has a special character. It undoubtedly focuses on human relation to God, not on fellow human beings. Yet it involves a creational pattern as well, namely, the pattern of succession of days. It is therefore not quite so direct an expression of the orderliness of God's character as are the first three commandments. As we shall see, it forms a kind of mediating point between the commandments concerning God and those concerning one's neighbor. For the moment, it is sufficient for us to observe the way in which it expresses a pattern of divine order. Human beings made in the image of God are to replicate God's order of work and rest in creation. They are to preserve a distinction between holy and unholy by distinguishing in their activity between the holiness of the Sabbath and the common character of the other days of the week.

The fifth commandment, Exodus 20:12, concerning honoring parents, is the first commandment dealing primarily with our responsibilities to other human beings. Some have argued that this commandment still expresses responsibility to God, since human authorities like parents represent the authority of God within a limited sphere. Certainly it is appropriate for the first commandment concerning other human beings to involve a unique relation to divine authority as a background element. Nevertheless, if we bear in mind what would be most obvious to an Israelite, this commandment belongs first of all with those involving responsibility to human beings.

The divine orderliness is expressed in this commandment in terms of preserving the created structure of the family and the orderly authority that it embodies. The family is also the proper place for the production of new life, in the form of offspring. Hence, the protection of the family is a preeminent form of honoring human life, life derived from God. In addition, because parents had a key responsibility for teaching their children about God and His law (Deuteronomy 6:6–9), the parents represent the primary channel through which knowledge of and conformity to the divine order is passed on and preserved for the next generation. An attack on the authority of parents is most grievous because it threatens the most precious heritage of Israel, its knowledge of God, and thereby also threatens possession of the blessings flowing from this knowledge ("that you may live long in the land the LORD your God is giving you," Exodus 20:12b).

The sixth commandment enjoins the preservation of human life itself, and the orderliness expressed in life. Human beings created in the image of God replicate on earth in their own persons a special form of divine order on earth. Their degradation into the disorder of death is a most serious disruption of divine order.

The seventh commandment enjoins orderliness in human sexuality. Since human sexuality is closely related to the creation of new life and new order in human reproduction, the preservation of orderly sexuality is a natural consequence of the call to holiness.

The eighth commandment enjoins the orderliness in human property. Theft violently disorders the relations of human ownership. Since human ownership is closely related to the dominion that human beings have been given, which in turn imitates God's dominion over the world, preservation of orderly ownership is a reflection of the order of God's rule over the world. In addition, property is an important support for sustaining and enhancing human life. The destruction or expropriation of property is therefore an indirect attack on the human life supported by it.

The ninth commandment enjoins orderliness in human speech. Lying speech used as a weapon against other human beings perverts the natural function of human speech, namely, to be an instrument of fellowship and dominion. Truthful human speech imitates the truthfulness and righteousness of God's speech and God's law.

The tenth commandment enjoins orderliness in the desires of human beings and in their hearts. Jesus pointed out that the overt actions violating the other commandments all originate in the heart of men (Mark 7:20–23). Disorderliness of the heart generates disorderliness in action.

Because human beings are made in the image of God and are called on to imitate God, we can also see various relations of analogy between the first four commandments and the last six; that is, we can see analogies between responsibilities to God and responsibilities to other human beings. For example, in honoring our parents we ought to imitate the honor that is due to our heavenly Father (Malachi 1:6). Similarly, in not killing but protecting human life in the image of God, we ought to imitate the practice of loving God and protecting his honor. The practice of not committing adultery but enhancing the order of marriage ought to imitate Israel's responsibility to be the faithful "wife" of God and not to prostitute herself with other gods (see Ezekiel 16; 23). The practice of not stealing but protecting human property ought to imitate the practice of dealing responsibly with God's property, i.e., everything that we receive from God (cf. Malachi 3:8–11). In not bearing false witness but speaking truthfully we ought to imitate the truth of God's speech. Our desire for the neighbor's good and not covetousness ought to imitate God's goodness, His love, and the purity of His own purposes.

The relation between the tabernacle and the law is further cemented by a certain amount of common order even in their arrangements. Recall that the Ten Commandments are placed in the ark within the Most Holy Place (Deuteronomy 10:1–5). In the spatial arrangements of the tabernacle we have already seen a pervasive theme of replication. The Holy Place in its shape and furniture imperfectly replicates the Most Holy Place. The priestly garments suggest that Aaron replicates the tabernacle as a whole. And so on. Within this context it is not unnatural to notice that the number of the commandments—ten—is replicated in the dimensions of the Most Holy Place. The context already suggests the idea of replication. Moreover, the tabernacle as a whole is made after a heavenly pattern, the same as the origin of the Ten Commandments (Exodus 25:9, 40). The form of the tabernacle must conform exactly to the verbal instructions of God (a kind of law) specifying its plan.

Next, notice that the order of the Ten Commandments suggests a transition from heaven to earth, just as does the order of the tabernacle from inside to outside. The first three commandments deal with heavenly order, i.e., responsibilities to God. The first commandment expresses the same message as the singleness of the tabernacle, of the ark, and of the throne of God, namely, that there is only one true God. The second commandment expresses the reality of the single way to God represented by the tabernacle. In particular, it expresses the fact that no image appears between the two cherubim over the ark. No Israelite is to make an image for any other dwelling place, in conformity with the fact that the central dwelling place in Israel, the tabernacle, has no image of God within it.

The third commandment enjoining honor of the name of God is a verbal counterpart to the practice of honoring the place of God. God's dwelling place is the place where He has put His name (1 Kings 8:29). Just as the name of God is the verbal expression of His character and His attributes, the tabernacle is the visible expression.

The fourth commandment corresponds to the transition from heaven to earth. That is, it enjoins sabbath observance as first of all a responsibility to God, and in this sense involves heavenly responsibility. But it also involves responsibilities downward to other human beings, sons, daughters, servants, aliens and even animals (Exodus 20:10). Because it involves observance of a periodic seven-day pattern, and because the pattern of day and night is controlled by the heavenly bodies (Genesis 1:14), it also reminds us of Israel's relation to the visible heavens as the good creation of God. Thus it corresponds in some ways to the Holy Place, where the seven lamps correspond to the light of seven days of the week. It forms a transition between the invisible heavens of the Most Holy Place and the earthly space of the tabernacle courtyard.

With the fifth commandment, then, we move out into the courtyard, as it were, and into the domain of responsibilities to other human beings. But fittingly the first responsibility mentioned is that of honor to human representatives, to those in authority, who still in some pronounced way represent God. The priests who minister in the courtyard of the tabernacle embody this same representative function in their own priestly way.

The sixth through the tenth commandments discuss various "horizontal" responsibilities, so it need not be the case that there is any order in them. But still some degree of order seems to be observable. Violations that cause more overt damage and are difficult or impossible to repair come first, followed by violations involving less serious disruption of the environment. Last comes the commandment concerning covetousness, a sin that though very serious does not overtly disrupt the environment around a person. We might also argue that the commandments start with the most elementary and basic responsibilities and move out to more complex responsibilities. Thus the sixth commandment enjoins the responsibility to preserve human life itself. This responsibility is most basic and all the other human responsibilities make no sense without it. Following this commandment comes one affecting our most intimate and basic relations, namely, sexual relations. Then two others touch first on the tangible possessions of neighbors, then on the intangibles, namely, their reputation and legal security. The commandment concerning covetousness is the most complex and most intangible, because it involves direct assessment of motives.

In fact, all the commandments reflect the perfect righteousness of Jesus Christ. Jesus Christ is the true God and as such is Himself the divine standard that we are called on to imitate. Jesus Christ is also true man and as such was perfectly obedient to God. He perfectly reflected God's standard in human life. He alone of all human beings consistently and thoroughly served God and no idol. He alone kept pure the proper way of worshiping God, following God's own commandments. He alone perfectly honored the name of God by perfectly revealing God in human form. He alone perfectly kept the sabbath by accomplishing the re-creation of the world, the purpose to which the sabbath pointed forward. He alone perfectly honored not only His human parents (Luke 2:51) but His Father in heaven. He alone single-mindedly sought and perfectly embodied the divine ordering and not the disordering of human life, sexuality, possessions, speech, and desires of the heart. All His achievements came to a climax on the cross. In obedience to God the Father, He surrendered to destruction and death His human authority, His life, His sexuality, His possessions, His power of speech, and His heart, in order that the Father would be obeyed and honored, and the disorders and death of humanity and creation be remedied.

Thus Jesus Christ perfectly kept the law, perfectly embodied it, and perfectly exemplified it. The mystery and wonder of His work is even greater than what we can express. Christ's work does not come as an afterthought appended to an already self-existing, self-sufficient law. The law of the Old Testament is not a mere datum or a mere code book, but the personal word of the great King of the universe. And who is this King? From eternity to eternity the Word was with God and was God (John 1:1). The King is the trinitarian God, Father, Son, and Holy Spirit. God the Son was always at work from the beginning. The law of

Moses is a reflection and foreshadowing of the absolute perfection and righteousness of Christ, rather than Christ being a reflection of the law. This conclusion confirms what we have already seen through the tabernacle. Both tabernacle and law express in complementary ways the communion with God that achieves full expression only through the coming of Christ and His uniting Himself to us by faith.

EIGHT

THE PURPOSES
OF THE TABERNACLE, THE LAW,
AND THE PROMISED LAND:
POINTING FORWARD
TO CHRIST

The tabernacle, the law, and the promised land are all intended to point forward to Christ. It makes sense that Jesus said, "Everything must be fulfilled that is written about me in the Law of Moses, the Prophets and the Psalms" (Luke 24:44). But within this single unified purpose of testifying to Christ we can still discern a multitude of subordinate purposes. We have already noted a trio of purposes, namely, to set forth a God-given order, to open access to communion and personal fellowship with God, and to show God's power to bless and curse (see chapter 5). The tabernacle and the law both testify to a triple set of facts, namely, that God is the origin and Creator of order, that the world expresses His personal presence in its order and its life, and that He is the Redeemer and Restorer of the order and life disrupted by sin. The land also expresses the same truths, since it derives from God the Creator, it expresses His personal blessing, and God has taken it away from the wicked Canaanites in order to give it to His redeemed people.

The Connections of Tabernacle Symbolism

We can see the way in which several points are unfolded when we recall the multiplicity of connections of tabernacle symbolism. First of all the tabernacle represents, copies, and models heavenly reality. But its symbolism is not merely a one-dimensional pointer to heaven. As we have seen (chapter 2), the tabernacle has a multiplicity of connections with Biblical teaching:

1. God dwells in heaven in the midst of His holy courtroom of angels and ministering spirits. The tabernacle as a dwelling place of God replicates heaven.

2. The whole universe has been created in a manner like constructing a house (Psalm 104:2–3; Amos 9:6; Proverbs 8:22–31; Isaiah 40:22). The tabernacle is analogous to the universe as a whole.

3. The tabernacle is connected to the temple, a larger replica of the same truths.

4. The tabernacle is suggestive of the Garden of Eden, which was a special dwelling of God where God met with Adam and Eve (cf. Genesis 2:15–3:8).

5. The tabernacle is a pattern for the people of God corporately, who become a dwelling place of God.

6. The tabernacle is a pattern for each individual believer, and for the priest in particular, since each individual becomes a dwelling place of God.

7. The tabernacle looks forward to the final dwelling of God, the new Jerusalem of Revelation 21–22.

8. The tabernacle prefigures Christ Himself, who is the ultimate dwelling of God with human beings.

9. The imagery in the tabernacle is also capable of recalling God's great acts of redemption in the Exodus.

10. The tabernacle points forward to God's future acts of redemption.

All these connections, especially 1–8, are part of the great Biblical theme of God's dwelling place. Hence, they all express the truth that God comes to us to be personally present and a source of personal communion. The cosmic scope of the connections 1, 2, and 7 particularly remind us that God is the source of all order. Connections 9 and 10 remind us that God is the Redeemer and Restorer. All of these connections of tabernacle symbolism have an inner unity, because Christ is the source of all (connection 8).

Likewise, the land expresses in some fashion many of the same connections, as we have seen (chapter 6).

The Connections of the Law

Because of the close inner connection between the tabernacle and the law, we may expect to find the law to exhibit the same connections as does the tabernacle. The law points upward to the character of God the Holy One. It points outward to the people of Israel and provides for them a standard to which they are to conform. They are to "be holy because I, the LORD your God, am holy" (Leviticus 19:2).

Next, the law points backward to God's original creation. For one thing, the distinctions between clean and unclean intensify the original separations that God made in creating the different regions of creation and the different kinds of living things. The law enjoins on Israel a special necessity to separate from crawling things and things symbolically associated with the fall, as part of Israel's calling to be a kingdom of priests. This obligation is analogous to Adam's responsibility to keep the garden and resist the serpent. In addition, the moral principles of the law articulate the relationships that human beings were created to have with God and with one another.

The law also points backward to God's act of redemption from Egypt. Sometimes it explicitly invokes God's past mercies and promises (e.g., Exodus 20:2; Deuteronomy 5:15; 1:19–3:29). At every point its contrasts between good and evil recapitulate the fundamental contrast between serving idolatrous masters in Egypt and serving God with freedom in a new redeemed situation.

Finally, the law points forward to its final embodiment and fulfill-ment. The very disobedience of the people of Israel testifies to the fact that they need God to act in a new redemptive way to write the law on their heart (Jeremiah 31:31–34). The insufficiency of animal sacrifices to cleanse from sin points to the necessity of a final, perfect sacrifice for sin. The people need a sacrifice that will fully bear the penalty for dis-obedience to the law and also create by its perfection a dynamically reproducing pattern of perfect obedience. Thus the law points forward to Christ. Christ will perfectly obey God and perfectly embody the righteousness of God expressed in the law (2 Corinthians 5:21). He will also perfectly satisfy the penalty and curse that comes to those who disobey God's law (Galatians 3:13).

In summary, the law like the tabernacle sustains connections in sev-eral directions, upward, outward, backward, and forward. In all these directions it expresses a fundamental unity in God's purpose, namely, the unity of Christ Himself. Christ is the preeminent Word of God, the Creator, the ultimate standard and embodiment of divine wisdom, truth, righteousness, order, life, and peace (John 1:1–4). He is Himself "the fullness of the Deity . . . in bodily form" (Colossians 2:9). He is the Truth (John 14:6), the ultimate reality of realities, the consummate righteousness that the law foreshadows. "For the law was given through Moses; grace and truth came through Jesus Christ" (John 1:17). He sus-tains "all things by his powerful word" (Hebrews 1:3). "By him all things were created" (Colossians 1:16). "In him all things hold to-gether" (Colossians 1:17). "He is the beginning and the firstborn from among the dead, so that in everything he might have the supremacy" (Colossians 1:18).

The law, then, like the tabernacle and the land, expresses the holi-ness, truth, beauty, and righteousness of God Himself. Its revelation comes with the absolute authority of God Himself and can never pass away. But in another sense it proclaims its own insufficiency and non-ultimacy. It is a shadow—a true and precious shadow, but still a shadow, of the surpassing glory of Christ. The ministry of the law in its own time was fading and is now superseded by the ministry of the gospel of the glory of Christ (2 Corinthians 3:1–18). Far from abolishing the law, the ministry of Christ causes us through the Spirit to have the "veil" over our hearts removed and to see the law in its true purposes, as a reflection and anticipation of the glory of Christ (2 Corinthians 3:14–18).

Moral and Ceremonial Aspects of the Law

Many people have traditionally distinguished between "ceremonial" and "moral" laws in the Old Testament. According to this view, ceremonial laws are those laws like the sacrificial laws and dietary laws that were destined to pass away. Moral laws like the Ten Commandments have permanent validity. Two distinct purposes are customarily associated with these two types of law. The ceremonial laws symbolize and foreshadow by means of temporary outward ceremonies the nature of Christ's redemptive work. The moral laws set forth the permanent standard for human righteousness and show what human beings who serve God are expected to do.

Obviously there is some truth and some value in this distinction. Some parts of the law, namely, the "moral" commandments, express in a more or less direct way universal rules for human behavior. "You shall not steal" is just as valid a rule now as it was for Israel. One significant purpose of such law is to guide the behavior of those who have come to know God, whether these people are Israelites or modern Christians.

Other parts of the law, namely, the "ceremonial" commandments, express rules applying directly only to Israel's circumstances or to the circumstances of particular individuals within Israel. For example, much of the instruction in Leviticus 6–7 and 21–22 is applicable in an immediate sense only to Israelite priests. Since the priesthood symbolizes mediation between God and human beings, and since such mediation is now fulfilled in Christ, we may properly argue that one main purpose of Leviticus 6–7 and 21–22 is to foreshadow the nature of the work of Christ as our perfect and holy high priest in heaven.

Likewise, the food laws operate to distinguish Israel from the surrounding Gentile nations (see chapter 7). Israel as the holy people are in communion with God through the tabernacle. The other nations do not have this privilege. With the privilege comes a unique responsibility to remain separate from unclean things (Deuteronomy 14:21). The holiness and separation of Israel foreshadows the holiness and separation of Christ, who by His work has now purified all foods (Mark 7:19; 1 Timothy 4:4–5).

The organization of the book of Deuteronomy also reveals a rough distinction between moral and ceremonial parts.[1] As Moses indicates, the Ten Commandments in Deuteronomy 5 are given by the direct voice of God, whereas the other ordinances are spoken by Moses under God's direction (5:22–33). The Ten Commandments are the "covenant" (5:2–3), to which God "added nothing more" (5:22). They alone were written with the finger of God on the two tablets that Moses received directly from God (5:22). The subsequent commandments in the rest of Deuteronomy are then explicitly described as "all the commands, decrees and laws you are to teach them to follow in the land I am giving them to possess" (5:31). Deuteronomy repeatedly invokes the phrase "in the land" (e.g., 5:31, 33; 6:1, 3, 10, 18, 23; 7:1; 8:1). Thus all the commands from 6:1 onward are qualified by the geographical boundaries of the land. Some commands are clearly of much broader scope (e.g., the command to love God in 6:4–5). But many others are explicitly tied to the land (e.g., Deuteronomy 19:1–13 depends on the setting up of cities of refuge in the land). Many of the laws are thus "ceremonial" laws in the sense that their observance depends on the unique holiness of Israel and the unique holiness of the land of promise, the new Eden.

Hence, Deuteronomy itself separates a moral part, the Ten Commandments in Deuteronomy 5, from a ceremonial part, the "commands, decrees, and laws" of Deuteronomy 6–31. But the distinction is a rough one, since some obviously moral commands are included in the later chapters.

However, the simple distinction between moral and ceremonial laws does not reveal the full richness of God's law. Though useful up to a point, it pays attention to only a few aspects of Old Testament revelation.[2] And if used unthinkingly, it threatens to separate into two disparate pieces what God has undeniably joined together. The tabernacle as a *whole* and the law as a *whole* bear witness to Christ. The order of the tabernacle and the order of the law express a profound unity belonging to Mosaic revelation. This unity prefigures the final unity of the one way of salvation through the one Lord and Savior Jesus Christ. Hence,

the law itself contains no special terminology neatly separating ceremonial and moral. Many chapters contain primarily ceremonial and primarily moral law side by side and mixed together (e.g., Leviticus 19;
Deuteronomy 22; 23; Exodus 23).

Some laws do express divine standards in a universally binding way,
while others are adapted in one way or another to special circumstances
in Israel. Hence, on a rough basis we may distinguish between what is
universal and what is special to Israel's circumstances. Yet this distinction is often a matter of degree. For example, the principle of honoring
one's parents is universal. Yet when it is expressed in Exodus 20:12, it is
combined with one very particular specification, namely, "that you may
live long in the land the LORD your God is giving you." Taken most
literally and most narrowly, this qualification can apply only to the people of Israel to whom God is giving the land of Palestine, and then only
during the period in which they possess the land, not, for instance, after
they have been cast out of it for disobedience. Nevertheless, Paul in the
New Testament does not hesitate to invoke this commandment in a
Christian context and to suggest that "long life on the earth" is the
result (see Ephesians 6:2–3). Paul does perceive a universal principle in
the commandment. But he does so only by reckoning with the fact that
Israel's life in the land typologically symbolizes a universal reconquest
and renewal of the whole earth through the work of Christ.

The Ten Commandments are generally considered to be the central
Old Testament expression of the moral law. Yet here we have one commandment, the fifth, which contains clear reference to a ceremonial
item, namely, the land and life in the land. Some other less striking
particularities characterize other commandments from among the Ten
Commandments. The Sabbath commandment in Deuteronomy 5:15
specifically appeals to the fact that the people were slaves in Egypt and
that the people owe allegiance to God because of His redemption. The
commandment against graven images in Exodus 20:4–6 presupposes a
social and religious context in which literal image-making was a genuine temptation. The commandment against coveting in Exodus 20:17
lists typical objects that would tempt Israelites to coveting, but not all
of which would be meaningful in a modern industrialized society.

To crown it all, the whole of the Ten Commandments is pointedly preceded by a powerful claim of God to Israelite allegiance. He says, "I am the LORD your God, who brought you out of Egypt, out of the land of slavery" (Exodus 20:2). This most significant contextual note does not literally apply to anyone but Israel. If we use these commandments apart from this all-significant context, we lose sight of the motivation and backing for all of them. The Ten Commandments are not moralism or a legalistic way of salvation, but a call to life motivated by gratitude for God's compassion and deliverance. We can retrieve the correct use of the commandments only by invoking a typological analogy between redemption from Egypt and redemption from sin by Christ. That is, we argue that though we have not been literally redeemed from Egypt, we have been redeemed from what Egypt symbolized and foreshadowed, namely, bondage to sin. Egypt is a "type" or foreshadowing of the domain of sin. Redemption from Egypt is a kind of foreshadowing of redemption through Jesus Christ. Consequently, we who are redeemed are to be motivated to obey God's commandments just as Israel was. Such an analogy between Israel and us does indeed exist, as Paul affirms in 1 Corinthians 10:1–13. But it is a symbolical analogy, an analogy between two levels, like the ceremonial analogies of the so-called ceremonial laws. Hence, the Christ-centered analogies of the ceremonies and the permanency of moral demands are inextricably linked.

We can illustrate the richness of the law starting from the other end as well. Consider the laws that prohibit Israelites from touching unclean things and eating unclean foods. Such laws are generally classified as ceremonial because Christians are not bound to observe them literally (see Colossians 2:20–21; 1 Timothy 4:3–5; Mark 7:19). Nevertheless, these laws still express permanent principles. "Touch no unclean thing" is quoted by Paul as a backing for his injunction not to be yoked together with unbelievers (2 Corinthians 6:14, 17), because it embodies the general principle of separation from moral disorder. The dietary laws also express the general truth that God has created all orders of living things, that this order also has been corrupted through the fall (see Genesis 3:17–18), that this order is to be redemptively restored through the renewal of the word of God, and that God's priests are to be radically separated from the corruptions of the fall. Believers in God are themselves to play a role in carrying out renewed discriminatory dominion over the lower creation and over the effects of the curse. Hence, though the exact form of observance of the food laws has changed, they express a multitude of permanent principles. They point backwards to creation and fall, upwards to the divine creative order, outwards to the domain of human responsibilities towards unredeemed humanity and the lower creation, and forwards to the hope for final redemption and renewal of the heavens and the earth (Isaiah 65:17; Romans 8:21–23).

Thus it seems wisest to me not to draw a sharp distinction between ceremonial and moral law, but to study all of the law most carefully in the endeavor to appreciate its depth, the richness of its connections, and the unity of its purposes in foreshadowing Christ.

I have stressed the fundamental unity of the law not only because the law finds its fulfillment and realization in one goal, the one Lord Jesus Christ, but also because I think that Israelites themselves would perceive the law as a unity. In one sense all the commandments are summed up in the one, "Be holy because I, the LORD your God, am holy" (Leviticus 19:2). There is only one God, and devotion to Him involves the holistic response of the whole person.

> The LORD our God, the LORD is one. Love the LORD your God with all your heart and with all your soul and with all your strength. These commandments [all of them, finding their unity in God] that I give you today are to be upon your hearts. Impress them on your children. Talk about them when you sit at home and when you walk along the road, when you lie down and when you get up. (Deuteronomy 6:4–7)

Yet within this fundamental unity Israelites themselves could easily sense some relative distinctions. Surely the commandment in Deuteronomy 6:4–5 about loving God with all your heart is the great commandment to which all others are subordinate (cf. Matthew 22:37–38). The Ten Commandments as the heart of the law express in a most fundamental way our obligations first of all to God (commandments 1–4) and next to our neighbor (commandments 5–10). The rest of the law is largely an outworking of the implications of these central obligations. Hence, Jesus can point to the fundamental character of the two great commandments, to love God and to love one's neighbor, in that order (Matthew 22:37–40). The two central commandments are deep and permanent moral principles. It should be no surprise then that the Ten Commandments, as an expansion of these two principles, also embody permanent principles, though they simultaneously particularize the principles to Israel.

The two great principles of loving God and loving one's neighbor also suffice to awaken Israelites to the possibility that not everything in the law is equally permanent. The food laws and the sacrificial laws are not directly deducible from general principles of love. Do they therefore have a special, temporary purpose? Perhaps. Israelites might not be at all certain, and would not need to be certain because their own obligations for their immediate future were clearly defined. But would changes come in the more distant future? What would happen when salvation was definitely accomplished, by an even more remarkable and thorough deliverance than the exodus from Egypt? It would be fitting to be open-minded on such a question. Moreover, these food laws and sacrificial laws involve the use of the lower creation, plants and animals, in a special symbolic way. Israel is forbidden to do some things that other nations may do (Deuteronomy 14:21). Such special boundaries on the use of the lower creation seem in themselves to be temporary in view of the comprehensive dominion given to human beings in the original creation in Genesis 1. Such restrictions by their very nature suggest something introduced as a symbol for the necessity of remedying the disorders of sin and the fall.

These impressions available to Israel would be strengthened as Israelites compared the law of God and their own situation with the surrounding nations. How did Israel differ from the surrounding nations, and how was she like the other nations? In particular, did other nations have the same laws as their own standards? With respect to the first four of the Ten Commandments, the other nations were polytheistic idolaters, whereas Israel was enjoined to be loyal to one God exclusively. This distinction set Israel apart. But since God is the only true God, the God of the whole world, it is clear that the nations were deeply blinded and were guilty for not worshiping God alone (cf. Isaiah 41–48; Romans 1:18–32). With respect to commandments 5–9 from the Ten Commandments, the other nations did acknowledge the same basic standards, though with confusion and in the midst of much disobedience to standards that were formally acknowledged. Even today, almost all societies recognize that it is wrong to disrespect parents, to murder, to commit adultery, to steal, or to bear false witness. No society can completely suppress the most basic principles of fairness, of not doing to others what you would not want done to you. And societies that go too far in suppressing these standards simply disintegrate and disappear from the face of the earth. Thus, Israel can see a measure of agreement by other nations, because the great principle of loving one's neighbor is universal.

In the case of food laws and sacrificial laws, on the other hand, the standards of other nations by no means conformed to the standards for Israel. In at least one key case, the law itself indicates that the standards were never intended to be the same (Deuteronomy 14:21). In some cases, of course, disagreement with other nations might only mean that the nations were blind. But at other times it might mean that the standards for Israel herself were temporary and symbolical. Apart from special revelation, how could other nations have come to see the necessity of keeping things in just the way that they were kept in Israel? Hence, Israelites themselves might easily sense that these special laws set Israel apart as a holy people not only in a unique way but also in a temporary way. Distinctions between foods and types of sacrifices could never be the essence but only a symbol of the essential holiness of Israel and the holiness of God who dwelt in the midst of Israel.

Thus the distinction between permanent principle and temporary symbolical form is not merely some artificial idea from a later age or from later revelation; it was embedded already in the original Mosaic revelation to Israel. Israelites would naturally not have all the answers immediately, but they would have a vague, almost subconscious sense of there being a distinction between what was more central and what was less, between what was more permanent and universal and what might possibly be temporary. At the heart of their experience would be a covenantal relation to God and a trust in God. Pious Israelites would have included in their experience of God an expectation that God would in His own time clarify what was imperfectly known concerning the deeper significances and purposes of the revelation of Moses. For us to read the law of Moses now in the light of further Old Testament revelation and even New Testament revelation is not a violation of law's intentions but their realization.

The Tabernacle, the Law, and
The Land as Elementary and Deep

The tabernacle, the law, and the promised land all present us with a fascinating depth behind an elementary exterior. Depending on whether we look at their surface or their depths, they can be regarded either as elementary and simple, or as rich and profound. Though such a situation seems paradoxical, it is a natural result of the functions and purposes of these institutions within their own environment. On the one hand the tabernacle, the law, and the land are given to Israel during a time of immaturity or childhood, before Christ has come. Hence, they convey principles of salvation in an elementary pictorial form. They can rightly be described as temporary structures (Hebrews 9:8–10; Galatians 3:17–25) serving as guides only until Christ comes. The law embodies "basic principles of the world" (Galatians 4:3, 9–10; Colossians 2:20–23), elementary teachings that Christians should have gone beyond. The land was the concrete expression of God's promise. As such, it was only a pointer to "the city with foundations, whose architect and builder is God" (Hebrews 11:10). Taking possession of the land did not constitute the final sabbath rest, but was a foretaste of it (Hebrews 4:8–11).

On the other hand, precisely because they point forward to Christ, the tabernacle, the law, and the land also involve a depth dimension. They are rich with meaning once our eyes have been opened to see their true significance and the way in which they depict Christ (see 2 Corinthians 3:1–18). Even within their Old Testament context the tabernacle and the law already showed the nature of redemption. They set forth the holiness of God and the standard to which human beings are to conform. The land and its associated promise reminded Israel that God had loved the undeserving. Salvation was a gift, but the gift implied an obligation to thank and obey God the giver. The tabernacle showed the necessity of sacrifice, substitution, priestly representation, and cleansing to remedy the damage of sin.

The Israelites in the Old Testament did not always grasp the significance of the tabernacle, the law, and the Promised Land; but that failure was due to the "veil" over their hearts (2 Corinthians 3:14–16), not to an intrinsic lack of meaning in God's word. We do not need to impose an extra alien idea in order to find connections with redemption in Jesus Christ. The connections are there from the beginning. Yet our understanding of the tabernacle, the law, and the land can undergo further deepening now that Christ has accomplished redemption. Things that were only hinted at in the Old Testament become clearer now. When we have the second half of the story presented in the New Testament, we can become more confident that we know how the first part was intended to predict this second part.

A look at the tabernacle, the law, and the land in detail confirms this paradoxical duality of elementary teaching and depth. The tabernacle is a kind of child's picture book of elementary teachings. God is holy. You cannot approach Him. You need a mediator and sacrifice. The most basic theological facts about the tabernacle are simple and obvious. The tabernacle expresses truths in shadows, i.e., elementary outward forms. Yet the truths to which the shadows point are as deep as redemption itself. Who can appreciate the full depth of meaning in the statement that Jesus is "Immanuel," God with us, God making His dwelling or "tent" with us? Who knows the depths in the claim that Jesus is the Bread of Life or the Light of the world, corresponding to the bread of the Presence and the lampstand?

Now let us look at the law. The food laws are again symbolic in nature. In form they touch only on externals and do not "clear the conscience of the worshiper" (Hebrews 9:9). Yet they also symbolize a deep truth, namely, the holiness of God and the necessity for His people to separate from spiritual uncleanness.

The Ten Commandments are rightly considered to be the heart of the law. Viewed on a superficial level, they confine themselves mostly to elementary things. Do not worship other gods. Do not make idols. Do not murder. Do not commit adultery. As we have already observed, commandments 5–9 are so "elementary" that almost all societies recognize their validity. Viewed superficially, they forbid only what almost everyone knows is wrong. Many moral people, like the rich young man of Luke 18:21, think that they have kept these commandments—or at least most of the commandments, most of the time. Yet we know from the history of Israel that Israel needed just such an elementary list, and was not able to keep the commandments even on the most superficial, literal level.

Modern expositions of the Ten Commandments have nevertheless seen a great depth of meaning in the Ten Commandments. When we read the commandments carefully within the larger context of God's revelation, we can indeed see that they hint at a greater depth of obedience, not merely blind, limited literal observance. For instance, the tenth commandment, concerning coveting, throws light on all the other commandments by suggesting that evil desires and evil intentions are sinful, in addition to the actual acts of murder, adultery, and theft. The law also commands Israel to "circumcise your hearts" (Deuteronomy 10:16) and promises such circumcision in the future (Deuteronomy 30:6), thereby indicating that the law touches on the inward responsibilities of cleanliness of heart.

The commandment to love your neighbor as yourself (Leviticus 19:18) shows that positive actions of help as well as negative prohibitions against damaging one's neighbor are included. On an elementary level we are prohibited from literally murdering our neighbor. But on a more advanced level, we can infer that we are enjoined to act positively to try to preserve and enhance the life of our neighbor. The commandment not to steal has an elementary level on which it simply forbids taking another person's property. On a more advanced level it can be seen to embody the positive principle of taking care to preserve and enhance another person's property and well-being. And so on with the other commandments.

Most of all, we must reckon with the fact that all the commandments are the commandments of God the righteous King. The commandments are reinforced by appeals to the fact that "I am the LORD" (Leviticus 19:18) and "be holy because I, the LORD your God, am holy" (Leviticus 19:2). When we see the law as a pointer to the character of God and His holiness, infinite depth is suggested. When we read the law in the context of the whole Bible, we can see that it expresses the righteousness of Jesus Christ Himself. Since we are to be imitators of Christ and to reflect His righteousness (1 Peter 2:21; 2 Corinthians 3:18; Romans 8:29), the law is also relevant to us.

The Promised Land was a third elementary reality. All the ordinary routines of one's life took place there. Inheritance, farming, harvest, eating and enjoying one's produce, management of livestock, seasons of the year, war, international commerce, were all based on the existence of this land, with its particular natural (actually, God-given) resources and with particular geographical relations to neighboring lands. The land was in a sense the most basic, elementary reality among all the realities of ordinary Ancient Near Eastern life. It was one's stable environment, the thing that one could take most for granted. Yet, in the case of Israel, it was the special gift of God; it was His promised inheritance to Abraham, through whom blessing would come to all nations (Genesis 17:4–8). It was freighted with theological meaning. What happened to the land signified the people's relation to God, in blessing or curse (Deuteronomy 28). Hence, the land as a sign or symbol of God's goodness opened an inviting window onto the infinite riches of God's choice of Israel, His mercy, His goodness, and His anger against sin (Exodus 34:6–7).

In summmary, a balanced treatment of the tabernacle, the law, and the land takes into account both their externality and their depth. All three institutions necessarily had an externality and an insufficiency. Their very insufficiency was a reminder to Israelites of the fact that reality was in the future to supersede shadows. It simultaneously reminded them that in the meantime the shadows did have a depth dimension, in that they pointed to heavenly reality and its future realization on earth.

The Righteousness Set Forth in the Law

The tabernacle and the law are characterized by meticulous and thoroughgoing order. The land as well is parceled out to the people in an orderly way (Joshua 13–21). All these reflect the orderliness and order-creating character of God. As an integral and central part of this order, the tabernacle and the law set forth standards to which Israel is to conform. The holiness of the tabernacle is to be reflected on a subordinate level in the holiness of the holy people, who are to "be holy because I, the LORD your God, am holy" (Leviticus 19:2). Since the people are a kingdom of priests (Exodus 19:6), they are to imitate the holiness of the Aaronic priesthood. When they conform to the Ten Commandments, they reflect the holiness of the commandments themselves, a holiness exhibited in the fact that the commandments are kept in the ark in the Most Holy Place of the tabernacle.

The most basic principle of righteousness is the imitation of God: "be holy because I, the LORD your God, am holy" (Leviticus 19:2). God is Himself the standard and origin of holiness and righteousness. Human beings created in God's image have a natural responsibility to imitate and embody God's character on their own created plane. In terms of responsibilities to God, in the first four of the Ten Commandments, Israel is to imitate God's own zeal to protect the holiness and uniqueness of God's own person and claims. In terms of responsibilities to other human beings, Israel is to take care to preserve what God has created and ordained: human authority (commandment 5), human life, human sexuality and procreation, human property, human reputation, and human desires.

The imitation of God can be subdivided into two parts, namely, the imitation of God's care for things by a similar exercise of care oneself, and the imitation of God's bounty by reciprocal giving back to God. We have obligations to care for the world that God has created (commandments 5–10) and obligations to give back to God in thanksgiving the honor that is due to Him alone as Creator (commandments 1–4). Actually, these two parts are two perspectives on the entire field of ethics. Giving honor to God is not only an act of thanksgiving for His bounty but also an imitation of the zeal that God has for His own name—it is imitation ultimately of the intra-trinitarian honor that the Father gives to the Son and the Son to the Father (John 5:23; 8:54; 14:31). Caring for the world is not only an imitation of God's original care but a form of thanksgiving to God for what He has made. Nevertheless, for practical purposes we may sometimes distinguish one form of service as more prominent. Let us call the imitation of God "replication" of His action, and giving back to God "restoration" of His goods.

In the fourth commandment in Exodus 20:8–11, replication of God's action is clearly more prominent, since Exodus 20:11 specifically appeals to the fact that God made the heavens and the earth in six days. In the first three commandments restoration is more prominent, since the giving of exclusive honor to God is only giving what is owed back to Him. Many other commandments can be viewed easily from either perspective. The negative prohibitions against murder, adultery, theft, and false witness can be viewed as imitation of God's care for these aspects of human life; but since the commandments are negative in form, they could also be viewed as injunctions to leave God's human creation as one finds it, i.e., to restore it to God without corrupting it.

These distinctions become useful mostly in other areas. For example, the grain offering represents primarily restoration, since the grain that one has produced through God's providential care for agriculture is restored to its original owner. The fellowship offering represents primarily replication, since in eating the holy food of the feast one commits oneself to conformity to the character of the God with whom one has fellowship. One takes into oneself the life-giving power of God that the food symbolizes.

When God's holiness and His standards have been violated, some other distinctions may come into play. When we have sinned against God, we not only owe Him the thanksgiving that was always owed, but also an additional debt, namely, the debt of sin itself. We must pay a penalty in the form of punishment. Thus, when we deal with cases of wrongdoing, restoration is transformed into punishment. We also have a continuing obligation to imitate God or replicate his holiness. When sin has come in, replication of God's holiness must take the form of abolition and destruction of sin. Thus replication takes the form of destruction. In a rough way, these two motifs correspond to the other main forms of sacrificial offering. The sin offering (and the guilt offering as a variant form of sin offering) symbolizes primarily the need for punishment. The burnt offering symbolizes the need for entire consecration or holiness. In the context of sin, such consecration includes entire destruction of sin.

Actually, the sacrificial offerings delineated in Leviticus 1–5 have a great deal in common, so we must not exaggerate their differences. The punishment of sin and the destruction of sin are both a replication of God's holiness, which is intrinsically averse to sin. The punishment of sin and destruction of sin also constitute a kind of restoration of the situation disrupted by sin, so that it returns to an ordered situation of righteousness. Thus all the aspects of human response to God are involved in one another. We always respond as whole persons to the whole God.

Christ fulfills all the aspects of Old Testament sacrifice, as we have seen (chapter 3). Yet we can still distinguish aspects of His work. Replication consists primarily in Christ's imitation of His Father (John 5:19–23). We in turn replicate Christ's character as we are transformed into the image of Christ (2 Corinthians 3:18). Restoration consists in Christ's rising to new life in His resurrection. We in turn are to present our bodies to God as a living sacrifice (Romans 12:1–2). Punishment consists in Christ's bearing our sins (1 Peter 2:24). Consecration to God consists in Christ's death and resurrection, plus our death and resurrection through Him: we die to our old man through Him and are raised as new people (Romans 6:3–7; Colossians 2:20).

Blessing and Curse from the Law

The tabernacle speaks of both blessing and curse. God dwells in the midst of Israel in a unique way, and His presence bestows on Israel a unique privilege and unique blessing. Through Him they are enabled to inherit the land of Canaan. Yet the tabernacle is simultaneously a source of curse to those who violate its holiness. Those who enter its precincts unauthorized are threatened with death. After Israel sins God sometimes appears at the tabernacle to pronounce judgment (Numbers 12:5–10; 14:10–11).

The law has the same double-pronged effect. Israel is blessed above all other nations by having wise statutes and laws (Deuteronomy 4:5–8; Psalm 147:20). The laws set forth a way of life and blessing to those who keep them (Leviticus 18:5; Exodus 20:12; Deuteronomy 28:1–14). Simultaneously, they threaten a curse on the disobedient (Deuteronomy

27). The possession of the land betokens the character of Israel's relation to God (Deuteronomy 28:1–68).

The tabernacle, the law, and the land are given to the people of
Israel after they have been redeemed from Egypt (Exodus 20:2). They
are crowning blessings to those who have already received the great
salvific blessing of deliverance. Even the curses of the law can be
viewed positively as warnings and fatherly chastisement to wayward
sons, intended to awaken them and bring them back to the way of
obedience. In such functions the Mosaic law is parallel to the commandments given to Christians. Christian obedience does not earn our
salvation any more than Israelite obedience earned deliverance from
Egypt. Salvation is a gift. The blessings of God in Christ, like the blessings of the land, are a gift. Obedience follows in the form of the service
of gratitude (restoration) and imitation (replication) of the Deliverer.

The tabernacle, the law, and the Promised Land point in this respect to the gracious benefits of deliverance through Christ. Christ is
Himself the final embodiment of the tabernacle, the law, and the land.
He is God's dwelling with us (John 2:21), in conformity with the tabernacle theme. He is God's righteousness expressed to us (2 Corinthians
5:21), in conformity with the law theme. He is God's richest blessing to
us, our inheritance (Ephesians 1:14), the fulfillment of all the promises
of God (Ephesians 1:3–4; 2 Corinthians 1:20), in conformity with the
theme of the Promised Land. We ourselves are to imitate or replicate
Christ's character in ourselves. We are to be temples of the Holy Spirit
(1 Corinthians 6:19) replicating the tabernacle. We are to be new people, "created to be like God in true righteousness and holiness"
(Ephesians 4:23), replicating the law. We are to be filled with the fullness of God and His blessing (Ephesians 1:3; 3:19), replicating the land.
In the new covenant each Christian becomes a tabernacle, beholding
the glory of Christ (1 Corinthians 6:19; 2 Corinthians 3:18; 4:6). The
kingdom of God is our proper inheritance (Matthew 5:5, 10; 6:33). The
law is written on our hearts (Jeremiah 31:33). Thus the law, understood
as fulfilled in Christ, can serve as a "lamp to our feet and a guide to our
path," a guide for the righteous living of a Christian (Psalm 119:105).

The built-in insufficiency of the tabernacle, the law, and the land
also point to Christ. Longings for deep communion with God can never

be fulfilled in the Old Testament, because the tabernacle veils bar the way. Definitive forgiveness of sin can never be obtained in the Old Testament, because animal sacrifices do not suffice to cleanse the heart or to abolish sin permanently (Hebrews 9:9; 10:2). The law when understood in its depth pointed to the absolute perfection and holiness of God. Sinful human beings cannot stand before God's perfection; they are always condemned. Circumcision of the heart was promised to Israel in the future (Deuteronomy 30:6), but the law bluntly pronounced Israel to be hard of heart (Deuteronomy 29:4; 32:5). The blessings of the land, good as they were, were temporary: they were sometimes interrupted by war and famine, and always terminated by bodily death.

The law, then, condemned Israel for its sin. It provided also for some relief through the animal sacrifices, but these sacrifices never gave final cleansing nor did they result in circumcision of the heart. The more we read the law in depth, as a pointer to the absolute righteousness of God rather than an elementary list of rights and wrongs, the more we see the desperate character of the human situation. We are condemned by God and alienated from Him. There is no human remedy. Israelites were thus shut up under the curse of the law in order that their longings for future deliverance might grow, that they might return to the promise of blessing given to Abraham, and they might look forward to a final deliverance and circumcision of the heart. The curses of the law in this respect functioned not simply as a kindly chastisement by a heavenly father, but as a shadow of the final punishment in hell. When Christ came, He came to die under the curse of the law, to suffer the punishments of hell, in order that we might be freed from the curse (Galatians 3:10–13). Thus Christ's suffering is the fulfillment of the curse of the law. In this respect we ourselves ought to look to the law not to understand what we undergo but to understand what Christ underwent on our behalf.

The tabernacle, the law, and the land seem, then, to have two contradictory purposes, to bless and to condemn. Actually, the two are harmonized in Christ. To begin with, the land as a blessing of God foreshadows the permanent blessings of Christ. But the temporary character of the blessings, and even more strikingly their eventual reversal into a curse for disobedience, remind Israel of her insufficiency and point to what Christ had to suffer to win permanent blessing.

The tabernacle and the law foreshadow the holiness and righteousness of God. On the one hand, they anticipate the holiness and righteousness of Christ that we are to imitate, and thus set forth a standard for our obedience. On the other hand, they set forth the unreachability of the divine standard and the necessary condemnation falling on the disobedient. In doing so they anticipate the suffering of Jesus Christ for us and the pains of hell that fall on the unrepentant.

The men of the Reformation spoke of three uses of the law of Moses. The law was, first, a restraint to the wicked; second, a schoolmaster that by condemning us points to the remedy in Christ; third, a standard for Christian obedience. Our own discussion confirms the validity of the second and third uses. The first use is also valid, since it is true enough that even unbelievers cannot avoid knowing God's standards (Romans 1:32). The threat of punishment either directly from God or through state authorities keeps unbelievers from doing some of the wicked things that they would otherwise do. When unbelievers obey God's standards in this way they are fulfilling God's purposes of restraining the outbreaks of evil.

If we would indicate relative importance, however, we would do well to rearrange the traditional order. First and foremost, in terms of eminence, the law points forward to Christ. This preeminent function includes within it the other two. By foreshadowing the righteousness of Christ it becomes a guide to Christian living. And by foreshadowing the universal righteous punishment of evil through Christ, it threatens punishment for sin, and thereby restrains evil even among those who have not yet willingly bowed their knee to Christ.

The Interpretation of Mosaic Law in Hebrews

The book of Hebrews contains a discussion of all the major aspects of Mosaic revelation and confirms the interpretations that we have already set forth. Let us review them one by one.

First, look at the tabernacle. According to Hebrews 9:1–14 the tabernacle was an earthly sanctuary. It symbolized the heavenly sanctuary and pointed forward to the work that Christ would complete.

Next, consider the sacrifices. According to Hebrews 10:1–10, the animal sacrifices showed their imperfection and pointed forward to the final substitutionary sacrifice of Christ.

Next, look at the priesthood. According to Hebrews 7:1–8:6 the Aaronic priesthood by its imperfection showed the need for a new and greater priesthood after the order of Melchizedek. Christ has now become a high "priest forever in the order of Melchizedek" (5:6).

Next, consider the people. In Mosaic times the nation of Israel was made a kingdom of priests (Exodus 19:5–6). Hebrews 10:19–25 shows that all Christians now have the privileges of the high priest, in that they are able to enter the Most Holy Place through Christ. We have become the people of God who are called to enter God's rest (Hebrews 4:2–3; see Galatians 3:6–29).

Next, think about the land. Hebrews 4:8–11 indicates that the rest in the land of promise typified the heavenly rest with Christ that is our goal.

Next, look at the law. Hebrews 8:5–13 and 10:15–18 draw a connection between the "new covenant," enjoyed by Christians, and the Mosaic covenant of Hebrews 8:9. The Mosaic covenant includes all the elements just listed above, but prominently among them it includes law. In the new covenant, "I will put my laws in their minds and write them on their hearts" (Hebrews 8:10). "My laws" in this verse refers back to the laws of the Mosaic covenant, which had been violated by Israel (8:9). The new covenant thus continues the standards of righteousness of the Mosaic covenant. Yet radical transformation is also in view. The first covenant as a whole, with tabernacle, sacrifices, priesthood, land, and law, is "obsolete" and "will soon disappear" (8:13; cf. 7:12, 18–19). Hebrews does not go into detail about what results from this transformation of law. But we see hints of the implications not only in the radical alteration of the total institution of priesthood (7:18–19), but in sacrifices (13:15–16), food regulations (13:9), and promised land (13:14; 11:10, 16; 12:22–29). The transformation does not mean lawlessness, but love (13:1–6) and obedience to authority (13:17). At the heart of obedience is the constancy of Christ's righteousness and love (13:8).

The book of Hebrews thus contains a remarkable amount of instruction touching on the relation of the Mosaic covenant to Christians. This richness is summed up in the book's opening verses:

> In the past God spoke to our forefathers through the prophets at many times and in various ways, but in these last days he has spoken to us by his Son, whom he appointed heir of all things, and through whom he made the universe. The Son is the radiance of God's glory and the exact representation of his being, sustaining all things by his powerful word. After he had provided purification for sins, he sat down at the right hand of the Majesty in heaven. (Hebrews 1:1–3)

The Son as the exact representation of God's being brings to a climax all earlier revelations of God, and His glory outshines them all.

NINE

THE PUNISHMENTS AND PENALTIES OF THE LAW: PREFIGURING THE DESTRUCTION OF SIN AND GUILT THROUGH CHRIST

S ome of the laws of Moses describe punishments that fall on those who disobey. How do we understand these punishments? This area is a particularly sensitive one, because of modern aversion to punishments of any kind. Some people are tempted to say that these parts of the Old Testament contain inferior ideas deriving from Israel's imperfect understanding rather than from God. But such a response greatly misunderstands the character of Mosaic law. Israel was indeed an imperfect nation, but the laws in Exodus through Deuteronomy are God's words to Israel, not Israel's response to God. Jesus confirms the absolute authority of these words when He says, "Do not think that I have come to abolish the Law or the Prophets; I have not come to abolish them but to fulfill them. I tell you the truth, until heaven and earth disappear, not the smallest letter, not the least stroke of a pen, will by any means disappear from the Law until everything is accomplished" (Matthew 5:17–18). Hence, we must see the punishments of the law as part of the positive communication deriving from God Himself.

The Righteousness of God's Punishments

The punishments are easy to accept once we deal with the perversions and misunderstandings in our own hearts. Modern culture is averse to punishment because it does not understand God nor does it understand the seriousness of sin. We need to reject many ideas of modern culture in order to accept God's word. God is infinitely holy and good. Sin is rebellion against Him, an infinitely serious violation of His majesty and a despising of His goodness. The righteous punishment for sin, according to the standard of God's own righteousness, is eternal death. If we can see the true seriousness of our sin, we will no longer object to God's supposed severity but marvel at His mercy.

We can approach the same issue from another angle. God loved Jesus Christ His own Son supremely. And yet by God's own plan Jesus was condemned to death (Acts 2:23; 4:25–28). God hated sin so much that even Jesus had to suffer when sin was laid on Him. Here we see the true awfulness of sin. Moreover, if there had been another way to save the world, God surely would have spared His own Son from a horrible death in order to do it. The awesome character of Jesus' death therefore shows how righteous God is. Sin must be punished. God's righteousness requires it. There is no other way. Punishment, then, is built deeply into the order of the universe; in fact, it is an aspect of God's own order, of His way of dealing with sin. We do not like to hear about punishment because it reminds us of the seriousness of sin. But we must hear about it if we are to wake up to the true horror of our sinfulness and flee to the remedy, namely, flee to Christ. Thus punishment in this life can have a positive side. It can make us wake up to our need. C. S. Lewis has said that "God whispers to us in our pleasures, speaks in our conscience, but shouts in our pains."[1] Pain is a warning that our lives are amiss. Come to Christ before it is too late!

Thus we never have a right to complain that God's punishments are too severe. Within this life, punishments are less than we deserve apart from Christ. Moreover, when we are God's children, we can have confidence that He is disciplining us for our good (Hebrews 12:5–13). "No discipline seems pleasant at the time, but painful. Later on, however, it produces a harvest of righteousness and peace for those who have been trained by it" (Hebrews 12:11). Discipline also has a role on a human plane, when parents discipline their children. Of course, a good parent takes care to set a good example and spends much time giving positive instruction and guidance to children, like the father in Proverbs 4:1. But good parents will not shirk their duty to punish children when the children go astray. Such punishment, if given consistently and in love, gives the children a most concrete warning of the long-range consequences of evil behavior. "Do not withhold discipline from a child; if you punish him with the rod, he will not die. Punish him with the rod and save his soul from death" (Proverbs 23:13–14). "He who spares the rod hates his son, but he who loves him is careful to discipline him" (Proverbs 13:24).

God's punishments in the Old Testament always foreshadow God's final judgment. They warn us that judgment is impending and symbolize on an earthly plane the character of the judgment. Thus, as we have seen, the substitutionary punishments that take place in animal sacrifices foreshadow the punishment and destruction that is due for sin, and the complete consecration to God that is required of true worshipers. This punishment and destruction fell on Christ on the cross, where He became our substitute. Christ's utter consecration to God is vindicated in His resurrection. We who trust in Christ share the benefits of His work. We are freed from punishment and destruction and are consecrated to God through Christ's sacrifice (Hebrews 10:10, 14). Those who do not believe in Christ and are not united to Him must suffer punishment and destruction in their own persons in hell. In a similar way, we should understand all the punishments in Israel's history as warnings and foreshadowings.

The punishments of God are never arbitrary, but fit His own holy character. Sin always involves an attempt to play God, to usurp God's authority, and to be one's own standard of right and wrong like Adam and Eve in the Garden of Eden. In sin we engage in an attempt virtually to destroy God's authority and claim on us—to destroy God if we could. The fit punishment for such rebellion is a replica of the crime. "As you have done, it will be done to you" (Obadiah 15). Since we have attempted to destroy God, we are ourselves destroyed by God in hell. Or else Christ as our representative bears the destruction for us on

the cross. (Lest readers misunderstand, let me say that in Biblical contexts destruction of human beings never implies literal nonexistence or
annihilation, but frustration and rendering powerless.) The smaller
judgments of God within history, whether in the form of illness, suffering, or physical death, all confront us with smaller forms of destruction
and powerlessness; they thereby anticipate the great judgment.

The fit payment for sin is both punishment and destruction, as two
aspects of one whole. Fit punishment includes powerlessness and,
hence, the destruction of our powers. Conversely, fit destruction includes destruction of our longings for fulfillment. Hence, it involves
pain and frustration, i.e., punishment. Within this life such payment
can serve to awake us to our danger and our guilt, if we are repentant.
For those who are unrepentant, it serves as the first foretaste of greater
punishment at the last judgment.

Another way of understanding the appropriateness of punishment is
to see it as an implication of love. God the Father loves the Son. Just as
any human father will want to defend his son against enemies, God the
Father reacts against any dishonor to Christ and will punish it.

One final analogy may help to drive home the point. A wise human
father will not only endeavor to warn a young son but spank him for
disobedience if he gets too near a busy street. Similarly, the son will be
punished for trying to play with the father's power tools. The father
gives his son an immediate pain signal to warn him, because the son is
not yet able to calculate the more distant consequences of toying with
danger. Similarly, in our relationship to God certain areas are off limits,
because God is using His power tools. The entire tabernacle is off limits
for Israel, except under certain carefully specified conditions that protect the priests from the danger. Moreover, even the tabernacle itself is
only a shadow of the real areas of power.

God's holiness and righteousness are in fact the real power tools.
God because of His righteousness undertakes to cleanse the world from
evil. And He will do so through the power of Christ's death and resurrection. But we must keep out of God's workshop. We must stop play-
ing God. We must submit to His way of doing things. Punishment on
earth is God's signpost warning us of approaching danger. Presumptuous

people are like madmen dancing nonchalantly into the business end of a sawmill.

The analogy with the sawmill is imperfect, because we are guilty and not merely ignorant. We ourselves are part of the refuse from which God must cleanse the world. But we must not be embarrassed or embittered by punishment. God's goodness does not contradict His punishments. Rather, the coming together of goodness and punishment points to a deep mystery, the unfathomable wisdom by which God righteously saves wicked people. For God to create the world shows infinite power and wisdom. For God to destroy wickedness and injustice shows infinite power and wisdom. For God to destroy wickedness while rescuing wicked people shows infinity squared, namely, the infinity of the punishment and goodness and justice that are united together in the crucifixion and resurrection of Christ. Here God's power tools are harnessed for our good.

One of the most general principles of God's justice is the principle of similar measure. "As you have done, it will be done to you, your deeds will return upon your own head" (Obadiah 15). Jeremiah 50:29, Habakkuk 2:8, Joel 3:4, 7, and other passages articulate the same principle in varying forms. The famous law of punishment, "eye for eye, tooth for tooth" (Exodus 21:24), embodies the same principle in a specific juridical context. It was never intended as an excuse for personal vengeance but as a directive to judges making decisions regarding penalties in cases of injury (Exodus 21:22–25). The death penalty for murder comes in the same form, "Whoever sheds the blood of man, by man shall his blood be shed" (Genesis 9:6). Genesis 9:6 is an exceedingly significant passage because it is spoken to Noah immediately after the flood. The character of Noah as representative of all his descendants and the otherwise universal context of the passage (Genesis 9:7, 11–19) show that here we are dealing with a principle of truly universal scope, and not merely with something specially tailored to Israel as a holy nation. The same principle comes up in New Testament teaching. "For in the same way you judge others, you will be judged; and with the measure you use, it will be measured to you" (Matthew 7:2). "Give back to her even as she has given, and pay her back double for what she has done. Mix her a double portion from her own cup. Give her as much torture and grief as the glory and luxury she gave herself" (Revelation 18:6–7). "For they have shed the blood of your saints and prophets, and you have given them blood to drink as they deserve" (Revelation 16:6).

Penal Authority Given to Human Beings

The principle of similar measure applies both to judgments by God, such as the judgment on Babylon in Revelation 18:6–7, and to judgments by human authorities, such as the penalties of "eye for eye, tooth for tooth" in Exodus 21:24. But we must be careful in making the transition from God to human authorities. God's authority is original and absolute, while all human authority is derivative and limited. God's judgments are always perfectly holy and righteous, while human judgments are tainted by sin. God's judgments are based on perfect, exhaustive knowledge of the facts of the case, while human judgments must be based on partial, imperfect knowledge. Human governmental authority is subject to great abuse, as when it was used to try to force Daniel and his friends into idolatry.

Nevertheless, even with all these reservations, the Bible definitely teaches that the authority of human state governments and the authority of human parents is a limited but legitimate authority given by God (cf. Romans 13:1–7; Ephesians 6:1–3). We must resist the modern temptation to rebel against all authority whatsoever. Such modern rebellion is rooted ultimately in rejection of God's authority (Romans 13:2). It overlooks the fact that God sets up kings and deposes them (Daniel 2:21). Since it regards differences in status and authority as pure chance, it is naturally contemptuous of the claims based on such differences.

In the Mosaic law God gives to human beings—to Israel in particular—authority to execute penalties for certain crimes. In fact, the human authority to punish is attested even earlier, in Genesis 9:6. God might have kept all prerogatives to punish for Himself, but He does not do so. In the case of murder, the awesome responsibility of executing the death penalty is assigned to finite, sinful human beings ("by man"). Undeniably there is a risk here. Human beings with the best intentions may make a grievous mistake because their knowledge is finite. And frequently their intentions are corrupt. But by assigning this task to human beings, God confirms one aspect of their dominion as image bearers of God.

Human government at its best is indeed a blessing from God. Most obviously, government can protect the innocent from criminals (Romans 13:3–5; 1 Peter 2:14). But the punishments of human government, since they reflect nothing less than divine authority (Romans 13:1–2), are also a little reminder of the coming final judgment of God. Human authorities as image bearers of God ought to reflect in some measure divine justice as they carry out their duties.

We can learn something about principles of God's justice as we reflect on the specific penalties of Old Testament law. Such laws derive from God, so we know that the penalties are always just. But when human beings are given responsibility to execute penalties, the penalties involved are only a finite image of God's own penalties and justice. There is always a decisive difference in the nature and scope of their authority. As Jesus says, "Do not be afraid of those who kill the body but cannot kill the soul. Rather, be afraid of the One who can destroy both soul and body in hell" (Matthew 10:28). Once we recognize the decisive distinction, we can also see similarity. Justice on a human level is a shadow of that great act of justice and mercy where Jesus Christ bore the just penalty for our sin. Hence, all the Old Testament penalties point forward to the justice of God at work in the sacrifice of Christ.

Simple Examples of Just Recompense on Earth: Murder and Theft

We can see clearly how things work in the case of the death penalty for murder in Genesis 9:6. Let us suppose that person A has deliberately killed person B. The same penalty is in return executed on person A: the executioner, by God's authority, deliberately kills person A. Such a penalty corresponds to the nature of the crime. "As you have done, it will be done to you" holds true. The punishment is a kind of replication of the crime, except that it returns the crime back on the criminal. Thus this punishment, operative as it is on the level of human government, reflects the divine principles of replication and imitation that we have already seen.

How do we understand the principle of just recompense in the case of theft? According to Mosaic law thieves are required to pay back something to the owner from whom they have stolen. The amount paid varies with the situation: sometimes double, sometimes four times, sometimes five times (Exodus 22:1, 4, 7). The situation is more complex here, because we must try to understand whether there is some reason for the various quantities of repayment. The easiest starting point is with the related statutes concerned with reparations for accidental damage and for borrowed things (Exodus 21:28–36; 22:10–15). The person who is responsible for accidental damage or who has borrowed something is required to make good what the owner has lost. A singlefold restitution takes place in order to match the loss. In the case of theft, by contrast, the restitution is usually double (Exodus 22:7). What principle is at work here?

The logic behind simple singlefold restitution is fairly clear. In a typical case Bill borrows, say, an ox from Al and restores the ox to Al afterwards. The restoration of the ox restores balance or harmony and brings the situation back to its original normalcy. If the ox dies while Bill has it, Bill is unable to restore full normalcy. So Bill does the best he can by supplying a substitute ox of equivalent value (Exodus 22:14). Or suppose that Bill makes a pit and Al's ox falls into it and dies. Bill accidentally caused damage to Al's property. Bill cannot bring Al's ox back to life (the best restoration), so again he does the best he can by offering Al a substitute ox. The dead ox undergoes a substitutionary exchange with the living one, and so the dead ox becomes Bill's (Exodus 21:33–34). The end result is that Al's property is restored to its original integrity (as best as possible), and that Bill suffers exactly the amount of loss for which he was actually responsible (the difference in value between a live ox and a dead one).

Note that a principle of restoration is at work. Even in as simple a case as this one, people are to imitate what they see in the tabernacle and in the general principles of God's justice. They are to take heed to abide by the created order of God. In a way the restoration is simultaneously a replication of the original situation. When the borrowed ox is restored to its owner, the borrower replicates the original order that was temporarily set aside by the borrowing. If the borrowed animal dies, the borrower can no longer restore it, but he restores a replica of it—a substitute animal. Thus the principle of substitution embedded in this practice is simultaneously an instance of replication. Once again, this imitates an aspect of the tabernacle and the creation of God, namely, the principle of replication.

What decisive difference arises when we deal with theft instead of borrowing or accidental damage? In the case of theft the thief intended to appropriate the property permanently without the owner's permission. Bill steals an ox from Al. If Bill is apprehended with the ox alive in his possession, then the ox is returned to Al. The return of the ox restores the balance in the same way as with borrowing. But theft in distinction from borrowing carries with it the evil of intending specific damage to Al's total supply of property. Bill intended damage to Al and simultaneously advantage to himself. Hence, the principle of "as you have done, it will be done to you" involves an act in the reverse direction, of damage to Bill and advantage to Al. An ox is forcefully taken from Bill and given to Al, just as Bill earlier forcefully took an ox of Al's and had it given to himself. The total result of this process is that Bill repays *double*. The repayment of the first ox is simple restoration, while the repayment of the second ox is punishment for the criminal intent.

The nature of the punishment is obviously significant. Not just any punishment will do, but only a punishment that matches the crime. A suitable match is achieved by replicating or reproducing the effect of the crime, only in the reverse direction. If Bill stole from Al, he must give to Al the same amount. This process of replication in reverse is exactly what we saw in the case of murder as well. As a general rule, punishment in similar measure implies that the punishment should replicate the effect of the crime, only in reverse. Such a punishment embodies the basic principle of replication that is integral to God's created order. Moreover, a punishment of this kind also embodies a kind of restoration of balance. Injury to one is balanced by injury to the guilty party. For convenience, however, I prefer to reserve the term "restoration" for the act of returning the original stolen ox. Restoration is appropriate in the case of borrowing, whereas punishment as an additional burden is appropriate in the case of theft.

In summary, double payment is the appropriate penalty for theft. The penalty must involve two parts, restoration of the original and punishment for evil intent. The double quantity involved is not an arbitrary amount, but is based on what is fitting. Through this rationale we also help to resolve an important exegetical question. Interpreters of Exodus 22:4 and 22:7 are not sure whether these texts describe restoring the original plus one more or restoring the original plus two more.[2] The linguistic data of the texts by themselves do not point with absolute clarity to either one of these alternatives. But on the basis of the general principle of due recompense, the interpretation involving restoring the original and one more seems much more likely. Moreover, once we have penetrated to the principle behind the particulars, we are much more confident that the instances of double recompense are the rule, while recompense of four or five times represents the exception.

This punishment for theft reflects on a human level the nature of our obligations to God for our sin. Payment for sin must include both restoration and punishment. In restoration we must restore or repair the damage done to others and to God's honor. In punishment we must in addition bear damage in ourselves corresponding to our evil intent.[3] Both of these two sides to our obligations are fulfilled in Christ. Christ's suffering and death were God's punishment for sin. Christ's earthly life of righteousness and His resurrection are His restoration of righteousness to God. In the promise of new creation, based on Christ's work, we have hope for full restoration of the universe from the damage of all sin. In the suffering of Christ on the cross we have full payment for the punishment of sin as well as vindication of the honor of God.[4]

What do we now say about the fourfold and fivefold recompense in Exodus 22:1? The passage specifies that if an ox or a sheep is stolen and is not found alive, the thief must pay the owner five oxen in return for one stolen ox, or four sheep in return for one stolen sheep. Everyone has difficulty with this verse because no explicit reason is given why these cases differ from the general principle of twofold repayment (see 22:7). Several speculative reasons have been offered, but in the nature of the case none can be viewed as definitive.[5] I would suggest that we take our clue from the only direct information that we are given distinguishing the case of verse 1 from those of verse 4 and verse 7, namely, the issue of whether the ox or sheep is found alive in the thief's possession. If the animal is alive, the thief restores double, according to the pattern that we have already seen. But if the ox or sheep is not in the thief's possession, the process of restoration cannot take place according to the normal pattern. The thief's further action in disposing of the beast has introduced a further element of guilt, in that he has intentionally damaged the possibility of making things good to the owner. Before the action of disposition, he was liable for two animals. After the action the guilt is doubled. He must pay two animals to restore balance, and then two more animals for the additional guilt and liability. By this process we get a total of four sheep.

But now why five oxen for an ox? I do not know. We may have reached the limit of our ability to account for recompense in terms of the principle of balanced punishment and restoration. What distinguishes the ox? In Israelite times in an agricultural economy, the ox was the single most expensive possession and simultaneously the least dispensable possession that an average Israelite might have—other than land or a house that could not easily be stolen. The theft of an ox could easily threaten an average family with poverty, and the additional guilt involved may be what warrants the additional payment. There may also be a principle at work similar to Exodus 22:5. For accidental damage to a field, restitution is made *from the best* of the field. That is, in order to make sure that restitution is complete, the best quality product must be given as a substitute. Such a principle would certainly be just in the case of other forms of substitutionary restoration. In the case of the five oxen, the serious threat to the owner's livelihood warrants a fifth ox to make sure about the fullness of repayment. I am not satisfied with this explanation, but neither am I satisfied with alternative explanations that I have seen.[6]

My analysis also helps us to understand the appropriateness of recompense being made to the original owner. Just as in a case of borrowing the borrowed item must be restored to the original owner, so the thief must give back the original item to the owner. And since in the initial act of theft advantage flowed from, say, Al to Bill, in the second act of repaying double advantage flows back from Bill to Al. As James Jordan observes, "Restitution is not made to the state, but to the man robbed. The state is not wronged in any of this, and the wrong done to God is satisfied by sacrifice."[7]

One further question remains. Does Proverbs 6:30–31 indicate that a person stealing on account of hunger must pay back sevenfold? The text runs, "Men do not despise a thief if he steals to satisfy his hunger when he is starving. Yet if he is caught, he must pay sevenfold, though it costs him all the wealth of his house." In context, the word *sevenfold* is a metaphorical way of expressing the completeness of the penalty rather than its literal quantitative proportion.[8] Hence, this text is not in tension with the principles developed above.

Using the same principles of recompense we can explain more thoroughly the penalty of capital punishment for murder (Genesis 9:6). Suppose Bill deliberately kills Al. In analogy with theft, proper recompense involves two elements. First, restore what has been damaged (restoration). Second, have the offending party subjected to the same process in reverse (punishment). The first stage would involve raising Al back to life, while the second would involve Al killing Bill under the supervision of legal process. But of course human beings are unable to achieve full recompense in this situation. Only God can bring Al back to life. Such a resurrection will indeed take place at the last day, but until then all human reflection of God's justice will necessarily partake in pre-eschatological imperfection. Since perfection cannot be attained immediately, what is actually done in a case of murder? The dead man must be left dead. There is no restoration. But at least the second part of the process, namely, punishment, can be carried out. The avenger of blood, i.e., the nearest family representative of Al, kills Bill under the supervision of legal process, as outlined in Numbers 35. Note that the element of reciprocity is carried out as fully as is practicable. Since Al himself is dead and cannot participate in the judicial retribution, the nearest of kin substitutes for him.

Recompense in the case of manslaughter follows the same general lines. Manslaughter is the accidental taking of human life. Rather than being analogous to theft, it is analogous to the cases in Exodus 21:28–36 where there is accidental damage to property. If Bill is responsible for the death of Al's sheep, perfect restoration would involve Bill bringing the sheep back to life. Since Bill cannot do this, Bill substitutes a live animal. There is no double recompense here because there was no evil intent. Likewise in the case of human death with no evil intent only a singlefold repayment or restoration would be appropriate. Ideally, the raising of the dead person but not the death of the manslaughterer is called for. But the dead person cannot be raised. The requirements of recompense can only be met when the person guilty of manslaughter takes refuge in a "city of refuge" whose character symbolically anticipates the eschatological refuge of salvation in Christ. By pointing to the promise of restoration of all things, including the restoration of life, the city of refuge and the death of the high priest are crucial pivots responding to the desire of the avenger of blood for satisfaction.

We can also make sense of the provisions in Leviticus 6:1–7 for repentant thieves. The thief must offer a sacrifice to deal with his sin against God. He must also restore singlefold to the person robbed (6:5). This situation corresponds to the distinction between accidental and deliberate damage to another person's property in Exodus 21–22. As a general rule, accidental damage results in singlefold repayment (restoration), while deliberate damage results in double repayment (restoration plus punishment). The difference between the two resides in the evil intent. Now in the case in Leviticus 6:1–7 the thief has repented of his evil intent. The situation has thus become like one of accidental damage. But the thief adds one-fifth (6:5). The figure of one-fifth is not further explained in the text of Leviticus 6, but the easiest supposition is that it represents a tithe of the double repayment. The thief thereby testifies that he would otherwise be liable to the whole penalty, just as the tithe of crops testifies that they are all owned by God.

Furthermore, we can now understand the principles regarding penalties for false witnesses. Deuteronomy 19:15–21 contains the basic instructions for dealing with cases of false witness. The appropriate penalty is described in Deuteronomy 19:19: "Do to him as he intended to do to his brother." The immediate context of Deuteronomy 19:19 appears to suppose that the case is resolved before the innocent party suffers damage. The first stage of recompense—restoration—is unnecessary, because no measurable damage has occurred. The false witness has been detected early enough, before the intended damage was achieved. But the second stage—punishment—where the false witness receives equal damage, is still appropriate. We may therefore generalize to cases not directly covered by the passage in Deuteronomy. Suppose that monetary damage had already been inflicted by a false witness whose testimony was believed. Due recompense would presumably require the double payment characteristic of theft; that is, it would include restoration plus punishment.

Up to this point I have concentrated on the questions concerning the type and quantity of recompense required for various crimes. Yet we should not suppose that God's wisdom is manifested only at that level. There are obviously practical social benefits to these arrangements. The provision for repentant thieves in Leviticus 6:1–7 provides tangible, practical incentive for a thief to repent, since he will not have to repay as much. The provision for fourfold or fivefold repayment in the case of animals that have been disposed of (Exodus 22:1) also has practical value. It supplies practical motivation for a thief not to dispose of stolen property, and thereby makes it easier to get a full restoration. Moreover, the thief is not shut up in prison where he may become worse, but forced to do something constructive by paying someone else. The injured person rather than the state receives recompense, which not only helps to heal the injury but shows to the thief the proper direction in which his energies should be directed.

The basic motivational problems of the thief are also addressed as best they can be in the form of outward actions. The problems of crime are all rooted in the failure to love one's neighbor. For example, the thief is keenly aware of his own desire for someone else's goods but has little concern for the well-being of the owner. He is unable to love the other person who owns the property and unable to see things sympathetically from that person's point of view. When the thief is caught and forced to repay, the structure of recompense forces him at least in a minimal way to adopt the other person's point of view. He is made to feel the same deprivation that the other person felt. In the case of capital punishment, of course, the murderer cannot thoroughly feel the experience of death until he is dead, and then it is too late. But even the fact that death is approaching gives him some idea.

Capital punishment certainly does not solve the problems completely. Only the resurrection of the dead person, the repentance of the criminal, and the criminal's union with Christ's death and resurrection would suffice to deal with the root of the matter. Only the power of the Holy Spirit, sent to apply the work of Christ to human beings, can heal the root of sin in human hearts. Christ's work also includes the promise of dealing with the results of sin, including death itself. Because of the power of Christ's resurrection we have a sure hope for the resurrection of human beings at Christ's return (1 Corinthians 15:12–58). Until then God has given certain powers of punishment to human beings, including the power of the sword (Romans 13:4), i.e., the power of the death penalty. But the judicial activity of human beings, important and legitimate as it is, cannot bring forth justice in a final, perfect form. The insufficiencies of the best human justice are one more pointer to the necessity for hope in Christ and His divine justice.

The argument that we must not use capital punishment—or any punishment—because it does not achieve a perfect and final reciprocity of results must be set aside. Rather, we have hope for the return of Christ and know that until then human justice does contain imperfections.

In general, the whole structure of punishment and restoration of balance that is operative in Old Testament penalties points forward by virtue of its own nonultimacy to the final and perfect restoration to come in Christ. It is a subtle reminder of what sort of world we live in: a world in which there is evil, but also a world where God's justice is at work to abolish evil and repair its damage, a world whose hurts will be entirely repaired, restored, and balanced out in the final working of the justice of God at the last judgment.

The Significance of the Injured Party: God and Human Beings

We should note that the injured party has a definite role in the process of recompense in all of the cases that we have discussed. Damage done to the injured party must be repaired, if possible, by restoration of the same amount or a substitute. In addition, if the party doing the damage has evil intent, the injured party is involved in a double repayment, punishment as well as restoration. In the case of theft, the injured party receives whatever the thief loses. In the case of murder or manslaughter, the avenger of blood, i.e., the nearest of kin who represents the dead person, kills the murderer or makes sure that the manslaughterer is forced to remain in the city of refuge.

Once we have understood this principle of recompense and the involvement of the injured party, we can make good sense of the relation of God to human beings in the process of recompense. First, note the obvious problems. Every sin is an offense against God, and as such merits not only physical death but eternal death in hell. Yet in the Mosaic law not every sin receives the death penalty. In fact for some sins no penalty at all is specified in the Mosaic law. If every sin is an infinitely serious offense against the majesty and holiness of God, how do we understand the differences in penalties in the Mosaic law?

In part the distinctions arise from differences in knowledge. God knows all things, including the secrets of the heart, and so is in a fit position to give judgment corresponding to the true facts of the case. But in many cases human beings cannot determine guilt. The testimony of only one witness is insufficient (Numbers 36:30; Deuteronomy 17:6; 19:15).

But in addition to the differences in knowledge, we must take account of differences in the injured party. Any sin "injures" God in the sense of being an offense against Him and an abomination to Him. Moreover, though an attack against God's deity and lordship never succeeds, its intent is to escape God's authority. It aims at overthrowing God as God, by making oneself or some idol into a god. As we have seen from some of the examples above, action with intent to destroy receives the same penalty as would actual destruction (e.g., Deuteronomy 19:19). Since the sinner attempts to destroy God, the fit penalty is the destruction of the sinner in hell—or else the destruction of a substitute, namely, in the death of Christ as a substitute for the sinner. Thus even the last judgment and its outcome can be understood as an operation of the basic principles of recompense and balancing: "As you have done, it will be done to you."

Short of the last judgment, God acts in history to punish sin by sending afflictions, suffering, and physical death. Though these penalties stop short of ultimate destruction, their tendency is in the direction of disintegration, and hence they are foretastes of the final judgment. In general, God can and does punish sins against Himself according to the principles of His own just character.

What criteria do we use when human beings are involved in executing punishment? God's right to punish does not yet imply any right for human beings to punish. State governments have such rights only because God has given limited but genuine authority to governmental agents to bring wrath (Romans 13:4). From the cases above and the way in which the injured party is involved, we can conclude that the authority of human beings covers only those cases in which human beings are injured.[9] Only then is some human being fit to exact the penalty, namely, the injured human being. Moreover, in the typical penal case in Mosaic law, the ruling authorities are mentioned either not at all or only tangentially (e.g., Deuteronomy 17:9). Undoubtedly elders, judges, kings, and others with ruling authority would have played a role in making sure that proper procedure was followed in determining guilt (Deuteronomy 17:6; Numbers 35:24–25). But in the cases discussed above the injured party always has a central role in execution of the penalty. The injured party, rather than the state as such, has this central role because of the principles of reciprocity and balance involved in God's justice. When Al deliberately damages Bill, God's justice fittingly pronounces a recompense exactly in reverse. Bill, not merely God Himself acting in His own person, receives authorization under the eye of governing authorities to restore the balance by bringing the same damage on Al. In short, Biblical principles of justice enable us to begin to understand why human beings are involved in punishment and why some sins receive more severe punishment than others.

In all this process we must bear in mind the most fundamental reality, namely, that human beings are created in the image of God. Israel in particular, as a redeemed nation restored to fellowship with God, is called to a life of imitating the holiness of God (Leviticus 19:2). Human beings are to imitate or replicate the character and action of God. Human relations to one another must replicate the justice of God's relation to human beings. Just as offense against God calls for recompense from God, an offense against other human beings calls for recompense from human beings. Human judicial activity, partial and imperfect as it is, replicates the judicial activity of God.

The fulfillment of human justice as well as the fulfillment of divine justice is found in Christ. Christ fully bears God's penalty for sin on the cross (2 Corinthians 5:21). He simultaneously bears the penalty of unjust human judicial activity by the Jewish leaders, by Herod, and by Pilate (Acts 4:27–28). The injustice of human judges is overruled by the justice of God who accomplishes salvation. In Christ's resurrection God pronounces His approval on Christ's work and simultaneously judges the injustice of the human courts (cf. Acts 3:13–15). Christ will come at the end of this age, not only as the Divine Judge, the Word of God (Revelation 19:13), but as the Man whom God has appointed to judge the world (Acts 17:31). Thus the judicial activity of all human judges throughout history will find its completion in this final judgment of Christ the perfect King and Governor (Isaiah 9:6–7; 11:1–9).

In the meantime, during this age, human state authorities have a limited but legitimate role, as we have said (Romans 13:1–7). All rule and authority, power and dominion, have been subjected to Christ (Ephesians 1:21–22). Hence, even human governments are included under His rule. When they fulfill their duties properly, they are reflecting Christ's justice on an earthly plane and are to be submitted to for the Lord's sake (1 Peter 2:13).

PART TWO

UNDERSTANDING SPECIFIC PENALTIES OF THE LAW

FALSE WORSHIP, HOLY WAR, AND PENAL SUBSTITUTION: PREFIGURING THE SPIRITUAL WARFARE OF CHRIST AND HIS CHURCH

I have now accomplished in large measure my main purpose of show-ing the way in which the law of Moses testifies to Christ and how it is relevant to us in all its parts. But I believe it is profitable to devote extra space to judicial laws, partly because they are the most neglected and partly because they have been misunderstood. I also say this be-cause the principles of justice embodied in them will be of help to us as we think about the obligations of modern states, which are one and all under the authority of God and the rule of Christ.

In principles, the laws of God in the Old Testament have im-plications in many directions: for economics, for state responsibilities, for family, for individual morality. I shall focus on only one area, that of state responsibility for punishing crimes.

We begin with a particular case, namely, the penalty for seduction to false worship in Deuteronomy 13:1–18. We shall spend some time on this case, because of its importance in revealing principles of justice and their application to Israel as a holy nation. In subsequent chapters we shall then go on to examine in detail many other cases of judicial penalties set out in the Mosaic law.

Just Recompense for False Worship in Deuteronomy 13

Deuteronomy 13:1–18 instructs Israel on how to deal with false prophecy and seduction to false worship in its midst. A false prophet is to be put to death (13:5). Even if a member of your own family entices you to false worship, that person is not to be spared (13:6–11). If a whole city goes astray into idolatry, the city is to be destroyed (13:12–18). The guilty city is destroyed in the same way that the Israelites destroyed the Canaanite cities when they entered the land of Canaan: nothing at all is left (13:15–17; exactly as in Deuteronomy 7:2; 20:16–18; Joshua 6:21). The people are especially warned to keep away from the "cursed" things (13:17; see also Deuteronomy 7:26; Joshua 6:18). The special word ḥerem is used in these cases signifying items "consecrated to God for destruction."

How are the general principles of just recompense operative here? First of all, the city committed to false worship is sinning against God. This sin like all other sins deserves destruction in hell. Those who attempt to destroy God will themselves be destroyed. But as usual, this type of observation does not help us to understand how the Israelite recompense for this crime differs from the recompense for any other crime. We should therefore ask the question whether any human beings are injured in addition to the direct insult against God. The passage itself indicates that a "detestable thing has been done among you" (13:14), suggesting that the people are polluted by the idolatry among them. The related verses concerning small-scale rebellion have a similar note: "you must purge the evil from among you" (13:5); "all Israel will hear and be afraid, and no one among you will do such an evil thing again" (13:11). The city becomes a "whole burnt offering" (13:16), which certainly suggests that a purification is taking place in the process.

We conclude, then, that the city engaging in false worship has committed an offense against Israel, not merely against God. False worship within the land of Palestine pollutes the people. As in the case of theft and other crimes, the proper recompense involves two aspects. (1) Restoration: the guilty city is responsible to restore Israel to purity; and (2) punishment: the guilty city is to suffer the same penalty in the reverse direction. The destruction of the city accomplishes both aspects simultaneously. First, the city functions as a whole burnt offering (13:16). Those who offer the offering, i.e., the people of Israel, are purified by the act of offering. This act not only removes the evil from among them but also signifies a penal substitution: the city bears the penalty that otherwise Israel would bear. Second, since the city has polluted Israel, Israel must in reverse fashion pollute the city. Since the city has already suffered a first radical pollution by its act of idolatry, the only way for Israel to bring further pollution on it is by utter destruction. Cases dealing with individuals rather than whole cities involved in false worship (13:1–11) are to be understood along the same lines. The discussion is less elaborate, but we can assume that the same principles are operative.

In what capacity are the people of Israel involved in this recompense? The fact that Israel undertakes an operation of war against the rebellious city makes us think of the connection with war waged by modern states. But clearly not everything is the same as in a modern state. In the case of an individual involved in false worship, as in 13:1–11, the witnesses begin the execution and then all the congregation joins (vv. 9–10; cf. 17:7). People with special authority, such as elders and judges, would presumably be involved in supervising the weighing of evidence (cf. 13:14; 17:4; Numbers 35:24). But such authorities have no explicit role in the execution itself. The crime involved here is not an offense against governmental authorities but against the congregation. The congregation is polluted, and so it must engage in the action leading to purification. Israel is involved in recompense because it is a holy people whose holiness has been profaned. This particular crime is a crime precisely because of the holiness of Israel. The structure of recompense makes sense only when we appeal to this holiness and to the processes by which it is violated and restored.

When we apply this insight to the warfare in 13:12–18, we see that we are dealing not with ordinary war but holy war. When a city turns to false worship, it puts itself into a situation similar to the original

Canaanite cities of the land of Palestine. The means of dealing with the city is to apply the same justice as was applied in the conquest under Joshua. The whole city is destroyed and devoted to destruction. Even within Israel there is a clear distinction between this type of war and wars against nations beyond the borders of Palestine (Deuteronomy 20:10–18). The distinction makes sense in terms of the principles of just recompense. Idolatrous cities within the land of Palestine pollute the holy land (Numbers 35:33–34; Leviticus 20:22–26) and threaten to pollute the holy people. The pollution of holiness is itself an injury that must receive just recompense from the injured party.

The Significance of Holy War: Justice and Purity

Our observations up to this point can provide further insight into the principles of holy war. Holy war establishes justice and purity in the land of Palestine during the conquest. In addition, in the case of a rebellious city, holy war maintains justice and purity after the conquest. Since God is just in His actions at all times and places, we expect a fundamental agreement between the two stages. The same basic principles of justice and of balanced recompense should be operative at both stages. So let us look at the conquest of Canaan. The conquest is first of all God's providential act to punish the Canaanites for their sins (cf. Leviticus 20:23; Genesis 15:16). In this respect it is like any other case where God punishes sin. God is the just and holy Judge of all the earth. His own righteous character implies that He must and will punish sin. In some instances one nation becomes an instrument for punishing another, even when the first nation acts unrighteously or arrogantly (cf. Isaiah 10:5; 1 Kings 17).

But in the Canaanite conquest the human actions of the Israelites are just, unlike the actions of the Assyrians and many other conquerors. The actions of destruction are approved by God, even though less radical destruction by other nations might be labeled "cruel." Why does God approve this holy war? Because God Himself commanded it. If we understood nothing more, we would still be bound to accept it as just. But in fact we can understand more. The earlier inhabitants of Canaan had sinned grievously and were polluting God's Promised Land (Genesis

15:16; Leviticus 18:24–25). When Israel enters the land with God in her midst, the land is in effect claimed for God, consecrated by His presence and given to Israel. The claims of the Canaanite nations to the land are forfeited. The Canaanites represent polluters of the land and potential polluters of the holiness of Israel in her own land. Thus the process of recompense goes into effect: Israel destroys the nations in recompense for the pollution that they would do to her.

The same standards that apply to the Canaanites must in fact also apply to Israel. How can that be the case? Let us stand back for a moment to see the overall process of God's redemption. Remember that God's standards of justice and God's rule are completely universal (Daniel 4:34–35). All human beings are ruled by God and owe allegiance to God. But since the fall, not all human beings are equally submissive to God's rule, and not all the earth equally conforms to His justice. The salvific presence and blessings of God were in the Old Testament uniquely focused on Israel. Hence, in a sense we may speak of God "becoming king" over Israel (Deuteronomy 33:5) and His reign as something that comes and takes hold of the world progressively through the great events of redemptive history (cf. Zechariah 14:9; Isaiah 52:7; Matthew 6:10). The coming of God's reign is simultaneously the coming of His justice and the enforcement of His standards over new people or new regions. The Israelite conquest of Canaan is one such establishment of God's reign. Of course we can describe the conquest as Israel's act of maintaining her purity. Equally the conquest is God's act of maintaining His purity as He in His holiness symbolically "enters" the land through the ark, the tabernacle, the priests, and the law itself which is kept in the ark.

Since God's standards of justice are truly universal, we are bound to ask how Israel comes to be under God's rule without suffering the same fate as the Canaanites. How can anyone approach God's presence without dying on account of sin? Does a different standard apply to Israel? The Old Testament contains ample indications that God brings the Israelites under His rule by a process of holy war similar to the conquest of Canaan. In the case of the Canaanites the approach of God and His rule means consecration to utter destruction. In the case of Israel the approach of God involves the use of substitutes that are consecrated to destruction: the Passover lamb substitutes for the firstborn of Israel, and animal sacrifices substitute for the people more generally.

The Old Testament also speaks of the fact that God was being faithful to His promise of Abraham, Isaac, and Jacob (e.g., Exodus 6). Israel received mercy on account of the fathers (cf. Romans 11:28). If we go all the way back to Abraham, we find once again that Abraham enjoyed the blessing and promise on the basis of substitution: in Genesis 22 Abraham was willing to sacrifice Isaac as a whole burnt offering (22:2), and at the last minute a ram was substituted. Since the whole of Abraham's future and the future of the promise was bound up with Isaac (Hebrews 11:18), Isaac here represented the whole nation of Israel in one person (see the similar reasoning in Hebrews 7:9–10). In Genesis 15:9–21 God put Himself under oath to fulfill the promise, in a symbolism involving not only animal sacrifice (15:9–10) but also the hint that God Himself, as symbolized by the flaming torch, may be subject to destruction (15:17).[1] Abraham's faith in God's promise (Genesis 12:1–4; 15:6) implicitly looked forward to Christ as the offspring who will definitively accomplish the fulfillment of the promise.

Other passages confirm the connection between Abraham's faith and ours (Romans 4:22–25), between the Passover and Christ (1 Corinthians 5:7), and between the sacrifice of Isaac and the resurrection of Christ (Hebrews 11:18–19; cf. Galatians 3:16). "Baptism into Moses" in the cloud and in the sea mentioned in 1 Corinthians 10:1–13 prefigures baptism into Christ, which in turn points to Christ's substitutionary death and resurrection (Romans 6:1–11). A whole host of typological events in the Old Testament prefigure the substitutionary sacrifice of Christ. In sum, Israel came under the dominion of God by experiencing death in the form of symbolic substitutes. The same basic principles of holiness, pollution, and recompense that we have seen everywhere apply to Israel too. Israel was distinguished from the Canaanites only because of faith in promises and in symbolic institutions of substitution. These institutions pointed forward to Christ. God's holy war was waged against Israel too (see Exodus 32:25–35), but in crucial cases substitutes bear the penalty inflicted by the war.

Holy War, Christ, and the Church

All these passages in the Old Testament have a bearing on us in the New Testament period. The parallel between baptism into Moses and baptism into Christ (1 Corinthians 10:1–13) already suggests a deep and fruitful connection. The "baptism" of Israel in the Red Sea is a picture of going down into death and being saved from death on the other side of the sea. Such symbolism of death in the Old Testament is fulfilled in the reality of Christ's consecration to death. In the Crucifixion, Christ as penal substitute bore the penalty of destruction that should have come to us because we have rebelled and tried to pollute God's holiness. Christ is not only our substitute but one through whom we experience spiritual death and resurrection (Romans 6:1–11; Colossians 2:20–3:4).

Hence, as Christians we ourselves are victims of holy war. We have been crucified with Christ (Galatians 5:24; 2:20), and we have died with Christ (Colossians 2:20; Romans 6:3–5). Our flesh has been subjected to destruction (Galatians 5:24). But since Christ was raised from the dead, we also enjoy new life (Romans 6:4). The work of Christ represents a dramatic advance in the accomplishment of salvation, not only because reality supersedes symbol, but because the Old Testament symbols typically did not prominently include the note of resurrection. The animals who were sacrificed did not come to life again. As a rule, the law of Moses killed but did not bring to life (2 Corinthians 3:6–18). It revealed God's standard but did not produce in the hearts of Israelites genuine inward conformity (cf. Jeremiah 31:31–34).

We have established, then, that Israelites were subject to holy war through substitution, just as Christians are. But Israelites after their consecration were also active participants in holy war on God's side. The same is true of Christians. The book of Revelation depicts a holy war of cosmic proportions in which Christians are involved. In this war they must maintain their confession and their purity in the face of every kind of opposition springing from Satan. Revelation even presents us with specific parallels between Christ's holy war and the holy war in the Old Testament. The seven trumpets of Revelation 8–11 are reminiscent of the trumpets sounded for the fall of Jericho in Joshua's holy war. The effects of the seven trumpets and the seven bowls of Revelation 8–11 and 16 are similar to the plagues on Egypt, which was a different phase of Old Testament holy war waged by God Himself. The conspiracy of kings in Revelation 17:12 is reminiscent of the conspiracies in Joshua 10–11. The fall of Babylon in Revelation 17–18 is reminiscent of the fall of Jericho. And so on.

The process of holy war is described in less imagistic language in Ephesians 6:10–20. Satan and his agents undertake to pollute and destroy the holiness of Christians; Christians in turn engage in war leading to the destruction of Satan (Revelation 12:11; 20:10).

What are we to conclude on the basis of these New Testament passages? Should Christians engage in holy war? Do passages such as Deuteronomy 6:15–21 apply to us? Certainly the passages do apply to us. For one thing, we have the general principle that the Old Testament applies to us (2 Timothy 3:17; Romans 15:4; 1 Corinthians 10:11; Matthew 5:17–20). We also have specific New Testament injunctions from Ephesians 6:10–20 and from Revelation confirming the thrust of the Old Testament passages. We are not importing something alien to the Old Testament. Rather, the Old Testament all along pointed forward to Christ and spoke in symbolic form of just this holy war that we are called on to wage (Luke 24:25–27, 44–49).

But a fair understanding of the Old Testament requires that we take notice of its own indications of the preliminary and shadowy character of some of its institutions (cf. Hebrews 9:8–14). Before Christ came to fulfill God's plans of redemption and holy war, His purposes could be realized properly only in a preliminary way, through foreshadowing. This process of foreshadowing had several features. (1) A genuine analogy and continuity exists between the Old Testament institution and its fulfillment in Christ. (2) The continuity enables Old Testament saints to participate in the benefits of Christ's work in a preliminary way, and so to be saved and to experience His justice and holiness. (3) The coming of Christ brings a reality and an accomplishment that supersedes Old Testament symbols in depth and finality. Old Testament symbols are fulfilled in and replaced by reality.[2] (4) Old Testament symbols proclaim their own nonultimacy (e.g., the law brought death and not the promised life, 2 Corinthians 3:6–7). (5) The resurrection of Christ introduces a new era where the Spirit is operative with heightened power, the power of the resurrection, in order to bring spiritual life.

Applying these principles to the case of holy war, we see the following. (1) New Testament holy war does continue the holy war of the Old Testament. (2) Old Testament holy war enabled the Israelites to enjoy a foreshadowment of the purificatory power of Christ. (3) Whereas Old Testament holy war was waged primarily against human opponents, on the level of symbol, New Testament holy war is waged against the ultimate opponents, Satan and his demonic assistants. In our age wicked human beings do become the agents of Satan in a limited way, but the fight is preeminently with superhuman forces of wickedness in the heavenly places (Ephesians 6:12). Christ Himself accomplished the definite victory in this holy war. Paul speaks of Christ's triumph over the Satanic hosts when he says, "Having disarmed the powers and authorities, he made a public spectacle of them, triumphing over them by the cross" (Colossians 2:15). During Christ's earthly life His actions of casting out demons proclaimed His authority and prefigured the great triumph over Satan through the cross.

(4) Old Testament holy war had a built-in insufficiency. The fight was primarily with human beings, the shadows of spiritual wickedness, rather than with the demonic sources of wickedness. Moreover, the fight did not result in ultimate cleansing. The offering of a city as a whole burnt offering, as in Deuteronomy 13:16, shared in the insufficiency of all Old Testament sacrifices (Hebrews 10). (5) The power of Christ's resurrection is able to raise the dead. In this fact there is a decisive advance over the Old Testament. To be sure, Abraham's faith and the sacrifice of Isaac became an Old Testament symbolic basis for Israel's redemption, but Old Testament acts of redemption never circumcised the hearts of the Israelites and never extended much beyond the bounds of Israel. Holy war waged against Israel brought redemptive results because of the substitutes, but holy war against the Canaanites brought only disaster to the Canaanites. But now during the New Testament era there is an advance. Holy war is waged through baptism and union with Christ. The flesh is crucified (Galatians 5:24). Human beings are not simply destroyed as were the Canaanites, but raised to life because of Christ's resurrection. This situation is the foundation for

widespread evangelism. Now the whole inhabited earth has become the new land that is to be conquered in God's name (Matthew 28:18–20). We are to wage holy war. But the nature of that holy war is redefined because of Christ. Holy war takes the form of evangelism rather than physical conflict. In particular, there is hope for modern wicked people in a way that there was no hope for the Canaanites. When wicked people repent and are baptized into Christ, they undergo destruction and resurrection. They are consecrated to destruction in a way analogous to what happened to the Canaanites. But they do not stay dead and destroyed because Christ raises them. When they come to Christ in faith, they experience both death to the old life and resurrection to the new life.

Applying Deuteronomy 13:1–18 Today

Now that we have understood more about holy war, we can consider Deuteronomy 13:1–18 once again. Deuteronomy 13:1–18 describes the continuation of holy war in the land once it is conquered. For one thing, the procedures for destroying a city match the procedures for Joshua's war against the Canaanite cities, including even the semi-technical term for things consecrated to destruction (herem, 13:17). In addition, the structure of recompense and reciprocal payment involves the threat of pollution to Israel and Israel's restoration through sacrifice (13:16). Hence, we find how this passage applies to us by connecting it to our own phase of holy war.

First and foremost, this passage prefigures Christ's own war against Satanic hosts. Spiritual wickedness had polluted humanity and the earth. Christ acts to bind the "strong man" and to destroy the works of the devil (Luke 11:20–22; 1 John 3:8; John 12:31). Israel as God's son (Exodus 4:22–23) acts by the authority of the true heavenly Son and so foreshadows the actions of Christ's against spiritual wickedness in heavenly places. In fact, just before the beginning of Israel's holy war to conquer Canaan, a figure appears to Joshua who is "commander of the army of the LORD," whose very presence makes the ground holy (Joshua 5:13–15). Many interpreters have thought that this figure is one pre-incarnate appearance of Christ, and I think that they have good grounds for their view. But even if the figure is an angel rather than Christ Himself, he prefigures the activity of Christ as the ultimate commander of the Lord's armies, the King of kings and Lord of lords (Revelation 17:14; 19:16).

On a secondary level, the passage from Deuteronomy 13 also has relevance to Christians, because they wage spiritual holy war in imitation of Christ's victory and based on it (Ephesians 6:10–20). How do we apply the passage on this level?

The false worship that occurred during and after Joshua's conquest profaned the land and the holy people. They in return were required to give recompense. What is the proper analogue in our modern situation? What injury is done and what guilt is incurred in modern holy war? There are several possible types of injury analogous to the Old Testament situations.

Punishment for False Worship

First, any sin is an injury against God and will be repaid by Him at the Last Judgment (cf. 1 Corinthians 3:17). But we have already seen that sins against God do not in and of themselves involve human beings in responsibility for retribution.

Second, suppose that false worship or seduction to false worship occurs within the church, i.e., within its membership. The church is a holy people (1 Peter 2:9) and is profaned by this evil in its midst. Double payment is required, first to restore the church to purity (restoration), then to render the offender profane by an action in the reverse direction (punishment). The same principles operative in Deuteronomy must be operative in the modern case. In particular, the church as the injured party must be active in retribution in order to conform to the principles of justice in the Old Testament. The punishment of the offender is accomplished by the church's excommunicating him. Paul counsels the church on its duty of excommunication in 1 Corinthians 5:1–8, and Jesus gives similar counsel in Matthew 18:15–18 (note especially 18:17). In excommunication, the church expels the offender from its fellowship, and declares that the person is henceforth separate from the holy community. It also advises its members to treat the person like an unbeliever. Like all unbelievers the person is to be treated with love and respect, in the hope that the person may eventually repent and be united to the Christian fellowship of believers. In one respect, however, excommunication is even more serious than simple unbelief. People who have once been part of the Christian fellowship have more grievous responsibility if they reject what they have known (Hebrews 10:26–31). Not only is the offender officially put outside the holy community, but "consigned to Satan" (1 Corinthians 5:5) by an act invoking Christ's authority and power (1 Corinthians 5:4). This act does not render the offender profane merely on the level of symbol; that is, it does not "fight flesh and blood" (Ephesians 6:12) by destroying the body of the offender. Rather, it renders the offender profane on the level of judicial reality: it subjects him to the authority of Satan.

The duty of excommunication is clearly taught in the New Testament, but too seldom practiced in evangelical churches. Out of a false sense of pity and mercy we often refuse to act against sin. We thereby make the same mistake as lenient parents who refuse to discipline their children. We set a bad example for all other Christians, we contaminate the body of Christ with spiritual pollution, and we fail to honor Christ and make known His purity and holiness. In addition, we do no real good to offenders themselves. We neglect to give them a solemn warning of the danger of their position, and we fail to call on them to renew their allegiance to Christ. Of course, error can also arise at the opposite extreme, if we deal with offenders harshly. Then we neglect to act on the basis of the reality of Christ's ability to bring people to repentance.

Restoration from False Worship

So far we have talked only about one aspect of the penalty for false worship, namely, punishment. There must also be restoration. The church's purity has been damaged and must be restored. If we used a direct analogy with the Old Testament, we might still expect the church to inflict physical death on the offender, in order to purify itself by burnt offering (Deuteronomy 13:16). In the Old Testament a person who has touched a dead body must not only stop touching the dead body and have it removed from his presence permanently, but must go through a cleansing ceremony to be restored. So the church must not only stop the contact of Christian fellowship with the spiritually dead, but must undergo cleansing. What cleansing? A burnt offering? Yes, our cleansing must use the only final and all-sufficient burnt offering for cleansing, namely, the sacrifice of Christ. The church is united with Christ in the heavenly realms (Ephesians 2:6). The finality and perfection of Christ's sacrifice, together with His resurrection, the permanency of His presence in the church, the efficacy of His intercession (Hebrews 7:25–28), and the vitality of the church's union with Christ, guarantee continual cleansing from sin (1 John 1:7–9). In this respect Christ's work fulfills and surpasses the Old Testament. The church offers as its burnt offering not the excommunicated person but the finished work of Christ, continually applied through the power of His resurrection. The vitality of Christ restores the church to new life.

Third, suppose that false worship occurs outside the church. Is the church injured? For insight on this issue, we need to consider again the Israelite situation. In Deuteronomy 13 the holy people are profaned by evils taking place "among you" (13:1, 3, 14). Apparently no distinction is made between native Israelite and the sojourning foreigner. Seduction to false worship brings profanation if the act takes place within the holy land (13:12), in physical proximity to the holy people. Is such physical proximity and presence in the holy land always the significant factor? In the Old Testament the holy people apparently have no obligation for holy war in times when they are dispersed among the other nations (cf. Jeremiah 29:5–7). The geographical and political separation of the people from other nations is evidently part of their sanctification and the sanctification of the land.

Now what about the church? The church during its growth is dispersed among the nations and is in the world without being of it (John 17:15–16). The church's sanctification does not spring from geographical and ordinary political separation from others, but from the power of Christ's word (John 17:17–26). The significant dividing line is not a spatial separation, but the spiritual separation denoted by the distinction between church members and nonmembers.

Hence, in this respect it appears that the church lives in a situation more like that of the Jews dispersed in Babylon, or like Abraham living in Canaan. We mingle socially and politically with unbelievers, but are separated by participation in the promises of God. In another respect, however, the church is nevertheless unlike the dispersed Jews. The dispersed Jews should have had hopes for returning to Palestine. We hope for the coming of Christ. In the meantime, we are to spread the gospel and "make disciples of all nations," not simply wait passively for the end of this age (Matthew 28:18–20).

Better yet, we may properly say that the church is a heavenly community. Christians have their true citizenship in heaven (Philippians 3:20). By being united to Christ they are, as it were, carried up to heaven. In worship they meet with the heavenly assembly (Hebrews 12:22–24). They are seated with Christ in the heavenly realms (Ephesians 2:6). Their life is now "hidden with Christ in God" (Colossians 3:3). By temporarily participating in the holy community, a backslider has had a taste of heavenly reality in a sense (Hebrews 6:4–6), but only in a sense. The book of 1 John says of backsliders that "they went out from us, but they did not really belong to us. For if they had belonged to us, they would have remained with us; but their going showed that none of them belonged to us" (1 John 2:19).

It is difficult to see, then, how the church is profaned in a direct and fundamental sense through the false worship of outsiders. Such outsiders are firmly confined to earth and do not tread upon the church's heavenly holiness and privileges. But if there is no injury to the church, there is also no penalty that the church must inflict. This conclusion is confirmed when we make a direct comparison between false worship by outsiders and false worship by church members. The latter is certainly more serious. The insider does profane the holiness of the church, and greater responsibility belongs to the person who is more privileged ("everyone who has been given much, much more will be asked," Luke 12:48). Now in the case of an insider, a church member, excommunication puts the offender into the position of being an outsider. Hence, it seems that the person who starts as an outsider would simply remain an outsider, without further penalty.

In a sense the whole world has now replaced the land of Palestine, which was the Old Testament holy land on a symbolic plane. The conquest of Palestine filled the land with God's holiness and presence and brought His justice into practice in the land. This process was a symbolic foreshadowing, as we have seen, of holy war that is now waged on a cosmic scale. Jesus Christ has authority over all parts of the earth (Matthew 28:18; Ephesians 1:21). In principle Christians by their union with Jesus Christ inherit the earth (Matthew 5:5; 1 Corinthians 3:22). The manner of conquest, however, is by the forces of the gospel of Christ and the power of His resurrection to bring spiritual life to outsiders. We conquer our own "Canaan," i.e., the whole world, not by executing people with the sword but by bringing them to union with Christ, whereby they experience spiritual death and resurrection (Ephesians 6:13–18, cf. 2 Corinthians 10:3–5). Thus our manner of dealing with outsiders is fundamentally different from the practice of Israel in Canaan. The difference exactly matches the nature of this new age, which is introduced by Christ's resurrection and is continued by His reign in heaven.

At the close of this age, Christ does come to wage a war of destruction against unbelievers (2 Thessalonians 1:7–10). Physical, geographical, and political separations return in full force at the end, when the world is completely cleansed from evil and unbelievers are physically separated in hell. Thus, the physical and political separation of Israel foreshadows the judgment of the end of the age.

Until the time of Christ's coming, then, false worship is to be met with the spiritual power of the gospel, not with physical punishments.[3]

ELEVEN

PRINCIPLES OF JUSTICE
FOR THE MODERN STATE

All of God's justice finds its climax and fulfillment in Jesus Christ and His work. All the treasures of God's wisdom are hidden in Him (Colossians 2:3). Christ's sacrifice does not abolish justice or replace justice with mercy, but shows the way in which God's justice and mercy come together (see Psalm 85:10–13). What implications does God's justice have for the modern state?

The Nature of State Responsibilities

Since the beginning of time, God has always been Lord and Ruler of the world and everything in it. Christ was the Word of God, the Second Person of the Trinity, from the beginning (John 1:1). He came into the world as the One who had always been its lawful Ruler (John 1:10–11). But He came also as the Messiah, the God-man who would redeem the world and fulfill the purposes of God's rule. Christ's death and resurrection established Him as Messianic, saving Lord and Ruler over all authorities, including state authorities (Matthew 28:18; Ephesians 1:21–22). "God placed all things under his feet" (Ephesians 1:22). He is "head over every power and authority" (Colossians 2:10). State authorities in the New Testament as in the Old derive their authority from

155

God (Romans 13:1–7) and perform legitimate functions in bringing "punishment on the wrongdoer" (Romans 13:4). The Old Testament also requires kings and judges to rule according to God's standards of justice, both Israelite rulers (Deuteronomy 25:2; 2 Chronicles 9:8; Isaiah 10:1; Jeremiah 22:2–3; 1 Kings 2:3) and others (Proverbs 16:12; 29:4; 31:4–5; Psalm 82). Since all authority derives from Christ, all authorities are answerable to Him. All actions of the state ought to conform to God's standards of justice revealed in Christ.

To this much nearly all Christians assent. But disagreements arise among Christians over the details. Christians disagree first of all over the question of whether Christians should actively participate in the exercise of state power. Christians in the Anabaptist tradition argue that the state's authority to punish wrongdoers is incompatible with the Christian's responsibility to show mercy. Most Anabaptists recognize that for the good of society some people must serve as officers of the state, but they prefer to leave the responsibility to others besides themselves. By contrast, Christians in Roman Catholic, Reformed, Lutheran, and modern Baptist traditions have usually affirmed the legitimacy of Christian service in the state, but they have sometimes understood the state's role in different ways.

We must avoid being overly dogmatic on questions about which Christians have disagreed for centuries. Problems arise over these matters partly because the New Testament does not give a great deal of specific, direct teaching concerning the relationship of the state to God's authority. The Old Testament contains considerable teaching of this type, but Christians have not always agreed on the manner in which the Old Testament is relevant to us. We must recognize our own fallibility. We must recognize that our own understanding of Scripture is imperfect. We must realize that sinful tendencies in our own hearts and in the culture around us may push us into biases. A false kind of mercy in us wishes to avoid any thought of punishment. Or a false kind of justice wishes to use the state harshly to eliminate all evil from the world immediately.

Even though the path is difficult, we have a responsibility for the sake of Christ's glory and for the sake of more consistently obeying Him to think through the implications of His justice for our lives. So let us proceed.

The modern state derives its authority from God and from Christ (Romans 13:1–7). Yet it does not have all the prerogatives of Christ, or even the prerogatives of the church. For example, it cannot pronounce pardon for sins. Pardon and forgiveness before God come only through Christ. Only God Himself can forgive sins. Though the church cannot pronounce pardon on its own authority, it nevertheless has a real judicial power of "binding and loosing" (Matthew 18:18; John 20:23) through the presence of the gospel and the power of the Holy Spirit. The church acts with Christ's own authority and as His representative when it pronounces judgments in accord with His teaching. In a fundamental sense the pardon of God is a judicial pronouncement from heaven, and can be received only from God's heavenly presence. Christ's death on the cross on earth satisfied the divine penalty for sin. We appropriate His pardon when by faith we are united to Christ in heaven. Both individually and corporately we are seated with Christ in the heavenly realms (Ephesians 2:6). The state, by contrast, is firmly confined to earth. Even though it has divine authority, it does not give us access to heaven.

Thus in a sense the Anabaptists are quite right in seeing a pronounced distinction between the task of the state and the task of Christians. Christians who are united to Christ have a heavenly citizenship (Philippians 3:20). They have access to the assembly of saints on the heavenly Mount Zion (Hebrews 12:22–24). They practice mercy on the basis that the Lord has been merciful to them (Matthew 6:14–15; 18:21–35). By contrast, Christ has not been merciful to the state, united it to Himself, or exalted it to heaven. It is an earthly institution that ought to reflect God's justice.

Nevertheless, I would argue that Christians can properly serve as officers of the state. They must simply recognize that the obligations of the state are not identical with the obligations of the individual Christian or of the church. Jesus' instructions about forgiving and showing mercy set forth a pattern of justice that fits the situation of Christians united to Christ, but does not fit the situation of state obligations. State authorities are "God's servant" according to Romans 13:4. Christians who are officers of the state obey Christ and function as genuine servants of God when they supervise the punishment of a criminal. But state action is limited to an earthly sphere of governmental authority. The same Christian who as a judge pronounces judgment may as a Christian pray for the criminal, exhort him to repent, and perhaps even give him some gift to bring happiness into his life.

There is no inconsistency or even psychological tension between these two sides to Christian behavior. For the criminal's own good the criminal must feel the weight of God's preliminary punishment. He must be reminded of the more ultimate consequences of crime when God's last judgment comes. He must see a little earthly picture of God's justice in order that he may perhaps realize the seriousness of God's justice in its more ultimate forms. To withhold punishment from him is like withholding a legitimate discipline from a child. Reluctance to punish manifests not love but false sentimentality and escape from responsibility. At the same time, Christians want to present to the criminal a positive message of hope and new life based on the gospel. Only Christians, not the state institution as such, have the equipment to bring such a message, for only they are united to Christ in the heavenly realms. Only they are clothed with Jesus Christ (Romans 14:14) and so have the spiritual armor of Ephesians 6:10–20 to do battle for the souls of human beings.

Thus we may say that state-supervised punishments present a kind of shadow of God's judgment, while Christians through the gospel present the reality to which that shadow points. That is, Christians present the reality of Christ's penal death and the reality of hell awaiting those who do not put their trust in Christ. When human beings have injured other human beings, both the shadow and the reality need to be presented. The shadow punishment rectifies an immediate human wrong on an earthly plane. When coupled with gospel proclamation of the reality of ultimate judgment, the shadow itself is filled with meaning as a pointer to Christ. But by itself it is only a shadow and does not bring deliverance from spiritual death.

Thus I think that Anabaptists have a genuine insight into the distinction between Christian obligations and state obligations. But they have stopped short of the fullest exercise of love and mercy. Punishment does have a role in genuine mercy. It is a reminder of the consequences of sin. People who sin need such a reminder, and if we really love them we will give them what they need. We are not to shrink from punishment when God enjoins it, as He does in Romans 13:1–7. Moreover, our neighbors need the state and its punishments for their good. The basic principles of loving God and loving our neighbor as ourselves push us into a positive commitment to supporting the state in its proper God-given functions. In short, a fuller view of love and mercy recognizes not only the need but the appropriateness of state-supervised punishments as a shadow along side of the Christians' responsibility to show forth the glory of Christ.

Principles for Just State Punishments

What penalties are just for the state? In this area also we meet much disagreement. Christians have agreed in large measure over what things are sins, but over the ages there has been much diversity of opinion over what sins warranted official punishments and over what the punishments should be. Again we must be cautious.

Our best course is to start with the principles of justice that we have already derived from the Old Testament, and to supplement our insights by delving into both the Old Testament and the New Testament in greater detail. We must also keep before us three complementary principles with respect to the state.

First, the state derives its authority from God, is answerable to God for its actions, and must endeavor to embody in its laws and its punishments the standards of God's justice.

Second, the state has a limited authority, an authority over a limited territory on earth. It cannot release criminals or pardon them on the basis of Christ's sacrifice, because access to Christ is by way of faith in Christ and spiritual union with Him.

Third, the state deals with injuries against other human beings, not injuries against God.[1] Such a limitation arises from the differences between the role of God and the role of human beings in executing punishment. As we have seen in chapter 9, distinct punishments correspond to the two types of offense. Injuries against God are redressed by

God, both in a final form in hell and in a preliminary form through disasters brought by God. Injuries against human beings are redressed by the victim or a representative of the victim. Typically, redress takes place by repayment to the injured party. The state can never be responsible to make sure that people give redress to God, either by compelling them to faith, or by consigning them to hell. It does have responsibility to see that human injuries are redressed, but such redress is often imperfect.

In fulfilling its responsibilities, the state must not insist on attaining divine perfection. It cannot wait until all the facts are in before judgment is pronounced; it must rely on a looser principle like "guilty beyond reasonable doubt." Moreover, it cannot hope to redress all wrongs. It must be content with partial redress in many cases. The very imperfections of human justice are one way, as we have observed, that such justice continues to provide a pointer to the ultimacy of God's justice.

In particular, the limitations of the state require that due legal process must be used. No penalty ought to be executed until guilt has been established. Evidence given against accused persons must be adequate to convince human judges of their guilt. Moses indicates that two witnesses are necessary for conviction (Numbers 35:30; Deuteronomy 17:6; 19:15). This provision appears to be a matter of general principle, so general in fact that it can be invoked even in the case of divine testimony (John 8:17–19; 1 John 5:8–9). But this provision also embodies common sense. Human judges would be unable to render a confident decision if they have only the witness of one person against the witness of the offender. In practice, this provision also protects people against malicious witnesses (Deuteronomy 19:16–21).

If I am correct in thinking that independent corroborating evidence is the important issue, material evidence such as fingerprints might also be used as a substitute at times for a human witness (such appears to be the case in 1 John 5:8–9; Deuteronomy 22:13–17). On a more general level, the practice of weighing evidence and counting a person innocent until proven guilty is so clearly wise that it has deeply embedded itself in Western justice. Such practice fully conforms to God's justice and the principles of state responsibility.[2]

Next, the state is obliged to act only when disputes and injuries are not settled privately. For example, if a thief repents and restores to the owner what he has stolen, as in Leviticus 6:1–7, the case would never come to court. Similarly, if one man hits another and knocks out a tooth, the offender and the injured person can negotiate a monetary payment. Only if the injured person was not satisfied with what the offender offered would he bring the case to court, and then the judges would inflict the specified reciprocal penalty (Leviticus 24:19–20). Thus in many cases the penalties in the Old Testament represent not a penalty used every time, but a maximum penalty.[3] They fix a limit on the requirements of restitution and a limit on the demands for vengeance. In the case of certain serious violations, however, the penalty must be enforced as is and cannot be diminished (Numbers 35:31; Deuteronomy 13:5, 8–9; possibly 19:21).[4]

In my judgment, the same principles apply now. Generally speaking, the state should take a hand in actual punishment only when the offender and victim are unable to negotiate a suitable solution more privately. Sometimes the privately negotiated solution might include the offender's apology and spiritual reconciliation as well as monetary restitution. Because of its potential spiritual dimensions, such a path is clearly superior. Judges or other official mediators would of course aid the negotiation and take care to protect the victim.[5] However, murder and crimes involving usurpation of state authority cannot be dealt with privately, because of their extreme seriousness (cf. Numbers 35:31) and the lack of the authority on the part of the state to pronounce pardon.

The earthly character of the state and the imperfect, shadowy character of its justice resemble the situation of Israel in many ways. There is something to be learned from Israelite law about ways in which God's justice can be concretely embodied and practiced by imperfect agents in an imperfect world. But as we examine the Old Testament we must constantly be aware as well of the way in which Israel and its institutions foreshadow the great work of Christ. Only in such a way will we learn deeply about God's justice. Only so will we also avoid certain mistakes in interpreting the implications of Mosaic law. As we have seen from chapter 10, the passage in Deuteronomy 13 about false worship, when properly understood, points forward to Christ's victory over demons and the church's activity in excommunication, not to a holy war conducted by a modern state. Generalizing from this example, we may say that we need special circumspection when we deal with Old Testament penalties that express the special holiness of Israel and punish profanation of her holiness.

In all the cases that we undertake to analyze, we will focus on the twin features of restoration and punishment, sometimes called "retribution." Each crime deserves a penalty that justly fits it, a penalty that restores damage and brings balanced punishment on the offender. When cases come before the state, the state is responsible before God to ensure that just retribution takes place. In some cases, fit punishment may also achieve subsidiary results in terms of deterrence and rehabilitation. That is, the threat of punishment for a particular crime may motivate some people not to engage in the crime—it may deter them. The type of punishment may also on occasion prove to be a means of reintegrating the offender into society in a positive way. The thief who is forced to repay may learn the value of honest work in the process (cf. Ephesians 4:28). Deterrence and rehabilitation are thus extra secondary benefits flowing from just practices on the part of the state.

But now we must introduce a caution. The present atmosphere of humanism tempts us to formulate punishments *exclusively* on the basis of factors of deterrence and rehabilitation. According to modern humanism, retribution is barbarous. Kindness should motivate us to seek the other people's good by encouraging them not to commit crime in the first place (deterrence) or helping them out of a pattern of crime (rehabilitation). Humanism understands nothing of restoration and punishment because it does not acknowledge a divine order and the reality of divine wrath against sin.

Despite its plausibility, basing punishment exclusively on deterrence and rehabilitation is ultimately inhumane. As C. S. Lewis eloquently argues, the elimination of restitution and retribution converts the offender into an object to be manipulated rather than a person responsible for wrongdoing.[6] Moreover, no boundary remains between crime and personality problems. Why not deter people beforehand by shutting them up or operating on their brains before they have the temptation to commit a crime? In addition, rehabilitation becomes a code-word for unlimited bondage. The criminal is restored to society not when he has paid his debt, but whenever the therapist is satisfied that his personality has been sufficiently readjusted. No form of torture is excluded if the effect promises to be suitable to the rehabilitator. For these reasons we must resist the plausible attractions of current humanism and continue to maintain the appropriateness of reasoning in terms of retribution and fit recompense.

Modern culture has infected and corrupted even Christian thinking more deeply than we may realize. We must train ourselves to exercise unusual self-control, patience, sobriety, and wisdom in considering issues of punishment. Partly because of modern culture, we are tempted at times to operate wholly in terms of deterrence. We feel uncontrolled indignation against crime and then advocate unjustly harsh measures to deter it. At other times, we are tempted to operate wholly in terms of rehabilitation. We feel uncontrolled sympathy for offenders and then advocate unjustly lenient measures in hopes of rehabilitating offenders through kindness. We are not used to conforming our thinking and our sentiments to standards of justice. We must be prepared to make adjustments.

In the arguments that follow I do not claim to have infallible answers. But I would ask you to keep an open mind and to consider not only my arguments in favor of certain punishments, but also my arguments in chapter 14 against the present-day preference for punishment in the form of imprisonment ("doing time").

TWELVE

JUST PENALTIES
FOR MANY CRIMES

W e may now proceed to analyze laws and penalties with regard to
particular types of crimes. Mosaic laws with regard to crimes
may conveniently be grouped together on the basis of the general nature of the crime. Crimes of theft and cases of accident both involve
damage to the property, and so they relate most directly to the eighth
commandment, "You shall not steal." Similarly, crimes involving damage to or destruction of human life are most closely related to the sixth
commandment, "You shall not murder." We shall consider separately
the crimes related to each of these commandments.

Penalties for Theft and Accident

Let us begin with the matters concerning theft and accident, related to
the eighth commandment. As we saw in chapter 9, the penalty for theft
and for accidental destruction of property embodies a clear-cut reciprocity and balance. Accidental destruction must be balanced by restoration
of a substitute (Exodus 22:5–6; 21:36; Leviticus 24:18). If an animal
engages in a destructive act, the owner is normally responsible in only a
diminished way, and hence the penalty is correspondingly diminished
(Exodus 21:28–36). A monetary payment given to the person damaged

is the fit penalty. But if the animal has previously had a history of goring, and the owner does not keep it in, he is fully responsible (Exodus 21:29, 36). This type of case is obviously generalizable into a principle of full responsibility when there has been a previous problem.

Thievery must be balanced by double payment, restoration plus punishment, because there was evil intent. The thief restores the original item as a borrower would, and then gives a second item so that the thief suffers the same penalty that he inflicted on the owner. Both restoration and punishment are involved.

The sacrifice of Jesus Christ fulfills the principles of restoration and punishment in the fullest possible way. Full punishment for all the sins of the redeemed and full restoration of the cosmos to God are implied. His sacrifice is even construed in Scripture as like a monetary payment or ransom. "For you know that it was not with perishable things such as silver or gold that you were redeemed from the empty way of life handed down to you from your forefathers, but with the precious blood of Christ, a lamb without blemish or defect" (1 Peter 1:18–19). But Christ's sacrifice does not eliminate the responsibility of the state to redress wrongs on its limited human plane. In fact, if the state properly executes its responsibility, it produces on earth little pictures or shadows of Christ's great work. It will be a positive but limited aid to the process of bringing the nations to Christ and causing God's will to be done on earth as it is in heaven. Since theft and accident still injure the owner in the same way that they did in the Old Testament, there is every reason to think that the human penalties should be the same now.

If my interpretation of Exodus 22:1 is correct, thieves who have destroyed or sold what they stole are required to pay fourfold to the owner. The general principle of balanced recompense, rather than some special situation in Israel, appears to lead to this result. If so, the same general principle applied today leads to the same result. The same penalties would be appropriate, specifically, fourfold restitution for items that the thief has disposed of.[1] A thief who steals the most expensive and useful item in the culture that is subject to being easily stolen, i.e., an automobile or truck, is required to pay fivefold if the item has been sold or destroyed. But because of the uncertainties surrounding the intent of Exodus 22:1, it might also be argued that a general policy of double payment is best.[2]

But other considerations weigh in favor of a lesser amount of restitution. In typical cases in modern postindustrial societies, stolen items are resold to a "fence" at greatly reduced prices, partly because used goods typically bring a much reduced value even on the open market, partly because disposing of stolen items is not easy. Hence, a thief who is required to repay double the market value will actually end up paying the victim many times what he gained through the sale of stolen items.[3] Moreover, since the market resale value of used items is on the average something like half the price of a new item, payment of double the value of a new item already represents virtually fourfold compensation. Such factors regarding the differences between new and used manufactured products were not typically present in the Israelite situation. But the Old Testament law does recognize the general principle that the value of an item can be depreciated on the basis of its remaining useful life (e.g., Leviticus 25:15–16, 50–52). On this basis, as well as because of the uncertainties in understanding the rationale for fourfold and fivefold payment in Exodus 22:1, I think that a general rule of double repayment is best.

According to Mosaic law, thieves who cannot pay the penalty for their crimes are to be sold into servitude for their theft (Exodus 22:3). The same logic of justice is operative here. The thief must be forced to pay even if such action involves selling the price of his future work. The time in which the thief would be in servitude should be just enough to pay for the damage done.[4] We must beware of importing into this practice the modern connotations of slavery. In the Old Testament context the period of servitude is limited. The offender can always be rescued from servitude by a relative or friend who is willing to pay the value of the remaining period of labor. The offender can even rescue himself from servitude if he earns enough money through a second spare-time job (Leviticus 25:49). The situation is somewhat similar to our modern system of parole, except that a private citizen buys the labor of the offender and simultaneously becomes the parole officer. The buyer receives authority to supervise the offender during the time of parole and also receives responsibility to care for the offender. The system is in fact probably more workable as well as more just than the present parole system, since the employer remains in much more regular contact with the offender and can discipline him immediately for transgressions of duty.

This last case concerning the thief who cannot pay is of course more difficult than the previous cases. But the principles of justice and balanced recompense suggest that the same solution is as valid in our day as in Israelite times. Variations are possible in which the state would more directly supervise the parole and the schedule of repayments.[5] We may debate what arrangements in detail are most workable, and whether some variation on the parole system can be made into a suitable vehicle for supervision.[6] But the general idea is clearly useful as well as just. Besides being a true execution of just recompense, such a penalty has practical value. When the thief loses what he hoped to gain, he is made to experience the other person's point of view. When a greater value of goods is involved, the thief must come to realize the greater value. Moreover, in being forced to serve other people for a time, he unwillingly receives an illustration in his own body of the principle that the person who has been a thief must learn to work hard and honestly (Ephesians 4:28). If all goes well, the thief may at the end have found a useful vocation. The process far exceeds in its wisdom the present criminal system, which bottles thieves up in prison in a situation of frustration, groups them together with others of like mind, and frequently intensifies the inclinations to criminality.

Nowadays some criminals are allowed to "pay a debt to society" by doing meaningful work for the state or for some charitable cause. But such a course is still wrongheaded. The thief's debt is not to the state or to society but to the injured person. We help the thief understand better the nature of his crime as well as conform to Biblical principles of restoration and punishment when we follow the Old Testament practice more directly.

Repentant Offenders

According to Leviticus 6:1–7, the robber who repents and wishes on his own initiative to make things right is required to restore the amount stolen, and to add a fifth (a tithe of the double payment of an unrepentant thief). In addition, he must make a guilt offering to God. The logic leading to this result is not completely certain. Apparently, the guilt offering pays for the robber's sin against God. Such an offering is now fulfilled in the sacrifice of Christ. In addition, the robber must make restoration to the injured person. I take it that repentance plus the acknowledgment of guilt by the symbolic tithe compensates for the evil intent of the original act.[7] Thus repentance plus the symbolic tithe fulfills the punishment aspect of repayment. This initial compensation moves the situation back to the equivalent of borrowing and implies that only singlefold restitution or restoration is then necessary to bring the situation back to a just balance.

Thus this case does embody in a reasonable way the principles of just retribution. But the bearing of this case on judicial principles is still not so clear. Leviticus 6:1–7 does not directly encompass all cases of theft, but only cases in which the robber or false witness has successfully evaded punishment. The offender has only to remain silent in order to continue to profit from its results. In fact, this passage may be even more specialized. The passage lists various types of fraud but lacks the usual term for theft (*gnb*); it explicitly mentions false oaths (6:3, 5). These and other features suggest that the whole passage concerns cases where the victim suspects the offender but cannot legally prove guilt.[8] In such a situation the victim takes the suspect before the court and the suspect swears an oath to prove that he did not defraud his neighbor of property (Exodus 22:11). But suppose the offender escapes by swearing falsely. Later, he feels guilty. Leviticus 6:1–7 gives him a remedy. It requires a guilt offering, not because of the initial fraud or robbery, but because the offender has desecrated God's name by a false oath. This special case still appears to express a general principle, namely, that repentance on the part of an offender who is not caught reduces the payment to singlefold recompense.

But now suppose that a thief is caught, and then begs forgiveness. The victim nevertheless demands double payment and takes the thief to court to obtain it. We are confronted with two possible alternatives. First, it may be that Leviticus 6:1–7 is basically irrelevant to questions of judicial process. It contemplates only the case when the offender is

not caught. Or it may be that Leviticus 6:1–7 embodies a general principle to the effect that repentance on the part of any offender reduces
the penalty to a simple restoration plus a tithe or token of previous evil
intent.

Some tentativeness is called for here, because Leviticus 6:1–7 by
itself does not explicitly specify in what way it might illustrate a general
rule. Other cases in the law do indicate that penalties are to be adjusted
according to the degree of responsibility attached to the offender (see,
e.g., Exodus 21:28–30, 22). In general, the penalties mentioned in the
Mosaic law are maximum penalties, some of which may be mitigated by
extenuating circumstances.[9] If the thief "turns himself in," in a manner
parallel to Leviticus 6:1–7, his repentance is clearly genuine and mitigates the evil intention involved. A reduced restitution would seem to
be appropriate. But what if the thief repents only *after* he is caught and
the wheels of justice begin to turn? Obviously an expression of apology
is of some value, but how can the officers of the court tell for certain
that repentance is genuine rather than merely a ruse to escape the due
punishment?

Though there is room for leniency on the basis of mitigating circumstances, there is no provision for pardon in the modern sense,
namely, a release of a guilty, convicted criminal on the basis of mercy
or promises of reform. For the convicted person, even an expression of
repentance ought not to bring relief. Repentance pays for sin, not because of its innate qualities, but because it unites us to Christ and to
the efficacy of his death and resurrection. Sin must always be punished.
Repentance does not diminish the punishment, but by uniting us to
Christ transfers the punishment from ourselves to Christ the substitute.
All this process is a heavenly reality now for those who are united to
Christ by faith. But the state's own limitations and its earthly character
imply that it does not reflect this aspect of Christological substitution in
its own sphere. The state does not have power to bring Christ down to
earth to substitute for the criminal, nor does it have power to raise the
criminal up to heaven to participate in the benefits of Christ's sacrifice
accomplished once and for all. It does not have the church's authority
to judge the sincerity of a profession of faith. Hence, the state can find
no just way to pardon parallel to the way that Christ grants pardon.

Penalties for Murder, Attempted Murder, And Manslaughter

We now turn to crimes involving destruction of human life, then to crimes involving damage to human life. Both of these types of crimes are related most directly to the sixth commandment, "You shall not murder."

We may begin with a comparatively clear case: murder. In Genesis 9:6 God specifies the civil penalty for murder. The context in which it is given, namely, the instructions affecting all of Noah's descendants after the flood, indicates its universal scope. The special holiness of Israel cannot be in view, since Israel as a distinct, separated people had not yet arisen.

We have seen also how the death penalty for murder embodies the principle of balanced, reciprocal recompense. "As you have done, it shall be done to you." If Al kills Bill, the appropriate reciprocal penalty is for Bill to kill Al. Since Bill is not alive to do the deed, the avenger of blood, the nearest of kin, stands in his stead (cf. Numbers 35:9–34).

The coming of Christ brings amazing redemptive and spiritual resurrection. Christ's atonement does have power for healing conflicts between human beings as well as the fundamental conflict between God and human beings. But His atonement does not immediately remedy all physical death; that remedy will come only at the resurrection of the dead. In the resurrection of the dead all unjust taking of human life is remedied and answered for. Christ on the cross bore the punishment of death in order that through His resurrection life we might participate in the resurrection ourselves. Thus Christ acted both to bear punishment for the violation of human life and to restore that life.

In the midst of the changes brought about by Christ's resurrection, the authority of the state over civil penology is confirmed rather than abolished (Romans 13:1–7). In particular, the mention of the sword in Romans 13:4 indicates the legitimacy of the continuation of the death penalty. Only at the resurrection of the dead does the task of the state legitimately come to an end.

The death penalty is therefore still the appropriate penalty for murder.[10] Initially, we might presume that because of the reciprocity, the nearest of kin should execute the penalty. However, there is an argument (appearing below) in favor of shifting the responsibility of executing the penalty to the state.

What should we say about cases of attempted murder? The Mosaic law does not speak directly concerning the penalty for attempted murder, perhaps because it is difficult in many cases for judges to determine that a particular crime is attempted murder in distinction from attempt to cause serious injury (Exodus 21:18–19, 23–25). This case is therefore more doubtful in character. Deuteronomy 19:16–21 seems to indicate that the intention to do a thing, if legally demonstrable, constitutes guilt on the same level as the actual doing of it. On this basis I deduce that attempted murder deserves the death penalty. As I have already observed, in this and other cases the maximum penalty is to be enforced only when (a) the crime is legally demonstrable beyond reasonable doubt; (b) there are no mitigating circumstances.

What do we say about manslaughter, that is, accidental killing of a human being? In ancient Israel the penalty for manslaughter was flight to a city of refuge until the death of the high priest (Numbers 35:9–34). Some thought it necessary to perceive the principle here and adapt this case to our circumstances. We do not have cities of refuge or an earthly high priest.[11] No evil intention is involved in the case of accidental killing. The parallel with recompense for accidentally destroyed property (Exodus 21:33–36; 22:5–6) would indicate that the proper recompense would be for the offender to restore the dead person to life. Since this option is not possible, the offender goes to the city of refuge with its redemptive symbolism. The provisions of the law present us with a picture of a person fleeing to safety from the consequences of his acts. In addition, the cities are a special gift of God to the Levites, the special holy tribe (Numbers 35:6). Deliverance from the offender's confinement comes with the death of the high priest, again suggesting holiness and sacrificial atonement through death. As if this much were not enough, the key passage in Numbers 35 gives as the reason for upholding the law the following: "Bloodshed pollutes the land, and atonement cannot be made for the land on which the blood has been shed, except by the blood of the one who shed it. Do not defile the land where you live and where I dwell, for I, the Lord, dwell among the Israelites"

(Numbers 35:33–34). In the case of murder this statute is fulfilled through the death of the murderer. In the case of manslaughter, this statute must be fulfilled through the death of the high priest as a substitute for the manslaughterer. In both cases blood must be shed to undo the pollution of the land.

Principles of general equity, as well as the specific content of Genesis 9:6, clearly enjoin the death penalty as a universal penalty for murder, even if the murder is unconnected with the promised holy land. But if the murder is connected with the land, the blood of the murderer has the additional value of cleansing the ceremonial pollution of the land. In the case of manslaughter things are not so clear. How might the fact of the holiness of the land, the holiness of Israel, the holiness of the Levites and their city, and above all the holiness of the high priest have affected the exact form of the penalty?

If we tried mechanically to match a modern penalty to the ancient one, no penalty that could be devised would exactly match the nature of the offense. One aspect seems to be that the offender must go to the special holy city until the land is purged by the blood of the high priest. A second aspect may be that the offender associates himself with the symbolism of refuge and redemption, thereby pointing forward to the hope of restoration of life. A third aspect may be that since the unrestricted freedom of the offender has been the occasion for death, his freedom is carefully restricted until there has been another death.

With this much information in view, the closest mechanical parallel might be for a manslaughterer to be required to appeal for refuge to a church in another city, and to remain in this city under the oversight of the church until the death of its principal pastor. But the symbolism is imperfect, since a pastor is hardly a high priest and a type of Christ. Moreover, the land is not specially marked as holy and hence is not polluted in the same way as was the land of Israel.

We penetrate a little deeper by reflecting on Exodus 21:28–30. If an ox gores and kills a person, the ox is to be stoned and its flesh not eaten (indicating its uncleanness). Just as the blood of a human murderer cleanses the pollution of the land, the blood of the ox cleanses the land from the death that the ox caused. Thus the death of the ox fulfills the provision of Numbers 35:33–34 exactly. An interesting extra factor enters if it was known in the past that the ox was dangerous. The owner of the ox is partially responsible. The ox is stoned as before, but the owner also is put to death. Exodus 21:30 indicates that the owner may or may not be allowed to ransom himself by paying a monetary ransom. How do authorities determine whether or not a ransom is to be permitted, and if so how much? Exodus 21:30 does not say specifically, but the answer is clear enough. The degree of responsibility of the owner depends on his degree of negligence. How frequently had the ox gored in the past and shown an irascible disposition? Had the owner been warned privately by neighbors or publicly by the authorities? Had the owner taken any measures to try to make sure that the ox was always penned up? Had he taken mere token measures or thorough measures? Obviously, a whole continuum of cases might present themselves, and the authorities must be given some discretion to decide each case on its merits.

The important points to see are (1) that the blood of the ox satisfies the provision of Numbers 35:33–34 in a technical sense and (2) that the owner nevertheless bears some responsibility in proportion to his negligence. It appears that the blood of the ox satisfies the special provisions relating to the holiness of the land. If so, we may well suspect that the remaining penalties relate to the obligations of the owner apart from the holiness of the land. The owner receives the death penalty if his gross negligence shows him totally thoughtless of human life. The proper retribution is for the community in turn to show itself "thoughtless" about his life and put him to death.[12] On the other hand, if the owner has shown less than gross negligence, the death is treated more on the plane of accidental death. But he is still responsible to recompense the family of the deceased, just as an accidental destruction of property must be recompensed (Exodus 22:5–6). Since he is partially responsible for the death itself, he must be "partially killed." Of course one cannot achieve this result literally, but ransom money substitutes for the owner's life. A smaller amount of money would substitute for a smaller amount of the owner's life in case of lesser degree of responsibility. The ransom money would naturally be paid to the family of the deceased, and so would function simultaneously as ransom (substitutionary punishment) and as restoration.

The case in Exodus 21:28–30 therefore agrees with the solution at which we might arrive merely by reasoning from general principle. The manslaughterer has done damage accidentally, just as in Exodus 22:5–6. Hence, the just penalty is a singlefold recompense or restoration to the deceased. Since the deceased cannot be restored to life, the manslaughterer pays money as a substitute, thereby also repairing what can be repaired in the economic damage done to the family of the deceased.

Now let us return to the modern context. Actually the full structure of Numbers 35:22–28 is preserved in our modern context. Christ has died the death of the great high priest once and for all. His blood is permanently efficacious, since He lives forever to make intercession (Hebrews 7:25). He continually recleanses all the pollutions of the earth. Hence, the manslaughterer need not seek out a special city of refuge in order to protect the holiness of the land. In fact, to introduce a provision today such as waiting for a pastor's death would obscure the finality and permanent efficacy of Christ's sacrifice. The manslaughterer may thus remain where he was, but must still indemnify the family, in an amount weighted by his negligence. Even if no negligence is involved, the families ought justly to split the cost of the disaster (cf. Exodus 21:35).

Penalties for Bodily Injury

Cases of bodily injury are in some respects like cases of death. In both cases the full remedy and full rectification is found only in the resurrection of the body, which restores human beings to full bodily integrity. Christ bore bodily injury on the cross partly in order that He might pay the penalty to God for our bodily injuries to one another. He was raised to life in order that we might be restored to full health ourselves. But the full restoration comes only at the time of the resurrection of the dead. In the meantime, the justice of the state must operate on the same basis as in the case of murder. The state cannot repair damage to people's bodies, neither can it unite people to Christ. It must operate on earth.

In cases of human bodily injury, the principal passages Exodus 21:18–32 and Leviticus 24:19–20 speak of cases where one human being directly inflicts injury on another. Modern cases like car accidents or accidents at work for which the employer might be partially responsible would be handled like other cases of accidental damage discussed above. In cases of injury where there is evil intent, full recompense would involve responsibilities analogous to the responsibilities for theft. Just as the thief restores the original property, the offender should restore the hurt by causing the person to be healed and paying for time lost (Exodus 21:18–19). Just as the thief pays a second amount in punishment, in order to suffer the same damage that he inflicted, the offender suffers equal bodily damage (Exodus 21:23–25; Leviticus 24:19–20).

But there are still some difficulties in the process. The two sides of the penalty can seldom both be carried out together. In the case where the person is injured and recovers (Exodus 21:18–19), it would be impossible for human beings to inflict exactly equivalent injury on the offender. On the other hand, in the case where there is permanent loss of eye, hand, or tooth (Leviticus 24:19–20), no full repair of the damage is possible. In addition, in cases where two people fight together, it is usually difficult if not impossible to assign responsibility to only one side. It is more appropriate to divide the responsibility and see to it that both suffer equally. Hence, if one has already suffered loss of eye or tooth, the other must suffer the same loss. And if one has suffered the pain and inconvenience of temporary incapacitation, the other must suffer the pain of paying for it. Presumably the victim could ask for ransom money instead of the literal loss of eye or tooth, as is suggested by Exodus 21:30.

As we have noted, Exodus 21:18–19 and 21:22–25 involves cases of fighting where responsibility for the results may in a sense be divided between the two people involved. But in some cases clear-cut responsibility for bodily injury can be assigned to one party alone, as in the case of mugging or armed robbery, if the criminal inflicted an injury on his victim. General principles of equity suggest that a double penalty is called for, in the form of restoration plus punishment. On the other hand, the usual intention in mugging or robbery is not really to injure people but get their money. Injury, if it occurs, is an "accidental" though still culpable result. On this basis one might argue that only a singlefold penalty is called for, combining restoration and punishment. I am not sure which of these arguments represents greater justice. Leviticus 24:19–20 appears to be a general statement about penalties, not qualified in the same way as is Exodus 21:18–25 by the context of fighting. Thus it may be some evidence in favor of the idea of a singlefold penalty.

If we were to decide that a double penalty was appropriate, how would it work? In the case of a bodily injury that is later healed, double payment for the cost of healing and loss of time would be appropriate. In the case of permanent bodily injury, equivalent injury to the offender (punishment) plus payment to the injured person roughly equivalent to loss in earning capacity (restoration) would be appropriate. In all these cases the victim and the offender could negotiate a monetary payment to avoid the court-imposed punishment.

Penalties for Verbal Crimes

Verbal crimes are those related to the ninth commandment, "You shall not give false testimony against your neighbor." These crimes also are related to Christ's atoning work. Christ was put to death due to an accusation of being a false prophet, which is the most grievous form of false witness. By faith we receive the benefit of His punishment and we are united to His truthfulness. Our new status in Christ does not relieve but rather confirms our obligations to our neighbor. The state still has responsibility to redress wrongs in this area.

In the Mosaic law an act of false witnessing, if proven, receives the same penalty that would have fallen to the person witnessed against (Deuteronomy 19:16–21). This penal structure is a simple embodiment of the principle of just reciprocity; it should therefore have the same form today. Slander and libel outside the context of courtroom testimony can be handled on the same basis. If malicious intent to do harm is proved, the slanderer must repay for damage already caused and pay a second amount as punishment for intent to do harm. If no evil intent is involved, single restoration is appropriate as in the case of unintentional damage to another person's property (Exodus 22:5–6).

False witnessing represents a case in which exact balanced reciprocity appears to be violated in one respect. Deuteronomy 19:19 appears to indicate that the penalty is to be inflicted by the people, "you," rather than by the person witnessed against. But false witnessing attacks the integrity of the courts as well as the person who is witnessed against. It thereby threatens to pollute the society (Deuteronomy 19:19b). Hence, the larger society as well as the injured party has an interest in the punishment. The mention of "purging evil" in 19:19 should make us cautious. Such language may indicate a particular concern to protect the special holiness of Israel. But such language by itself does not constitute conclusive evidence that the holiness of Israel is decisively affecting the nature of the penalty. For example, the discussion of murder in Numbers 35:33–34 includes a note about how blood pollutes the land. The pollution of the land makes the execution of the murderer all the more necessary, since otherwise God's wrath comes on Israel. But the appropriateness of the death penalty for murder is not confined to Israel, as Genesis 9:6 shows.

Penalties for Profanation of the Holy Community

We now turn to those crimes having to do with violations of worship and holiness, that is, violations related most directly to commandments 1–4 of the Ten Commandments. Penalties for seduction to false worship and for false worship have been discussed in chapter 10 and appendix A. False worship within the church, if not repented of, leads to excommunication. No civil penalty follows, since excommunication together with the resurrection power of Christ in the community fully answers the reciprocity involved in justice.

If false worship is repented of, the same procedures are involved as in the case of the repentant thief in Leviticus 6:1–7. Singlefold restoration to the church, i.e., restoration of its purity, is enough. Such purity is indeed restored through the presence of Christ, and excommunication need not be employed as an additional penalty. The result at which we have arrived by applying the logic of retribution is in exact agreement with the New Testament instructions given for dealing with offenses in the church (Matthew 18:15–20; 1 Corinthians 5:1–13).

Blasphemy, witchcraft, sorcery, and other crimes involving occult worship would appear to belong to the same category as false worship.

As usual, we may begin by asking who is injured by such acts. The Old Testament does not give much explicit information about the reasons for penalizing these crimes, but presumably they attack the holiness of Israel in the same way as does false worship. Just as in the case of false worship, Israel must meet the offense by waging holy war and destroying the pollution from its midst. The death penalty is therefore the specific punishment within the context of Israel as the holy nation.

The modern equivalent of these crimes is an attack on the holiness of the church from within its midst. Thus I conclude that the same penalties are appropriate as for false worship. The church excommunicates unrepentant offenders, but no civil penalty follows in the case of offenders already outside the bounds of Christian fellowship.

We must recognize, however, that some forms of occult practice involve additional crimes. For example, Molech worship and some forms of Satanism can include human sacrifice. These practices are instances of murder and merit the same penalty as other forms of murder. Or take a more difficult case. Some forms of blasphemy involve slander of Christians and of the church as a societal institution. Such blasphemy involves the same type of liability as would other cases of slander. Since a direct attack on the holiness of the church is not in question, it appears to me that the completed work of Christ does not radically change the nature of reciprocal responsibilities involved in such slander. Christians individually and the church corporately should obviously endeavor out of love to pray for the offender and exhort him to repent. But if repentance is not forthcoming, the responsibilities of love may also include giving the offender, through the justice of the state, a reminder of his responsibilities and a shadow-picture of the more ultimate consequences of his acts. In short, Christians may in some cases take unbelievers to court, though always with reluctance.

Though I accept this possibility in principle, I must also say that in practice most cases of slander are likely to be so puny in comparison with the responsibilities of spiritual warfare that wise Christians will not divert their energies in such directions, even as Paul shrugged off the slanders by non-Christians against his ministry (1 Corinthians 4:13; 2 Corinthians 6:8). Christians must always bear in mind their responsibilities before the Lord to return good for evil (Matthew 5:43–48; 1 Peter 3:9).

Some practices of witchcraft and black magic involve the attempt to cause evil to come on other people through preternatural means. In actual fact, practicers of magic do not accomplish what they think they are accomplishing. Christ rules even over the demons (Ephesians 1:20–22), and His people are protected from the evil one (1 John 5:18). But there are nevertheless some complexities to this issue. For example, sometimes Satan is permitted by God to attack human beings (Job 1–2). But one of Satan's deceptions in occult practices is to seduce people into thinking that the power is theirs rather than Satan's, and to think that they rule rather than God. In any case, people using black magic intend evil. We have already argued on the basis of Deuteronomy 19:15–21 that a legally demonstrable attempt to do harm is punishable on the same basis of reciprocity as a successful attempt. Hence, I judge that black magic ought to be punished when the attempt to do evil is legally demonstrable. The type of punishment would correspond to the nature of the attempt.

Next, what about violation of the fourth commandment, that is, sabbath breaking? Sabbath breaking attacks the holy day of Israel and the sign of God's covenant with Israel (Exodus 31:13–17). Some theologians believe that sabbath observance is fulfilled in Christ in such a way that no distinction of days remains in the New Testament period. If they are correct, the sin of sabbath breaking in the Mosaic period corresponds to the sin of breaking covenant with Christ in the New Testament period. Any sin is, in a broad sense, breaking covenant with Christ, but the definitive form of breaking covenant is apostasy (such as is discussed in Hebrews).[13] If not repented of, the penalty is excommunication from the church and the final penalty from God is eternal destruction in hell.

I see the Sabbath as an institution deriving from creation and continuing until the consummation, so that God still requires a distinction of days. Christ through His resurrection and ascension has entered the sabbath rest. Christians are united to Christ and so already share in the first installment of the rest. Still, Christians have not yet entered rest in its consummate form (Hebrews 4:11). Their citizenship is in heaven

(Philippians 3:20) but they also live on earth in bodies of earth. As long as we are on earth, we celebrate Sunday, the day of Christ's resurrection, as our distinctive day of rest. The sin of sabbath breaking in the Old Testament does indeed point forward to the sin of breaking covenant with Christ. But we must also continue to deal with sabbath breaking as a sin on a literal level.

Supposing this is the case, we must still consider the issue of penalties. Once again this crime pertains to the special holiness of Israel. "This will be a sign between me and you for the generations to come, so you may know that I am the LORD, who makes you holy" (Exodus 31:13). Profaning the Sabbath pollutes Israel's covenantal relation to God. Thus sabbath breaking in our own day has a status similar to false worship and blasphemy. No civil penalty is appropriate for unbelievers, though believers need to be protected from being forced by unbelieving employers to work on the Sabbath.

What ought the church to do with church members who break the Sabbath? If we reasoned in a mechanical fashion, we might conclude that excommunication is the appropriate penalty. However, (1) the passage from the Old Testament to the New Testament involves moving from shadows to realities. The role of the Sabbath changes in the process. Literal sabbath keeping does not now play nearly so central a role in our worship as it did in the Old Testament. (2) In view of the theological uncertainties involved in assessing whether there is any literal sabbath observance at all, we must follow Paul's advice to live in harmony with Christians with whom we disagree on minor points (Romans 14:1–15:7). Of course, we should endeavor to convince other Christians of the view that we think is right, but we should not penalize Christians who disagree with us.

Finally, we should consider briefly Mosaic laws involving penalties for aggravated, serious violations of the ceremonial distinctions and separations of the law. Irremediable violations are punished by being "cut off" from Israel. Such is the penalty when a person eats yeast during the feast of unleavened bread (Exodus 12:15, 19), makes holy anointing oil or incense (Exodus 30:33, 38), works on the Sabbath (Exodus 31:14), eats a fellowship offering while unclean (Leviticus 7:20–21), eats the fat of an offering (Leviticus 7:25), eats blood (Leviticus 7:27; 17:14), sacri-

fices an animal other than at the tabernacle (Leviticus 17:4, 9), eats a
fellowship offering on the third day (Leviticus 19:8), lies with a woman
during her monthly period (Leviticus 20:18), officiates in a sacred offering while unclean (Leviticus 22:3), does not deny himself on the day of
atonement (Leviticus 23:29), fails to celebrate the Passover when able
(Numbers 9:13), sins defiantly (Numbers 15:30–31), or fails to be purified after touching a dead body (Numbers 19:13, 20).

What does "cutting off" involve? Conceivably the language could
imply exile or being deprived of special privileges of holiness. But Exodus 31:14–15 undeniably uses the language "cut off from his people" in
a context where the death penalty is in view. Similarly, a comparison of
Leviticus 18:29 with Leviticus 20:11–14 seems to show that the death
penalty is in view. On the other hand, comparison of Leviticus 18:29
with Leviticus 20:20–21 appears to present us with a case where "cutting off" corresponds to a penalty of childlessness. We cannot be completely certain how to reconcile all these texts. The most plausible solution is to regard the language of "cutting off" as a general expression for
God's curse. It indicates that God undertakes to punish the offender,
perhaps by bringing him to an early death. In fact, such appears to be
the meaning of the phrase in Leviticus 20:1–5, where the text explicitly
identifies God as the one who accomplishes the "cutting off," and indicates that God will undertake to cut people off even if the community
fails to execute the death penalty (20:4–5).[14] If so, the penalty of "cutting off" involves punishment by God for sins against God, but does not
in itself specify a punishment for damage to horizontal relations among
human beings.

All the sins for which "cutting off" is a penalty, with the possible
exception of sabbath breaking (Exodus 31:14–15) and sexual crimes
(Leviticus 18:29),[15] are violations of temporary symbolic distinctions
and separations. Several features might potentially alert Israelites to
their temporary, symbolic character. (1) The general dominion given to
human beings in creation seems to be restricted. (2) The symbolic associations with death, the fall, the curse, and remedies for sin indicate
how these distinctions function to separate Israel from the other nations
and confirm her status as a kingdom of priests with unique privileges
and responsibilities deriving from the presence of God in her midst. (3)

The lack of awareness of such distinctions among the nations surrounding Israel reinforce Israel's uniqueness. These factors would alert Israelites themselves to the shadowy but nevertheless temporarily serious character of the distinctions. The distinctions symbolize the necessity of utter and consistent holiness on the part of Israel as she dwells in God's presence and especially as she approaches God at the tabernacle and on special holy days. These symbolic distinctions therefore point forward to the utter consecration of Christ as well as His being cut off as a substitute for our unholiness. The penalty is fulfilled in the crucifixion of Christ and in the cutting off of unbelievers in hell. In addition, these statutes remind Christians of their obligations to "be holy because I, the LORD your God, am holy" (Leviticus 19:2; 1 Peter 1:15–16) and of the seriousness of apostasy (Hebrews 10:26–31).[16]

Clearly, then, these ceremonial laws in their literal form are all irrelevant to the duties of the modern state.

Penalties for Violent Usurpation of Authority

Under the fifth commandment we may group all crimes against authority. I would include in this group not only civil rebellions, seditions, and guerrilla war, but striking one's parent, cursing one's parent, kidnapping, and all forms of crime that use threats of bodily injury to accomplish the crime (e.g., armed robbery and rape using a weapon). To see why all these crimes may be called crimes against authority, we must reckon with the basic reality that human beings are made in the image of God. To use force against the body of another human being is therefore very serious business. People can rightly do so only when God gives them authority over other human beings. Parents, state authorities, and masters of Israelite slaves have such authority, but even their authority is limited. When an unauthorized person usurps such authority, he does so in defiance of legitimate authority. The state in particular is the institution of last resort to keep distinct legitimate and illegitimate uses of force.

In Israelite society in Mosaic times, the authority of parents, masters, elders, judges, and kings was closely intertwined. Prior to the settlement in Palestine, Israel's encampments were organized along genealogical lines—tribes, extended families, households, and nuclear families (Numbers 2; Joshua 7:16–18; Exodus 18:25). During the settlement in Palestine the land was parcelled out along genealogical lines. Since most of the people continued to live close to their inherited land, Palestinian villages would have been made up mostly of relatives in an extended family. In these situations most legal cases would have been supervised by elders or leading men in the extended family (Exodus 18:19–26; Deuteronomy 21:19–20; 22:15–21). The elders would usually be one's grandfathers, granduncles, uncles, and their cousins. In practical terms the functioning of the extended family and the functioning of the "state" would be virtually the same. A meeting with the elders at the city gate (Deuteronomy 22:15–21) was simultaneously a formal meeting of the family leaders in order to officially decide the business of the clan. The king or judge ruling over all Israel would become involved only in difficult cases (Deuteronomy 17:8–20) or cases of outside threat of war. Such cases would be like a muster of the entire clan to deal with the difficulty. All in all, family and "state" were much more interwoven in Israelite society than what we are accustomed to.

Parents have God-given authority over their children, as is signified by references to the rod (Proverbs 13:24; 22:15; 23:13–14; 29:15). Not surprisingly, the same Hebrew word is used for authority on a larger scale (the word *scepter* in Genesis 49:10; Numbers 24:17; Psalm 45:6; and elsewhere). Moses' rod, the rod of a shepherd, signifies his shepherding authority over the people of Israel. Thus, the authority of rulers is similar to the authority of parents. They are to look after people and protect them from injustice as well as discipline them when they stray. Judges may in some cases beat a guilty person (Deuteronomy 25:1–3), just as parents are given authority to punish children with a rod (Proverbs 13:24; etc.). In many cases judges and parents only need to threaten to use bodily punishment. Obedience is forthcoming because of the threat. Of course, leaders and parents may also use rewards as inducements, and wise leaders frequently do (cf. Joshua 15:16; Luke 19:16–27). Anyone may offer a reward. Only the person with special authority may give a bodily punishment.

Consequently, for an unauthorized person to use the rod or its equivalent is to usurp authority. All usurpations of human authority are, of course, usurpations of authority given by God; hence, they imply simultaneously usurpation of divine authority. In fact, usurpation of authority is one picture of the nature of all sin. All sin proclaims the ultimacy of the sinner over God and sets up the standards and the behavior of the sinner as more ultimate than God. It thus usurps to itself a godlike authority. Sin receives punishment as God exerts the rod of His authority against the sinner. God thereby "restores" the true picture of who is in charge. He also gives the sinner balanced punishment corresponding to the nature of the crime.

On the cross Christ received the punishment of God's rod. As a result we are delivered from God's wrath, and simultaneously God's kingdom is established. God triumphed over the hosts of wickedness through Christ (Colossians 2:15). God's authority to punish sin and also His power to establish righteousness were simultaneously asserted in a definitive way. Thus in Christ the abuses of authority were in principle overturned, and in Christ at His second coming fully righteous authority will be established everywhere on earth. Until the Second Coming the state has legitimate responsibility to oversee its earthly execution of justice. Among other responsibilities, it redresses crimes against earthly authorities.

On this earthly plane, usurpation may take place with various degrees of seriousness. Civil rebellions, seditions, and guerrilla war all attempt a wholesale overthrow of civil authority. Since they intend the destruction of the authority, they themselves deserve destruction. The just penalty is the death penalty.

Crimes with a threat of bodily injury, such as armed robbery and armed rape, do not intend wholesale overthrow of the authority, but only the setting up of a rival authority for a temporary, limited purpose. Of course, such crimes deserve the normal penalty that would be due when no violence is used. But in addition I judge that they merit a beating, just as temporary, limited rebellion by a child against parental orders merits a spanking or beating. Since the offender has illicitly usurped the use of a rod or its equivalent, the rod is in turn used against him. Such is the nature of balanced punishment according to the general principle, "As you have done, it will be done to you."

Some degree of confirmation of this view is found in Deuteronomy 25:1–3. Deuteronomy 25:1–3 specifies that judges may beat a guilty person if he deserves it. But when does a guilty person deserve beating? Nowhere in Mosaic law are we presented with a crime for which beating is the penalty, except Deuteronomy 22:18. That passage involves a newlywed man who falsely accuses his bride of not having been a virgin. The newlywed man has evidently not been guilty of false witness (for which the penalty would be death) but of rashly and foolishly making judicial judgments in a family area over which he has genuine authority. He is beaten, then, for irresponsible use of authority, which has some similarity to limited forms of usurpation of authority. Deuteronomy 25:1–3 seems to contemplate a wider range of cases in which beatings would be appropriate. No such cases can be supplied, unless we infer that there is a more general principle concerning usurpation of authority. The analogy between parental authority and state civil authority does suggest that both kinds of violation of authority ought justly to be punished with the rod.

What about kidnapping? In Israel kidnapping would usually be for the purpose of selling a person into slavery (Exodus 21:16). Since in the Israelite context slavery signified bondage to sin and return to Egypt, we must be careful about generalizing to our own context. Conceivably nowadays the just penalty for kidnapping could be permanent servitude for the kidnapper.

But the most serious issue in kidnapping appears to be the use of violence against another human being. The kidnapper attacks God through an attack on a human being made in God's image. He radically disrupts the victim's God-ordained calling or assignment in life. Hence, kidnapping is an exceedingly serious sin against God and against the person kidnapped.[17] The kidnapper's violence is a general violence, not confined to one narrow goal. To be sure, kidnappers usually hope to use their violence only for a limited time. But they have no fixed limit either in time or in purpose. Delivery of a ransom does not guarantee release. Unlike the case of armed robbery, nothing the victim might do can realistically give release. The kidnapper is in effect setting up a mini-state of which he is head and under which the victim dwells. This implication of kidnapping becomes crystal clear when we see modern cases of kidnapping, hostage taking, and airplane hijacking. Despite repeated appeals by legitimate authorities, kidnappers refuse to obey but rather set up a reign of terror within their little circle. Kidnappers attempt to destroy the state within their circle. The just penalty is the destruction of the kidnapper in death, executed by representatives of the state.

Next, let us consider violations of parental authority. Parents may themselves be guilty of abusing their authority, as in modern cases of child-beating and neglect. Surely this area is a most difficult one, because the normal prerogatives of parents' authority and state authority come into tension. None of us can produce very satisfactory answers. In such cases I believe that some discretion must be given to judges, just as discretion is given to parents themselves in dealing with difficult cases with their children. The judges are being forced to take into their own hands some judgments normally left in the hands of parents.

It is quite reasonable to argue that blatant abuse of the rod constitutes repudiation of genuine parental responsibility. Parents who repudiate responsibility thereby forfeit legitimate claim to responsibility. That is, their claim to parental authority is forfeited. Their abuse shows them to be no better than children or fools unfit for authority, and consequently the state may act to assign authority to a kinsman. Obviously, wise state officers would want in any case to consult with relatives of the family in dealing with such a difficult matter. The nuclear family is not all there is to family, since grandparents have a definite role (1 Timothy 5:4). State action to transfer guardianship to a near relative is not an arbitrary reassignment of authority but moves along God-ordained lines. Since the most immediate authority belonging to parents has effectively disappeared, the more tenuous authority that remains in the more extended family must function as a substitute.[18] Such a practice would appear to be analogous to the case in Exodus 21:26–27, where a servant is removed from the authority of a master because of physical abuse.[19]

Now let us consider children's rebellion against parental authority. Mosaic law specifies the death penalty for children who curse parents, strike parents, or are incorrigible (Exodus 21:15, 17; Deuteronomy 21:18–21). The statutes speak directly of the male child, but are clearly generalizable to daughters. The statute about incorrigibility speaks of "purging the evil," which might imply some reference to the special holiness of Israel (Deuteronomy 21:21). Moreover, the family line is the means through which the knowledge of God is passed on (Deuteronomy 6:6–9), the Promised Land is inherited, and the descent to the Messiah as the offspring of Abraham is traced. We must therefore be cautious about whether the severity of the penalty has been affected by the special holiness of Israel.

First, consider incorrigibility. A careful reading of the relevant statute, Deuteronomy 21:18–21, shows that we are not dealing with a temporary pique on the part of parents whose anger has broken out of bounds. The son has entrenched himself in a permanent pattern of rebellion that the parents are powerless to alter (21:18b). The matter is brought before the elders. As in all judicial cases they would be bound to check the veracity of the claim.[20] Moreover, in a typical case, parents out of sentimentality are the last people in the community to admit the truth to themselves about the hopelessness of their son. Here we have reassuring protection against arbitrariness.

Once we take these facts into account, we can see that the conduct of an incorrigible son constitutes general rebellion against parental authority. The just penalty is death. As he has attempted to destroy legitimate authority, so he is himself destroyed by legitimate authority.

For similar reasons, general rebellion against state authority, in the form of incorrigible repeated refusal to obey positive commands of the state, merits death. Blatant refusal to carry out a penalty assigned by the state also merits death (in analogy with Deuteronomy 17:12), because the penalty structure is the state's last appeal in its own use of authority. To refuse this appeal is to move outside the bounds of all authority.

Cursing father and mother is a more difficult case. Like the issue of blasphemy and cursing God, this sin may have a penalty intensified by the special holiness of Israel and the holiness thereby pertaining to the Israelite family. First of all, we must realize that within Israelite society cursing was closer to black magic than a modern utterance of "go to hell" would be. The utterer intended damage to the other person. Hence, it would be tantamount to blasphemy. Like all blasphemy within Israel, it warranted the death penalty.

But what happens in a nonholy society where blasphemy has a different status? We must then deal with this crime as an injury to the parents, not as an injury to the holiness of Israel. Depending on the nature and seriousness of the curse, it might be a comparatively light matter or it might be tantamount to the general repudiation of parental authority. The parents would be the injured party. They would also be the first to judge the seriousness of this attack on their authority. If it was a limited attack, they would administer a spanking or beating. If it was a wholesale attack, they would proceed to take the child to civil authorities and the death penalty would still be appropriate.

Striking father or mother would appear to me to present us with the same complexities as does cursing father or mother. The same penalties would be involved.

The death penalty for wholesale violation of parental authority may seem harsh to modern sentiments. But I would argue that it is not only just but realistic. Parental authority, even if very imperfectly exercised, takes place in the context of personal relationships and natural pressures in the direction of love. Parents have many advantages over the state. If a person does not receive instruction from parents, the chances of receiving instruction from the state's more impersonal discipline are nil. The person who rebels in wholesale fashion against parents will also rebel against the state and create general destruction and disorder until eliminated. It is mere sentimentality to refuse to come to grips with this reality.

The state and parents together have been given a monopoly on bodily punishments.[21] Any person who takes punishment into his own hands usurps this special authority and insults legitimate authority. On these grounds, it seems proper for the state to administer punishment in the case of crimes of bodily injury and murder. Murder in Israel was avenged by the nearest of kin, as we have seen. But this requirement was far more practical in a society in which close relatives regularly lived close together. Moreover, the practice of relatives living together and of relatives avenging death was tied in with the fact that relatives inherited neighboring plots of land through the Israelite system of inheritance of the Promised Land. Murder threatened the blood lines and the inheritance system, and constituted a threat to the holiness of Israel not equivalent to its damage nowadays.

Speed laws and many other rules seem wise in a modern society for the sake of protection and general order. Violation of these nonmoral rules does not, it seems to me, constitute blatant repudiation of state authority or usurpation of state authority. The analogy with parental authority is illuminating. Parents may impose nonmoral household rules for the sake of the proper functioning and well-being of the household. In like manner the state has a discretionary authority based on what seems best according to common wisdom. In the case of parents, punishments for older children may take the form of temporary loss of privileges or deductions against an allowance. Such punishments are appropriate partly because some violations may take place through mere negligence rather than through evil intention. In addition, the parents wish to train older children to calculate more distant consequences of their acts and to live in the light of more distant consequences. Monetary penalties involve distant consequences through the loss of purchasing power. Similar reasoning appears to be valid in the case of state punishments. Because money is the regular means for quantifying gain and loss, monetary penalties are usually the most suitable form for the state to use in imposing penalties on mature offenders.

By contrast, fools and younger children need corporal punishment because they do not calculate more distant consequences (Proverbs 10:13; 13:24; 22:15; 23:13–14; 26:3; 29:15). Pain as an immediate consequence represents virtually the only effective way of giving them a reasonable picture of consequences. But it must be understood that such punishment should avoid serious physical harm and be no more painful than is appropriate for its purpose. On the one hand, we must not use a mere pat on the bottom or the back. Pain should be forceful enough and unpleasant enough to get the offender's genuine attention and make him consider whether his misdeed was worth the cost. On the other hand, we should avoid punishment that debilitates or runs some danger of permanent harm. Deuteronomy 25:1–3 wisely sets a limit of forty lashes, lest "your brother . . . be degraded in your eyes." If excess of shame constitutes a reason for limiting the punishment, surely the possibility of physical harm does also. Since the limit in Deuteronomy

25:1–3 concerns cases involving adult men, parental punishment of children must naturally stop much more quickly. Colossians 3:21 and Ephesians 6:4 also warn us against excessive punishment.

Penalties for Crimes Against Servants

A considerable number of Mosaic statutes introduce special provisions for crimes committed against servants. Servants do have firm legal protection, but the character of the reparations to servants is degraded. This whole area is a very complex one, because servitude in Israel was associated with Egyptian bondage, which in turn signified spiritual bondage and death (cf. Leviticus 25:42–43). The normal principles of balanced recompense no longer work in quite the same way because the servant's status is subordinate, not merely from a political point of view, but from the point of view of the symbolic significance of the nation of Israel as a whole and the symbolic significance of its holiness code. Thus, only by understanding the significance of these statutes in their own redemptive context would it be possible to infer general principles from them. Such an investigation is outside the scope of this work, but a suggestive beginning has been made by James B. Jordan and Gary North.[22]

THIRTEEN

JUST PENALTIES
FOR SEXUAL CRIMES

N ow we must consider sexual crimes, that is, those that are related
  most directly to the seventh commandment among the Ten
Commandments.

Principles Involved
In Understanding Mosaic Sexual Law

God has designed the sexual bond to symbolize and express the deepest
communion and complementarity between a man and a woman in marriage. On the most basic level, sexual crimes all involve violations of this
purpose. Human sexuality is also important because it is the means for
procreation, by which the earth is to be filled with people made in God's
image (Genesis 1:26–28; 5:1–3). In one respect all reproductive capaci-
ties of living things are finite, created analogues of God's life-giving
power, by which He produces a world revealing His character and
human beings who image Him in a special way. Human reproduction is
exalted above animal and plant reproduction by the fact that it flows
from personal communion between man and woman and by the fact that
it results in new image-bearers of God.

Since the Fall human sexuality is corrupted by sin. Those descended from Adam have sinful natures (see Romans 5:12–21). Marriage and reproduction are corrupted by accusation (Genesis 3:12), strife (Genesis 3:16), and misuse of sexual intercourse. The bond between God and His people, which is like a marriage bond, is also corrupted by spiritual adultery on the part of Israel.

Christ as Redeemer brought the definitive remedy for sexual sins as well as other sins. His own life on earth showed sexual purity coupled with the fullest love for both men and women. In contrast to Israel's spiritual adultery, Christ in His humanity was perfectly faithful to God the Father. In the crucifixion Christ was forsaken by the Father (Matthew 27:46), bearing the pain of a severed relation like that of a severed marriage bond. The new life of Christ's resurrection contains the power to purify the church and to present her to Himself as a spotless bride (Ephesians 5:25–27). Christ also presents a model for human husbands and wives to imitate (Ephesians 5:21–33) and through the Holy Spirit provides the transforming power to conform Christian husbands and wives to His image, so that they display in their own marriages a reflection of His love (Ephesians 5:17–21; Colossians 3:15–19). The love now displayed in the church and in Christian marriages will be perfected at the second coming of Christ (1 Corinthians 13:8–13).

The calling of Christians is a high one. If they are single, their bodies and their sexuality as well as all other aspects of their lives are to be wholly devoted to the Lord (1 Corinthians 7:25–35). In particular, fornication is forbidden (1 Corinthians 6:12–20). If Christians are married, they are to embody in their marriage the purity, the commitment, and the perfect love of Christ for His church. Mosaic regulations concerning divorce do not lower the standard for sexual purity, but involve a concession to human sinfulness (Matthew 19:3–9).

The Bible's standard for sexual behavior is clear. But what should the church do in cases where it is violated? Offenders must be counseled to repent and to pursue righteousness afresh. If offenders persist in not repenting, they must be excommunicated (1 Corinthians 5:5). If they do repent, they are forgiven through the power of Christ's sacrifice. The church as a corporate holy community is also continually purified through Christ.

Repentant offenders must then be helped in practical ways to renew their love and their purity. But renewal is seldom easy. People's tangled lives present us with many hard issues concerning cases of adultery, divorce, and remarriage. Theologians disagree concerning the answers.[1] At least two routes are possible:

1. We could take as our main guide the permission to divorce laid out in Deuteronomy 24:1–4. The church, like Old Testament Israel, is God's holy community. Perhaps, like Israel, it should officially permit divorce and remarriage in a wide range of cases even though it does not morally approve.

2. We could take Matthew 19:3–9 as the main statement, and understand it as overriding or altering the provision of Deuteronomy. The church is a more exalted holy community than was Israel. We are united to the risen Christ. In view of this union, a return to the original standard of perfection is required, and the church can no longer permit divorce and remarriage except possibly in cases of adultery and fornication.

In fact, in all probability neither of these solutions represents a complete answer. Deuteronomy 24:1–4 must be used cautiously, for three reasons: Jesus' teaching seriously qualifies it; possibly it is more relevant to the duties of the state than the church; and the new holiness and redemptive power associated with the New Testament church may influence the church's internal practices. On the other hand, Matthew 19:3–9 must also be used with caution. Jesus is not primarily laying down a basis for the operation of church courts, but articulating the perfect standard for marriage based on creation. He does not focus on the question of what to do when others have already violated the standard, but on what the standard in fact is. What is the goal toward which God renews us through the power of His kingdom? It is not easy to deduce the church's corporate duty concerning offenses, because the passages in question are not directly focused on this question. I must therefore refer readers to the extended discussions of divorce and remarriage elsewhere.[2]

As usual, the justice of Christ is embodied fully in His crucifixion, His resurrection, and His reign in heaven. His justice and purity ought also to be reflected progressively in the purity of the church (Ephesians 5:25–26). We know also that Christ's justice is partially and temporarily represented in the state's responsibility to execute earthly justice in the case of sexual crimes. To this earthly responsibility we now turn.

We confront unusual complexities when we consider the laws of Moses regarding sexual crimes. To begin with, for some types of sexual crimes Mosaic law treats men and women differently, because their situations and responsibilities in Israelite society differed. For example, if two engaged or married people have sexual intercourse, the man is guilty. The woman is not unless it can be shown that she willingly consented (Deuteronomy 22:22–27). The Bible is realistic about the fact that men are almost always the offenders in violent sexual crimes, and that they can frequently succeed in overpowering women. Second, in the case of unmarried girls, the girl's father is integrally involved in some of the processes (Exodus 22:17; Deuteronomy 22:15–17, 21, 29), because in Israelite culture fathers had responsibilities for their daughters' marriages not fully equivalent to their responsibilities for their sons. To consider matters thoroughly we would have to engage in an extended discussion of the theology of man and woman, but we cannot do so here. Suffice it to say that, in general, just laws take into account the actual social setting, not a hypothetical setting.

In ancient Israel, engagement was similar to marriage from the standpoint of penalties (Deuteronomy 22:22–30; Leviticus 20:10). In late twentieth-century American society, engagement may not have the same meaning, since engagements can be made and broken rather freely. Again, such differences must surely be taken into account, because social setting may affect the significance of some sexual acts. Marriage itself is a socially recognized institution. The exact sequence of social and ceremonial events leading to marriage as a socially recognized and sanctioned bond may differ from society to society. This social and not merely private side to sexual acts is foreign to the consciousness of much of modern Western society, but it is exceedingly important not only for understanding the significance of Mosaic law but for adapting its principles to our situation.

I am convinced that this area of sexual crimes is more difficult than most of the other areas in Mosaic penal law. Because of the relation of sexuality to larger society, and because social structures are subject to change in a way that human nature as such is not, more complex adaptations may be necessary to apply the principles to our situation. In addition, our knowledge of ancient Israelite society is quite imperfect. With our partial information we may incorrectly assess the significance of a particular injunction through misunderstanding its impact on society.

I intend to do the best I can with the available information and to show how general principles of justice and recompense apply in the case of sexual crimes. But more tentativeness is necessary in this area.

Penalties for Fornication

Let us first consider cases concerning the sexual intercourse of two unmarried, unengaged people. Deuteronomy 22:28–29 and Exodus 22:16–17 indicate that the man is forced to marry the woman without possibility of divorce. If the father of the woman refuses to give her in marriage, the offender must nevertheless pay a marriage present. We cannot be absolutely certain, but Exodus 22:16 appears to have in view a case where the woman consents, whereas Deuteronomy 22:28–29 has in view a case where the woman is forced into sexual intercourse. The penalty may possibly have been the same in both cases, but it is much more likely that the amount of fifty shekels in the case of forced intercourse includes an extra penalty.[3] Fifty shekels is a large amount for the times, not only in comparison with the wage of a laborer, but also in comparison to the redemption price for a woman, specified at ten shekels for a woman under twenty years old and thirty shekels otherwise (Leviticus 27:4–5). Usually women married before becoming twenty, so that lower figure of ten shekels gives some comparison.

How do these penalties manifest the principles of just recompense? We find out best by asking who is injured and who is paid back. The man and woman are not dealt with equally, partly because the woman may have been forced into intercourse, but also because the father's protection and authority over the woman has been violated, and the woman's position in Israelite society is far more compromised than the man's. Loss of virginity puts the woman socially under reproach, makes her a poor prospect for marriage, and opens the possibility of her becoming an unprotected spinster. In addition we must reckon with the issue of psychological and emotional pain to the woman. Some of the secondary effects of the man's crime are impossible to calculate.

In all the cases of penology that we have already discussed, it appears to me that the basic principles of reciprocal recompense leave out of account secondary effects and emotional trauma, however serious these effects may be. For example, who can estimate the emotional trauma involved if a thief steals an heirloom whose value is mostly emotional? Precisely because no one but God can properly assess all these secondary effects, we must leave it to God to do so. The human powers of civil justice cannot extend this far, and so they must stop short with a kind of inevitable imperfection. Surely such must be the case with sexual crimes as well. Our longings for perfect justice and peace will not be satisfied until the Second Coming. Judicial restraint that refuses to right all wrongs but sticks to what it can do with reasonable consistency not only abides by the limits that God has given to human judicial authority but also speaks of the hope of something better.

Violation of sexual purity is a serious sin against God. But civil penalties do not rectify sins on this level. The penalty imposed on the man suggests that civil justice focuses on the more public, societal implications of the man's act. The man has forced the woman and her father into a situation of accomplished sexual union. Sexual union should to the surrounding society signify marriage. But the man has forcibly appropriated the sign of marriage rather than received it by consent and by giving a marriage present. He has stolen away a privilege with respect to the father's child. He must still pay the normal marriage present. So far we have singlefold recompense or restoration. The restoration does not, of course, bring the situation back to exactly what it was beforehand. Such an exact restoration would be impossible. Rather, the restoration has the effect of making the situation like a normal one in which the father gives his daughter in marriage.

But now there must be punishment in addition to restoration. Since the man has forced the father into the position of giving his daughter, the father in turn forces him not only to assume all the obligations of marriage but to continue in them. He cannot divorce her. Thus the forcing of the father's hand is reciprocated by the forcing of the offender's hand. In addition, the marriage payment in Deuteronomy 22:29, in the case of forced intercourse, probably involves something like double the usual amount, so that like the thief the man has paid a monetary penalty for his evil use of violence against the woman.

The father has an additional option, namely, to withhold his daughter. In this case the offender pays for the marriage without enjoying it, and thereby receives his penalty. Both restoration and punishment are involved. Restoration takes the form of returning the woman to her father's household. Then the offender must pay the marriage present as punishment for forcible appropriation of what was not his. Once again the monetary penalty would presumably be doubled in case the offender forced himself on the woman.

All the action is seen primarily from the standpoint of the father rather than the daughter. From the standpoint of modern American customs, such a viewpoint appears to be not only queer but demeaning to the daughter. But this appearance is illusory. We must take account of two cultural factors. (1) In ancient Israel daughters were customarily given in marriage at a young age.[4] They would not have had the maturity to make an independent decision. (2) Marriages in Israel were primarily viewed—as they still are in many non-Western societies—as familial, social, and economic institutions. Moreover, decision-making by whole families, even extended families, was a more common practice than we as individualistic Westerners are accustomed to. Consequently, marriages arranged by parents seemed natural. Nevertheless, as Roland de Vaux says, "parental authority was not such as to leave no room for the feelings of the young couple. There were love marriages in Israel."[5]

Since intercourse between unengaged, unmarried people still produces fundamentally the same social damage as it did in Israel, it would appear that the same principles of penology should apply now. In fact, since in this situation the Mosaic penalties appear to derive wholly from general principles concerning justice, there is no reason why we should not consider having basically the same penalties today. We can in this case carry over the provisions of the Old Testament in considerable detail. Certain adjustments need to be made because of the altered social relations between fathers and daughters. The parents of the woman, in consultation with the woman, play the primary role if she is under age, while the woman herself, in consultation with her parents and/or elders of her church, plays the primary role if she is of age.

The remaining difficulty is that American society and many other modern societies have no custom of marriage presents given by the bridegroom and his family to the bride's family. How did the marriage present function in Israelite society? Some have suggested that it was purchase of the bride, but de Vaux argues persuasively that it was more like "a reward for . . . accepting the proposal of marriage."[6] De Vaux also suggests that "it is probable that the father enjoyed only the usufruct of the mohar [marriage present], and that the latter reverted to the daughter at the time of succession, or if her husband's death reduced her to penury."[7] Thus the marriage present was treated as part of the daughter's property rather than the father's. Genesis 31:14–16 tends to confirm this idea when it indicates that Leah and Rachel complained that Laban "has used up what was paid for us" (31:15). Their complaint makes most sense if the marriage present was customarily in the father's control but was nevertheless understood to be for the daughter's benefit.

Among other things, the marriage present would have been an incentive for husbands not to divorce their wives and some financial protection for those who were divorced. The closest modern equivalent is alimony. General principles of justice do suggest the legitimacy of some form of alimony or a substitute for it. In marriage vows husbands commit themselves to care for their wives, and civil authorities may legitimately compel them to carry through this commitment.

In Israelite society the marriage present probably varied in amount depending on the social standing of the bride and groom.[8] For example, marriage to the king's daughter was a special privilege that could rightly command a special present (1 Samuel 18:23–25).[9] Such a practice makes sense because the economic standing of the two families would measure the relative economic well-being to which the woman would be accustomed, and hence would also influence the amount of support justly due in case of divorce. Similar factors would influence the amount of payment today (in fact, they already do in the case of alimony).

We do not have enough data concerning Israelite society to draw confident conclusions. But if we are right about the economic functions of the marriage present, the equivalent penalty today should provide financial support for the woman for a time period that would be sufficient to enable her to obtain some vocational training or make a vocational adjustment. The equivalent of six months' or a year's income of the average full-time working person does not seem unreasonable. Jacob worked seven years for Rachel (Genesis 29:18), but his time of service was probably much longer than the usual equivalent of a marriage present.

In conclusion, in the case of fornication that we are contemplating, the woman's family should have two options. The man may be compelled to marry the woman, without the possibility of initiating divorce proceedings. In addition, he pays the woman's family a cash sum or deduction from his wages (cf. Genesis 29:15–30; Joshua 15:16). The payment becomes a trust representing a permanent source of money for the woman's benefit. The payment is to be doubled in case of forced intercourse. The exact amount of the payment would have to be fixed with reference to prices in modern society. If the woman and her family decide against the marriage, the man must still pay the same amount as a penalty (Exodus 22:16–17).

Some major difficulties remain because of the differences between Israelite society and some recent aspects of Western society. In Israelite society young unmarried women were either virgins or prostitutes. Great social stigma attached to the loss of virginity, and so families protected their daughters until the time of engagement and marriage, which was usually at a comparatively young age. Judges naturally had an obligation to redress sexual violation of virgin daughters. But they had no obligation with respect to prostitutes and no obligation to protect the sexual purity of unmarried, unengaged young men. Such a system made sense within Israel because only the virgin daughters presented the judges with a case of immediate, demonstrable social loss.

But recent trends in the West have moved some elements of Western societies decidedly away from the Israelite situation. In some quarters promiscuity among single people not only flourishes but has a large measure of social acceptance. Hence, one could argue that loss of virginity does not represent a socially quantifiable form of damage, and if so, no penalty is appropriate. Moreover, one could argue on the basis of the more egalitarian roles of men and women in recent years that equal penalties should attach to both men and women in cases of fornication.

Arguments like these must be carefully weighed, but in this case I do not agree with their conclusions. If any Christians live within a modern society or subculture, they will on their own part wish for their own families and their own children to remain faithful to God's standards for sexuality. The state has a responsibility to act justly in defense of Christian families and any other families who hold to a Biblical standard of sexual morality. I believe this responsibility remains even if Christians and other advocates of nonpromiscuity are only a tiny fraction of the total population.

The state can still justly discriminate between the modern analogues of virgins and prostitutes in Israel. If a young woman is demonstrably promiscuous, neither she nor her family can claim special rights in a case of fornication. Her status is similar to that of the prostitute in Israel. She has suffered no demonstrable loss and so can claim no right to a penalty. But as in Israel, within a legal context a young woman is presumed to be chaste until proven otherwise.

What about the argument concerning the more egalitarian roles of men and women in recent times? Despite the social changes in recent times some things remain the same. Because of the creational differences between men and women, the two sexes are not at all interchangeable *in the area of human sexual intercourse*. Their respective contributions to sins of fornication are not equal but complementary. Moreover, the analogy between the sexual act in the context of fornication and the full significance of sexuality in the context of marriage points in the direction of understanding sexual responsibilities in a complementary rather than mechanically egalitarian way (see Ephesians 5:22–33). In particular, I believe that young men can never transfer their responsibilities to young women and complain that they deserve damages on account of loss of virginity. It is their own fault! On the other hand, young women have a right to the protection of their fathers and protection against unscrupulous men. These protections should not lightly be given up on the basis of abstract egalitarian overgeneralizations.

One final difficulty remains. We must consider whether modern cases involving rape of unmarried women are fundamentally different in character from the cases contemplated by Deuteronomy 22:28–29. It is possible that Deuteronomy 22:28–29 is not contemplating forced sexual intercourse between two strangers, but only the case of forced inter-course by a prospective suitor. In the common village setting of Israelite life, the young men and young women would know one another's names, unlike the anonymity of modern cities. Consequently, the typi-cal offender might be a seducer who, failing to persuade his partner, forced himself on her. Moreover, the key verb used in Deuteronomy 22:28 is different from the one in 22:25, suggesting to some interpreters that 22:28–29 is contemplating a case where the woman offers only token resistance.[10] The man catches her but does not really "force" her.

By contrast, it might be argued that modern urban rape cases are tantamount to adulterous rape. The modern rapist typically intends to violate a woman without knowing or caring whether the woman is mar-ried or not. Hence, it is arguable that the *intent* to commit adulterous rape ought receive the same penalty as adulterous rape.

The above argument has some merit, but I am not convinced that Deuteronomy 22:28–29 has such a restricted sense. To begin with, there is no significant difference in meaning between the verbs used in verses 25 and 28.[11] The operative contrast between verses 25–27 and 28–29 is not between resistance and nonresistance, but between a woman who is engaged and a woman who is not.[12]

Next, the story of Genesis 34:1–7 shows that cases of forced forni-cation involving virtual strangers would realistically have to be consid-ered within Israelite society. In the absence of any clear-cut, overt re-striction within the language of Deuteronomy 22:28–29, it seems altogether likely that judges would have understood verses 28–29 as ap-plying to cases with strangers as well as cases of genuine suitors. If so, the arguments become more complex. For instance, we must ask whether a stranger would know a woman's marital status merely from her style of dress. In many premodern societies, perhaps the great ma-jority of such societies, some distinctions in appearance distinguish mar-ried and unmarried women. The same was probably true for ancient Palestine, though we do not know for certain. The stories about Sarah in Genesis 12:10–20 and 20:1–7 indicate that confusion was possible. But perhaps Sarah dressed in a manner that confused or compromised normal dress codes, in order to comply with Abraham's duplicity. Even if dress codes did distinguish eligible women from others, cases of rape done at night would have potentially presented Israelite judges with difficulties similar to our modern urban cases. Biblical law as a whole does not seem to provide the kind of hints that would be necessary to restrict the scope of Deuteronomy 22:28–29.

In addition, when we turn to our modern cases of urban rape, the situation is not completely clear-cut. Modern American society, for example, still customarily distinguishes married women, engaged women, and eligible single women by means of the engagement ring and wedding ring. In most cases it would be difficult to demonstrate legally that a rapist had no knowledge of the woman's marital status, and without provable absence of knowledge a more severe penalty would not be justified.

In summary, the situations presented to us by modern urban rapes are not entirely analogous to the situations in Israelite society, and we must be cautious about the extent to which the same general principles would apply to all cases. But in the absence of clearer evidence to the contrary, I tentatively advocate treating all cases of forced intercourse with a sexually eligible woman (unmarried and unengaged) on the same legal basis.

Of course, from the standpoint of the woman's family the difference between anonymous rape and an exploitive suitor would be monumental. If the offender were a suitor, the father and the daughter might decide that marriage was the wisest option. If the offender were an unknown rapist, they would naturally decline marriage and settle for the monetary payment. The legal statute nevertheless does not discuss the difference directly—not because it was not important to the family, but because it was not relevant to the governing authorities. By placing the decision wholly in the hands of the family, the statutes leave the family with fullest control over all the questions relating to their future.

Penalties for Adultery

Next let us consider the crime of adultery. Who is injured and what penalty is executed by whom? In the Israelite setting, it seems that the larger society is injured, because the death penalty is executed not by the husband of the adulteress or the wife of the adulterer, but by "you," a general pointer to the society and its representatives (Deuteronomy

22:22–27). Moreover, in the case of an adulteress, if the husband alone were the offended person, we might expect that the husband would have the right to forgive his wife and release her from the penalty if he wished. But apparently no such option is contemplated within Israel. Of course if a husband caught his wife in the act of adultery, he could remain silent and no case would come to court.[13] But if other witnesses saw the adultery, they could bring the case before the courts on their own initiative. There is no explicit evidence for the possibility of the husband's forgiveness.

In addition, in a related case concerning promiscuity by an unmarried woman, the penalty is executed by the "men of her city" (Deuteronomy 22:21), which may again indicate some injury to the larger society. One possibility is that the structure of society itself is being attacked through an attack on the integrity of its most basic institution, the family. Or does the primary violation consist in attacking public vows that the community as a whole supports? The idea that marriage vows are primarily in view is not convincing, because the explicit language of Deuteronomy 22:24 mentions the guilt of "violating his neighbor's wife." If the emphasis had been on the vows, we would have expected reference to "violating the marriage vows" or some such language. Moreover, no explicit vows are involved in the case of promiscuity discussed in Deuteronomy 22:21.

How does adultery attack the family? In one sense, the intention of the adulterer or adulteress is to disrupt everything as little as possible socially, economically, and politically; they do not want to be caught. An attempt to destroy the state as a whole by rebellion or war might properly be met by destruction of the persons involved. But adultery involves a more subtle attack at a different level. We cannot be absolutely sure how the logic of justice operates. It may be that adultery represents simply a general attack on the structure of society, and thus destruction of the people involved is the appropriate penalty in any society.

But there is another possibility, namely, that the nature of the penalty for adultery is related to the special character of Israel. The family in Israel is the institution through which the commandments of God are passed on (Deuteronomy 6:6–9), through which inheritance of the promised holy land is passed on, and through which genealogical descent reaches out to the Messianic offspring who will bring final redemption. Thus the family in Israel has a special significance beyond what it might have in other circumstances. Adultery constitutes disruption of the orderliness and purity of the line of inheritance.

Moreover, sexual acts in general must not be considered as merely a private affair. They are intimately connected with the concerns of the larger society. Disorderly sexual acts introduce a fundamental disorder into society as a whole. Such disorder is particularly dangerous within Israel, since Israel as the holy nation must reflect the orderliness appropriate to God's character and God's dwelling place. In addition, human marriage is symbolic of the relation between God and His people (Hosea; Ezekiel 16). The symbolic dimensions of marriage may also have affected the penalties attached to these crimes.

Within the laws concerning holiness, we have observed a pervasive concern for the contrasts between life and death. This contrast may also provide a rationale for the penalties. Illicit sexual acts are an assault on the womb, which is the source of new human life. If the assault takes place on a woman who is unmarried and unengaged, it is remediable. But if not, the original assault on human life is punished by a parallel assault on the life of the offender. The larger society, and not just the victim, is involved in retribution because the holiness of Israel is compromised by this profanation of life within its midst.

Such observations provide an explanation for a number of otherwise puzzling facts. First, Mosaic law deals in a surprisingly different manner with a pair of analogous cases involving sexual intercourse, namely, (1) intercourse between an unmarried man and a married woman, and (2) intercourse between a married man and an unmarried woman. In the first case both man and woman are subject to the death penalty (Deuteronomy 22:22). For the second case, the Mosaic law does not provide any separate discussion. In the abstract it might be argued that we are invited to generalize from the first case, the reciprocal case of a married man and an unmarried woman. But such a conclusion is certainly mistaken. To begin with, the statutes in Exodus 22:16–17 and Deuteronomy 22:28–29 concerning seduction of virgins do not indicate the man's marital status. Technically speaking, these statutes cover a total of three cases, the cases of an unmarried man and a virgin, a married man and a virgin, and an engaged man and a virgin. Within a polygamous society, it is perfectly natural to understand the passages as actually applying to all three. If the male offender were engaged or married, he could be forced to take the girl as a second wife. The girl's father would thus have the same options as in the case of fornication: a marriage present and/or forced marriage without the possibility of divorce.

Moreover, Israelite popular sentiment viewed sexual indiscretion by a man much more leniently than sexual indiscretion by a woman. Popular sentiment would not on its own initiative have seen a direct parallel between male and female offenses. It seems clear that the statutes in Exodus 22:16–17 and Deuteronomy 22:28–29, involving obligatory marriage, were intended to apply to the case of a married man and a virgin, while no civil penalty was specified in the case of a married man and a prostitute.

If the concern of the law is partially with protecting the holy order of Israelite society and the integrity of inheritance, polygamous practice in Israel becomes intelligible. Polygamous practice may, of course, partly be a concession to human sinfulness, as was the case with divorce (Matthew 19:8). It also functioned to protect women's economic status, particularly in times when war decimated the male population. But in addition, at least sometimes polygamy functioned to protect the lines of inheritance and women's fuller participation in social religion. In the system of levirate marriage described in Deuteronomy 25:5–10, a man was supposed to marry his deceased brother's wife. When the living brother was already married, the practice necessarily involved polygamy. This levirate practice was instituted specifically to assure the preservation of inheritance (Deuteronomy 25:6; Ruth 4:5–6). Even apart from the levirate, the practice of polygamy assured that almost all women could enjoy marriage, not only for its economic and legal protection, but for the benefit of participating in the inheritance of the Promised Land. Women participated through their husbands and through sons who inherited from the husbands. The great reproach involved in childlessness thus becomes more intelligible (1 Samuel 1:1–16; 2:5).

Next, consider the case of intercourse between a married man and a prostitute. The Old Testament clearly indicates that prostitution is sinful (Proverbs 6:26; cf. Hosea 4:14). Yet no *civil* penalty is attached to the act. Why not? The child produced from union with a prostitute would be illegitimate and would not confuse inheritance through the male line. Moreover, sexual looseness on the part of a man does not fundamentally disrupt the order of Israelite society in the same way as does adultery with a married woman. The order of Israelite society guarantees that each woman will be under the authority and protection of one man, whether the man is her husband, or her father if she is a virgin, or perhaps a brother, uncle, or other relative if her husband has died. Her social status is largely determined through the man who represents her. Illicit sexual intercourse with a woman disrupts her entire connection with society and must necessarily be remedied. Prostitutes are the sole exception, because they themselves already inhabit the borders of society. On the other hand, a married man's relations to the surrounding society are not fundamentally altered or redefined by intercourse with a prostitute.

In addition, intercourse with a prostitute, unlike intercourse with a married woman, does not constitute a direct assault on the womb as the source of life. The prostitute voluntarily gives herself, whereas the married or engaged woman is under her husband's authority and is not free to do what she wishes.

These factors might also account for the penalty being the same for married women and engaged women.[14] The engaged woman would subsequently become married, and the child born would legally participate in the inheritance. Moreover, her womb is pledged to her fiance. Thus illicit intercourse with an engaged woman would confuse the order of Israelite society and assault the womb just as seriously as did intercourse with a married woman.

It also becomes clear why the death penalty is instituted in the case of the promiscuous girl in Deuteronomy 22:20–21. The girl is not executed for adultery—she may have had intercourse only with unmarried men. Neither is the girl executed simply because she is a prostitute (no such penalty is discussed in the Bible), but because she acted promiscuously "in her father's house" (22:21). The penalty takes place at "the door of her father's house." She has confused the integrity of her father's line and introduced disorder into the father's claim of authority over her and her womb. In addition she threatens to confuse the integrity of the line into which she marries and to introduce disorder into its authority relations. By contrast, no penalty falls on foreign women who may come into Palestine and function as known prostitutes. The statute in Deuteronomy 22:20–21 certainly would not apply to them, since Deuteronomy 22:13–17 clearly pictures a situation where the woman becomes married (not at all typical of women known to be prostitutes) and where the husband expects her to be a virgin.

Adultery, then, corrupts the order of authority in Israelite society, corrupts the line of inheritance, and attacks the womb as the source of life. Let us reason in the abstract about what a fit recompense should be within Israel. Just recompense implies first a restoration to the original situation. The line is to be righted. Children born from the union should be regarded as illegitimate. The legitimate authority of the husband or father is reasserted. Second, a penalty of equal weight is inflicted on the offender for evil intent. His and/or her own authority relations, line of posterity, and life is to be destroyed. Death appears to be the necessary penalty.

In our day, the order of society and genealogical descent no longer function to ensure possession of the Promised Land and to look forward to the promised Messiah. Union with Christ makes us inherit the fulfillment of the Promised Land (1 Corinthians 3:22). Faith and repentance result in the transfer of the pollution of our spiritual inheritance to the finished work of Christ. The death penalty is fulfilled in Him. The life/death contrasts in the holiness law no longer function as a symbolic testimony to Israel's special holiness among the nations. Rather, holiness is found in union with Christ and His resurrection to new life. But adultery is still a sin against God. Adultery still damages society, inheritance, and the womb on an ordinary plane. It deeply disrupts the proper meaning of sexual union for the society as a whole. It is not easy to establish the full nature and extent of such disruption. It is therefore not easy to see what the most appropriate penalty might be. At least three main alternatives can be envisioned:

1. Conceivably, the death penalty might still be appropriate because of the depth of destructive forces inherent in the act of adultery.

2. Conceivably, the appropriate penalty might be disruption of the offender's own sexuality, in the form of castration, inflicted by representatives of the society as a whole. In addition, a monetary penalty like the marriage present is the appropriate token of attempting to restore the offended party's violated sexuality.

3. Conceivably, a lesser penalty, perhaps only a monetary payment, might be all that was appropriate for social restitution, even though adultery is an exceedingly serious violation in the sight of God.

Is a monetary payment reasonable? In the case of two married persons, typically money would change hands between the two marriages involved, and the net result would be no change. Such a solution would seem to involve only a token penalty. What about forbidding the guilty parties from initiating divorce? This penalty would correspond to the fact that they have broken the marriage relationship on one level and they are forbidden the possibility of breaking it on another. But the penalty by itself does not seem to be very realistic, since often the offended spouse wants the divorce, and if not, could be pressured into doing so by repeated acts of adultery. Should there be no penalty? But this option does not deal with the undeniable damage to the spouses of the adulterers.

At a minimum it would seem that the offended spouse should be able to receive a divorce and a payment in money and property. Let us call this view the divorce-and-property position. We could argue for such a conclusion in the following way. Adulterous spouses break the vows committing them to exclusive sexual loyalty and family support. In the act of adultery they renounce marriage and family. In return, the injured spouse may renounce them (divorce) and retain control of the family (children and all property). So far we have singlefold recompense. All these actions constitute simply a recognition of the logical consequences of the act of adultery and ratify the consequences of the act publicly. In my opinion there should also be a penalty for special evil intent. Adultery is worse than desertion or mere failure in positive responsibilities to support. The adulterer, unlike the deserter, tries by concealment to steal rights that he can no longer lawfully claim. Such a penalty should perhaps be paid by both parties involved in adultery, since both are responsible for the damage. More likely it should come wholly from the outside party, since the adulterous spouse has already paid financially. The penalty should at least amount to the value of the modern equivalent of the marriage present. If both offenders are married, two separate sets of penalties are involved. If there are two divorces, both offenders will become financially destitute and both will end up with a period of servitude to pay off their fine.

In considering this position I am assuming that the state may justly allow people to divorce under some conditions. Does this position contradict Jesus' teaching against divorce in Matthew 19:1–12? Actually, it is completely compatible with Jesus' teaching. To begin with, Deuteronomy 24:1–4 indicates that Mosaic law did not legally forbid divorce, but regulated it and guarded against flagrant abuses. Some Pharisees of Jesus' day were using Deuteronomy 24:1–4 to justify the moral legitimacy of divorce (Matthew 19:7). Jesus in reply indicates that according to God's design in creation, marriage is intended to be permanent (Matthew 19:4–8). Divorces take place because of hardness of heart (Matthew 19:8). Jesus thus does not disagree with Moses or alter the law but reasserts the moral principle of permanency. When the state permits divorce, it does not thereby morally condone divorce but simply legally regulates a situation created by human sin. Its legal permission is in no way equivalent to moral approval.[15]

This divorce-and-property position differs on a technical level from the Israelite case of intercourse between a married man and a prostitute, for which there was no civil penalty. Why did intercourse between a husband and a prostitute remain untouched in Israel? Such intercourse did not corrupt the lines of authority, inheritance, and protection of the womb, as we have already observed. Thus it did not threaten the special holiness of Israel and her special relation to inheritance of the Promised Land. We would therefore logically expect that such intercourse would receive only the "ordinary" penalty for adultery, not the "intensified" penalty due to the special holiness of Israelite inheritance. But instead of an ordinary penalty we find no penalty at all.

The discrepancy is accounted for once we realize that divorce initiated by a woman is not contemplated in the context of Israelite society.

If the offended woman does not divorce her husband, what happens to the above penalties? No real penalty falls on the husband because as family head he remains in control of property and children. We might expect a payment to be levied against the prostitute. But of course the nature of prostitution makes it clear that the guilt attaches mainly to the husband for initiating the intercourse. The payment to the prostitute for her "services" tacitly includes acknowledgment of her release from the responsibilities of any penalty. Thus all of the penalties are dissolved, and we end up with a situation in which no penalties are imposed, a situation exactly equivalent to the Israelite situation.[16]

Why do women not initiate divorce in Israel? Perhaps the law of Moses was simply adapting itself to the existing form of Israelite society without thereby endorsing that form as an ideal (compare the analogous reasoning in Matthew 19:7–8). More likely, this situation also arises because of the unique significance of family authority and inheritance within Israel. Inheritance is passed on through the male line, so that we do not normally find unmarried women in charge of Israelite property (Numbers 27 is an exception, but note the concern that arises in 36:1–4 because of it). Divorce entails a loss against which women need to be protected, not a gain that they would seek.

The case of intercourse between a married man and a prostitute represents an interesting challenge for all interpreters. Those who advocate a more severe penalty for adultery, such as the death penalty, have difficulty explaining how justice is compatible with the lack of penalty for this particular case.

Tentatively, I think that the divorce-and-property position is best. But it is also possible that, even apart from the special holiness of Israel, the attack on the womb as the source of life still merits the death penalty in all cases where the attack is irremediable. I am aware of the difficulties and uncertainties concerning the significance of adultery. Therefore I would stress that we should remain open to a number of alternatives in this case. Many steps of inference are involved in drawing our conclusions.

Nevertheless, it does seem to me probable that the issues of family authority, inheritance, and the symbolic dimensions of human life and death have influenced the penalty system of the Mosaic law. If so, the penalties given there are influenced by matters pertaining to the special holiness of Israel. The violations merit more severe penalties, even the death penalty, because they have profaned Israel in her status of being a holy extended family. If so, modern cases must be dealt with on a different basis. We must reason out what should be just penalties on the basis of principles of justice. Conceivably, adultery is grievous enough as a civil crime, even outside the context of the holiness of Israel, to merit the death penalty. But we must work our way through the issues of recompense rather than simply assuming a pure continuity.

In a general way, adultery does unleash damage on the institution of the family. The family is such a central institution that it is arguable that such general damage to society ought to be recompensed by damage to the persons involved, in the form of the death penalty. Nevertheless, I am not at present persuaded of this view, partly because of the reasoning above about sexual intercourse between married men and prostitutes.[17]

The above reasoning with regard to adultery has assumed that both parties consented to the act of adultery. We still must consider the case of adulterous rape, that is, rape of a married woman or rape by a married man.[18] The rapist has caused injury both to the woman and to her family. The violence he brought on the sexuality, family, womb, and inheritance of the injured party is to be punished by reciprocal violence against his own sexuality, potential or actual family, and potential descendants. Tentatively, I would suggest that castration seems to be the fit penalty. But it is possible to argue that the general damage done to the woman and the surrounding society is so severe as to merit the death penalty. Again, disagreements are possible, in view of the discontinuities between the Israelite situation and ours. The rapist must also be required to do an act of restoration for damage done. In analogy with the case of fornication, I suggest that he should pay a monetary amount equivalent to the marriage present to the offended family.

One serious objection remains. Why should the penalty for nonadulterous forced sexual intercourse, as in Deuteronomy 22:28–29, be more lenient than the penalty for adulterous rape? In the latter case the act of rape is irremediable. In the former case subsequent marriage of the sexual partners represents a partial remedy restoring the injured person's sexuality, the lines of authority, and the inheritance.

The case of intercourse involving one or two engaged persons (not engaged to one another) still remains open. A solution to the question depends partly on our assessment of the type and degree of similarity between Israelite engagement and modern forms of engagement. Our information about Israelite society is imperfect. But when we operate in terms of general principles of justice, it seems that we can produce a tentative solution. Intercourse becomes irremediable only if engagement is "serious" and socially binding. In many non-Western societies there is some form of premarital arrangement of this type. In American society, engagement is poorly defined and does not seem clearly to have this value.

For the purpose of protecting engaged women against rape and untrustworthy suitors, it may of course be wise either to work for a social redefinition of engagement or, as would be much simpler, to provide in addition to the present loose form of engagement a more formal, legally recognized form, involving the knowledge and consent of the families and from which one party could withdraw only under penalty. Such an engagement would have a socially binding quality warranting the additional penalty in case of violation. In the situations created by the anonymity of modern cities, it would obviously also be wise to have a fixed form of sign connected with the engagement ring, signifying to potential attackers the risks they are taking. All these social details are of course a matter of general Christian wisdom rather than deduction from specific Old Testament directives.

I do not think anyone knows for sure why the penalties for sexual crimes in the Old Testament are exactly what they are. Perhaps the death penalty is the penalty for adultery merely because adultery is so serious a crime and merits the most serious penalty. Perhaps. But how and why is it so serious a crime? The seriousness of a sin before God merits hell, as we have observed. Christians naturally abhor adultery because of its attack against love and family. It is an attack on an institution symbolizing Christ's love for His church (Ephesians 5:22–33). But these facts by themselves do not enable us to determine what sort of penalty, if any, a sin deserves from civil authorities. The attack on society itself is a serious component in adultery, and certainly should be taken into account. But what exactly are the implications for the form of punishment? Unless we understand the Old Testament better than a minimum amount, we cannot tell for certain whether the special holiness of Israel has an influence on the nature and severity of the penalty. I believe that there is room for debate on this matter.

In any case, we must try to embody the general principles of God's justice in our laws today. The principle of "As you have done, it shall be done to you" is still valid as a guide to determining penalties for crimes today. We must reason on such a basis in trying to deal with the difficulties of sexual crimes.

Penalties for Sexual Perversion

Next, consider the question of sexual union between close relatives.[19] The basic Mosaic statutes are found in Leviticus 18:6–18 and 20:11–12, 14, 17–21. Mosaic law makes some distinction between different types of sexual relations between relatives. In Leviticus 20:11–14 the death penalty is prescribed for various types of sexual union that confuse the relationship of parent and child. The statutes include all the cases involving relatives by marriage (a man with his daughter-in-law, mother-in-law, or stepmother). By contrast, sexual relations with a sister-in-law or father's brother's wife are punished with childlessness(20:20–21). In case of a half-sister or father's sister or mother's sister, the consequences are vague: the persons involved shall "be held responsible" (20:17, 19). For other cases of sexual union between relatives, such as are discussed in Leviticus 18:6–18, no direct indication is given as to what penalty is appropriate. Leviticus 18:29 makes the general statement that they "must be cut off from their people." If this general statement is intended to cover all the cases mentioned in 18:6–23, as seems probable, a penalty involving disqualification from the sacred acts of Israel and perhaps exile may be in view. More likely, the "cutting off" designates an act of God rather than an act of human beings, and no specific civil penalty can be deduced.

Abraham married his half-sister (Genesis 20:12), apparently without God's disapproval. Yet the same practice is clearly disapproved in

Leviticus 18:9 and 20:19. Perhaps we should understand the prohibition in Leviticus as a special provision intended to be observed only within Israel as a holy community. Yet in his own day Abraham and his family were the initial form of the holy community, and it seems odd that he should not be subject to the same requirements. Perhaps the provision in Leviticus is an additional restriction, like the restriction of sacrificing only at a central altar (Leviticus 17:8–9), a restriction clearly not applied in Abraham's day. Or perhaps we are to understand that the narrative of Genesis, though not explicitly disapproving of the nature of Abraham's marriage, drops hints of such disapproval through the troubles recorded in Genesis 12:10–20 and 20:1–18. Perhaps the situation here is similar to the absence in the Old Testament of explicit disapproval of polygamy, even though it is not ideal (Matthew 19:5–6). The evidence in this area is complex, and we cannot achieve firm conclusions.

The passage in Genesis 2:24 about leaving one's father and mother may be relevant here. This passage appears to me primarily to enjoin that one should break the earlier legal, social, and emotional attachment in becoming married, so that the integrity and intimacy of the marriage bond is adequately realized. It is dangerous to deduce too much from this passage by itself, in order to deduce a disapproval of marriages between close relatives. Nevertheless, it is still reasonable, particularly in the light of later revelation of God, to see here already a vague hint to the effect that as a general rule marriages should rearrange family lines. If so, the prohibitions in Leviticus 18:6–18 can properly be viewed as spelling out general principles inherent in God's purpose in creation, rather than merely special restrictions due to the holiness of Israel. However, there are some exceptions to the principles in the case of marriage of a man to his sister or sister-in-law. For example, at the starting point of the human race, interchange of family lines was of course impossible. Seth would have married one of his sisters, and such a marriage would have been quite in accord with the purposes of God. The levirate marriage in Deuteronomy 25:5–10 represents another exception, introduced in a fallen situation to protect posterity and the inheritance of the land, both of which foreshadow the coming of Christ. Though the case of Abraham's marriage to Sarah is ambiguous, it is possible that it is another exception. Just as the origin of the human race as a whole required an exception to a general principle, so the origin of the Israelite people as a distinctive people of God may have involved an exceptional kind of marrying within the spiritual family. According to Paul, Christians ought to marry only other Christians (1 Corinthians 7:39; 2 Corinthians 6:14–18). If the same principle applied to Abraham himself, he might have had little choice but to marry a close relative.

On the other hand, marriage of a man to his mother, daughter, mother-in-law, daughter-in-law, stepmother, grandmother, or granddaughter would seem to be a more direct overstepping of the principle of Genesis 2:24, and as such is prohibited in every case. Thus also the penalty articulated in Leviticus 20:11–12, 14 is the maximum penalty.

Even if I am wrong about some of these details, we may assume that most of the kinds of sexual union between close relatives, such as are recorded in Leviticus 18 and 20, are always sins against God. In conformity with this view, we may observe that almost all societies up to this day have disapproved of at least some types of incest. Social standards and definitions for incest or forbidden sexual relations have indeed varied from place to place, but there have always been some such standards. Social standards are often imperfect and distorted, but they still manage partially to reflect God's standards.

Having decided that incestuous relations violate God's standards, we must also consider whether they deserve civil penalties. Let us first restrict ourselves to the "parent-child" form of incest discussed in Leviticus 20:11–12, 14. If adulterous union is involved, incest becomes a special case of adultery, and the arguments above apply. If incest occurs between two unmarried people, we must ask who is injured—the people themselves, clearly. But such injury is not legally actionable. Do they injure society? In a general way they do, because society as a whole depends on the family and its lines of authority. But how do we weigh the seriousness of this disruption? In Israel the disruption was all the more serious because Israel was supremely obligated to reflect God's holiness and order in her own orderly society. For Israelite society, the holiness of Israel was attacked by perversion in its midst. The statutes on incest contain the repeated phrase "their blood is upon their own heads." They occur in the context of preceding statements concerning the fact that the LORD consecrates Israel (Leviticus 20:7–8), a succeeding statement there being "no wickedness among you" (20:14) and at least one statute of a more clear-cut ceremonial order (20:18). All these elements suggest, though they do not make certain, a reference to the special holiness of Israel. The holiness of Israel involves the preservation of distinctions and separations at many levels, including not only separation from immorality generally, but distinctions between clean and unclean foods. Incest, bestiality, and homosexual acts ruin fundamental distinctions and thereby profane Israel's holiness. The penalty is the same as in the other cases of profanation of a fundamental kind. Only consecration to destruction cleanses Israel and imposes on the offenders a fit penalty, namely, a further stage of profanation. However, in the cases of incest mentioned in 20:20–21 a lesser penalty is sufficient. When the familial distinctions are not disrupted in quite so fundamental a way, childlessness is a fit penalty, since such a penalty disrupts the family line of the offenders.

I appear, then, to have arrived at some insights concerning not only parent-child incest but homosexual practice and bestiality. All three properly and justly warrant the death penalty in the context of Israel's holiness. In the context of the church, subsequent to the resurrection of Christ, they warrant excommunication (when not repented of).[20]

But outside the context of Israel or the church as a holy community, the situation is fundamentally different. We still have to reckon with the fact that sexual perversion disrupts the general order of society. Perhaps this fact by itself is enough to warrant a severe reciprocal penalty. If a person disrupts the order of society, society ought in turn to disrupt the order of the offender, possibly even in the form of maximum disruption, namely, the death penalty. How do we measure the severity of disruption here? I do not have clear answers, because the disruption involved is deep (pointing in the direction of a more severe penalty) and indirect (leaving us uncertain of the exact form of reciprocity that would be appropriate).

Because the nature of appropriate reciprocal penalties is difficult to assess, cases of incest and homosexual relations between consenting adults are among the most difficult to respond to. Homosexual rape should be dealt with on the same basis as rape against a married person.

The remedy of natural marriage is not available, and so the crime falls into the irremediable category even if it is perpetrated against an unmarried person.

Alternatives to My Position on Sexual Crimes

My results are somewhat tentative because of the complexity of the reasoning involved. But I am reassured when I consider the alternatives to my position. Any reasonable alternative must attempt to explain the data from Mosaic law in a consistent way, and must also deal with the issues of justice in modern social settings. There is no easy way to do both.

A rigid position stressing the uniqueness of Israel's holiness might claim simply that Old Testament penalties for sexual crimes are irrelevant. But sexual crimes still exist in modern society. What penalties are just? People in this rigid position can get no form of traction to start to deal with this question unless they are willing to reflect in depth on principles of justice. When they do so, Old Testament law will obviously be suggestive, and they may well arrive at the same practical conclusions as my own.

On the other hand, an opposite form of rigidity would argue that if God's laws are right for Israel they are right for us. People then attempt to apply Old Testament sexual penalties directly to modern society. But they must reckon with some difficulties. (1) In Israel the penalty for intercourse between a married man and an unengaged virgin was polygamous marriage. (2) There is no exact equivalent to a marriage present in modern Western society. (3) The significance of engagement and the relation of father to daughter in Exodus 22:17 seems different than in many modern societies. (4) In Israelite society there seem to be only two main categories of women who have never married: virgins and prostitutes. It is unclear how the law would apply to the promiscuous and other nonvirgin single women in modern society.

It is one thing to claim that Mosaic laws were just for Israelite society. It is quite another to claim that Mosaic law requires us to adjust modern society to conform exactly to the practices of Israel. The truth lies between the two extremes. At some points modern society needs reform. At other points ancient Israel society needs reform (remember that the prophets criticized existing society on the basis of God's word). At still other points societies may be structured in more than one way and still conform to God's standards.[21]

If, then, we cannot reasonably carry over Mosaic sexual law in a one-to-one way, we must assume the responsibility of trying to understand it. Only by discerning the principles of justice can we know what aspects are adjustments applying to particular features of Israelite society and what aspects represent permanent principles.

Once we take the step of trying to understand the law in detail, facts confront us that are difficult to account for. How do we deal with the intercourse between married man and virgin leading to polygamous marriage? How do we deal with the fact that Mosaic law is silent about intercourse between a married man and a prostitute, or between an unmarried man and a prostitute? Not only is it silent in a technical sense, but we can infer from cultural data that no civil penalty was contemplated.

Consider now some alternatives for modern society. We could specify the death penalty for all adultery. But how do we account for the fact that intercourse between a married man and a prostitute received no penalty in Mosaic law or in the Old Testament as a whole, and that intercourse between a married man and a virgin had a different solution?

We could specify the penalty of castration for all adultery. But outside of the context of modern medicine castration of females would be difficult. It seems wrong to claim that such a penalty represents a truly *general* principle of justice.

On the other extreme, we could specify no penalty for any sexual crime. But such an approach violates everyone's sense of justice. It does not address the questions of obvious injury to innocent spouses and sexual victims in cases of adultery and rape, and the more indirect injury to society as a whole from sexual deviations of various kinds.

We could specify imprisonment in the case of some types of sexual crimes. But the logic of just recompense never points in the direction of prison as a solution. How does such punishment really correspond to the nature of the crime? Moreover, prison is never used as punishment in the Mosaic law, even though the story of Joseph's imprisonment shows that it was a known alternative (Genesis 39:20).

We could specify monetary penalties for all sexual crimes injuring another person. Such a position is not so far away from mine, except in the case of penalties for rape. The case of rape is surely a difficult one, and my own view is therefore quite tentative. But it is at least arguable, not only that my proposed punishment corresponds much more exactly to the form of the crime, but that my punishment acts as an effective future deterrent. A fine or even a beating would almost surely be ineffective.

FOURTEEN

DETERRENCE AND REHABILITATION

I have now surveyed the major types of crime and have examined why the Mosaic law specifies particular penalties in each case. On the way I have also suggested what penalties might be appropriate in modern contexts on the basis of general principles of justice. My arguments have many times relied on detailed attention to the Old Testament texts. It is wise that we should immerse ourselves in the Bible in order to understand in greater depth the principles of justice relevant to any society. But it should also be noticed that I have never advocated blindly carrying over Old Testament laws into our own time. We must endeavor to understand the meaning and function of those laws in their own context and to understand the way in which they point forward to Christ in His perfect justice. The correct application of principles to our own times can only be achieved when we really understand the Bible. Such understanding is an ongoing challenge. I make my proposals tentatively because I realize that there is yet more to be understood.

The Use of the General Principle of Equivalence

Though I rely on the Old Testament as a basis for arguing about the appropriateness of various modern penalties, the same conclusions might conceivably be reached by other routes. For example, I can conceive of someone starting not with the Old Testament directly but with the general principle of equivalence, "As you have done, it shall be done to you." Merely by using this general principle, and without direct reference to the Old Testament at all, someone might conceivably arrive at modern civil penalties something like my own. We should not be surprised by the existence of such an alternative route. All human beings unavoidably have a general sense of justice, according to Romans 1:32. To be sure, they suppress, distort, and obscure what they know (Romans 1:18, 21). But they nevertheless do not escape the responsibility to act on the basis of their knowledge. Thus human beings do have some sense, however obscured, of the fitness of just punishment. They dimly sense the truth of the principle, "As you have done, it shall be done to you." And theoretically it is possible for them to see the implications of this general principle for particular crimes like murder and theft.

In some sense, therefore, it is valid to appeal to a universal sense of justice in the human heart. But such an appeal is beset with many serious pitfalls. Apart from Christ, our hearts and minds are darkened and rebellious (Ephesians 4:17–24). We suppress the truth that we know. Even when we are united to Christ, renewal comes gradually, in conjunction with the operation of the whole body of Christ and not just individuals (Ephesians 4:23–24; 4:11–16). We must beware of overestimating our abilities and underestimating the subtlety and insidiousness of sin. Moreover, God's justice, not the human sense of justice, is our ultimate standard. An appeal to a general human sense of justice easily gets corrupted into an idea of justice *apart from* God and His word. It tempts people back into love of self, lust for autonomy, and lust for defining justice to suit themselves and their narrow interests instead of God.

Hence, in actual fact, we need the presence of God, the instruction of His word, the ministry of the church and its sacraments, and perseverance in prayer to grow into a proper sense of justice. In spite of the clarity of God's general revelation, it will get distorted and suppressed unless we have the special aids that God's redemption provides. Even the general principle of equivalence, "As you have done, it shall be done to you," remains abstract and capable of manipulation and distortion, unless it is fleshed out by the richness of examples given to us in the Bible, and unless it is related to the personal God of the Bible, who is its source.

What do we conclude? We ought to listen carefully to the arguments of others, including non-Christians, who would appeal to general principles of justice. Fragments of truth remain even in the midst of distortion, and we may sometimes use such fragments to correct ourselves. We in turn might sometimes present to others arguments on the basis of general principles, without direct appeal to the Bible. But we ought not to expect much from either side of these exchanges. The most profound changes in our outlook and convictions concerning justice come from the cleansing and renewing power of God, who meets us through Christ as He is set forth in the Bible.

There is, therefore, a serious danger in trying to bypass the Bible's concrete expressions of God's justice. However, there is also a danger in the opposite direction. We could try to ignore questions of principle entirely, and without reflection apply the Mosaic law in a slavish, wooden way. Such a route would in fact be a contradiction of God's own intention. He wants us to meet Him and to digest His law into our own hearts. A robust response to Mosaic law leads us to embrace Christ with our whole being. Understanding and application of the particulars cannot be properly grounded simply on intellectual argument.

Even if there remain some disagreements about modern applications, the main points concerning the justice of God's judgments in the Old Testament and the way in which the Old Testament points forward to Christ remain untouched. As we read the Old Testament for its testimony to Christ, we encounter the ultimate source of purifying power, and so there is hope not only for us but for the larger society in which we live.

The Role of Deterrence and Rehabilitation

In chapter 11, I spoke of the dangers arising from fixing penalties on the basis of deterrence and rehabilitation alone. Only when we appeal to principles of justice and fit retribution can we avoid undue severity and undue leniency. Only so do we treat criminals as responsible human beings rather than as mere objects to be manipulated for the benefit of the larger society.

Prevention of crime (deterrence) and rehabilitation of criminals are nevertheless still significant concerns. In fact, at a deep level they are part of the structure of God's justice. Leviticus 1–5 present us with four main types of sacrifice, namely, burnt offering, grain offering, fellowship offering, and sin offering. In terms of emphasis these four types focus respectively on destruction of sinfulness, restoration to God of what is owed, fellowship with God and conformity to His image, and punishment for sin. They embody the intertwined principles of destruction, restoration, replication, and punishment. Up until now we have concentrated on restoration and punishment as fundamental principles involved in God's justice and in the determination of the proper penalty for crimes. But in the total picture of God's work, destruction of sin itself is also involved. Utter destruction is God's form of deterrence. Deterrence is thus also one aspect of legitimate punishment. Rehabilitation can also be an aspect, since replication of the image of God in renewed human beings is God's form of rehabilitation.

The ultimate form of deterrence is to be found in the destruction of sin through the crucifixion of Christ. As Paul says, "We died to sin; how can we live in it any longer? Or don't you know that all of us who were baptized into Christ Jesus were baptized into his death?" (Romans 6:2–3). "Those who belong to Christ Jesus have crucified the sinful nature with its passions and desires" (Galatians 5:24). The sinful nature with its tendencies to sin is mastered in a definitive sense at the time of Christians' conversions, as they are united to Christ. It is also mastered progressively through the process of sanctification. The power of Christ completely frees us from sin at the time of His Second Coming.

The ultimate form of rehabilitation is to be found in new life in Christ. "And we, who with unveiled faces all reflect the Lord's glory, are being transformed into his likeness with ever-increasing glory, which comes from the Lord, who is the Spirit" (2 Corinthians 3:18). "Therefore, if anyone is in Christ, he is a new creation; the old has gone, the new has come!" (2 Corinthians 5:17). We "put on the new self, created to be like God in true righteousness and holiness" (Ephesians 4:24), "being renewed in knowledge in the image of [our]

Creator" (Colossians 3:10). People renewed by the Spirit of Christ are once again the image of God and replicate His holiness. Their innermost desires are now controlled by the Spirit, not the flesh (Romans 8:5–11).

The state can obviously offer neither deterrence or rehabilitation in this glorious form. But as we have seen, the state is in its own way an agent of God under the rule of Christ (Romans 13:1–7; Ephesians 1:20–22). The state is responsible to reflect principles of God's justice on the shadowy, earthly level on which it operates. Hence, we rightly expect that the state will at least sometimes deter criminals in an outward sense, even though it does not change their hearts. We may also expect that sometimes state punishments will be an instrument of outward rehabilitation, in that they cause a former criminal to become a moral person. The outward acts of the state also bear witness to the more ultimate justice and judgment of God at the Second Coming. God may use these outward witnesses as prods for spiritual reflection. They can thus sometimes be an occasion for awakening criminals to the seriousness of their condition and opening their minds to hear the gospel.

But we must not expect too much of the state. Its powers are not worthy of being compared with the spiritual powers of the gospel and the spiritual armor of the Christian (Ephesians 6:10–20). People who do not trust in Christ and have no better hopes are nevertheless tempted to look to the state for some kind of salvation. The state is then expected to do what it can never do, and the results are disastrous. The dehumanizing effects when we forget justice and define the state's duty solely in terms of deterrence and rehabilitation are one example. Secular humanistic ideas of deterrence and rehabilitation can never provide good criteria for how to deal with criminals.

The Deterrent Value of My Proposed Punishments

Even though deterrence cannot safely provide the primary criterion for just punishment, it has some confirmatory value. The punishments that I have advocated in the previous chapters do arguably have a considerable deterrent effect. Their value as a deterrent becomes even clearer if we make one significant alteration in the normal criterion for deterrence. Ideally, people want the threat of a penalty infallibly to deter a possible offender from ever committing a crime. Unfortunately, criminals as a group tend to have poor ability to calculate the long range consequences of their actions. If they did calculate the consequences, they would reckon with the final judgment of God, and they would be deterred even without any threat of earthly penalties for their actions.

Hence, I think that it is appropriate to ask not only whether a prospective criminal will be deterred from a first violation, but even more important whether he will be deterred from a subsequent violation once he has felt the penalty from the first. The execution of a penalty brings home the consequences in a way that mere talk about a future penalty often does not. In the same way a son who is sorely tempted to do something forbidden by his father will often stay out of temptation only after he has tested the father's will once by succumbing to temptation.

We must also not expect that a penalty will deter criminals if criminals are very seldom caught. We can discriminate between effective and ineffective penalties only if we suppose that in the community in which penalties operate criminals get caught and punished with a reasonably high frequency—say, at least 50 percent of the time.

Using the above criteria, I believe that the penalties that I have suggested do have reasonable deterrent effect. In fact, these penalties are usually the least severe penalties that would have reasonable deterrent value. Thus we have here some argument that just penalties ought not to be much more lenient than what I have suggested. Let us now go through the major areas of crime one by one to verify this claim.

First, the area of theft. If thieves are caught and forced to pay a penalty, they are losing wealth rather than making it, and they lose all motivation for their crime. However, vandals might still not be deterred, because vandals are motivated primarily by hatred rather than by greed. But an owner who was repeatedly vandalized and who repeatedly received back fourfold compensation would become almost happy at the prospect of more vandalism. The vandal would then not be able to cause emotional unhappiness to the object of his vandalism, and so he would lose motivation.

Accidents that destroy property or cause human bodily injury or loss of life can of course not be wholly prevented. The use of a penalty is nevertheless a motive for everyone to use precautions.

Next, the area of murder. The threat of the death penalty has perhaps some value in deterring a first offense. But even this severe penalty cannot overcome the exceedingly strong impulses that are set in motion by hatred. What is more arguable is that the death penalty infallibly deters a second offense. No other penalty is likely to do so, since the impulses arising from hatred and wantonness are so uncontrollable by outward means.[1]

Next, the area of verbal crimes. No penalty except the death penalty can utterly deter unpremeditated slanderous outbursts, since these usually flow from hatred. But in the usual case of verbal crimes we are dealing with premeditated action. If the offender is caught and penalized, he does not of course achieve his goal against the other person, and he has no motivation for crime when the goal is not achieved. The principle of "as you have done, it will be done to you" means that a failure rate of something like 50 percent makes verbal crimes unprofitable.

Next, the area of crimes against the holy community. I argue that there should be no penalty in these cases. If there is no penalty, then of course these crimes will not be deterred. But this situation is appropriate if outside of Israel they are not crimes at all, that is, they are not offenses over which the state has responsibility. The most significant sins, like false worship and seduction to false worship, concern matters relating to the ultimate allegiances of human beings. Ultimate allegiances bind people in ways that they cannot easily be forced to give up. The first offense is not likely to be deterred effectively, even by the death penalty. Attempting to impose lesser penalties is just fooling around without coming to grips with the depth of the problem.

Next, the area of crimes against authority. Incorrigibility or repeated wanton violations of positive commands of the state can in the nature of the case be deterred only by the death penalty. Lesser violations of authority, if they take the form of folly, cannot be utterly deterred because fools by definition do not reckon with the consequences. For fools a punishment in the form of beating is likely to succeed better than a monetary payment or fine. Pain is immediate and cannot be ignored, whereas a fine affects only future purchasing power and hence does not come home to the fool, who does not calculate the future.

Next, the area of sexual crimes. Fornication is somewhat deterred if the fornicator is forced to marry and is thereby provided with a regular, legitimate channel for satisfaction of sexual desire. The monetary penalties attached when the fornicator does not marry are also some inducement to assume habits of life that will eventually equip the offender to discharge the monetary responsibilities associated with marriage. When marriage is available, when weighty monetary penalties attach to fornication with chaste women, and when prostitutes are legally available (though not free from moral disapproval), even a relatively foolish and promiscuous young man might conclude that it was more sensible to find his sexual satisfaction elsewhere than in seducing young virgins.

Adultery is somewhat deterred by the financial penalties involved. If the way is legally open for divorce, as I believe if should be, the person plotting adultery may be willing to obtain the divorce first. Even if the first offense of adultery is not deterred, the second will be if the injured spouse obtains a divorce.

But, adultery and divorce are also disruptive of the social order. Conceivably more severe penalties might be warranted in order not merely to try to prevent the individual act of adultery but to lower the statistical prevalence of adultery and divorce. Divorce, however, was only regulated in a minimal way within Old Testament Israel (Deuteronomy 24:1–4). State regulation and penalties with respect to these matters clearly do not deal with the fundamental root of the matter in the sinfulness of human hearts. As long as there are sinners, there will be disintegration of marriage relationships.

Rapists are not likely to be deterred by anything short of castration, since many of them are motivated primarily by desire for power and sexual mastery. Monetary payments or beatings will almost surely be ineffective.

The Rehabilitative Value of My Proposed Punishments

We can next ask questions about rehabilitation. Do my proposed punishments tend to rehabilitate criminals? Only through the gospel and the power of the Holy Spirit can criminals receive a new heart. Short of this change, no really thoroughgoing rehabilitation is possible. But we can still speak of a kind of earthly rehabilitation: sometimes a criminal ceases to commit crimes not merely because of fear of punishment but because of some sort of change in desires. Can such changes be created by appropriate punishments?

No set of punishments could guarantee change, because of the perverseness of human nature since the fall. Nevertheless, there are still some arguments in favor of punishments that match the crime. We have repeatedly appealed to the principle of reciprocity, "As you have done, it will be done to you." This principle expresses justice. Perhaps it is also most likely humanly speaking to lead to rehabilitation, for at least three reasons.

1. Just penalties are more likely to cause remorse. If criminals *feel* that their punishment is just, they are more likely to undergo some kind of remorse or repentance. Sometimes criminals' consciences are hardened (cf. 1 Timothy 4:2) so that they have a perverted sense of justice. But no one ever totally destroys a sense of God's justice within (Romans 1:18–20, 32). Criminals are certainly more likely to feel that a punishment is just if it is in fact just.

2. A special value attaches to the situation where the penalty imposed on the criminal is fundamentally the same as the one that the criminal imposed on the victim. The criminal is made to experience in his own life and his own person the effects that he brought on the victim. In the process the criminal is made to experience in at least some outward way the viewpoint of the victim. He is forced in some sense to think about the principle of not doing to others as he would not like to have it done to him, the negative side of the golden rule. All criminal actions arise from wickedness of heart. But more proximately, we may say that they arise from a deficiency in love for one's neighbor and inability to put oneself sympathetically in the other person's situation. The very nature of reciprocal punishment is to force the criminal into practicing what he does not practice of his

own accord. There is some hope that through this experience the criminal will come to a genuine insight into feelings of others and thereby be changed so that he is less likely to commit the same crime again.

In addition, if the punishment focuses on helping the victim, offenders are helped to appreciate the true consequences of their crimes. Such punishment reinforces the idea that crime is an offense against a victim, an injured party, not against society in the abstract. In the present prison system, it is too easy for criminals to make excuses for themselves or to blame society for their misery, because they are not made existentially aware of the damage to the victim. In our modern context, properly arranged and supervised meetings between victim and offender to discuss the injury and how to make proper restitution have proven quite effective in dealing both with the victim's anger and with the criminal's sense of responsibility. The percentage of repeat offenses is vastly reduced.[2]

3. Other things being equal, immediate punishments, rather than punishments inflicted over a long period of time, are more effective. Criminals often fail to calculate distant consequences of their acts, and in fact, the more distant future frequently has little existential relevance to them. Because of their deficiencies in reckoning with long range connections in time, immediate punishments are on the average more likely to bring home to them the true nature of consequences for criminal behavior. The punishments that I suggest tend to be punishments of an immediate kind, because they reciprocate crimes that themselves are immediate rather than spread over a long period of time.

The death penalty, however, is an exception to these reasonings. The death penalty destroys people rather than rehabilitating them. For this reason, along with other reasons, modern humanists shrink from inflicting the death penalty. It is nevertheless undeniable that God's justice does require the death penalty for murder (Genesis 9:6) and perhaps a few other crimes (incorrigibility and unrestrained rebellion against the state).

In the case of an authorized death penalty we should adjust our criteria of rehabilitation. We should ask whether any penalty is likely to rehabilitate criminals during their lifetime. Since the fall of Adam, all human life has limited duration. God never waits forever for sinners to rehabilitate. When the state is authorized by God to take human life in a particular case, that authorization is itself the signal that God wills the termination of the criminal's lifetime. Hence, the criminal's time for rehabilitation is the time between his crime and the execution of punishment. There is indeed still some possibility of rehabilitation within this time. It is not even clear that extending the time beyond a few days increases the probability of rehabilitation. Rehabilitation is not a matter of having lots of time but having a change of heart. It is arguable that the immediate prospect of dying is just as likely to focus a criminal's energies on repentance as is an extended period of not knowing when he will die.

With respect to this limited time period, the arguments above concerning the merits of my proposed punishments still apply. We trivialize the value of human life and the meaning of state authority if we do not take with utter seriousness the destruction of human life and the wholesale usurpation and destruction of state authority. We are toying with the criminal, rather than expressing to him the true seriousness of his crime, if we are not willing to inflict a penalty of reciprocal seriousness.

As in all cases of criminal punishments, so also especially in the case of the death penalty, Christians have a responsibility to communicate the gospel to those who are to receive penalties. Only through the power of Christ can either those who continue to live or those who must die know newness of life. Those who trust in Christ, whether they be dying thieves (Luke 23:40–43) or living disciples, are promised eternal life in the presence of the Father.

FIFTEEN

A CRITIQUE OF PRISONS

How do we evaluate the present systems of criminal justice in modern societies? Most modern societies use imprisonment as the primary form of punishment for crime. Some limited steps have been taken here and there to introduce alternative punishments, such as making thieves pay back for their theft. But such alternatives are the exception rather than the rule. For practical purposes we must focus attention on the value of imprisonment as a form of punishment.

First of all, we should distinguish carefully between using prison for punishment and using it as a means of custody before trial. The use of some form of custody until the time of trial is attested in the Bible itself (Leviticus 24:12; Acts 21:34; 23:35) and is widespread elsewhere. Sometimes no reasonable alternative is available. In such cases the temporary use of a prison is surely legitimate. To prevent this practice from becoming an unacknowledged or unintentional form of punishment, state authorities have an obligation to work for practices that promote speedy trial. In addition, the provision for bail works in favor of preventing unjust punishment in the form of confinement.

The deliberate use of prison for the purpose of punishing convicted offenders is quite another matter. In practice, it is a disaster. The statistics with regard to repeated offenders give a grim picture. Those who have been involved in prisons, either as state authorities or especially as prisoners, testify to their ineffectiveness, oppressiveness, and destructive tendencies.[1]

But I prefer to base my arguments on principle rather than on the actual results of the prison system. If I were to appeal only to actual results, I would leave open the possibility that prison reform could straighten out the system. I do not believe that any reform could be adequate, because the system is wrongheaded from the beginning.

To evaluate properly the principle of imprisonment, we must use Biblical criteria. As we have seen, a proper response to crime involves four elements: restoration, punishment, deterrence, and rehabilitation. Restoration and punishment must be our primary concern. But deterrence and rehabilitation can be significant secondary indicators of whether a proposed solution makes contact with the reality of the human condition.

Does Prison Justly Restore and Punish?

Does prison promote just restoration for crimes? Restoration means making things good to the victim of a crime. The victim's situation must be restored as far as possible to its original condition before the crime. Or if such restoration is not possible, some other kind of restoration to normalcy is appropriate, as when the thief gives back a substitute for a destroyed object, or when the fornicator is forced to marry his partner.

Prison in itself obviously restores nothing. Moreover, in cases where restoration involves the use of money, prison works against restoration by destroying the offender's capacity to work in order to obtain money to pay the victim.

Does prison promote just punishment? Just punishment, as we have argued, always fits the crime. It always matches the nature and the intensity of the crime according to the principle, "As you have done, it will be done to you." The only crime for which imprisonment would be the fitting penalty would be the crime of imprisoning someone else! A kidnapper might of course imprison the victim, and so one might deduce the penalty of imprisonment in this special case. But as we have seen in chapter 11, kidnapping also constitutes a usurpation of the authority of the state and as such merits the death penalty. The punishment of imprisonment does not cope with the full guilt attaching to kidnapping.

On a very general level one might argue that all crimes are abuses of the offender's social powers and his tacit agreements with society. Hence, such abuses are met by depriving the offender of interaction with society. But such reasoning grossly misconstrues the nature of crime. It pretends that crime is an offense against the criminal's social rights (i.e., an offense against the criminal himself) and also an offense against society as a whole (i.e., society in the abstract). Neither is true. Crime is an offense against the victim. It is a much more personal thing than this reasoning admits, and not seeing the personal character of crime is one of the criminal's main problems.

Yet another difficulty arises with respect to imprisonment. No plausible means exists for determining a just quantity of punishment. If the punishment matches the crime, as in my proposals in chapters 10–12, its quantity is automatically determined at least in a rough way. A theft of a small amount is met by a penalty proportional to this amount. The theft of a large amount is met by a penalty of a corresponding amount. But what do we do if we must use only the penalty of imprisonment? How much time in prison corresponds to the amount of a theft? We cannot say, because time and money do not directly match. How much time corresponds to murder? How much time to bodily injury? How much time to rape? How much time to adultery? Amount of time does not quantify any crime in a reasonable way.

We might perhaps propose to quantify some things by converting between quantities of money and quantities of time. An amount of time in some circumstances can be reckoned as equivalent to the amount of money that a person could earn during the given amount of time (see Exodus 21:19). But can we use such a criterion to deal with imprisonment? If the time really is equivalent to the corresponding amount of money, we should be satisfied with a monetary payment and not imprisonment. But in fact we are not satisfied, which indicates that the two are not really equivalent. Moreover, the question arises as to whether people who can command a higher salary should therefore be confined for less time. Such a position would offend all our sense of justice. Clearly imprisonment is not merely loss of working time, but in its essence something else altogether. What is it? An extreme form of slavery in which the wardens of the prison have much more detailed control in comparison with most historical instances of slavery? A form of slavery chosen to deprive the criminal of the normal pleasures of slavery, such as meaningful work, access to larger society, some degree of privacy, and social intimacy with spouse and family? What is this monster that we have invented, and how can it ever be just punishment?

Does Prison Effectively Deter and Rehabilitate?

Does prison deter crime? As long as the criminal is in prison, he is prevented from preying on the larger society. If and when he is released from prison, there is no guarantee whatsoever that he will not repeat his crime. Because doing time does not effectively match the nature of the criminal's crime, it does not effectively take away his motive for committing crime again.

An even more telling objection arises from the nature of the small subsociety or subculture within a prison. Prisoners are not totally prevented from preying on fellow prisoners. Murders, rapes, and thefts do take place within prisons. Such possibilities make a mockery of justice. The very thing that is supposed to be punishment becomes the scene of more crime. Prison does not thoroughly deter crime but simply transports crime to another location.

Moreover, the fact of crime within prisons suggests that the real desires of society may be less lofty than its altruistic rhetoric. The motives of a society as a whole are of course varied and confused. But a cynical analysis might suggest the following. The outside society is not really concerned with true deterrence but with its own comfort. By removing criminals from its midst it obtains the comfort of not having so much crime. Subsequently, it cares very little for whether crime is deterred inside the prison, as long as this crime is concealed and does not cause guilt feelings. To confine the prisoners for a lifetime would of course produce the greatest freedom from crime for the outside society. But the larger society would feel guilty about such a severe penalty. So it releases criminals after a time for the sake of comforting its own guilt feelings. The amount of time spent in prison is not determined by justice but by the interplay between social desire for freedom from crime and social desire for absence of guilt feelings. In all this interplay, society can act with perfect selfishness. At the same time it can pretend that prisons are intended to provide criminals with a rehabilitative environment, and hence it can congratulate itself for having motives of concern for the rehabilitation of criminals rather than their punishment. Such selfishness will naturally produce largely cynicism and not repentance on the part of criminals.

Does prison offer significant hope for rehabilitation? Criminals have the most hope for rehabilitation if they feel the justice of their punishment. As I have argued in the previous chapter, such results are far more likely under a system that takes care to think explicitly in terms of principles of reciprocity and justice. In addition, criminals have a greater chance to reform if they are in normal contact with normal society. They then have opportunity immediately to engage in just, socially profitable work and contributions to others. The abnormalities of prison life can never become a viable environment for training in righteousness. In fact, prison frequently produces results in the opposite direction because the morality of a subculture of criminals reverses the morality of normal society.

In addition to all these factors, prison presents dangerous temptations to injustice on the part of the wardens, guards, and supervisors of the prison. Let us grant that many who are charged with prison supervision act out of true good will and as a service to society. They often do so within circumstances that are personally very difficult for them and sometimes dangerous to their own safety. But there is another side that we seldom think about. Supervisors and guards are exposed to temptations that can easily bring out the worst in anyone. They supervise prisoners, some of whom are unpleasant people, sometimes vindictive, spiteful, deceitful, or obnoxious. Petty offenses and back talk from prisoners tempt supervisors to return evil with evil. The substandard morality of many prisoners tempts them to treat all prisoners as subhuman and to prejudge prisoners even before the prisoners do something against them. The prisoners have little effective way of making an appeal against injustice, and unjust acts on the part of supervisors are concealed within the prison from the eyes of the larger society. Thus injustice can be practiced with impunity. Supervisors have virtually totalitarian control over prisoners, and such absolute power tends to corrupt the human beings who possess it.

In summary, I would argue that the cases of injustice and sometimes gross inhumanity on the part of supervisors or guards are no accident but, a natural product of the unjust, unworkable character of the system. We should be surprised that the system does not turn out even worse than it is.

As a last resort, one might argue that at least prison represents a kind of shadow of hell. In this very vague sense it expresses a kind of justice shadowing the justice of God's judgment in hell. In reply I agree that prison imitates hell in one way. Just as hell isolates the damned and prevents them from contaminating the holiness of God's renewed world, so prison prevents its inmates from contaminating the larger society. So long as people are in prison they are deterred from preying upon the larger society. But this result is deterrence, not justice. In other respects the problems remain. (1) Whereas hell expresses the justice of God, prison does not. (2) In hell people may well be prevented from exercising their unrighteous desires against others, but in prison they are still capable of injuring fellow prisoners. (3) The troubles of supervisors and guards still show prison to be ineffective even as an image of hell. (4) If we think that prison is so bad as to be a shadow of hell, are we still willing to argue that it is less bad than my proposed alternatives?

Meanwhile, as long as the present prison system exists, Christians must do what they can on behalf of prisoners (Matthew 25:36–40). Through Prison Fellowship and other Christian organizations, many opportunities exist to bring to prisoners friendship, community support, and the gospel itself, which is the power of God for salvation. A convenient list of resources can be found in Van Ness, *Crime and Its Victims*, 193–217.

SIXTEEN

OUR RESPONSIBILITIES TOWARD IMPERFECT STATES

S uppose we grant that my proposed punishments for crime are more just than the current penal policies and practices of most states. What should we do to change the current situation?

Primary Responsibilities

A Christian's primary responsibility is to know Christ. The Apostle Paul forcefully summarizes this responsibility in Philippians 3:10–11: "I want to know Christ and the power of his resurrection and the fellowship of sharing in his sufferings, becoming like him in his death, and so, somehow, to attain to the resurrection from the dead." All the law and the prophets hang on the two commandments, loving God and loving one's neighbor (Matthew 22:40). Both love of God and love of neighbor are renewed through love of Christ and communion with Christ. The Bible says, "For in Christ all the fullness of the Deity lives in bodily form, and you have been given fullness in Christ, who is the head over every power and authority" (Colossians 2:9–10). Properly understood, a concentration on knowing Christ in His fullness is not a retreat from the world but an advance toward the fullness of the Origin of the world, the fullness of God Himself. Knowing Christ implies not ignoring the

241

world but seeing it for the first time properly, as an area over which Christ rules both as the Creator of the world (John 1:1–4; Colossians 1:15–17) and as its Redeemer (Colossians 1:18–20).

This focus on Christ is necessary not only because it is Biblical, but also because we need to beware of being swept away by matters of secondary importance. What non-Christians and even many Christians consider important may not always be of primary importance. Politics and economics are the two biggest areas of power by which we move the world and measure our own importance—so the worldly person thinks. But earthly political and economic power are only a shadow of the real power, the power of God's throne, His riches, and His justice. Paul prays that we may have the eyes of our heart enlightened to know:

> his incomparably great power for us who believe. That power is like the working of his mighty strength, which he exerted in Christ when he raised him from the dead and seated him at his right hand in the heavenly realms, far above all rule and authority, power and dominion, and every title that can be given, not only in the present age but also in the one to come. And God placed all things under his feet and appointed him to be head over everything for the church. (Ephesians 1:19–22)

Such power is the heritage of every Christian now: "And God raised us up with Christ and seated us with him in the heavenly realms in Christ Jesus" (Ephesians 2:6). Through Christ we have been given the power of prayer and the power to wage war "against the powers of this dark world and against the spiritual forces of evil in the heavenly realms" (Ephesians 6:12). Our weapons are the weapons of the gospel—righteousness, truth, faith, salvation, and the word of God—which we use in conjunction with prayer (Ephesians 6:18–20). In the deepest sense, we put on the "armor of light" as we put on the Lord Jesus Christ Himself (Romans 13:12–14).

Hence, we must avoid thinking that the kingdom of God is established primarily by means of political or economic power. Jesus counsels us about true economic power, heavenly power, when He says, "Sell your possessions and give to the poor. Provide purses for yourselves that will not wear out, a treasure in heaven that will not be exhausted, where no thief comes near and no moth destroys. For where your treasure is, there your heart will be also" (Luke 12:33–34). Concerning true political power Jesus points out to Pilate, "My kingdom is not of this world. If it were, my servants would fight to prevent my arrest by the Jews. But now my kingdom is from another place" (John 18:36).

Two errors arise in interpreting passages like these. On the one hand, some dismiss or ignore the passages and devote their hearts merely to earthly politics or economics. Either they end up worshiping power and riches like secularists, or they baptize them and try to establish Christ's heavenly kingdom using earthly, fleshly weapons. On the other hand, some interpret Christ's sayings in a dualistic sense, as a wholesale abandonment of this world. They see in Christ's sayings literal, external rules calling for renunciation of all use of political or economic power whatsoever. But to interpret Jesus as focusing on external prescriptions is to miss the consistent tenor of His teaching and His life. Jesus uses illustrations and rhetorical figures to reveal the essence of godliness at a motivational level. Jesus articulates primarily the heart of the matter, not the external arrangements. In agreement with this viewpoint we find that soldiers and tax collectors are not called on to abandon their tasks but to reform the way in which they do them (Luke 3:12–14). As a general rule the rich are not commanded to give away all their money, but to use it wisely and generously for spiritual good (1 Timothy 6:17–19). In short, far from being a renunciation of the world to the devil, Jesus' methods constitute the true means of redeeming the world. The creation itself, as well as human beings, is to be redeemed, to "be liberated from its bondage to decay and brought into the glorious freedom of the children of God" (Romans 8:21).

Christians share in Christ's purposes as they come to know Christ and the power of His resurrection and the fellowship of sharing in His sufferings (Philippians 3:10). Paul expressed his willingness to bear all kinds of human weakness so that the sufferings and resurrection of Christ may work through him.

> But he said to me, "My grace is sufficient for you, for my power is made perfect in weakness." Therefore I will boast all the more gladly about my weaknesses, so that Christ's power may rest on me. That is why, for Christ's sake, I delight in weaknesses, in insults, in hardships,

in persecutions, in difficulties. For when I am weak, then I am strong. (2 Corinthians 12:9–10)

Christians under persecution, or in prison, or sick, or handicapped, may all share in Paul's experience. Gospel power, the power of Christ, does not favor only those who are strong with human strength. In fact, when we recognize our weakness and humble ourselves before God we are most able to serve.

Because Christ is Lord of all the world (Matthew 28:18; Ephesians 1:20–22), whatever we do can be a service to our Lord. "Whatever you do, work at it with all your heart, as working for the Lord, not for men, since you know that you will receive an inheritance from the Lord as a reward. It is the Lord Christ you are serving. Anyone who does wrong will be repaid for his wrong, and there is no favoritism" (Colossians 3:23–25). Homemakers, do the dishes, the laundry, and the vacuuming for Christ. Love your husband or wife for the sake of Christ. Be diligent in prayer. Christians need to work hard at whatever tasks they have, and not to think that only political or economic greatness makes their work valuable.

Earthly Political Responsibilities

Though political responsibilities are not primary, such responsibilities do exist. Christians are to pray that God's will would be done on earth as it is in heaven. We are first of all to strive to do God's will in our own lives. But we are also to pray for His will to be done universally. The state, as I have argued, is a shadow form of the justice of God, and as such it too is obligated to conform to the rule of Christ. Hence, Christians must pray in particular that earthly states would conform to God's justice. "I urge, then, first of all, that requests, prayers, intercession and thanksgiving be made for everyone—for kings and all those in authority, that we may live peaceful and quiet lives in all godliness and holiness" (1 Timothy 2:1–2). We are to thank God for the benefits even of imperfect states ("thanksgiving"), but we are also to pray that kings and other state authorities would in all their actions reflect God's justice (1 Peter 2:14), so that "peaceful and quiet lives" come to those under their rule.

What other political responsibilities do Christians have? First of all, it is clear that private individuals ought not to take penalties into their own hands. Even if the state fails to execute the proper penalty for crime, we may not do so privately ourselves. Paul counsels Christians not to avenge themselves, but to let the Lord do the avenging (Romans 12:18–21). In the context Paul's command not to avenge is immediately followed by an argument that the state has God-given power to avenge (Romans 13:4–5). The state acting with God's authority is one means God uses to execute His own vengeance, but special God-ordained authorities are the *only* people with this responsibility.

May Christians work to cause the political overthrow of a blatantly unjust government? Political revolution is a complex issue that could easily fill a book by itself. Here I can only direct readers to the arguments of John Calvin, with whom I agree.[1] According to Calvin, private individuals are never authorized to revolt, but "popular magistrates" have a duty to curb the tyranny of kings.[2]

In situations of hostile, totalitarian control, the political responsibility of Christians in private life begins and ends with prayer and obedience to God, not men. But what shall we do in countries where Christians are allowed to participate directly in the political process through voting and holding office? All Christians should desire and pray for just government, but their responsibilities differ in detail because of the gifts and the tasks that the Lord has assigned to each one. Some will have politics as their main vocational responsibility. Many others will have other vocations and participate in politics to varying degrees, according to their skills, interests, and their discernment of the Lord's purposes for their use of time (Ephesians 5:15–16). We must all avoid the temptation to think that our particular task is the most important or to despise Christians to whom the Lord has given different responsibilities.

In both voting and holding political office Christians have to think about many issues besides the issues of just penalties for crime. For one thing, even if just penalties were specified by the statutes, unjust enforcement, through the prejudices and oppressions of judges, lawyers, or law officers, could result in gross injustices in practice. In addition, many other types of decisions confront legislatures, and on such issues Christians may have definite convictions. Many types of laws may affect the social, economic, and moral well-being of a country, and thus indirectly influence the social conditions exacerbating or inhibiting crime.

Votes must sometimes be cast for political candidates whose views are imperfect, and votes must be cast for political bills whose provisions and laws are imperfect, because the alternative to one particular imperfection is another, worse imperfection. We must beware therefore of judging harshly people who vote in favor of an alternative form of imperfection.

On the question of penalties for crime, we should endeavor to use God's standards for justice when we weigh the issues. To the extent that my proposals in previous chapters (primarily chapters 11–13) embody principles of justice, they are a suitable goal for our legislation. They provide guidance for making some basic decisions about what kind of direction should be taken in revising the present penal system. But even here we must issue some cautions. God wants us not only to attend to His standards but also to be wise about how best to bring about a situation where His standards are more fully reflected on earth. My cautions are as follows:

1. Thoroughgoing revision of the penal system can realistically be achieved only if modern societies as a whole change their ways of thinking about crime, punishment, and justice. Currently many Christians disagree with my views. Even if they could be brought to agree, many non-Christians would almost certainly not quickly agree, because they do not respect the Biblical basis for my arguments. In the West, educational and communications media are currently dominated by a secular humanist framework of thinking, so that changing the patterns of thinking of society as a whole requires much long-range work in a broad spectrum of areas. We must not become discouraged if we do not see quick political victories. We do best to concentrate our energy on knowing Christ, and on the health and multiplication of Christianity generally as described in Ephesians 4:7–16.

2. We must endeavor not to alienate in any unnecessary way those who disagree politically and those who fight against us politically (Romans 12:17–21). Christians using the spiritual weapons of the gospel and prayer may always have hope for winning over those with whom they disagree. Immediate desires for political victory should not obscure the fact that political opponents are real people with longings and hurts like our own at a fundamental level. Messages and deeds of kindness toward opponents are always appropriate as a manifestation of our desire to do good to all people (Romans 12:17–21; Galatians 6:10), and may perhaps open a way for sharing the gospel and winning them over.

3. The most profound transformations occur as the gospel works its way into a whole society. If a large portion of the population has come to be disciples of Christ over a long period of time, the work of the power of Christ on Christians and the broader influence of Christian moral standards even on non-Christians should create a situation in which there is very little crime. Individuals and families that become Christians become "a new creation" (2 Corinthians 5:17). They find new hope, new motivations, new moral standards, and a new supportive community—the church—to direct them toward productive service to others. The application of Christian principles to society shrivels the familial and social circumstances conducive to crime. Then it will not matter very much in practice what penalties are laid down by the laws of the state. Let us be diligent in working for the discipling of the nations, since such work followed by the second coming of Christ will alone make the present book into a mere technical dispute.

4. It is possible that states have authority to determine punishments using a good deal of discretion. John Calvin argues that though moral standards are permanent, different states may legitimately differ in the punishments imposed for violation of moral standards.[3] This argument deserves careful attention. Calvin supports his argument partly by appealing to the actual diversity of punishments used by various nations in various circumstances

and partly by appealing to the necessity for strict measures in time of war, pestilence, or disorders of the state.

I cannot completely agree with such arguments for the following reasons.

1. Careful study of Mosaic law does show a pattern and a rationale for punishments. Principles of God's justice appear to operate in the determination of what penalties are appropriate. It is natural to think that such general principles of justice extend to modern states.

2. In a fallen situation states tend to seek totalitarian power. We must beware of loosing the state from being subject to God's standards. The state ought to serve God, not just to do what is right in its own eyes.

3. Is it possible that a penalty for a moral violation could be unjustly severe or unjustly lenient? I think so. Surely justice enters into the question. And if so, not all penalties are equally appropriate, given a fixed set of societal circumstances. Then we are confronted once again with the unavoidable question of what constitutes a just penalty. My proposals at the very least suggest guidelines as to what is appropriate in "normal" situations.

4. In some of the abnormal situations that Calvin envisions, such as war and disorders of the state, the very existence or integrity of the state as an institution may be threatened by actions that normally would carry less severe penalties. Now, as I have argued in chapter 12, actions usurping state authority may be punished by severe penalties, even the death penalty for acts threatening actual destruction of the state. Thus some particular types of violation of moral standards might carry unusually severe penalties not because the moral violation in itself deserves the penalty, but because the moral violation is accompanied by an additional violation, the violation of state authority.

Despite these points of disagreement with Calvin, we can still learn some lessons from his arguments. The state may indeed have some discretion to introduce extraordinary penalties to meet dangers arising in extraordinary circumstances. The analogy between parental authority and state authority suggests that in both cases mature wisdom must be exercised in dealing with difficult cases. God's own character and the revelation of His justice in the Bible instruct both parents and state on how to be wise in their dealings. Subject to these instructions, both parents and states must be allowed some leeway to adjust themselves in dealing with complexities. But I also believe that the personal, rich, intimate character of parents' relations to their children justifies a much greater amount of discretion in their case than in the case of the state. If the state tries to adjust to too many exceptions or meddles too much and becomes a parent to all its citizens, it smothers their initiative and maturity and creates injustice despite good intentions.

Calvin's survey of the history of punishments has another lesson. It is not as easy for people to agree on just punishment as it is to agree on what is a crime and what is a violation of moral law. Given this history of disagreement, we should all exercise an extra measure of charity toward those who disagree with us.

SEVENTEEN

FULFILLMENT OF THE LAW IN THE GOSPEL ACCORDING TO MATTHEW

T he five books of Moses contain much teaching on law and punishment. But that teaching is properly understood and applied to our
present situation only when we see the significance of God's entire
work with Israel and the way in which He purposed for the Old Testament to reveal His justice and to look forward to Christ. Because of the
Christocentric character of all of Scripture, and because of the way in
which the Old Testament is completed by the New, it is wise to complete our study by looking briefly at what the New Testament says
about the Mosaic law. We shall concentrate on one important but often
misunderstood passage, Matthew 5:17–18. "Do not think that I have
come to abolish the Law or the Prophets; I have not come to abolish
them but to fulfill them. I tell you the truth, until heaven and earth
disappear, not the smallest letter, not the least stroke of a pen, will by
any means disappear from the Law until everything is accomplished."
Matthew asserts a comprehensive fulfillment on the part of Jesus, a fulfillment extending even to the smallest letter ("jot and tittle"). What
does this fulfillment involve?

Matthew 1–4

To understand this passage more fully, let us look first at its broader context in the Gospel according to Matthew. All four Gospels have an interest in showing that Jesus fulfills the Old Testament promises regarding the coming of the Messiah. But Matthew does so in unusual detail because he is writing to a Jewish audience. He repeatedly quotes from the Old Testament using a formula, "so was fulfilled what was said through the prophet" (Matthew 1:22; 2:15, 17, 23; 4:14).

Matthew begins with a narrative of Jesus' birth and early ministry in Matthew 1–4 and the Sermon on the Mount in Matthew 5–7. In these two sections Matthew concentrates particularly on Jesus' fulfillment of the five books of Moses. Already in Matthew 1:1–2 the genealogy assigns a special place to Abraham, thus recalling the special prominence of Abraham and his descendents in the book of Genesis. More broadly, Matthew shows that the life of Jesus is analogous in some striking ways both to the life of Moses and to the status of Israel as a whole nation.[1]

The genealogy begins the process by establishing that Jesus is indeed an Israelite, descended from both Abraham and David (1:1). Jesus' supernatural birth is reminiscent of the birth of Isaac, the representative of all Israel. After His birth Herod attempts to destroy Him, just as Pharaoh attempted to destroy the baby Moses. Jesus then goes down to Egypt and returns from Egypt, thus recapitulating the early movements of the Israelite nation. Matthew specifically points out this fact by quoting from Hosea 11:1, "Out of Egypt I called my son." In the original context of Hosea, the text is speaking about the past deliverance of Israel, God's son, from Egypt. But the deliverance of Israel through the Passover and the Red Sea symbolized a greater future deliverance (see Isaiah 51:9–11). Jesus the true Son of God, the final Son, identified with and recapitulated the experience of Israel in order that He might deliver her. And so Matthew can speak of the passage in Hosea being "fulfilled" in Jesus (Matthew 2:15), even though the passage in Hosea was not a direct prophecy.

The ministry of John the Baptist in Matthew 3:1–17 continues along these lines. John's ministry is the fulfillment of the prophecy in Isaiah 40:3 concerning a voice preparing the way of the Lord (Matthew

3:3). Isaiah in its context is speaking of a second Exodus, that is, the coming of God to save Israel in a deliverance greater than but parallel to the original exodus from Egypt (Isaiah 51:9–11). Isaiah's expression "in the desert prepare the way," alludes to Israel's original journey from Egypt to Canaan. Isaiah thereby shows that the great coming deliverance will be analogous to that original deliverance from Egypt, even in the use of the wilderness as the place for fellowship with God. John appears in order to fulfill Isaiah's prophecy. He appears in the wilderness and calls on people to repent, which reminds us of the unrepentance and hardness of heart of the Israelites on the way to Canaan. John also proclaims, "The kingdom of heaven is near" (Matthew 3:2). God is about to come and reign, in a way parallel to the establishment of His reign over Israel long ago (Exodus 19:5–6; Deuteronomy 33:5). In addition, John's baptism is reminiscent of the cleansing rites that Moses introduced to Israel. Those cleansing rites in turn reminded people of the deliverance from Egypt and idolatry through the "cleansing" waters of the Red Sea.

When Jesus comes to be baptized by John, John immediately sees an inappropriateness in the situation (Matthew 3:13–15). John's baptism signified washing sin away and was administered to those who acknowledged their sinfulness (3:6). Jesus is sinless and needs no baptism. In comparison to Jesus' sinlessness, even John himself is a sinner along with the rest, and needs to be baptized (3:14). But Jesus impresses on John the necessity of doing the seemingly inappropriate thing: "Let it be so now; it is proper for us to do this to fulfill all righteousness" (3:15). Once again the key word *fulfill* occurs. Jesus the sinless One is identifying Himself with the sinful position of His fellow Israelites by being baptized like them. His identification with them here anticipates His complete identification with sinners when He bears their sins on the cross.

Hence, for Jesus to be baptized is not improper, but supremely proper. It is fulfillment. God's plan is that Jesus should in His sinlessness be identified with sinful Israel. In this way "all righteousness" is fulfilled. Certainly Jesus' own action is righteous. But for *all righteousness* to be fulfilled means something more. This one act of Jesus somehow signifies the fulfillment of all the righteousness spoken in the law. Israel was a disobedient people; they did not obey the law and did not show righteousness. Jesus' act not only shows perfect righteousness but also shows the first stages of the unfolding of God's plan to save people from their unrighteousness.

Following the baptism a voice comes from heaven, "This is my Son, whom I love; with him I am well pleased" (Matthew 3:17). This voice first of all expresses God's special approval of the baptism. It is indeed the sign of "all righteousness" being fulfilled. Second, the voice combines the language of Psalm 2:7; Isaiah 42:1; and possibly Genesis 22:2. Thus it shows that the Law (Genesis 22:2), the Prophets (Isaiah 42:1), and the Writings (Psalm 2:7) simultaneously come to focus in Jesus. The language of Jesus being God's Son is also reminiscent of the earlier quote from Hosea 11:1, where Israel is the son. Israel's sonship and Isaac's sonship is now fulfilled in the coming of the true and final Son, the Son in the supreme sense of the word.

After these events Jesus is led into the wilderness (Matthew 4:1–11). He experiences temptations parallel to Israel's temptations in the wilderness. Whereas Israel succumbed to temptation again and again, Jesus as the true, obedient Son successfully resists. He counters the devil's temptations by quoting three times from the book of Deuteronomy, the book reflecting on Israel's experiences in the wilderness (Deuteronomy 8:3; 6:16, 13).

Jesus then begins His public ministry. He repeats John the Baptist's message concerning the coming of God's reign (Matthew 4:17). But in addition, He demonstrates God's saving power by beginning to gather disciples, the core of the new people of God, and by healing the sick, analogous to God's promise of delivering Israel from the diseases of Egypt (Deuteronomy 7:15; cf. 28:59–60).

The character of Jesus' ministry can well be summed up in His proclamation: "Repent, for the kingdom of heaven is near" (4:17). In Jesus' own actions of healing and casting out demons, the kingdom of heaven, that is, God's reign to save His people, was not only shown to be near, but actively manifested (12:28). The Old Testament prophets had looked forward to a final great day of salvation, when God would appear in glory (Isaiah 60:1–4, 19–22), when He would defeat His enemies (Zechariah 14:1–3; Zephaniah 3:8), when Israel would enjoy His blessing (Isaiah 65:17–25; Ezekiel 36–37). God would rule over all (Isaiah 52:7–10; Zechariah 14:9; Daniel 7:9–14). The phrase "the kingdom of heaven" or "kingdom of God" sums up this Old Testament expectation. In Jesus' ministry it becomes obvious that God's saving reign is to be established in two stages. Jesus' teaching and miracles bring in the first stage, when salvation is accomplished through Him. His second coming brings in the second stage, when salvation is brought to completion and consummation. Thus Jesus can say at one time that the kingdom of heaven has come already (Matthew 12:28; cf. 21:43) and at another that it will come in the future (13:43; cf. 20:21; 25:34; 26:29). There is no contradiction here, because God's reign is established in stages: first through Jesus Himself as the firstfruits, then in those who belong to Him (cf. 1 Corinthians 15:23). Many of the parables illustrate these truths by speaking of a process of growth or waiting before a final harvest or a final meeting (e.g., Matthew 13:24–43; 25:1–46).[2]

Thus the coming of the kingdom of God sweeps into its orbit virtually the whole of the Old Testament, since the Old Testament pervasively speaks of God, His rule, His kingly wisdom, and His salvation. This tremendous breadth of significance to Jesus' ministry nicely complements the details in the correspondences that Matthew is concerned to point out in his fulfillment sayings. The details do not indicate merely a slavish one-to-one mechanical matching. Rather, they anchor and confirm the magnitude of the massive global theological connections. Conversely, the global theme of the coming kingdom gathers under one head the meaning of all the details and demonstrates their organic relation to one another in the plan of God.

All in all, Matthew 1–4 shows a host of parallels with the events of the Exodus and Israel's experiences in the wilderness and sums up the significance of these parallels in the announcement of the coming kingdom. Matthew 1–4 thereby shows that Jesus fulfills the purposes and meanings contained in the earlier history of Israel. Since it is a narrative, Matthew 1–4 concentrates on fulfillment of the narrative portions of the five books of Moses. Matthew 5–7, by contrast, contains a large amount of teaching of Jesus. It thereby shows most specifically Jesus' fulfillment of the didactic portions of the books of Moses.

Matthew 5–7

Let us trace out in some detail the connections of Matthew 5–7 with the didactic and legal parts of Exodus through Deuteronomy. To begin with, Matthew 5 opens with an event parallel to Mount Sinai. Jesus speaks from a mountain to His disciples, as God spoke from Mount Sinai to Israel, His "discipled" nation. Jesus begins with a series of blessings, corresponding to the curses and threats that issue from Mount Sinai (Exodus 19:12–13, 20–24; cf. Deuteronomy 28:15–68).

These parallels between Matthew 5 and Mount Sinai do not seem to be merely accidental. Remember that Matthew 5 is placed immediately after the events in Matthew 1–4 that introduce the themes of fulfillment and the parallels with Israel's experience of deliverance and testing in the wilderness. Since Matthew 1–4 has already prepared us to expect parallels, we can say with some confidence that Matthew 5 is indeed to be understood as picturing a kind of new giving of the law from a new Mount Sinai. At Mount Sinai the voice of God spoke directly from heaven, and further revelations were mediated through Moses. In Matthew 5 the revelation comes through the voice of Jesus who is both God and the final Moses.

In the beatitudes Jesus sets forth blessings in an extravagant and paradoxical way. He promises truly extravagant blessings, namely, "the kingdom of heaven" (Matthew 5:3–9), "the earth" (5:5), to "see God" (5:8), and to be "called sons of God" (5:9). The blessings overthrow the existing order of things by being given to the weak rather than the strong and prominent. They set out standards for Jesus' disciples, the people who belong to God. The next few verses after the beatitudes (Matthew 5:13–16) show how the disciples are to be salt and light to the world, analogous to Israel's function of being a distinctly holy nation and a kingdom of priests (Exodus 19:5–6).

Following these verses setting forth the character of His disciples, Jesus embarks on an exposition of the law. Matthew 5:17–20 contains a comprehensive statement concerning the fact that Jesus has come to fulfill the Law and the Prophets. Because of the importance of these verses, we will devote a separate discussion to them below. Taken together, the verses 1–20 provide the introductory framework for the details given in the rest of Jesus' sermon. The remainder of the Sermon on the Mount in Matthew 5:21–7:29 can be conveniently divided into several sections, as follows:

- 5:21–37 Teaching related to some of the Ten Commandments
  - 5:21–26 Murder (See also Exodus 20:13)
  - 5:27–32 Adultery (See also Exodus 20:14)
  - 5:33–37 Oaths (relating to misuse of God's name, Exodus 20:7, and possibly also to the commandment not to bear false witness)
- 5:38–47 Principles of retribution
  - 5:38–42 Balanced recompense (related to Exodus 21:24–25; Leviticus 24:20; Deuteronomy 19:21)
  - 5:43–47 Love your enemy (See also Leviticus 19:18)
- 6:1–18 Specific practices of worship
  - 6:1–4 Almsgiving
  - 6:5–15 Prayer
  - 6:16–18 Fasting
- 6:19–34 Worldly cares
- 7:1–23 Discriminating between good and evil
  - 7:1–6 Judge yourself first
  - 7:7–12 Ask for good gifts
  - 7:13–23 Two ways, one to life and the other to destruction
- 7:24–27 The importance of obeying Jesus' words
- 7:28–29 The authority of Jesus' teaching

All of the sections of the Sermon on the Mount deal in some way with abuses and misunderstandings of the law that had arisen in Jesus' day. In particular, Jesus repeatedly stresses the significance of correct motives. His focus on the heart contrasts with the externality and legalism promoted by Pharisaic religion (see Matthew 15:1–20). According to Jesus it is not enough to refrain from murder and adultery in a merely external sense. One must keep one's heart from feelings of anger and lust. Such feelings lead toward murder and adultery and already represent sins of the heart.

Jesus' stress on proper motivations agrees with material found in the law. The tenth commandment concerning covetousness is entirely about motivation. The two great commandments to love God and love one's neighbor (Deuteronomy 6:5; Leviticus 19:18) include the level of motivation. The mention of circumcised or uncircumcised heart and hardness of heart recognize the necessity of inward cleansing (Deuteronomy 10:16; 29:4; 30:6). Yet Jesus' concentration on issues of the heart represents a shift of focus in comparison with the law of Moses. In agreement with the overall external, earthly character of Mosaic worship, the stress of the law is *predominantly* on externals. The Ten Commandments, as we observed in chapter 8, focus in their obvious meaning on the most obvious violations. The laws concerning clean and unclean foods separate good and evil on a basis of external symbolic order, not on the basis of clean and unclean hearts. The sacrificial system is rooted on earth and is only a copy of heavenly reality.

The most striking aspect of Jesus' teaching is its own intrinsic authority and its originality. The Pharisees and the scribes constantly appealed to earlier authorities. They said, "Rabbi so-and-so taught that we should do this or that." The earlier rabbis to whom they appealed were in turn dependent on the authority of Moses the original lawgiver. They constantly quoted from the law. But Jesus speaks on His own authority, as the new Moses. Matthew comments on the whole Sermon on the Mount by saying, "When Jesus had finished saying these things, the crowds were amazed at his teaching, because he taught as one who had authority, and not as their teachers of the law" (7:28–29). In fact, seldom except in situations of controversy does Jesus quote from the law.[3] Even in the Sermon on the Mount the bulk of Jesus' teaching contains no *direct* mention of the law (Matthew 6–7). And when Jesus does introduce teaching related to the law in Matthew 5, He several times says, "You have heard that it was said, but *I* say to you" (5:21, 27, 31, 33, 38). Thus Jesus indirectly claims to have an authority equal to the authority of Moses.

Jesus' teaching does not contradict the true meaning of the law of Moses, but neither is it a straightforward exposition of the obvious meaning of Moses. For example, Jesus intensifies the punishments of the law. Now that the kingdom of heaven is near, the copy is about to be superseded by the reality. The preliminary is about to be superseded by the final. Jesus therefore speaks of the final judgment, the judgment of hell, rather than merely the preliminary judgments embodied in portions of the law of Moses. "Anyone who says, 'You fool!' will be in danger of the fire of hell" (Matthew 5:22). "It is better for you to lose one part of your body than for your whole body to go into hell" (5:30). Jesus says to His disciples, "For I tell you that unless your righteousness surpasses that of the Pharisees and the teachers of the law, you will certainly not enter the kingdom of heaven" (5:20). Jesus here confirms what we argued with respect to punishments of the law, namely, that the external punishments enjoined by Moses foreshadow the ultimate punishments to be executed by God.

Let us now see how each of the sections of the Sermon on the Mount show a connection to the law of Moses. Matthew 5:21–37 takes up issues related to the Ten Commandments, in particular the commandments concerning murder, adultery, and misuse of God's name. Legalistic religion of Jesus' day tended to say that people were free from sin if they kept themselves from literal murder and adultery. Jesus corrects the misuse by pointing to the importance of motives. But He also points out the urgency of purity by speaking of severe judgments, including hell.

In His discussion of divorce in 5:31–32, Jesus corrects a further abuse. Deuteronomy 24:1–4 in its original context was a regulation and restraint on divorce. It tacitly permitted divorce but did not condone it. Some of the Pharisaic teaching, however, had used the passage as a justification for loose divorce practice. Jesus corrects this abuse, but also goes beyond the direct teaching of Moses by indicating that divorce is morally evil. His teachings are in harmony with Genesis 2:23–24, as we are reminded in Matthew 19:4–6. But in the context of Matthew 5:31–32 His teaching on divorce rests on His own authority rather than merely on an appeal to Genesis.

On the matter of oaths in 5:33–37 Jesus corrects an abuse illustrated in Matthew 23:16–22. Pharisaic teaching relieved people of the obligation to fulfill oaths if the oaths were not sworn using God's name but using certain substitutes, such as swearing by the temple or by the altar. But Jesus goes beyond the direct teaching of Moses by abolishing oaths altogether. Oaths are only necessary because of human sinfulness. In sinful situations where people do not always keep their word, oaths are a means of introducing stronger threats and obligations in order to protect the communication of truth. Indeed, even within the church the possibility of sin remains, so that Paul must on occasion call God to witness what he is saying (Romans 1:9; 2 Corinthians 1:23; 1 Thessalonians 2:5, 10). Jesus is not establishing another external rule to supersede the external rules of the Old Testament; if He were, it would not only contradict Paul but be in tension with His own constant focus in the Sermon on the Mount on the intentions of the heart.

Even though Jesus is not setting forth an external rule with no exceptions, His teaching does imply a change in the practice of His disciples in comparison with the time of Moses. The pure truthfulness of the kingdom of heaven is beginning to alter forms that were temporary measures foreshadowing that truthfulness.

In Matthew 5:38–47 Jesus corrects an abuse of "eye for eye, tooth for tooth." In the Old Testament this rule was intended as a guide for the judges, who were authorized by God to supervise the execution of punishments. But it was abused by people who saw it as an excuse for personal vengeance.

Jesus corrects the abuse but does not merely stop there. He does not merely say, "Do not seek personal vengeance, because vengeance belongs to God and to his specially appointed agents. Go to the state authorities and have them take up your cause." Rather, Jesus invokes the principle of balanced recompense in an altered way. The old rule said that if Al does damage to Bill, Al must in turn suffer equivalent damage and restore the damage that has been done to Bill. Jesus' new principle makes a subtle alteration. If Al does damage to Bill, Bill willingly has Al do it again. The damage goes twice in the same direction rather than being reversed. The intentions, however, are reversed by Bill's willingness to suffer loss and to do good to Al.

Something very peculiar is going on in Jesus' injunctions. The principle of retribution, "As you have done, it will be done to you," gets altered into a very similar but structurally transformed principle, "Do to others as you would have them do to you" (Matthew 7:12; Luke 6:31). Jesus does not directly say how His disciples receive power to give to other people in this way. But He does point to the origin of their behavior in God Himself. "Be perfect, therefore, as your heavenly Father is perfect" (Matthew 5:48). As members of the heavenly kingdom, His disciples are to replicate the pattern of their heavenly Father (5:45).

We receive one further hint from Matthew 5:43, "You have heard that it was said, 'Love your neighbor and hate your enemy.'" The actual Mosaic commandment is "Love your neighbor" (Leviticus 19:18). The added phrase "and hate your enemy" is found nowhere in the Old Testament but is a distortion of the meaning of the original. Jesus thus corrects a misunderstanding. But at the same time His emphasis introduces an atmosphere somewhat different from the atmosphere of Mosaic times. Moses never commanded the people to hate *their* enemies (see Exodus 23:4–5; Leviticus 19:17–18), but in a certain sense the Israelites were indeed to hate God's enemies, the Canaanites. The practice of holy war and the separation from evil peoples introduced an element that might properly be called "hatred."

Christians also are to hate evil (Jude 22). But because of the power of Christ's resurrection and the power of the gospel, evil people are often not simply destroyed but renewed and changed into good people. Retribution and destruction of sin operate differently after Christ has come as sin bearer. Thus Jesus' exhortations to give back good for evil are appropriate for those who are constantly renewed inwardly. As heirs of the kingdom of heaven (Matthew 5:3, 10) they are not merely to operate in terms of normal earthly patterns of retribution, but a heavenly pattern of giving good for evil because Christ did the same for them. In a special way Christ's death and resurrection bring about a new abundance of blessing and healing that give His disciples inward power.

Jesus' teaching in the Sermon on the Mount is still incomplete in some respects. He does not speak of all the implications of His death and resurrection until after they are accomplished (John 16:25). Nevertheless, what He says here is consistent with what we have seen about the unique calling of the church and of Christians individually. Since they are citizens of the heavenly kingdom their purity is continually renewed by their union with Christ. A special retribution to repair damage to their purity is no longer necessary.

Next, consider Matthew 6:1–18. Jesus' teaching corrects abuses of current religious practices concerning almsgiving, prayer, and fasting. As before He stresses the importance of the intentions of the heart. He goes beyond mere correction of abuse by pointing people to the reward coming from God the Father who is in heaven (6:1, 4, 6, 9, 14–15, 18), thereby reminding people of what He has said concerning the kingdom of heaven and its coming in His own ministry. The practices of worship are to be transformed inwardly because of the coming of a new era where God establishes His saving reign. The emphasis on inward intention as well as the mention of the new era indirectly implies the transformation of outward ordinances for worship, such as the temple, the sacrifices, and the Jewish feasts. Jesus does not here mention how such a transformation is to take place. But Matthew has earlier noted that Jesus is to be called Immanuel, meaning "God with us" (1:23). The definitive dwelling of God with human beings through Jesus must necessarily supersede the temple, which is the shadowy form of God's dwelling.

In Matthew 6:19–34 Jesus exhorts His disciples not to be anxious about worldly cares. Such exhortation runs parallel to Deuteronomy 8 with its reminder that "man does not live on bread alone but on every word that comes from the mouth of the LORD" (Deuteronomy 8:3). The Holy Place of the tabernacle, with its lampstand and bread of the Presence, testifies to the same need for people to look to God for their supply of needs. In some respects Jesus says what the Old Testament has said all along. But He also adds as its basis, "Seek first his kingdom and his righteousness, and all these things will be given to you as well" (Matthew 6:33). The mention of God's kingdom and treasures in heaven (6:19–21) orients His disciples toward the realities of the kingdom of heaven that is brought near through Jesus Himself and His ministry.

Matthew 7:1–23 contains several paragraphs dealing predominantly with problems of discriminating between good and evil. The distinctions of the law between sin and righteousness, between holy and common, and between clean and unclean are all part of the background for the distinctions that the disciples of Jesus must now make. But Jesus does not simply tell His disciples that the law is their basis for discrimination. He does not speak simply as a scribe might have spoken. Once again Jesus teaches with His own authority. In 7:1–6 Jesus teaches that His disciples must not regard themselves as lords whose first responsibility is to straighten out others. They must first make discriminate judgments concerning their own failures. Their heavenly Father knows what is good and what is evil and will give them good gifts (7:7–12). They must concentrate first of all on discriminating two ways, the way of life and the way of destruction (7:13–14). These two ways are to be distinguished by the fruit of obedience in life (7:15–27).

Jesus' teaching in 7:1–27 has some fascinating connections with many strands of Mosaic teaching. The general principle of just recompense is still operative. "As you have done, it will be done to you" becomes "For in the same way you judge others, you will be judged, and with the measure you use, it will be measured to you" (7:2). An analogous principle of justice, "Do to others what you would have them do to you," "sums up the Law and the Prophets" (7:12). The distinction of holy and common is taken up in the illustration with dogs and pigs (7:6). The discrimination between types of trees in 7:15–20 is similar to the discrimination between clean and unclean foods in Mosaic times. The building of the house on a rock, standing for obedience to Jesus' teaching, is analogous to the care in building the tabernacle, which depended on obedience to the teaching of Moses. But these connections are distant and vague in character. Jesus does not stress the connections in any obvious way, because His authority does not depend on establishing such connections.

Matthew 5:17–20

Now we return to the summary statement in Matthew 5:17–20:

> Do not think that I have come to abolish the Law or the Prophets; I have not come to abolish them but to fulfill them. I tell you the truth, until heaven and earth disappear, not the smallest letter, not the least stroke of a pen, will by any means disappear from the Law until everything is accomplished. Anyone who breaks one of the least of these commandments and teaches others to do the same will be called least in the kingdom of heaven, but whoever practices and teaches these commands will be called great in the kingdom of heaven. For I tell

you that unless your righteousness surpasses that of the Pharisees and the teachers of the law, you will certainly not enter the kingdom of heaven.

As we have seen, Jesus teaches on a mount in a manner analogous to Moses. He speaks as one who has authority (Matthew 7:29). He introduces new powers of a new kingdom (4:23–25), new blessings (5:1–12), new definitions of a circle of disciples (5:13–16). In the verses following Matthew 5:17–20 He will introduce fresh teaching relating to the law of Moses and to the Jews' religious service to God. The radical character of Jesus' teaching as well as the radical character of His ministry as a whole might well lead to the question, "Are you abolishing Moses? Are you starting all over again?"

Jesus anticipates just such questions in Matthew 5:17. In verse 17 He makes a general statement about both the Law and the Prophets. In verses 18–20 He focuses on the Law, because in the context of the Sermon on the Mount He is primarily engaged in fulfilling the Law (but "law" in verse 18 may easily be an inclusive use, covering "the Law and the Prophets" of verse 17).

In verse 17 He juxtaposes two possibilities, abolishing and fulfilling. Fulfilling is clearly the opposite of abolishing. But what kind of opposite is it? Some have supposed that in this verse Jesus is affirming that He will by His own obedience perfectly keep the law. But the context in Matthew concerns what Jesus teaches, not what He obeys. Doubtless fulfillment may have many ramifications, including Jesus' obedience to the law. But primarily Jesus claims that His own teaching fulfills the *teaching* of the law.

If so, *how* does Jesus' teaching constitute "fulfillment"? Some interpreters have argued that the word "fulfill" here means "confirm" or "establish."[4] According to this view Jesus reasserts the true meaning of the law against Pharisaic distortions, and thereby confirms its validity.

This view, I believe, is nearly correct. Jesus' teaching in 5:21–48 does vindicate the law against distortions and does harmonize with its true intention. But I would argue that in verse 17 Jesus claims something more. The coming of the kingdom of heaven means a fundamental advance in the working out of God's purposes. God's promises of His reign and His salvation, as given in the Old Testament, are being accomplished. What the law foreshadowed and embodied in symbols and shadows is now coming into realization. What was earthly and preliminary in the function of the law is now fulfilled in heavenly realities. Jesus' teaching represents not simply the reiteration of the law but a step forward, bringing the purposes of the law into realization. The law is to be written on the hearts of His disciples (see Jeremiah 31:31–34). Jesus does not assert merely a static continuation of the force of the law, but rather a dynamic advance—in fact, the definitive fulfillment.

What was temporary and shadowy in the form of the Old Testament law is superseded, now that God's glory and kingly power are being manifested in the very person of Jesus and in His ministry. The promise of the kingdom of heaven involves the intensification of all that served to manifest God in the Old Testament. All is transformed by the supremacy and weightiness of God Himself coming to save. The law also undergoes transformation. The final revelation of God is surely in harmony and resonance with the old; indeed, it involves the coming of the old into the destiny to which it pointed. But also this new and climactic revelation bursts the bounds of what anyone could have reckoned from the old.

Commentators have expressed this view in a variety of ways. For example, Calvin says,

> By these words [Jeremiah 31:33–34] he [God] is so far from departing from the former covenant, that, on the contrary, he declares, that it will be confirmed and ratified, when it shall be succeeded by the new. This is also the meaning of Christ's words, when he says, that *he came to fulfil the law*: for he actually fulfilled it, by quickening, with his Spirit, the dead letter, and then exhibiting, in reality, what had hitherto appeared only in figures.[5]

The first sentence from Calvin might appear to be asserting no more than mere static confirmation of the law. But the later contrast between reality and figures, and the idea of the new succeeding the old, introduce an element of advance.

John Murray says,

> Hence what Jesus means is that he came to realize the full measure of the intent and purpose of the law and the prophets. He came to complete, to consummate, to bring to full fruition and perfect fulfilment

the law and the prophets. Jesus refers to the function of validating and confirming the law and the prophets and includes much more than the fulfilment of the predictions of the Old Testament regarding himself. He means that the whole process of revelation deposited in the Old Testament finds in him its completion, its fulfilment, its confirmation, its validation. Still more, it finds in him its embodiment. To use John's terms, "grace and truth came by Jesus Christ" (John 1:17).[6]

The words *confirm* and *validate* by themselves might assert only static maintenance of the law, but Murray introduces terms like *complete* and *consummate* to indicate an advance.

Donald A. Carson gives a more precise formulation as follows:

> Jesus fulfills the Law and the Prophets in that they point to him, and he is their fulfillment. . . . Therefore we give *plēroō* ("fulfill") exactly the same meaning as in the formula quotations, which in the prologue (Matthew 1–2) have already laid great stress on the prophetic nature of the Old Testament and the way it points to Jesus. . . . [J]ust as Jesus fulfilled Old Testament prophecies by his person and actions, so he fulfilled Old Testament law by his teaching. In no case does this "abolish" the Old Testament as canon, any more than the obsolescence of the Levitical sacrificial system abolishes tabernacle ritual as canon. Instead, the Old Testament's real and abiding authority must be understood through the person and teaching of him to whom it points and who so richly fulfills it. . . . Jesus is not primarily engaged there [in Matthew 5:21–48] in extending, annulling, or intensifying Old Testament law, but in showing the direction in which it points, on the basis of his own authority (to which, again, the Old Testament points). This may work out in any particular case to have the same practical effect as "intensifying" the law or "annulling" some element; but the reasons for that conclusion are quite different.[7]

Carson's idea of fulfillment clearly agrees with all that we have seen up to this point in studying Matthew and his theology of the kingdom, as well as what we have derived from our study of the Mosaic law itself. Carson preserves the normal force of "fulfill" within the context of Matthew, and explains how Jesus can confirm the law and make advances as He gives the rest of the Sermon on the Mount.

One major alternative is to interpret "fulfill" as meaning simply "confirm" and nothing more. In such a case it would imply maintaining the law in place, but would not imply any sense of advance or transformation of the law. But there are major objections to this alternative.

1. The Greek word *plēroō* does not normally have the sense "confirm."[8] Though the theological idea of fulfillment implies confirmation, it is richer than mere confirmation. Induction from other instances where the New Testament speaks of fulfilling the Scriptures indicates that the bringing to realization of forward-pointing aspects of Old Testament revelation is in view.[9]

2. Literal confirmation of the law, in the sense that every letter of the law still requires the same form of obedience as in Old Testament times, is in tension with what the rest of the New Testament and Matthew as well indicates about changes in the observance of the law (Matthew 5:33–37).[10]

3. It is difficult under this view to explain why the text uses the Greek word *plēroō* ("fulfill") rather than the words *bebaioō* or *histēmi* ("establish, confirm"), since the latter words would be less confusing.[11] The use of *plēroō* with the sense "confirm" would be all the more confusing because elsewhere Matthew repeatedly uses this same word *plēroō* as a significant key word to state his theme that Jesus fulfills the whole Old Testament.[12]

4. The meaning "fulfill" is more compatible with the breadth of Matthew's teaching on fulfillment in the kingdom of heaven. The kingdom of heaven involves dramatic, spectacular advance over Old Testament religion, as well as building in harmony with it.[13]

Once we have determined the force of "fulfill" along the lines indicated by Carson, the meaning of the subsequent verses is easier to establish. Some further quotes from Carson's commentary may serve to indicate the correct lines of interpretation. With regard to verse 18 Carson says,

> The reference to "jot and tittle" establishes [the extent of Old Testament authority]: it will not do to reduce the reference to moral law, or the law as a whole but not necessarily its parts, or to God's will in some general sense. . . . The two "until" clauses answer [the question

of duration of the Old Testament's authority]. The first—"until heaven and earth disappear"—simply means "until the end of the age": i.e., not quite "never". . . but "never, as long as the present world order persists." The second—"until everything is accomplished"—is more difficult. . . . *panta* ("everything") is best understood to refer to everything in the law, considered under the law's prophetic function—viz., until all these things have taken place as prophesied. This is not simply pointing to the Cross. . . , nor simply to the end of the age. . . . [T]he entire divine purpose prophesied in Scripture must take place; not one jot or tittle will fail of its fulfillment. . . . Thus the first "until" clause focuses strictly on the duration of Old Testament authority but the second returns to considering its nature; it reveals God's redemptive purposes and points to their fulfillment, their "accomplishment," in Jesus and the eschatological kingdom he is now introducing and will one day consummate.[14]

Concerning verse 19 Carson continues,

The entire Law and the Prophets are not scrapped by Jesus' coming but fulfilled. Therefore the commandments of these Scriptures—even the least of them (on distinctions in the law, see on 22:36; 23:23)—must be practiced. But the nature of the practicing has already been affected by vv. 17–18. The law pointed forward to Jesus and his teaching; so it is properly obeyed by conforming to his word. As it points to him, so he, in fulfilling it, establishes what continuity it has, the true direction to which it points and the way it is to be obeyed. Thus ranking in the kingdom turns on the degree of conformity to Jesus' teaching as that teaching fulfills Old Testament revelation.[15]

Thus Matthew 5:17–19 asserts in a sweeping and direct fashion what the rest of Matthew illustrates in detail: Jesus in His person and His ministry brings to realization and fulfillment the whole warp and woof of Old Testament revelation, including the revelation of the law. The whole law points to Him, and its purposes find their realization in Him. All the commandments of the law are binding on Christians (7:19), but the way in which they are binding is determined by the authority of Christ and the fulfillment that takes place in His work.

When we become disciples of Christ, our lives are transformed by our fellowship with Him. We become participants in the kingdom of heaven (5:3, 10), under the care of our heavenly Father. We become imitators of our Father (5:45), so that Jesus' commandment makes sense, "Be perfect, therefore, as your heavenly Father is perfect" (5:48). Such is the fulfillment of that great commandment from Moses, "Be holy because I, the LORD your God, am holy" (Leviticus 19:2).

As disciples of Christ we are to "obey everything I have commanded you" (Matthew 28:20). Since Jesus commands us to practice and teach even the "least of these commandments" of the law (5:19), we are bound to do so. But we do so as disciples who have learned how to discern the function of the law of Moses as a pointer to the realities of Jesus Christ our Lord. The way in which each law is fulfilled in Christ determines the way in which it is to be observed now. Since the law foreshadows the righteousness of Christ and the kingdom of heaven, the practice of the law in the deepest sense takes the form of replicating the character and grace of Christ in our lives and imitating our heavenly Father. To have this fellowship with and obedience to Christ is no burden, as Christ Himself says, "Come to me, all you who are weary and burdened, and I will give you rest. Take my yoke upon you and learn from me, for I am gentle and humble in heart, and you will find rest for your souls. For my yoke is easy and my burden is light" (Matthew 11:28–30). The rabbis spoke of commitment to the true God and His law as "the yoke of the kingdom of heaven," "the yoke of the law," and "the yoke of commandments."[16] But the rabbis did not anticipate that the law would be fulfilled in the yoke of Jesus Christ.[17]

Pentecost in Matthew

The coming of Jesus represents a transformation of the law and of its relation to God's people. How, then, is the law of Moses to be fulfilled now, in this new age, in the light of the resurrection of Christ? We can answer the question properly only by understanding the nature of Christ's work and its consequences.

The transformation of the law does not take place all in a moment. There are at least two stages, specifically, the stage of Jesus' earthly life and the stage following His resurrection. If we wish, we may make finer distinctions and list even more stages, as they are given to us in the outline of Luke—Acts: angelic announcements of the dawn of salvation

(Luke 1), the birth of Jesus (Luke 2), the beginning of John the Baptist's public ministry (Luke 3:1–20), the baptism of Jesus (Luke 3:21–23), the beginning of Jesus' public ministry (Luke 4:14–15), the Passion (Luke 22:1–23:56), the Resurrection (Luke 24:1–12), the Ascension (Acts 1:9–11), Pentecost (Acts 2), the spread of the gospel to Samaria (Acts 8), the first Gentile converts (Acts 10), and so on.

Luke, by providing us with the book of Acts, shows in some detail how Christian faith works out in the context of Jesus' completed work of salvation. We see the church struggling over the status of Gentiles and the relevance of the law of Moses (Acts 11; 15). We see that the Holy Spirit, as opposed to distinctive obedience to Jewish law, constitutes the mark of salvation and incorporation into the chosen people of God (11:17; 15:8–11).

Matthew, by contrast, gives us no second volume; there is no Matthean form of the book of Acts. He does, however, give us a brief sketch of the meaning of Acts through the final words of his book, namely, the Great Commission of 28:16–20. These words indicate the nature of the transition to the new, postresurrection era, because, as we shall see, they express in a brief form some of the same truths that we find in the more elaborate picture in Acts.

The Great Commission in Matthew is first and foremost a commission to spread the gospel. In this respect, it condenses the same truths that Jesus expresses in the commission in Acts 1:8 and the subsequent narrative of Acts. Acts spells out how the gospel spread, beginning from Jerusalem but not stopping until it reached Rome, the center of the Empire and therefore a fitting symbol of the universal outreach of the gospel.

But the Great Commission is not merely a bare command to spread the gospel. It contains a promise and an assertion as well. "Surely I will be with you always, to the very end of the age," Jesus promises. The promise of continued presence at all times and places ("all nations") points to the fact that His presence takes a new form—the form defined more precisely by the Pentecostal giving of the Spirit. Such presence of the Spirit, which is also the presence of Jesus Himself, empowers and motivates the proclaiming and discipling. Second, the Commission contains an assertion, "All authority in heaven and on earth has been given to me." This assertion serves to announce the realities most closely associated with the ascension of Christ and His sitting at God's right hand. It thus briefly adumbrates the fuller narrative in Acts 1 and the interpretations of Christ's rule in the New Testament epistles. Moreover, it also directly supplies backing for the Commission: "Go therefore, . . ." that is, "go on the basis of My universal authority and claim to the allegiance of all nations." It thus anticipates the declarations in Acts of Jesus' Lordship (Acts 2:36; 10:36, 42; 17:31). In sum, Matthew 28:16–20 anticipates in highly condensed form the complete narrative given in the book of Acts.

Obedience to the Law in the Great Commission

Notably, God's commandments have a continuing role according to the Great Commission. Those who receive the gospel are to be taught "to obey everything I have commanded you." Moreover, the Commission includes not merely announcement of the truth but "making disciples." A disciple is nothing without a master whom he must obey. The master, in this case, is clearly Jesus, and what the disciples obey is "everything I have commanded you."

The rest of the Gospel of Matthew is organized in such a way that it leads naturally up to these verses. As is widely acknowledged, the Gospel contains five large blocks of Jesus' teaching, namely, Matthew 5–7 (the Sermon on the Mount), Matthew 10 (instructions on sending the Twelve), Matthew 13 (parables concerning mysteries of the kingdom of heaven), Matthew 18 (shepherding and caring for one another in the community), and Matthew 22–25 (prophetic denunciations and warnings, including parables about rewards and judgments). A comparison with Mark and Luke shows that Matthew has sometimes arranged this teaching material topically rather than merely chronologically. These blocks are closely linked to the phrase "everything I have commanded you" in 28:20. By the very organization of his gospel Matthew has provided a kind of handbook of Jesus' teaching relevant to the postresurrection duties of disciples.

Among the duties of disciples we must include obedience to the Old Testament law. "Everything I have commanded you" naturally includes the Sermon on the Mount, and within the Sermon it includes Jesus' statement about the continuing force of the law:

> I tell you the truth, until heaven and earth disappear, not the smallest letter, not the least stroke of a pen, will by any means disappear from the Law until everything is accomplished. Anyone who breaks one of the least of these commandments and teaches others to do the same will be called least in the kingdom of heaven, but whoever practices and teaches these commands will be called great in the kingdom of heaven. (5:18–19).

The claims in both 28:18–20 and 5:17–20 are sweeping and powerful. On this basis some people have understandably not hesitated to draw strong inferences about the obligation of Christians to practice thorough, meticulous observance of the entire law of Moses:

> [Christ] says that a person's relation to the kingdom of God is determined by meticulous observance of the least details of the law. The breaking of the very least stipulation of the law generates God's displeasure; taking an erroneous teaching position with respect to the details of the law (e.g., that the exhaustive details of God's law no longer bind Christians or this period of history) does the same.[18]

But, as we have seen, the word *fulfill* and various other elements in the Sermon on the Mount point away from understanding New Testament obedience to the law of Moses as a purely static continuation of the Old. They imply a profound transformation of the law, because the law is brought to fulfillment. The kingdom of God has come. The last days—eschatology in a broad sense—have begun. Similarly, the Great Commission itself contains suggestions of the same transformations and discontinuities.

To begin with, the Great Commission speaks of making disciples "of all nations." The kingdom of God breaks the bounds of Israel and the elements in Mosaic law that functioned to separate Israel from all other nations. Matthew alone of all the Gospels has the radical statement, "Therefore I tell you that the kingdom of God will be taken away from you and given to a people who will produce its fruit" (Matthew 21:43).

Next, the Great Commission indicates a change in criteria for membership in the people of God. In Acts, of course, many Jewish

Christians of the Pharisaic party still continued to believe for a time that salvation came by incorporation into the Jews and practice of Jewish distinctives (Acts 15:5). Matthew refutes this idea, not directly as in Acts 15, but through an indication of the true basis for membership in God's people, when he speaks of "baptizing them in the name of the Father, and of the Son and of the Holy Spirit" (Matthew 28:19). What is the meaning of this baptism? Baptism as a cleansing rite fulfills the baptism of John the Baptist, which in turn was partly based on the cleansing rites specified by the Mosaic law. John warned people not to rely merely on their external membership in the Old Testament covenant people (Matthew 3:9–10). An eschatological judgment was coming that would sift them for their fruit (Matthew 3:10–12). In the light of coming judgment, they should repent, confess their sins, and be baptized as a symbol of the washing away of sin. The baptism mentioned in 28:19 goes beyond John's baptism, in that it is baptism "in the name of the Father, and of the Son and of the Holy Spirit." That is, this new baptism brings people into enjoyment of fellowship and blessing from God. It is parallel to the Aaronic priestly blessing of the law, which placed the name of God on Israel (Numbers 6:22–27). Significantly, the name of God now explicitly includes the name of the Son. He has died and risen, and thereby supremely revealed God and definitively opened the way to fellowship with God.

Being part of God's people is thus inaugurated by baptism, rather than by circumcision and becoming a Jew. One continues as a part of God's people by being a disciple of Jesus. A Jew of Jesus' time would have characterized his Jewishness above all as being under "the yoke of the law"—including circumcision and food laws that most vividly separated Jews from Gentiles in society. By contrast, the Great Commission characterizes the people of God by loyalty to their ever-living Master.[19] To be sure, such loyalty never implies antinomianism, but rather obedience to the teachings of the Master. These teachings, not the Law of Moses, constitute the immediate reference point for the disciple's obedience. These teachings of the Master come in their newness and in their fullness of revelation, as well as in their continuity with the Law of Moses, and the affirmations of the validity of the Law in 5:17–20.

Moreover, the teachings and the personal presence of the Master must always be held together, as they are in the Gospel of Matthew. The Great Commission itself vigorously proclaims both Jesus' teaching ("everything I have commanded you") and Jesus' personal presence to authorize, empower, and apply the teaching ("surely I will be with you always, to the very end of the age"). The Master is not a mute, idealized example, whom each person honors in the way that seems best in his own eyes. One who claims to be a disciple of the Master must show his honor and obedience to the Master very concretely, through keeping His commands.

Conversely, obedience is not a mechanical response to an abstract, disembodied commandment. The commandment is always the commandment of the Master, who Himself perfectly embodies and mightily empowers obedience through His love and personal communion through His name. This communion is inaugurated in baptism in His name, which identifies the disciple with His death and resurrection and His life forevermore.

The two sides to discipleship are aptly illustrated by the two sides to the organization of Matthew's gospel. The five teaching blocks are interspersed with five narrative blocks. Whereas the teaching blocks expand most pointedly on the commandments of the Master, the narrative blocks expand on the meaning of His personal presence, His blessings of healing, His fellowship with sinners, and His friendship with His disciples. Both the teaching blocks and the narrative blocks are brought to a climactic fulfillment in the Passion Narrative (Matthew 26–28), which fulfills both His life and His teaching.

The Broader Role of the Old Testament In the Great Commission

When we take into account the theme of fulfillment in the whole of Matthew, we cannot rigidly isolate the role of the law of Moses from the role of the Old Testament in general. The Old Testament as a whole, as well as the law of Moses in particular, finds fulfillment in the life and work of Jesus Christ. Old Testament psalms and prophecies throw additional light on how the legal parts of the Old Testament have a forward-pointing function.

In Matthew, it is possible that the various blocks of teaching and narrative each focus to some degree on the theme of fulfillment of some part of the Old Testament. The first narrative block (chapters 1–4) has a remarkable number of parallels with the narratives of Mosaic times. The first teaching block (chapters 5–7) has parallels with the teaching of Moses.

When we come to the second narrative block (chapters 8–9), we find a focus on the expansion of Jesus' ministry and of the kingdom of God. God's rule extends to the sick (8:14–17; 9:1–8), the unclean (8:1–4), the Gentiles (8:5–13), the demonized (8:28–34; 9:32–33), the dead (9:18–26), the physical elements (8:23–27), and the sinners (9:9–13). The narrative also includes a saying that hints about the expansion of the kingdom beyond the bounds of Old Testament order (9:14–17) and ends with a statement about the necessity of expansion in view of the great harvest (9:35–38). The teaching block in chapter 10 picks up on the same theme, as Jesus commissions the Twelve to participate in the expansion. Thus both narrative and teaching blocks correspond to the great period of expansion in the Old Testament, namely, the conquest under Joshua.

The third narrative block (chapters 11–12) shows the growth of misunderstanding, misinterpretation, and opposition to Jesus' ministry. The corresponding teaching block (chapter 13) contains primarily parables expounding the mystery of the kingdom. The idea of wisdom versus lack of wisdom becomes prominent. The disciples know the fundamental mysteries, whereas they are concealed from others (13:11). This contrast relates to the theme of wisdom and foolishness in Old Testament Wisdom Literature. The very genre of parable revives something of the Old Testament *mashal* or proverb, characteristic of Wisdom Literature. Matthew 13:34–35 explains Jesus' parabolic teaching by quoting from Psalm 78, a kind of wisdom psalm that encourages Israel to draw wise insights from the lessons of history. The quote itself speaks of bringing to light "things hidden since the creation of the world," an achievement possible only through the wisdom associated with creation (Proverbs 8). In Matthew 11:25–30 Jesus again speaks of revealing hidden wisdom and uses language about Himself and His "yoke" similar to what Jews had traditionally associated with personified wisdom (see Sirach 53:23–28).

The fourth narrative block (chapters 14–17) and teaching block (chapter 18) may have some focus on the responsibilities of shepherding God's people. Certainly the idea of caring properly for God's people is prominent in the teaching in chapter 18. The figure of shepherd and sheep is invoked in 18:10–14. The narrative demonstrates that Jesus, not the official religious leaders, is the true leader and shepherd of the people of Israel. Two feeding miracles occur (14:13–21; 15:29–39), as well as a statement about "the lost sheep of the house of Israel" (15:24) and criticism of the Pharisees as false shepherds (15:1–20; 16:1–12). Peter's confession (16:13–20) highlights that Jesus is the Christ, the Son of David. But Jesus knows, as Peter does not, that the Son of Man, like David, must undergo suffering for the sake of the flock (16:21–28). These materials therefore have a relation to the Old Testament figure of the Davidic king. They thereby fulfill the historical narratives that rehearse the ups and downs of the monarchy, as the leaders succeed or fail to be true shepherds. The relevant materials are found in Judges through Kings. Chronicles, Ezra, and Nehemiah are somewhat less directly related to these concerns, since they were written from a postexilic point of view, when there was no reigning king. Leadership came from governors (Nehemiah) and priests (Ezra). But the question of proper shepherds for the people was still a real one.

The fifth narrative block (19:1–21:22) and teaching block (chapters 21–25) are predominantly prophetic in nature, as Jesus speaks of the fall of Jerusalem, the final judgment, and criteria for punishment and rewards. These materials clearly represent Jesus as fulfilling the prophetic ministry of the Old Testament.

If the above analysis is correct, each narrative block is to be linked most closely with the following rather than the preceding teaching block. Such a division is also suggested by the repeated refrain, "When Jesus had finished saying [these things]," which Matthew uses to terminate the major divisions of his work (7:28; 11:1; 13:53; 19:1; 26:1).

Some further confirmation of this scheme is perhaps found in the curious fact that some key word or idea near the end of each teaching block sends us back to the Old Testament. Thus the mention of "rock" in 7:24 is reminiscent of the rock theme in the Old Testament wilderness. In addition, the idea of having God's teaching as the foundation for one's life is pervasive in the Mosaic law. The "sword" in 10:34 is reminiscent of the battles of Joshua's conquest. The mention of "treasures" of teaching in 13:52 is reminiscent of the Old Testament meditations on the treasure of wisdom (cf. Proverbs 2:4; 8:10–11, 19, 21; 16:16; Job 28). In 18:23 the mention of a king sends us back to the history of Old Testament kingship. Finally, the note of final judgment expressed in 25:46 sums up the prophetic oracles of judgment in the Old Testament.

In addition, the end of each narrative block presents us in each case with some clear-cut linkage with the corresponding Old Testament material. The first narrative block ends with a passage in which Jesus is healing and beginning to call disciples, thus forming the core of a new people of God. This action corresponds to the formation of the people of Israel in Genesis and Exodus. The narrative in 8–9 ends with Jesus' statement about the abundant harvest, which is easy to relate to the expansion and conquest of Joshua. The narrative in 11–12 ends with a statement about Jesus' true brother and sister and mother, reminiscent of the statement in Proverbs 7:4 about wisdom as a sister. Chapters 14–17 end with a reference to kingship in v. 25, reminiscent of the theme of kingship in Judges through Kings. Chapters 19:1–21:22 end with Jesus' prophetic sign of cursing the fig tree, which is reminiscent of Old Testament prophetic symbolic actions.

Not all of these correspondences are equally clear, and one may perhaps doubt whether Matthew planned this whole scheme of correlations. God as the Divine Author was of course aware of all possible correlations, but are we sure that we know what significance He intended at every point? Some caution is necessary when we are in doubt. But no one would doubt that Matthew is very interested in exploring throughout his gospel how Jesus fulfills the Old Testament. The fulfillment, as Matthew understands it, is pervasive, but often takes subtle and startlingly transformed shape.

The crucifixion makes the paradoxical character of fulfillment particularly apparent. Let us consider one by one how the various portions of the Old Testament are fulfilled within the Passion narrative of Matthew's gospel.

First, look at the fulfillment of the books of Moses. Jesus inaugurates a new covenant, parallel to the covenant inaugurated by Moses through the Passover (26:17–29). But He functions at this point not primarily as a new Moses who gives instructions to a whole nation of people, but as the father who presides over an intimate celebration with His family, and even more notably as the lamb who dies for the people. The Last Supper signifies not merely a repetition or equivalent of the Old Testament, but a transition from symbolic, shadowy sacrifice (the lamb) to final, real sacrifice (Jesus). Hence, we have a transition also from symbolic deliverance from Egypt to real deliverance from sin (26:28). We enter not into Canaan but into the kingdom of the Father (v. 29).

Second, look at the fulfillment of Joshua's conquest. Jesus pointedly refuses to use the sword (26:51–56). All His "army" deserts (v. 56). But He conquers evil and the devil by steadfast obedience (v.v. 36–46). Through His own completed work He opens the door to the new Promised Land of conquest, namely, the whole world (28:18–20).

Jesus is the fulfillment of the wisdom of Old Testament poetry in the very moment when He is treated like a fool (27:42). The multitudes misunderstand and fail to be wise even in their final interpretation of one of His utterances (27:47–49). His own last utterance quotes from the Psalms, one of the poetical books closely associated with wisdom. "My God, my God, why have you forsaken me?" But what kind of quote is this? On the surface it apparently testifies to lack of understanding, lack of wisdom, as seen in the word "why." Yet by quoting the psalm Jesus also demonstrates His understanding that He is dying as the representative sufferer, the final David. He fulfills the plan of God as prophetically foreshadowed in the psalms.

Next, Jesus is the King. But unlike earthly kings He comes to serve (20:25–28). He is the "King of the Jews," but is called such only in mockery (26:27–31; 27:37). His crown is made of thorns (26:29).

Finally, Jesus dies because He is accused of being a false prophet (26:65, 68). But in the act of dying He fulfills His own prophecies concerning His death (16:21; 20:17–19; 20:28; 21:33–42), as well as the prophecies of the Old Testament (26:31, 54, 56; 27:9–10).

Thus, fulfillment is pervasive in the gospel of Matthew. But particularly in Jesus' crucifixion, fulfillment takes deep and surprising forms, which only God in His wisdom knew beforehand. God confronts us with the scandal of a crucified redeemer. Jesus was condemned as criminal, blasphemer, and deceiver by all the prestigious people of His day, including those most knowledgeable in the Old Testament. But deeper still, we can detect underneath it all a yet more appalling note: the Scripture testifies that God the Father pronounced His condemnation because He bore our sins (20:28; 26:39; 27:46; cf. Galatians 3:13; 2 Corinthians 5:21). Who can fathom such an event?

Only a few days later, this very Jesus, who died an ignominious death, awesomely claims, "All authority in heaven and on earth has been given to me" (28:18). This supreme reversal in position fulfills all the vindicatory events and promises of the Old Testament. What does it mean for Jesus' disciples? The disciples have their loyalty defined simultaneously as loyalty to their Master and obedience to His teaching. In His resurrection, Jesus is the same Master as before, and yet He is transformed in body and exalted in authority. Contemplating the depths of the crucifixion can only increase our conviction of both the continuity and the discontinuity between then and now. In continuity, the *same* one who died has been vindicated. In discontinuity, the curse of God has been superseded by blessing, the body of dust by the body of heaven.

In my opinion, the same deep continuities and discontinuities must be introduced at least to some degree with regard to Jesus' teaching, because of the close relation between Jesus' person and teaching in the gospel of Matthew. In the Great Commission Jesus says, ". . . teaching them to obey everything I have commanded you." In this phrase He affirms strongly and clearly a thorough continuity with His previous teaching. At the same time, Jesus' command to go to all nations apparently contradicts His earlier command, "Do not go among the Gentiles or enter any town of the Samaritans. Go rather to the lost sheep of Israel" (10:5–6). Superficial reasoning would say that "everything I have commanded you" clearly includes 10:5–6, and so the disciples are bluntly commanded to do what they must simultaneously teach is forbidden. We cannot say merely that Jesus supersedes the earlier command in 10:5–6. The phrase "everything I have commanded you" affirms and endorses the command at the same moment in which it is supposedly superseded.

Only the structure of fulfillment, I would suggest, is rich enough to encompass this phenomenon in a harmonious unity. "Everything I have commanded you" must not be interpreted as mechanical, unreflective obedience to Jesus' words when taken in the abstract. "Everything" indicates comprehensive obedience; but simultaneously "I have commanded you" indicates the context of personal fellowship and understanding in which true obedience arises and is nourished and directed. Understanding Jesus' commandments, as well as understanding the Old Testament, vitally depends on appreciating that commandments as well as direct prophecies point forward to climactic fulfillment in the cross. Commandments and prophecies alike are to be interpreted as part of a story leading to a climax.

Hence, in particular, the instructions to the disciples in 10:5–6 are not an abstract, universal command for all circumstances. Rather, the restriction to Israel follows naturally from the fact that the coming of the kingdom of God through Jesus and His ministry confronted Israel with a crisis (10:7, 15, 32–42). The abundance of the harvest and the limitations of the workers also called for a limited focus for their ministry (9:35–38). More significant, the disciples are imitators of their Master, who "was sent only to the lost sheep of Israel" (15:24).

But the Crucifixion and the Resurrection redefine the scope of Jesus' "being sent" and His outreach (28:18, 20). So likewise these events *must* inevitably redefine the scope of the disciples' being sent. When we understand 10:5–6 in the light of the crisis leading to Jesus' crucifixion, we can properly grasp its purpose and general principle, namely, that the disciples are empowered by Jesus to extend His own ministry. They go in His name and with His authority and must restrict themselves to the task for which Jesus Himself is sent. Having understood the verses in this way, we can see that the same command needs fresh embodiment in altered form after Jesus' resurrection. In fact, the command is fulfilled in the Great Commission rather than being contradicted by it.

To put it another way, personal fellowship with Christ means fellowship with the crucified and risen Christ. And those events of crucifixion and resurrection, by their very nature as climactic fulfillment, redetermine the nature of obedience for us now. The whole Old Testament is properly observed by us now, not when we treat it as an abstracted word, dusty legal specifications, or mere ancient history, but as the word that is fulfilled in Christ. His own life, death, and Resurrection, as recorded in Matthew, define the sense of fulfillment, and thereby give us guidelines whereby, in continued fellowship with Him as our Master, we begin to see what remains the same and what is transformed within the system of revelation foreshadowing Him.

In summary, the whole Old Testament—Law, Conquest, Wisdom, History, Latter Prophets—is indirectly prophetic, pointing forward to the definitive fulfillment in Jesus Christ. But fulfillment, when it comes, does not endorse a flat, prosaic, purely unimaginative, and strictly straightforward reading of the Old Testament. Rather, there are unfathomable depths to the wisdom of God. All the wisdom is found in Christ (Matthew 11:25–30), and His wisdom is truly accessible to those who come to Him in humility. But humility begins with acceptance of that final scandal presented by Matthew, the scandal of the Cross and the Resurrection.

Christocentric Interpretation of the Old Testament

Let us, then, confront the major question again. Does Old Testament law remain in force now, or is it altered by the coming of Christ? Are the periods of the Old Testament and New Testament continuous with one another, so that the law is the same? Or are they discontinuous, so that the law is altered? Must we choose between affirming continuity or affirming discontinuity?

Simply to assert one side of this polarity is too simple. In the purpose of God, complexities and difficulties have been woven into Scripture itself, and we will never succeed in evading them as long as we are in this world. But these complexities are a sign of the richness of God's revelation. No hermeneutical trick will magically dissolve them, nor should we want it to.

For example, some people might suppose from a superficial reading of Matthew that Matthew asserts almost pure continuity of the law and enjoins us merely to keep the same old law in the same form as always, only now empowered with the presence of Christ. In fact, however, the coming of Christ is the coming of the kingdom of God, the climactic fulfillment of all to which the Old Testament pointed. Reality supersedes shadows. Thus radical transformation of the law is included.

Conversely, some people might suppose from a superficial reading of Paul that Paul primarily asserts only discontinuity in the law. The law is dead and gone, not to be obeyed, virtually irrelevant for Christian living (cf. Ephesians 2:15; Romans 7:1–6; Galatians 2:19). But Paul too sees the law as comprehensively fulfilled in Christ (Romans 15:4–6; 1 Corinthians 10:1–13; cf. Romans 8:4; 13:10–14). When understood properly it is a most impressive means of communion with Christ (2 Corinthians 3:15–18).

The apparent differences between Matthew and Paul arise largely from the differences between their immediate concerns and goals. Paul asserts the abolition of the law loud and clear, lest anyone miss it and destroy the unity of Jews and Gentiles as free people in Christ. Matthew asserts the continuation of the law loud and clear, lest anyone miss it and think that Jesus is not the true Jewish Messiah. But at a deep level they agree. Matthew's assertions are qualified by the idea of fulfillment, which involves radical transformation through Christ's crucifixion and resurrection. Paul's denials are qualified by his vigorous affirmations concerning the character of the law: it is God's prophetic revelation looking forward to Christ and still now revealing Him in His righteousness and mercy. The law is abolished in the sense that the fulness has come and the temporary has come to an end. The law continues in the sense that seen in the light of Christ, it still speaks His word to us. In short, we may speak either of abolition or of continuation, as we wish, provided we understand the depths and richnesses involved in what we should affirm in a total picture.

Suppose that we primarily notice in the law its temporal symbolic functions, its curse, and its focus on the structure of Israel. We see its inferiority in form to the "writing of the law on the heart" through the Holy Spirit (2 Corinthians 3:3–11). We may say that it is abolished. But then we must qualify that assertion by observing that its revelation of God continues to function in illumining the meaning of the righteousness of Christ and the final work of Christ. Conversely, suppose that we view the law as an articulation of principles of righteousness, and through Spirit-enlivened interpretation we see its pervasively Christological character. We may say that it continues to bind us, not when misinterpreted as a dead letter, but specifically in its character as revelation of Christ our Lord. But then we must qualify by observing that it reveals Christ by proclaiming the preliminary and insufficient character of the institutions and acts of salvation before His coming.

We might attempt to resolve this complexity by saying that the Ten Commandments, as an expression of the moral law, continue in force, while the rest is abolished.[20] Such a formula has a great deal of truth, when treated as a first approximation. As a rule of thumb, it can serve new Christians well. The Ten Commandments do play a strikingly central role in Mosaic revelation, and do articulate permanent moral principles. But under close scrutiny this formula reveals insufficiencies. A neat, pure separation between moral and ceremonial is not to be found in Matthew as a whole or in Matthew 5:17-20 in particular.

Moreover, no simple and easy separation between types of law will do justice to the richness of Mosaic revelation. As we observed in chapter 8, obviously moral principles are articulated outside the Ten Commandments (Leviticus 19:18), while conversely some of the Ten Commandments contain at least minor "ceremonial" or "culturally specific" elements connected with the specific situation of the Israelites. The focus and implications of the Ten Commandments are most fully and properly understood only when we read them in the context of the more specific laws elsewhere, and then the ceremonial element can be separated less than ever. In the context of the books of Moses, the Ten Commandments, the other laws, the priestly institutions, and the events of the Exodus and wilderness wandering necessarily interpret one another. And all of these must now be interpreted in the light of their fulfillment in Christ. The entirety of this Mosaic revelation simultaneously articulates general moral principles and symbolic particulars: it points forward to Christ as the final and permanent expression of righteousness and penal substitution (with moral overtones) but is itself, in that very respect, a shadow (with ceremonial overtones).

In one sense, recognizing the complexities is already part of the solution. It is part of growing in understanding what the Bible really says, as opposed to what we might imagine it to say. Moreover, in the light of our reflections on Matthew we can formulate hermeneutical strategy in a more positive way. Our interpretation of the Old Testament and the New is to be Christocentric, as Matthew itself is Christocentric. That is, we are to understand that the purposes and will of God as revealed in the whole Bible come to focus in the person of Christ and in His triumphant accomplishment of salvation in the Crucifixion and Resurrection.

The same lesson is conveyed by other New Testament writers as well. Luke records a postresurrection meeting of Jesus with His disciples, in which He sums up His previous teaching:

> "This is what I told you while I was still with you: Everything must be fulfilled that is written about me in the Law of Moses, the Prophets and the Psalms."
>
> Then he opened their minds so they could understand the Scriptures. He told them, "This is what is written: The Christ will suffer and rise from the dead on the third day, and repentance and forgiveness of sins will be preached in his name to all nations, beginning at Jerusalem." (Luke 24:44–47)

Understanding "the Scriptures"—the comprehensive term for the whole Old Testament—centers on seeing their relation to the events of Christ's life (see the further discussion in chapter 1).

Similarly, Paul says that "no matter how many promises God has made, they are 'Yes' in Christ" (2 Corinthians 1:20). The book of Hebrews speaks of climactic revelation in Christ by saying, "In the past God spoke to our forefathers through the prophets at many times and in various ways, but in these last days he has spoken to us by his son, whom he appointed heir of all things, and through whom he made the universe" (1:1–2). The author also goes on to show in some detail the relation of Christ to the Old Testament priesthood and practices of holiness.

The book of Revelation is a veritable mosaic of Old Testament allusions, all centered on the revelation of God and of Christ. The gospel of John contains fascinating allusions to Old Testament feasts and symbols, all finding their fulfillment in Christ.

To be Christ-centered in interpretation is not, however, to be Christomonistic. Not only in Revelation but in Paul, in John, and in Matthew the central work of salvation in Christ's life is the work of the Trinitarian God—the Father, the Son, and the Holy Spirit. The revelation of God through Christ is a revelation of the full Godhead (e.g., Revelation 4:1–5:6; 1:4–5; Romans 8:11; John 14:10; 16:14–15; Matthew 3:16–17; 26:39–42; etc.). Moreover, Christ has become our Redeemer and Re-creator because from all eternity and prior to His incarnation He is already the Creator (Colossians 1:15–20). We therefore repudiate the collapse of distinctions found in Barthian theology.

To read the Old Testament Christocentrically need not mean collapsing creation into redemption or suppressing the revelation of God the Father in the Old Testament. Rather, it means appreciating the Old Testament for what it is in the design of God: a witness, foreshadowing, anticipation, and promise of salvation as it has now been accomplished by the work of the triune God in Jesus Christ Incarnate. So to read the Old Testament means that we do not hastily attempt to read off of the surface of its text immediate moral applications, either in the area of personal morality or in the area of political and social morality. The Old Testament does yield such applications, but does so in God's chosen way, not ours. To be specific, it reveals and is fulfilled in Christ, who is the fullness of the Deity (Colossians 2:9), the sum of wisdom (Colossians 2:3), and therefore also the comprehensive source and standard for practical righteousness both personal and social.

Such a Christocentric approach, though it may require patience on the part of moral activists, commends itself in several ways as superior to an approach defined primarily in terms of either continuity or discontinuity. Consider the following points in this connection:

1. Christ's climactic salvation includes within itself continuity and discontinuity in harmony. The faithfulness of the person of Christ, who is the one way of salvation, guarantees continuity (Hebrews 13:8); the transition from wrath to grace by His death in history guarantees discontinuity (Hebrews 9:26–28). Thus a focus on Christ moves us beyond an abstract dialectical movement between continuity and discontinuity.

2. Christ's work defines the true nature of continuity and discontinuity between Old and New Testament situations. Thus it provides a hermeneutical focal point for sifting claims about Old Testament application.

3. Christocentric interpretation demonstrably corresponds to the true nature of the Old Testament and God's design for its present-day use. It thus does not run such a risk of immediately falsifying the texture of the Old Testament by means of a biased framework or a selective set of questions. Of course, there is no way to avoid in principle the effects of sin on interpretation. Our own feeble conceptions of Christ and of His relation to the Old Testament must themselves be subject to criticism and modification in accordance with the Bible.

4. The New Testament documents endorse Christocentric understanding of the Old Testament, as we have seen in some detail from the gospel of Matthew. Christ-centered fulfillment, and not a principle of continuity or discontinuity as such, is the sustained theme of the New Testament, and we would be wise to follow its lead.

5. As all evangelicals admit, union and communion with Christ is the only valid source of sanctification and power for godly living. We shall not properly bring society under the rule of Christ unless we keep our grips on the way of salvation.

6. With respect to issues of public justice, our resting point must be found in our assurance that Christ is the majestic Judge of the universe (Revelation 1:12–20). In the day of His coming, "in righteousness he judges and makes war" (Revelation 19:11). All must stand before Him (2 Corinthians 5:10). As we are progressively conformed to Him and have "the mind of Christ" (2 Corinthians 3:18; 1 Corinthians 2:16), we will have a proper sense of indignation at injustice. At the same time, our zeal will be moderated by Christ's patience. No one will escape His justice, and so we can face patiently the fact that injustices are not always redressed in this life, and that political evils are often slow in being rectified.

APPENDIXES

APPENDIX A

FALSE WORSHIP
IN THE MODERN STATE

S hould a modern state punish false worship? If so, why? If not, why not? Most evangelicals recoil in horror against the idea that a modern state should punish false worshipers. I believe that their instincts are sound. But we must still seek to understand the practice in Israel with respect to false worship. We must also deal with arguments purporting to show that modern punishments for false worship might have a rational, Biblical basis. Recently, a viewpoint called "theonomy" has argued in favor of using Old Testament law as a precedent for the practice of modern states (see appendix B).[1] Greg Bahnsen, one of the principal advocates of the theonomic position, has lately expressed reservations about punishing false worship.[2] But his earlier published position is widely known and supported; it needs to be refuted. We must also realize that Christians in other times and places have sometimes used the power of the state to suppress false worship. Only a thorough grasp of Scripture is sufficient to assure us that our instincts are better than theirs.

The Point at Issue:
The God-given Authority of Civil Government

Let me first specify what the point in dispute really is. Should the *state*, in distinction from individual people, other agencies, and other institutions, undertake action attempting to stop false worship? In particular, should it enact and enforce laws that prohibit or penalize false worship? And should civil laws be enacted that give the state the legal power to punish those who engage in acts of false worship within its borders?

Let us carefully note what the discussion is *not* about.

We are *not* discussing whether false worship is a serious sin. Certainly it is. It is no accident that the prohibition of false worship comes first in the Ten Commandments. It comes first because false worship is a most grievous sin. The withdrawal of proper allegiance to the true God, and the offering of allegiance to a false god, is the most radical possible disruption of the very root of our responsibility to God. We dare not underestimate the horrible character of the consequences both in people's hearts and minds and in people's relation to God's creation around them.

Next, we are *not* discussing whether false worship has serious social, political, and ethical consequences of a destructive kind. It certainly does bring such consequences. Precisely because it attacks the root of what human beings are intended to be, in the long run it affects every aspect of human life. Moreover, because of the heavy responsibility that human beings have for exercising godly dominion over the subhuman world, false worship brings in addition a train of evil consequences to animals and plants and nonliving physical things. (One might think of the relationship in India running from idolatry to taboos concerning the subhuman world, and from there to India's problems in environmental management.)

Finally, we are *not* discussing whether we ought to work and pray for the eradication of false worship. Certainly we should. God detests idolatry and so should we. In the Great Commission in Matthew 28:18–20 Jesus instructs us not to make peace with false worship, or to leave it alone, but to "make disciples of all nations." As people hear the gospel and believe, they leave false worship behind and so false worship is progressively eradicated.

Rather, we *are* discussing what are the proper godly *means* by which false worship ought to be suppressed. Do we use the means of proclaiming the gospel? Do we follow the Great Commission? Or do we use state laws to suppress false worship by force? Do we appeal to people to repent? Or do we have the state threaten them with earthly penalties for their false worship? Do we attract people by our deeds of kindness and love, and pray for God to kill the root of idolatry in them through applying the power of Jesus' sacrificial death? Or do we have the state threaten them with bodily death, imprisonment, or banishment?

The New Testament makes it perfectly clear which is the correct means to use. The Great Commission in Matthew 28:18–20, Paul's letters, the examples of evangelism in the book of Acts, the picture of spiritual war in Revelation, and Jesus' statement about the spiritual nature of His kingdom (John 18:36) all assert the primacy of *spiritual* conquest through the gospel. Moreover, as I argued in chapter 10, the holy war theology in Deuteronomy 20 and Joshua actually reinforces rather than contradicts this conclusion. The Old Testament contains abundant indications that holy war in Israel is a type and a shadow pointing forward to a final spiritual war that is deeper and greater. The New Testament reveals more fully the nature of this spiritual war as a conflict with the demonic realm (Ephesians 6:10–20; Colossians 2:15). During this gospel age, the proper means of conquering false gods and false worship are spiritual in nature.

Hence, it is a radical mistake to carry over the practice of holy war on a literal plane, as Islam does. Islam does not believe in nor understand the crucifixion and resurrection of Christ as the basis for salvation and the re-creation of the human heart. It is therefore not surprising that Islam should resort to the crude external pressures of physical war. But we Christians who do understand the true nature of salvation have no such excuse.

Moreover, we must beware of a widespread twentieth-century mistake about the state. Many Western humanists expect the state to cure all ills. When they see a problem, such as suicide, drug addiction, oppression, war, poverty, sexual exploitation, racial hatred, or mere ignorance, they are greatly distressed. Their feelings of distress and indignation are in a sense proper, but because they do not admit that the root of these ills is found in human sin, they look for immediately engineered human solutions. After all, if human nature is basically good, the difficulty must not really be that intractable. It must be solvable, and solvable *now*. Any delay is reprehensible. The state has the maximum concentration of power and resources for the job. Hence, the state must institute a program to solve the problem. If the problem cannot be solved merely by throwing money at it, then a state-run educational program can do the job.

Accordingly, in the twentieth century we have seen the growth of huge state bureaucracies. Moreover, in many political arguments it is simply assumed that the state is the proper agent for the job. The debates tend to be confined to the question of expediency and quantity: whether the citizens are willing to foot the bill for still another program, and whether one program rather than another will be effective.

We must break out of this foolishness. The state is not god, nor is it the savior of humanity. It cannot remedy all ills. Moreover, contrary to humanist thinking, the state's legitimate authority is limited by God. The state does not have the right simply to meddle in any affair that it chooses. Only God has universal, unbounded authority. The authority of the state consists only in what has been delegated to it by God. The state must confine itself to doing those things for which it has a God-given responsibility.

Hence, when we see some difficulty in the world, we must not immediately clamor for state action to eliminate the difficulty. It is not enough merely to demonstrate that there is a difficulty, and that the difficulty is serious. We must always ask what are the just *means* for dealing with the difficulty. We must not blindly assume that state action is appropriate or approved by God. Prayer, individual action, action by churches, action by voluntary organizations, and other forms of action are all alternatives. State action needs to be justified as part of the legitimate sphere of authority given to the state. Such action is appropriate not merely if we can show that it might "help" in some pragmatic sense, but only if we can show in addition that it is *just* when measured by the limited authority that God has given to the state.

This general principle applies also to the question of false worship. False worship is a difficulty in the world; in fact, it is an exceedingly serious evil. State action to suppress false worship might "help" in some crude, pragmatic way. But does God give such authority to the state? That is the crucial question.

Theonomists have argued that in Deuteronomy 13:1–18 and Deuteronomy 17:2–7 God does give such authority to the state. But they have misunderstood the passages in Deuteronomy. Both Deuteronomy 13 and 17 reflect the theology of holy war in Israel. As I argued in chapter 10, the punishments in these passages are particular instances of the practice of holy destruction that was inaugurated with Joshua's conquest. Moreover, in neither passage is authority given to the *state*—it is given to the congregation of the people of Israel, in their capacity as God's holy people.

The death penalty maintains the purity of Israel in the Holy Land by a renewal of holy war against violators of Israel's holiness. The profanation of Israel's holiness receives due recompense by an appropriately measured action in the reverse direction. The holy people of Israel is the offended party. They undertake a further act of profanation of the offender (punishment) and a purification of Israel (restoration) by presenting the offender as an offering consecrated to destruction (Deuteronomy 13:16–17; cf. Deuteronomy 17:4, 7). These things foreshadow the work of Christ, who wages holy war against the demonic spirits of wickedness (Colossians 2:15). Hence, these verses are *not* applicable to modern states.

Once these primary issues are settled, there still remain a few further questions. Granted that evangelism is the primary means for overcoming false worship, might the state still have a subordinate role? Granted that the state's authority is strictly limited, might there be something in the Bible that indicates that the state does have an authority from God to punish false worship? Granted that Deuteronomy 13 and 17 are about holy war, and do *not* give the state any authority, might there still be a way of inferring principles from the state's general mandate to execute justice? These are the questions that we must persue. But note well: it must be *demonstrated* from the Bible, not merely *assumed*, that the state has authority to interfere in the area of worship. I claim that there is no such demonstration, but rather that Biblical evidence points the other way.

State Responsibilities:
Offenses Against Human Beings, not God

We must first seek to determine the scope of state responsibilities. In the area of punishment, I maintain that modern states are only responsible for punishing offenses against other human beings, not offenses directly against God. To understand the issue, we must distinguish sins from crimes. A sin is any offense against God. A crime is a legally reprehensible offense against another human being.

Sin describes damage to our relation to God; crime describes damage to fellow human beings. The two are not identical. Every crime is a sin, but not every sin is a crime. For example, coveting is a sin but not a crime. In the Old Testament no fixed civil penalty attaches to coveting. It is not a "chargeable offense" from the point of view of civil justice. Coveting (unless it leads to overt actions like theft or murder) does not directly damage other human beings, and so the state has no business in overseeing a process of restoration and retribution. Similarly, within the Mosaic period farming during the sabbath year was a sin but not a crime (see Leviticus 25:1–7). God commanded the people not to farm during the sabbath year. But no earthly court was allowed to punish people for violating God's command.

Every crime is a sin because God commands us to love our neighbors. Hence, every offense against a neighbor violates God's commandment and represents rebellion against Him. But not every sin is a crime, because some offenses against God do not *directly* harm other human beings.

Sins and crimes must each receive the appropriate punishment from the appropriate person. Sins are offenses against God, and thus they are always punished by God. Every sin intends to destroy God's authority and His claim on all of life. Consequently, it merits punishment in a corresponding form: the offender, or a substitute, must be destroyed by God. All people who sin must either go to hell or have Christ bear hell for them on the cross. Every sin therefore receives a punishment from God.

Crimes are offenses against other human beings, and hence they always ought to be punished by restoration and retribution paid to other human beings and supervised by human courts of justice. In typical legal cases in the Old Testament, like theft, murder, or false worship, the fundamental system of recompense involves the principle "As you have done, it shall be done to you," *by the offended party.* Governmental authorities supervise the procedures leading to penalties, but in the typical case they are not themselves the offended party. Moreover, the offended party in view is always another human being or a group of human beings. God is of course offended by every sin whatsoever. But not every sin merits state punishments. Nor is the kind of penalty determined by how God is offended, but by how other human beings are affected. The provisions of the law then point away from the idea that the state is responsible for offenses against God *as such.* The legal punishments supervised by earthly judges make sense only when they are viewed as the fitting payment for offenses against human beings.

In addition, the law of Moses includes cases where unqualified people touch holy objects or perform ceremonies in an unlawful manner. In many cases the text specifies that God brings death on such people (Exodus 28:35; 30:20–21; Leviticus 8:35; 10:2; 16:13; Numbers 18:3, 32).[3] The distinction between these situations and situations where human beings execute the death penalty is intelligible if we make the distinction that I am advocating, but is otherwise difficult to account for.[4]

Suppose, on the other hand, that we claim that the state is indeed responsible to punish offenses against God. We get ourselves into several difficulties:

1. How do we any longer distinguish between a sin and a crime? All sins that are legally demonstrable would appear to be the state's responsibility. But such an approach clearly does not correspond to the nature of Old Testament penal law.

2. How do we calculate the appropriate penalty? Since sins against God are infinitely offensive, it would appear to follow that every sin merits the death penalty in civil courts.

3. How do we explain the key role of the offended party in the Old Testament system? If God is always an offended party, then recompense must be made to God, or perhaps to the state as the representative of God. In actual fact, in the Old Testament law animal sacrifices represent the payment to God, while the penal-

ties of other kinds deal with offenses of a "horizontal" kind, offenses against other human beings.

Romans 13:4 says that "he [the state authority] is God's servant, an agent of wrath to bring punishment on the wrongdoer." Superficially, this text might appear to provide warrant for a very broad view of the state's responsibility. In fact, if it were taken in isolation, it could imply that the state must seek to punish all sins and to bring down God's wrath on sinners in the most thorough way that it can. Then every publicly provable sin becomes a crime, and presumably every sin would merit the death penalty. But no Christian with any sense interprets the verse in this extreme way. Clearly, state responsibilities are not simply identical with God's responsibilities; rather, they are limited. The state is rightly God's servant and God's agent for wrath *in the particular sphere of responsibility that God has delegated to it* (Romans 13:1-2, 7; 1 Peter 2:13-14). The limiting phrase is crucial. The rest of the Bible must help us to determine how the state's responsibilities are fixed. Hence, verse 4 of Romans 13 is in fact compatible in principle with my view of the limits of state authority.

In summary, state authority is limited to crimes, that is, offenses against fellow human beings. The state has responsibility to supervise acts of restoration and punishment for crimes but not for other types of sin. Offenses against fellow human beings are within its jurisdiction, but offenses against God are not (except, of course, if they are *also* offenses against human beings).

Now we are ready to apply this general principle to the case of false worship. False worship is an offense against God, but not against other human beings. Hence, it is not within the state's legitimate sphere of authority and ought not to be punished by the state. And so we have reached the conclusion we already anticipated when we observed that evangelism through the gospel was the primary means for eradicating false worship. Prayer and evangelism are the appointed means of God, and the state must not try to "supplement" these God-sanctioned means by enacting a law penalizing false worship.

But we still need to deal with two possible arguments that attempt to show that false worship comes within the state's sphere of responsibility in a less direct way. One argument claims that false worship is in fact an offense against other individual human beings. The other argument claims that false worship is an offense against the state. Let us consider each of these two arguments in turn.

False Worship: An Offense Against Other Human Beings?

Is false worship an offense against other human beings? In a broad, vague sense, false worship may "offend" other people, both people who worship the true God and people with competing forms of false worship. Muslims and Hindus are often "offended" by each other's presence and practices. But disgust or emotional repulsion or deeply rooted principial disagreement do not count as a legitimate basis for formal legal action. In Israel, if you did not like your neighbor's ugly house or cantankerous wife or his field overgrown with weeds, you had no basis for legal action. A legal offense must be some much more definite, concrete damage to a person or property, not merely a matter of "being offended." The word "offense" must be understood in a specifically legal sense.

But, in fact, false worship is likely to lead to specifically criminal offenses, offenses in the technical sense. Because of its radical character of rebellion against God, it tends to generate all kinds of immorality. If a man worships a murdering and lying god, or a god who cares nothing for morality, he and his family will likely become murderers and liars themselves. Moreover, such people set a bad example and tempt others around them to slide into false worship and immorality.

But once again one must respect the limited scope of state courts. The state is not given authority to punish human actions on the basis of distant indirect effects that those actions might have. For example, the state has no authority to punish covetousness, even though this sin of the heart leads to all kinds of other sins and crimes (Matthew 15:18–20; Ephesians 5:5; 1 Timothy 6:10). Nor does it have authority to punish fools or bad examples merely because they are bad examples. The state must restrict itself to the human acts that actually cause damage to other human beings; it is not given authority to meddle in the more inward precursor acts that feed the heart of sin.

False Worship: An Attack Against the State?

Now we must consider the claim that false worship attacks the state and should be punished as a crime against the state. In what way might false worship constitute an attack on the state? If the state is pagan or godless, false worship does not attack the state in any clear way. Some pagan states have even required worship of their leaders as an act of allegiance (a problem for Christians in the Roman empire). Only if the state is in some way Christianized does false worship become a possible issue.

For the sake of argument, let us suppose that a modern state has in some way acknowledged that its authority is derived from Christ and that its actions are accountable before Him. Several types of argument might try to show that false worship attacks such a state. (1) The spread of false worship among the citizens of a state threatens in the long run to lead to a repeal of the laws expressing the state's allegiance to God and hence to an overthrow of this specific form of state. (2) An attack on God is in itself an attack on a state owing allegiance to God. (3) An act of false worship is an act of treason because it in principle sets up a rival source of authority, namely, the false god. Similarly, seduction to false worship is seduction to treason. (4) An act of false worship or seduction to false worship within the bounds of a state's territory profanes the holiness of a state devoted to God. Let us consider these possibilities one by one.

False Worship Leads to Repealing Laws

When we speak of the possibility of repealing laws, we are viewing the state from the standpoint of modern democratic elections rather than in terms of authority given from God to the rulers. But let us temporarily operate within this perspective. If the current laws of a modern state allow for the repeal of a law by action of the citizenry, the citizens are within their technical legal rights when they try to repeal the law. Citizens who repeal a just law are acting foolishly and sinning against God, but they are not thereby made liable to civil punishment.

For example, suppose that citizens elect an ungodly lawmaker. The lawmaker in turn repeals a law requiring thieves to pay back double their theft, and replaces it with a law that gives prison sentences for thievery. What the lawmaker did was sinful, unwise, and unjust. The citizens were unwise to elect such a person. But the state cannot justly punish the citizens who voted for the lawmaker, nor could it punish the lawmaker for changing the law. Again, the distinction between sin and crime must operate here. The sins of the lawmaker and the citizens are in this case not crimes. No statute explicitly forbids them from altering the law.

On the other hand, suppose that current laws prohibit everyone from altering or repealing at least certain crucial statutes. Then no matter whom the citizens elect, the lawmaker would have no legal power to change matters. Only a violent overthrow of the government, or a kind of violence by those in authority, in which they deny their constitutional obligations, would be capable of doing violence to the state. It would be just to punish the violent act intending overthrow of the state. But voting as such does not directly imply such violence, and so would still not be punishable.

These general principles can now be applied to the specific case in which voters or lawmakers attempt to change a statute specifying that the state owes allegiance to the God of the Bible. If the law allows for changes in this statute, a change is a sin but not a crime. If the law does not allow change, the actual overthrow of the statute is treasonous. But the overthrow as such, not the mere presence of false worship somewhere among the citizenry, is what is punishable.

An Attack on God Is an Attack on the State

Romans 13:1–7 indicates that an attack on the state as such is an attack on God's authority. But the reverse does not follow. Every sin is in one way or another an attack on God's authority, but not every sin is liable to civil punishment (not every sin is a crime). Of course, false worship expresses disagreement with a specific, basic element of the state's commitment. But citizens may disagree with many basic elements in a state's constitutional basis without thereby attempting to destroy the state as a whole.

False Worship Sets Up a Rival Authority

False gods are indeed rivals to the true God. Hence, they represent attempts to destroy God's authority. But false gods are not direct rivals to the state in the same way. A rival government or guerrilla activity within the territorial bounds of a state is a very different kind of rival from false worshipers who still obey all the state laws. Of course, if the state puts in place laws directly forbidding false worship, some people may violate those very laws because of their strong allegiance to a false god. But the question is whether such laws do indeed express legitimate state authority.

False Worship Profanes the Holiness of the State

But is a state giving allegiance to God holy? All state authorities derive their authority from God and are the representatives of God in giving retribution (Romans 13:1-7). In a loose sense, then, they represent a certain presence of God. But this fourth argument presupposes that a state has received a special holiness by explicitly giving allegiance to God.

We must first of all remember that human action does not in itself create holiness. God must declare people and things to be holy, and any human actions involved in the process of consecration are subordinate to this divine initiative. In the case of the modern state, we do not have Biblical warrant for believing that there is a divine initiative resulting in consecration of a state at a particular time. In addition, a holy state would necessarily share some of the same basic attributes as the church: it would be a "holy nation" (1 Peter 2:9), whose actions embody the presence of Christ's reign in such a way that it becomes a temple of God. The same arguments used above concerning excommunication would appear to imply that banishment would be the proper penalty for profanation of the state. Purification of the state by a "whole burnt offering" (Deuteronomy 13:16) has as its fulfilled form purification by the continuing presence of the life-giving power of Christ's resurrection.

In the final analysis the situation created by a holy state is only hypothetical. Not only the absence of positive Biblical warrant but Christ's statement to Pilate about the distinctive character of His kingdom (John 18:36–37) exclude this route. Even theonomists, by their maintenance of a church/state distinction, appear to agree with me in principle at this point.

We have considered four possible ways in which false worship or seduction to false worship might represent an attack on the state. There may be more possibilities that I have not thought of. The very multiplicity of possible modes of attack expresses the fact that I am not at all certain how an attack occurs in any definite form. By contrast, an assassination attempt or an attempted coup is an attempt of a quite definite and direct kind to destroy the existing state. Since it is analogous to attempted murder and may involve literal attempted murder, the appropriate penalty is destruction of the persons involved by the representative(s) of the state who have been attacked. Such a conclusion follows from principles of just reciprocity. But no such conclusion follows in a case when we cannot see clearly that there has been an attack.

We must beware of extending the idea of treason to an unreasonably wide area. Because of human sin, states love to extend their powers and their claims to allegiance to unwarranted lengths. In the past, worship of the state's gods has sometimes been positively required in order to avoid the charge of treason (cf. Daniel 3; 6; Revelation 13:8). If the state's authority is very closely tied with the authority of God, why shouldn't such a conclusion follow? But our consideration of possibility (3) above shows the fallacy in the argument. If the state's authority derives from God, an attack on the state is one form of attack on God. The converse result, namely, that an attack on God is one form of attack on the state, would follow *if* God's authority is derived from the state. When states idolatrously confuse their authority with the authority of God, they begin to make just this mistake, and draw the conclusion that they must enforce worship of their god.

The whole argument about attack on the state also looks implausible when we return to the situation of ancient Israel. Israel did have a holy state in certain respects. The kings in the Davidic line were specially marked out by God as the predecessors of the Messiah and received a rule analogous to the Messiah's (Genesis 49:10). In this situation Israel knew what it was to have plots for seizing the throne. But it seems implausible to claim that false worship and seduction to false worship were to be viewed on the same level with seditious plots. False worship was not a special attack on the rulers but merely an attack on the holiness of the people as a whole.

Even Jeroboam's false worship in 1 Kings 12:25–33 confirms this viewpoint. Jeroboam did not fear that false worship would lead to rebellion but rather that true worship would lead to allegiance to the Judean king. Jeroboam was simply working with the maxim that accepting the authority of God implies accepting the authority of the state, as we have seen in (3) above. Of course, Jeroboam's fears were mistaken, because he had been given legitimate authority by God (1 Kings 11:31–39). But Jeroboam did use false worship in hopes of furthering the division. He was attracted not mainly by some superficial feature of false worship (false worship also occurred in the southern kingdom), but because false worship over which he had control (cf. 1 Kings 12:31–32), which was physically located in his territory, and over which he was the acknowledged leader (1 Kings 12:33; 13:4) could be exploited to consolidate his power. Jeroboam illustrates the point already made about the tendency of the state to extend its powers and use religion for its own purposes.

The most fundamental error involved in the extension of state prerogatives is a confusion between heaven and earth, between Christ's reign from heaven and the state's reign on earth. Christ does exercise authority over both heaven and earth, according to Matthew 28:18. Hence, all earthly obedience to God's standards is obedience to Christ, empowered by His heavenly power. Conversely, all earthly disobedience to Christ simultaneously attacks His heavenly prerogatives. All sin is sin against Christ. But what about false worship in particular? False worship endeavors to attack heaven in a most blatant way by substituting a false god for the true one and undermining at its foundation human commitment to God's holiness. By doing so it does not, however, institute an immediate attack on any state's earthly powers, even though these powers derive from God.

Ancient Israel was profaned by false worship not because it carried state powers but because it was an earthly replica of God's heavenly holiness. The church is profaned by false worship within it not because it is a social organization on earth containing Christians but because it is the body of Christ, united with Him in heaven. Christians are exalted to heaven with Christ, according to Ephesians 2:6, but the state never is. It remains a kingdom of this world (John 18:36). It cannot grant forgiveness on the basis of Christ's death, and neither can it raise the spiritually dead to life. Modern states should indeed practice the principles of God's justice, but they always do so within the limits of their earthly powers. The life-giving powers of the gospel do not belong to the state as such, but to the church, to whom the gospel is committed (Matthew 16:16–19).

My conclusion, then, is that false worship as such does not injure the state in any direct and fundamental way. Therefore no reciprocal retribution from the state is called for. Some forms of false worship, such as human sacrifice, satanic sexual rituals, and slanderous blasphemies, involve crimes against other human beings and are punishable as such. But they are not punishable merely because they are forms of false worship.

Of necessity, my arguments above have been based almost entirely on general principles of justice rather than on specific texts. The texts Deuteronomy 13:1–18, Deuteronomy 17:2–7, and other texts concerning false worship do not make a pronouncement on whether there is any injury to the state. Their silence concerning injury to the state might be taken as negative evidence, but arguments from silence are precarious. When we leave aside these texts, neither side, pro nor con, can present texts that make direct pronouncements on the question at hand.

Since the arguments are all based on general principle, there is greater possibility for disagreement. It may be that I have overlooked something. But I can do no better than set forth my present position. I do believe that we should not seriously advocate state punishment of false worship unless we can find a clear Biblical basis for it. And no such basis is forthcoming. On the contrary, the limitations of state authority in the Bible argue against it.

Practical Reasoning

In addition to all these reasonings, we may also look at some practical difficulties likely to arise from instituting penalties for false worship.

Practical difficulties can never constitute the primary grounds for rejecting a position with Biblical sanction. But they may nevertheless suggest
that we need to reexamine whether we do indeed have Biblical sanction for a position.

For the sake of argument, then, let us envision a situation in which
the population of a particular nation has become largely Christian. Suppose that by legal, constitutional means the state expresses its allegiance
to Christ. The laws are altered so that the state will now inflict a penalty
on those engaging in false worship or seducing others to false worship.

The first practical difficulty is in deciding what penalty is appropriate. According to my arguments above, we cannot safely base ourselves
directly on an Old Testament text. Neither can we easily determine the
exact nature of the violation of state authority involved in false worship. Without these controls, it is most difficult to establish what would
be a just penalty. With respect to the issue of deterrence, a minor penalty would almost certainly function mostly as a nuisance and would not
thoroughly deter false worship. Those who are committed to worshiping
other gods often make that commitment as part of their ultimate allegiance, so that even the death penalty might not deter them from practicing false worship until they are caught.

The next practical difficulty is in specifying what counts as false
worship. In Israel, cases of false worship involved clear-cut devotion to
"other gods" (Deuteronomy 13:2; 17:3), that is, gods like Baal, Ash-
taroth, Molech, and Marduk. But we cannot use Deuteronomy as a direct model for the modern state. Hence, many questions remain open.
Are we to say that modern Jews and Muslims worship the God of Abraham, Isaac, and Jacob because they claim to do so? Or are we to say
that they are engaged in false worship because they do not properly
know the true God through Jesus Christ? What are we to say about
Mormons and Jehovah's Witnesses, whose doctrine of Christ is defective? What are we to say about some Roman Catholics who may get
involved in the worship of images? What are we to say about secularist
worshipers, worshipers of money, power, sex, fame, comfort, and self?

Obviously, no form of false worship could rightly be punished by
the state unless it were legally demonstrable. Worship of Baal that is

confined to mental prayer is not punishable (unless later confessed). But what is legally demonstrable depends on how specific the legal statutes are. Statutes could in principle be formulated that would quite narrowly confine themselves to easily identifiable cases like worship of Baal. But such statutes would be irrelevant to the typical forms of false worship in modern Western society. May the statutes legitimately be formulated so as to cast their net more broadly? Why or why not? As long as we are unclear about how false worship attacks the state, we have all too little guidance. In principle we can imagine advocates of some particular Christian theology, Roman Catholic or Reformed or Arminian or Baptistic, writing their theology into the constitution of the state and then claiming that all worship contrary to their theology is an attack on the state. I know of no modern Christian who advocates such a procedure, but once we open the door to broad state inference in religious worship, just how can we forbid such religious tyranny?

Many more difficulties arise because of a possible tension between state punishment of false worship and the evangelistic purposes of the Great Commission in Matthew 28:18–20. Many bad effects might result from a state-imposed punishment for false worship, but I will concentrate on two.

First, the gospel may be less well heard. Because of their spiritual blindness unbelievers have a great inclination to misunderstand and distort the message of the Christian faith (2 Corinthians 4:4). State punishment for false worship is likely to make things harder. Because they overrate political power to begin with, unbelievers are likely to believe that Christianity is fundamentally a political power play. Christian religion looks like a weapon for coercion or political manipulation rather than a gospel of grace.

Next, Christians are likely to have fewer opportunities to proclaim the gospel to non-Christians. Suppose that the state imposes the death penalty for certain types of false worship. Just before the penalty goes into effect, citizens who are committed to these types of false worship will face hard decisions. Do they continue living where they are? If so, do they give up their previous commitments? Do they confine themselves to mental acts of worship that are not legally punishable? Do they continue to worship secretly and run the risk of being discovered? Do they worship openly and become martyrs for their cause? Do they leave the country so that they can practice their religion freely in some other place?

Some people, perhaps a good many, would probably decide to leave the country under those circumstances. To the extent that exile results, the Christians living in the Christian state cut themselves off from natural contact with unbelievers. Moreover, non-Christian states are more likely to raise severe barriers against Christian evangelization if they think that the result of such evangelism in the long run may be a takeover by Christianity and its consequent suppression of other worship.[5]

The net results of such processes of misunderstanding, exile, and barrier-raising would seem to run contrary to the means that God normally uses for discipling the nations during this age. He scatters His people among the nations and thrusts them out (Acts 8:4; 11:19) into situations where they are truly in the world but not of it. A radical difference exists between the geographical purity of Israel as a physically separated, holy nation and the heavenly purity of the church as a spiritually separated, holy nation (1 Peter 2:9–10; 1:1). Hence, state attempts to suppress false worship confuse what is appropriate in these two distinct circumstances, with their two distinct kinds of purity.

In any case, our priorities as Christians are determined by Christ our King. In Matthew 28:18–20 He commands us to wage spiritual war in His name against the peoples of the world in order to subdue them to His allegiance. We do so through the proclamation of the gospel and the process of discipling. We may well be highly suspicious of operations of state power that tend to interfere with the accomplishment of our primary task.[6]

Now let me consider some further objections to my position.

Objection 1: The Possibility of Reviving Holy War

Postmillennialists might foresee another possibility concerning the applicability of Deuteronomy 13. Suppose that the world is largely converted to Christ before His second coming, as postmillennialists believe will be the case. It might be argued that the church will then come into possession of the whole world and that such possession should subsequently be maintained by holy war waged against violators. But there are some insuperable obstacles to such a conclusion.

1. In this scenario the mode of carrying on holy war seems to change in midstream. The initial achievement of conquest uses the means of spiritual union with Christ in His death and resurrection. The subsequent maintenance of conquest however uses a difference means, namely, physical separation and the death penalty. It is difficult to justify such a shift in the nature of holy war other than on the basis of a pronounced shift in the presence of Christ when He appears bodily to judge the world. As we have observed from Deuteronomy 13, the manner of initially conquering Palestine is fundamentally the same as the manner of preserving the conquest by eliminating idolatry. In like manner, in our day conquering and preserving conquest use the same rules. We should not undertake to alter Christ's rules for conquest given to us in Matthew 28:18–20.

2. The above conclusion still depends on the supposition that the church would be profaned by physical proximity to false worship. Since the true holiness of the church consists in its access to and presence in heaven, and since John 17:14–19 makes a clear distinction between being in the world and being contaminated by it, physical proximity to false worship does nothing to profane the church, whether or not we are in a postmillennial situation.

3. Even those Christians who advocate the most thoroughgoing use of Old Testament law recognize the unique and unrepeatable character of holy war in Israel. In particular, theonomists deny that holy war is to be renewed within this age.[7]

Objection 2: The Possibility of Inciting God's Anger Against the Whole Society

We must also consider the possibility that false worship incites God's anger against the whole society in which it occurs. False worship is a most grievous sin, an abomination in the sight of God. In God's eternal reckoning, at the Last Judgment, this sin and all other sins deserve the punishment of hell. But God also inflicts punishments within history, sometimes in the form of war, famine, pestilence, or captivity (Revelation 6:1–8; Amos 1:3–2:3; Isaiah 13:1–19:25; Ezekiel 25:1–32:32; etc.). It could therefore be argued that the practice of false worship within any society threatens the whole society with historical destruction and that the fitting penalty is destruction of the offenders.

Does God hold a whole society responsible for the offense of some? In a sense yes, but in another sense no. The judges and leaders of a society commit sin not only when they practice private wrongdoing but when they refuse to reprove and to punish unjust acts (cf. Isaiah 1:16–28; Micah 3:9–12; etc.). Sometimes a society has become so wicked that even the presence of a few righteous people does not suffice to turn away God's judgment (Ezekiel 14:14, 20). But even then, God in His judgment is capable of discriminating between the guilt of society as a whole and the innocence of the righteous people within it. For example, in the story of Abraham's intercession for Sodom and Gomorrah (Genesis 18:22–33), God promised not to destroy the towns if He could find even ten righteous people there. In the end, ten such righteous people could not be found, but God still rescued Lot and his family. Though Lot was far from a perfect model of righteousness, 2 Peter 2:6–9 says concerning the incident,

> If he [God] condemned the cities of Sodom and Gomorrah by burning them to ashes, and made them an example of what is going to happen to the ungodly; and if he rescued Lot, a righteous man, who was distressed by the filthy lives of lawless men (for that righteous man, living among them day after day, was tormented in his righteous soul by the lawless deeds he saw and heard)—if this is so, then the Lord knows how to rescue godly men from trials and to hold the unrighteous for the day of judgment, while continuing their punishment.

Similarly Ezekiel 14:14, 20 mentions that if Noah, Daniel, and Job were in a wicked country, "they could save only themselves by their righteousness." In fact, Noah, Daniel, and Jeremiah were each righteous people whom God preserved in times when God's judgments came against the great wickedness of their society.

From Biblical passages like these I infer that Christians within a wicked society have several types of obligations before God. First, God commands them to abstain from personally practicing the sins of the surrounding society. Second, God obliges them to warn non-Christians and reprove them for their sins. Noah, Lot, Daniel, and Jeremiah all warned their contemporaries concerning God's standards and His judgments (2 Peter 2:5; Genesis 19:7, 9, 14; Daniel 5:22–28; Jeremiah 26; etc.). Of course, such reproof ought to be done in love. Christians should always be ready to speak to non-Christians about the gospel, which is the only proper remedy for their wickedness. Christians must pray for the conversion and repentance of non-Christians.

Third, when Christians are in positions of authority, they must exercise their authority in accordance with God's standards and make sure that they discharge the obligations belonging to their offices—no matter how wicked the surrounding society or even their coworkers may be. In particular, Christians ought to work for the establishment of just laws and their enforcement. We ought also to pray for God to put a stop to wickedness. Ultimately wickedness is destroyed through the second coming of Christ. But in a less comprehensive fashion, wickedness is destroyed both through the repentance of wicked people and through the establishment and enforcement of just laws.

Do we therefore have an obligation to act against the practice of false worship within the surrounding society? We must certainly warn against it and reprove it. We must pray for its abolition. But does God also command us to set up state laws against it? If so, then God will certainly hold us responsible for failure. But if not, we who are Christians do not anger God by not doing so.

God certainly does abhor false worship. But we can deduce a civil penalty from this fact only by using a circular argument. The argument may be summarized as follows. If indeed a civil penalty is warranted, then guilt falls on a whole society for not maintaining the penalty. Hence, the false worshipper is guilty of bringing potential destruction on the whole society. Hence, he ought to be punished for his damage to the society. Hence, a civil penalty is warranted. This argument in favor of a penalty only succeeds by assuming at the beginning what it ought to prove, namely, that God requires all societies to suppress false worship by means of civil penalties.

In conclusion, then, I believe that no civil penalty ought to be used to suppress false worship. The arguments that have been used in favor of such a penalty are not sound. God wants us to eradicate false worship using His proper means, the means of prayer and evangelism. Obedience to the Great Commission constitutes the proper fulfillment of Old Testament holy war and the principles of justice in Deuteronomy 13:1–18. The Old Testament is indeed to be applied today. But we shall not really understand Deuteronomy 13:1–18 and we shall not really obey it unless we take into account its relation to Old Testament holy war against Canaan, holy war against Israel through substitutionary sacrifice, and holy war in Christ.

In the deepest sense, we shall not understand what it means unless we understand that God intends the passage to point forward to the fulfillment of justice and recompense in Christ. Christ's victory over the principalities and powers of wickedness (Colossians 2:15) forms the basis for our deepest insights into Old Testament holy war. And His victory gives us our foundation for confident proclamation of the gospel. Through Christ's power, and using His means, we can combat false worship in a just way.

APPENDIX B

EVALUATING THEONOMY

A merican and European cultures are losing their roots in the Bible. As a result, the culture is disintegrating and terrible sins and sufferings crop up all around us. What can be done to halt this decline? The movement called "Christian Reconstruction" finds the answer in the return to the Bible as our standard for all of life. Christian Reconstruction is currently making a wide impact in evangelical circles and even beyond into the secular world. How shall we evaluate it?

One central aspect of Christian Reconstruction is the conviction that Old Testament law in its details is still binding today. This conviction is usually called "theonomy," from the Greek words *theos* ("God") and *nomos* ("law"), because God's law is the standard for human conduct. However, in the last few years some of the advocates of Christian Reconstruction have become uncomfortable with the theonomic thesis in its original form.[1] I shall concentrate on theonomy, rather than Christian Reconstruction as a whole, because theonomic ideas are the most closely related to the issues raised in this book.

Major Concerns of Theonomists

What concerns motivate theonomists? In what respects does theonomy conform to Biblical teaching, and where if at all does it go astray? To begin with, we must recognize that theonomists do not agree with one

311

another at every point. Disagreements and quarrels have arisen among
the representatives. Moreover, theonomists are people, not just ma-
chinery in a movement. They share all that frustrating and challenging
variety of sins and righteousness, weaknesses and strengths that characterize the body of Christ. But a good many deep, Biblically rooted concerns make up the common core of theonomy and lead to the enthusi-
asm of its supporters. The supporters themselves are for the most part
well aware of their core principles. But outsiders have perhaps too often
heard only some passing fragment of the whole, e.g., that theonomists
think we should return to the gold standard or that they think homosexuals should be executed. Whether or not we end up agreeing with all
their conclusions in detail, we should appreciate that such conclusions
make a good deal of sense within the total framework of principles
adopted by theonomists. Viewed from inside, the conclusions are not
absurd, nor it is possible to refute them by some simple appeal to a
proof text or to common sense.

What then is at the heart of theonomist views? Greg L. Bahnsen
provides the fullest articulation of the position in his book *Theonomy in
Christian Ethics* and in revised form in *By This Standard: The Authority of
God's Law Today.*[2] Bahnsen provides a convenient summary in the following ten theses:

1. Since the Fall, it has always been unlawful to use the law of God
   in hopes of establishing one's own personal merit and justification, in contrast or complement to salvation by way of promise
   and faith; commitment to obedience is but the lifestyle of faith,
   a token of gratitude for God's redeeming grace.

2. The word of the Lord is the sole, supreme, and unchallengeable
   standard for the actions and attitudes of all men in all areas of
   life; this word naturally includes God's moral directives (law).

3. Our obligation to keep the law of God cannot be judged by any
   extrascriptural standard, such as whether its specific requirements (when properly interpreted) are congenial to past traditions or modern feelings and practices.

4. We should presume that Old Testament standing laws continue
   to be morally binding in the New Testament, unless they are

rescinded or modified by further revelation. [Bahnsen adds further explanation of "standing law" in a footnote.]

5. In regard to the Old Testament law, the New Covenant surpasses the Old Covenant in glory, power, and finality (thus reinforcing former duties). The New Covenant also supercedes [sic] the Old Covenant shadows, thereby changing the application of sacrificial, purity, and "separation" principles, redefining the people of God, and altering the significance of the Promised Land.

6. God's revealed standing laws are a reflection of His immutable moral character and, as such, are absolute in the sense of being nonarbitrary, objective, universal, and established in advance of particular circumstances (thus applicable to general types of moral situations).

7. Christian involvement in politics calls for recognition of God's transcendent, absolute, revealed law as a standard by which to judge all social codes.

8. Civil magistrates in all ages and places are obligated to conduct their offices as ministers of God, avenging divine wrath against criminals and giving an account on the Final Day of their service before the King of kings, their Creator and Judge.

9. The general continuity which we presume with respect to the moral standards of the Old Testament applies just as legitimately to matters of socio-political ethics as it does to personal, family, or ecclesiastical ethics.

10. The civil precepts of the Old Testament (standing "judicial" laws) are a model of perfect social justice for all cultures, even in the punishment of criminals.[3]

At the heart of theonomy is the fundamental conviction that God's word is the only proper standard for evaluating all human action, including the actions of government officials and the laws made by civil legislators. This particular thesis deserves the support of all Christians, for a very good reason. Confessing the lordship of God necessarily implies bowing to His will and realizing that He, rather than any human being, is the sovereign, all-wise Judge of the world. The authority of civil government like all other human authority is wholly derivative. Human beings, including officers of the state, are answerable to God for their every action.

This emphasis on evaluating politics, economics, business, and social action by the Bible is sorely needed in our day, as theonomists observe. Listen to Greg Bahnsen's indictment:

> It is not accidental that the glaring socio-political and criminal problems of the late twentieth century concern matters where our society has turned against the specific directives of God's law. Humanism has been taught in our schools and media; it has been practiced in economics, medicine, politics, and our courts. And the results have been a social disaster. Human life is treated as cheap. Sexual purity is an outdated concept. Truth and honesty have little place in the "real world" of business or politics. Repeat offenders and crimes which go completely unpunished belittle the criminal justice system. Prison reform is desperately needed. In short, humanism has proven its ineffectiveness in case after case. Where can we turn for socio-political wisdom which can effectively counter the degeneration and disintegration of our culture? The only acceptable answer will be to turn to God's directives for social justice, and those are (for the most part) found in the Old Testament commandments to Israel as a nation, a nation facing the same moral problems about life, sex, property, and truth which all nations must face, including our own.[4]

In short, theonomists are motivated by three deeply Biblical concerns. The first is zeal for the lordship of Jesus Christ. Christ is King of kings and Lord of lords (Revelation 17:14; 19:16). All of our lives must submit to Him. Nothing less than thorough obedience to God in every area of life is the fitting response to His glory, perfection, and bountiful grace. Second, they are motivated by love for God's law. "Oh how I love thy law! I meditate on it all day long" (Psalm 119:97). The law reveals God in His purity and justice. It also provides precious direction for our path: "Your word is a lamp to my feet and a light for my path" (Psalm 119:105). Such sentiments cannot be dismissed as merely the inferior sentiments of the Old Testament era, for Paul too affirms the holiness and spirituality of the law (Romans 7:12, 14). Third, theonomists have a deep concern for healing the hurts of modern society, including especially the elimination of tyrannical use of state power.

Theonomists know that the ills of modern society run deep, as deep as the horrible depths of sin, and that the remedy must be equally deep and radical.

In addition, we should mention one element that has not yet come into view: postmillennialism. All of the leading representatives of theonomy are postmillennialists; that is, they believe that eventually the great bulk of humanity will come to give allegiance to Christ and a great triumph of righteousness and blessing on earth will ensue prior to the second coming of Christ. Greg Bahnsen assures us that postmillennialism is not logically essential to the fundamental theses of theonomy, and surely he is right.[5] Bahnsen's ten theses given above nowhere require a particular view of the millennium. On the other hand, Rousas J. Rushdoony and Gary North are equally right in observing that postmillennialism and theonomy naturally go together.[6] The postmillennialists desire most vigorously to uphold the principle that Jesus Christ is enthroned and reigning over all authorities and powers (Ephesians 1:21–22). Moreover, they are motivated to reflect on the implications of the Bible for society because they think that these reflections can actually be applied in the future. As people come to acknowledge Jesus as Lord, His reign advances. When Christianity triumphs numerically, wide-scale transformations of society become not only realistic possibilities but required duties. Thus we may profitably begin now to work out what alterations bring society into conformity with Biblical standards and values.

Before we venture to criticize theonomy, let us learn from some of the good emphases of theonomists. Do we have zeal for Christ's universal lordship equal to theirs? Do we love the law of God with equal fervency? Do we show equal concern and work equally hard for healing the hurts of modern society? We must be ready to rethink our attitude toward the law. Many of us reject theonomy because we think that the Mosaic law is harsh. But the real problem is with us, not with the law (cf. Romans 7:12, 14). We have swallowed so much of the modern humanistic thinking that our own judgments and emotional reactions are corrupted. We confuse mercy with vague good will, justice with tolerance, love with sentimentality. Like all sinners we have something in us that would like to be free from God's standards altogether. We desire to abolish God's standards rather than have the standards honored by substitutionary death of Christ in payment for their violation.

The Mosaic laws were given by God, as the Old Testament itself, Jesus, and the apostles affirm (Deuteronomy 5:22–33; Matthew 5:17–20; Romans 3:2; 2 Timothy 3:16–17). The Canaanite wars and the execution of rebels were not Israel's substandard ideas but obedience to God's commands. When we find ourselves disliking these things in the Old Testament, we should take opportunity to wonder not whether the Old Testament is wrong but what is wrong with us. We need to study and pray over our Bibles until God grants us an appreciation in depth of the holiness of God, His hatred of sin, and His unfathomable wisdom in the expression of His justice in the law.

Interpreting Old Testament Law[7]

How then do we apply the Bible to modern society? Theonomists are convinced that the Old Testament law, even in its details, is applicable to modern society, while some of their opponents are convinced that the life, death, and resurrection of Christ introduced a new era in which the Old Testament law is no longer directly binding.[8] The issue is not easy to resolve because it depends partly on the hermeneutical frameworks and the sets of questions that one has when one approaches texts of the Old Testament.[9] For simplicity I confine myself to comparing theonomy with only one kind of antithetical position, namely, the "intrusionist" ethics of Meredith G. Kline.[10] Kline argues that Old Testament social and political law is not immediately applicable to us because it was tailored to the special situation of Israel. Israel as a holy nation prefigured the holiness of God's heavenly kingdom and the holiness belonging to the consummation of all things. For example, the wars against the Canaanites prefigured the Second Coming, when Christ wages a final war against all His enemies (Revelation 19:11–21). Special penalties were appropriate for Israel because of its unique role as a prefigurement of Christ's kingdom. Ethical practices belonging most properly to the kingdom of God in its final manifestation "intruded" in certain ways into the practice of Israel.

To see in action the differences between these two systems, theonomy and intrusionist ethics, let us consider a particular example. Leviticus 19:19 says, "Do not plant your field with two kinds of seed." This commandment is part of the Bible. It is God's expression of His character and His will for us. The commandment is therefore relevant to us, as part of the totality of the expression of the will of God. But just how is it relevant? Does it perhaps express a universal standard for human agricultural procedure, based on the creational principle that God made each kind of plant a distinct kind? Or does it symbolically express one element of the holy separation that Israel was to practice as a distinct "kingdom of priests" (Exodus 19:6)? Israel's observance of special distinctions between clear and unclean foods and the observance of special festival days functioned to mark Israel as a holy nation, specially set apart for God's blessing and called to a special holy service. Does this particular statute function as one instance of this special separation? If so, the statute has a lesson for the church, since the church is "a royal priesthood, a holy nation, a people belonging to God" (1 Peter 2:9). The food laws that separated Jew from Gentile have ceased to function on a literal plane as the symbolic mark of the holy community (Ephesians 2:11–22), but the same principle of holy separation still binds the church (2 Corinthians 6:14–18). We are not to mix good and evil. The way in which we observe the principle of Leviticus 19:19 is simply adapted to the new circumstances introduced by the life, death, and resurrection of Christ (Ephesians 2:16).

How do we decide how Leviticus 19:19 applies to us? The hermeneutical framework advocated by theonomy tells us to expect the whole Old Testament law to be binding on us. God's character is always the same and Jesus explicitly affirms the abiding validity of the law (Matthew 5:17–20). The hermeneutical framework advocated by Meredith G. Kline and other intrusionists tells us that the Mosaic law as a total system is no longer binding on us. The Mosaic law was specially designed as an instrument to convey typological truth concerning Israel as a holy nation. Since this typological function is fulfilled in Christ and in the consummation of all things, the literal observance of the law in its details is abrogated (Ephesians 2:15).

Actually, both theonomic and intrusionist interpretation, when understood in their very best form, include important qualifications. Bahnsen in advocating theonomy takes note of the changes due to differences in culture and due to the advance in the redemptive plan of God.[11] Kline in advocating an intrusionist approach indicates that there is continuity in the faith-norms of the Old Testament, in some of its life-norms, and in the principles of God's justice.[12] But such qualifications are sometimes minimized or forgotten by enthusiastic followers of these approaches. For the sake of illustration, it is actually better for us to deal to some extent with more stereotyped, popularized versions of the two positions. We thereby expose the general tendencies of the positions, without concerning ourselves immediately with all the details.

Neither of these frameworks by itself can solve all our problems. Theonomy rightly insists on continuity based on the unchanging moral character of God. And in principle it recognizes that the New Testament explicitly declares that some laws (e.g., food laws) need no longer be observed literally because they have been fulfilled in Christ.[13] But because its up-front emphasis is so heavily on continuity, many followers of theonomy find themselves under heavy pressure to insist on straight-line continuity of application for all the Mosaic laws except those that are explicitly altered in the New Testament. Leviticus 19:19 is never explicitly altered in the New Testament, and so by this reasoning we must assume that it remains in force.

In fact, Bahnsen and many other leading representatives of theonomy think that Leviticus 19:19 is not to be literally observed.[14] My point is merely that their explicitly articulated hermeneutical principles push in the other direction. For example, in a summary Bahnsen lists as one basic principle, "We should presume that Old Testament standing laws continue to be morally binding in the New Testament, unless they are rescinded or modified by further revelation."[15] Strict, wooden application of this principle would appear to imply continuation of Leviticus 19:19 in force.

But it could also be argued that Leviticus 19:19 is to be included with the food laws as a ceremonial ordinance. Bahnsen indicates his awareness of this possibility in principle when he says, "The New Covenant also supercedes [sic] the Old Covenant shadows, thereby changing the application of sacrificial, purity, and 'separation' principles, redefining the people of God, and altering the significance of the promised land."[16] Doubtless Bahnsen would consider the principles of Leviticus 19:19 to be among the "separation" principles whose application is altered. But how do we tell in practice what counts as a "separation" principle? How do we tell what elements in Mosaic statutes are shadows and in what way they are shadows? How do we tell what is ceremonial and what is moral? We get some significant clues concerning these questions from the New Testament, but what do we do in a case like Leviticus 19:19 that is not explicitly alluded to in the New Testament?

For several reasons it is not sufficient merely to observe that keeping types of seed separate is one kind of separation. For one thing, all the laws in Leviticus 19, including those that are most obviously permanent and moral in character, function in some way to mark Israel as holy and separate from the other nations (18:1–5; 19:2). Second, it would be quite easy to argue that keeping the types of seed distinct is a principle of separation based on creation, and therefore of permanent validity. Third, the immediate context of Leviticus does not provide decisive information about the permanency of this statute. The verse 19:19 contains two other statutes with similar concerns. But the same possible questions arise concerning the permanence or temporary character of all three statutes. Leviticus 19 as a whole contains a large number of ordinances by which Israel is to be holy (19:2). Israel's holiness was partially of a symbolical, ceremonial kind; and, sure enough, we find some ordinances in Leviticus 19 that have usually been regarded as ceremonial (e.g., 19:5–8, 23–25, 26a, 27–28). But Israel's holiness also involved moral purity. Mixed in with these ceremonial ordinances are other ordinances partly of a practical kind (19:9–10; of course with moral implications) and partly of a moral kind (19:15–18, 26b, 29). In the verse right before verse 19 is the great command to love your neighbor as yourself (v. 18).

Finally, some of the penal laws given to Moses involve a principle of separation, as we have seen in chapters 10–13. The punishment for false worshipers, false prophets, and blasphemers maintains Israel as a holy community, in its purity and separation from idolatry. The punishment for homosexual acts preserves before Israel the separation of sexes in their roles towards one another. The key book *Theonomy* assures us that the Mosaic penalties for such practices are universally binding.[17] But how do we know that some distinction between penalties regarding special purity and penalties regarding general offenses might be at work here just as it might be at work among the statutes of Leviticus 19? My arguments in previous chapters show that the Old Testament, as the foreshadowing revelation of Christ, is richer than what we have been led to expect. In particular, it does indeed contain penalties qualified by the special holiness of Israel (chapter 10). We must not jump to quick, overgeneralized conclusions about the status of all penalties whatsoever.

Bahnsen in one place distinguishes "between laws reflecting God's *justice* and those based upon His *redemptive* purposes—i.e., moral law and restorative law, the former *defining* sin while the latter aims at salvation from sin."[18] The former laws are permanent, while the latter change in form with the changes in redemptive epochs. This distinction is useful up to a point, in that it provides a Biblically-based rationale for why some rules are permanent and others are not. But the distinction is not always easy to use in practice. Bahnsen himself indicates that we are not dealing here with a "watertight" distinction but only with a significant diversity in "first order functions of the two classes of commands."[19] Typically, Mosaic laws involve both purposes in inextricable unity. All the laws point forward to Christ, both to His justice and to His redemption. Every law including Leviticus 19:19 defines some sin at least with respect to Israel. Every law expresses God's justice, inasmuch as the special ceremonial laws all express in symbolic form the absolute holiness of God and the necessity of separation from evil doing. In a broad sense every law has redemptive purpose, because the law is intended to be a slave master leading to Christ (Galatians 3:24–25). Laws that are primarily moral may include a note about salvation (Deuteronomy 5:15).

To distinguish their primary function Bahnsen notes that God's moral standards reveal our condemnation while ceremonial law shows "the means of salvation *per se*."[20] But this legitimate distinction about first order functions helps us least in just those cases where there might be doubt. For example, if refraining from sowing with two kinds of seed is indeed a universal agricultural principle, literally binding on all farmers, then the verse states something that is a sin for all times and places. It primarily functions to set forth a definition of sin and to condemn us for its violation. If on the other hand the verse expresses a principle of Israel's special separation for holiness, it primarily functions to point to the holiness of Israel and the tabernacle which in turns points to the final holiness of Christ in His sacrifice. To which category does this statute actually belong? If we know beforehand how to classify this statute, the classification will tell us its function. But in actual practice we tend to determine the classification of the statute by first understanding its function.

I think that Bahnsen understands his distinction in the same way that I do. We are supposed to determine the classification of any statute by first understanding its primary function. Understanding its function reveals whether it primarily defines sin in a universally binding way or whether it primarily articulates the way of salvation in a manner conditioned by the redemptive historical context. We thereby determine in what respects it is permanently relevant to our redemptive historical situation. The chief remaining difficulty is that it is not always easy to determine the primary function, particularly because several functions may sometimes be interwoven.

Theonomy at its best takes considerable note of discontinuities introduced by redemptive history and in particular by the coming of Christ. But because it is so interested in learning abiding principles of justice from the Old Testament, it focuses primarily on those aspects that are unchanging. The burden of proof is then placed on the person who would assert that there is change. When a framework of this kind rigidifies, as it sometimes does among followers of the movement, people insist on carrying over whatever is not decisively shown to be altered.

If we follow a rigid form of theonomist hermeneutical framework, we cannot evade the conclusion: no one text in the Old Testament or New Testament explicitly or decisively indicates the abolition of literal observance of Leviticus 19:19, and therefore it continues in force. We are bound to observe it. But the real question is not whether we observe it but how. What does the text enjoin? For what purpose? Does God express a permanent agricultural principle or a principle of Israelite symbolic holiness? No one text in the Old Testament or New Testament explicitly or decisively indicates the answer in *either* direction. In particular, nothing proves conclusively that this statute is *not* ceremonial. The principle of preserving distinctions and separations here may be of the same ceremonial order as the principle of clean and unclean foods.

The fact that the distinction of seeds has some basis in creation does not really count against this possibility. When Israel maintained distinctions between clean and unclean foods, she had to depend every moment on the order of creation that guaranteed the existence and preservation of distinct kinds of animals. But the separation between clean and unclean was nevertheless a temporary measure reexpressing a principle of creation on a heightened symbolic plane until the coming of fulfillment. Of course, in the case of food laws we are confident that we have understood correctly because there are some explicit New Testament passages on the subject (Mark 7:19; Colossians 2:21; 1 Timothy 4:3–5). But what about other Old Testament laws? Can we be sure that the New Testament will mention explicitly every case where an alteration of observance of law is appropriate? Might not there be room for deciding some issues on the basis of more general context of Old Testament and New Testament teaching together? We presume to dictate to God the form that the New Testament must take if we rigidly require the New Testament to mention every case before we are ready to admit that it may be ceremonial.

In the light of my earlier observations in the body of this book, readers may be able to guess my actual view on Leviticus 19:19. This statute is indeed a temporary law enjoining a special symbolic orderliness (see chapter 7). Hyperbolical care for orderliness symbolizes and reinforces the general orderliness of the law and the order-creating character of God the law-giver. Orderliness is maintained by distinguishing not only types of animals, but also types of seed. Moreover, certain types of mixture, such as the garments of the high priest (composed of gold, linen, and wool), the anointing oil, and the incense are associated with holiness and are therefore forbidden to ordinary Israelites (Exodus 30:22–38). If a field is used for both vineyard and grain, its produce is holy (Deuteronomy 22:9). Israel is obliged to maintain these special distinctions as part of the general practice of distinguishing the holy and the common, and this practice in turn is necessary because of the presence of the holiness of God and the holiness of the tabernacle in her midst.

By such distinctions Israel foreshadows the ultimate distinctiveness of the life-giving order that comes through Jesus Christ. The temporary symbolic character of Leviticus 19:19 is suggested even in Mosaic times by three factors: (1) it is elsewhere specifically connected with the requirements of holiness (Deuteronomy 22:9); (2) it is not directly deducible from the two great principles of loving God and loving neighbor; and (3) it apparently introduces a restriction on the wide-scope dominion given to human beings in creation (Genesis 1:26–28).

My concern, however, is not to answer questions with respect to Leviticus 19:19, but rather to examine how we go about obtaining answers concerning any Mosaic text. A general recipe of "assume continuity until proven otherwise" will not get us far.

With this example in mind, we might think that the safest course is to follow the intrusionists in denying the direct applicability of the Old Testament. But difficulties of a converse kind await us. Does our hermeneutical principle say that no Mosaic statute is binding unless specifically reiterated in the New Testament? It follows that Leviticus 19:19 is not binding. But then it becomes all too easy to miss the binding principle exemplified in Leviticus 19:19, namely, the principle of separating good from evil (2 Corinthians 6:14–18). Crudely used, this framework threatens to forbid us access to the divine wisdom and justice displayed in the Old Testament. Moreover, it makes us unable to follow the apostles when they argue ethically on the basis not of their own immediate God-given authority but of the Mosaic law (e.g., Ephesians 6:2).[21]

In the argument above I made a rigid form of theonomist hermeneutics look bad by choosing Leviticus 19:19 as the test case. But I might make rigid intrusionist hermeneutics look bad by choosing some other passage. Some passages like Leviticus 19:15 and 18:23 that are not directly reiterated in the New Testament express abiding principles, and it would be easier for our sinful nature to evade their requirements if we eliminated them and tried to deduce everything from the two great commandments of loving God and our neighbor.

How do we avoid some of the dangers that have cropped up in this examination of Leviticus 19:19? Let us stand back from the particular example and reflect on the general principles involved in arriving at conclusions in matters of ethics.

We may start with one of the theses of theonomy. God's word is the proper standard for evaluating all human action, including the actions of government officials and the laws made by civil legislators. As John M. Frame has argued, God's lordship implies that He specifies the standards for all evaluation, that He is always personally present to us as the one to whom we must respond in a personal relationship of love, and that He controls our situation so as to create opportunities and responsibilities towards our environment.[22]

Corresponding to these three ways in which God rules over us are three perspectives in terms of which we may approach ethical questions. The first perspective, the normative perspective, focuses on the rules in Scripture, God's norms for human conduct. The second perspective, the attitudinal or personal perspective, focuses on personal attitudes. The third, situational perspective, focuses on what is best for our situation.[23] From the normative perspective, we must conform to God's standards as expressed in Scripture. From an attitudinal or personal perspective, we must be motivated by love for God. From a situational perspective, we must promote the praise and honor of God in our situation.

Within a Biblical world view these three perspectives ultimately harmonize with one another, because God is the source of all. Moreover, each perspective when rightly understood encompasses the others. The normative perspective encompasses the personal, because God's law (the norm) instructs us concerning the importance of the heart and the motivation of love. The normative perspective encompasses the situational, because God's norms instruct us on the necessity of taking account of the situation (e.g., 1 Corinthians 8:7–10). The situational perspective encompasses the normative, because God is the most significant person in our situation, and God's laws are the most significant ethical facts about our situation. We cannot possibly honor God in our situation without taking into account what He says about it. The situational perspective encompasses the personal because our own dispositions as well as the existence of other people and their needs are part of the situation to which we are called to respond.

Though the three perspectives harmonize in principle, human beings in their sinfulness have a tendency to distort the truth, and the
possibilities for distortion are enhanced when they use only one perspective. For example, modern situation ethics blatantly distort Biblical
truth. It one-sidedly uses a situational perspective to deny that God's
norms are part of the definition of our situation, and that only by paying attention to the norms may we rightly judge what the consequences
of our actions will be for the honor and praise of God. By contrast, the
Pharisees of Jesus' day one-sidedly used a normative perspective. They
appealed to a constant norm, the sabbath law, in order to show that
Jesus broke the law. They failed to understand that the true intention of
the sabbath law involved an adaptation in the case of special circumstances of human need (Luke 6:9–11; 13:15–16) and special authority
(Luke 6:1–5).

The same dangers confront us. When using the normative perspective we may rightly observe that God's moral character is unchangeable
and that therefore the moral norms are always the same. But then it is
easy to overlook the fact that the special character of Israel as a holy
nation involved the observance of ceremonial ordinances that expressed
God's character and norms in a way adapted to a unique situation. Thus
the theonomists run the danger of using the appeal to unchanging
norms in order to prejudice the question of whether the great bulk of
Mosaic legislation is adapted to the unique situation of Israel. In other
words, they background the situational perspective, and this move may
make them underestimate the difficulty and complexity of disentangling
the abiding principle from the particularity of its application to Israel.

Conversely, when using the situational perspective we may rightly
observe that all of God's word given to Israel was adapted to Israel's
needs and situation. The Israelite nation lived with an agricultural, pre-
industrial economic and civic organization. More important, she lived
in a situation before the coming of Christ, when she needed to enjoy
the benefits of salvation in symbolic form before the salvation itself had
been definitively accomplished or consummated. In such a redemptive-
historical situation the entire geopolitical structure of the nation typologically embodied anticipations of Christ; covenant, king, priest, and
Israel's corporate status as son (Exodus 4:23) all foreshadowed Christ's

unique holy role. But when we concentrate on the situationally unique position of Israel, it is easy to overlook the fact that these very special arrangements foreshadowed a universally binding pattern, a permanent norm, namely, the pattern of Christ's own righteousness and perfect fulfillment of the law. Thus the special character of the Israelite law simultaneously expresses universal norms. Intrusionists run the danger of using the appeal to the special situation of Israel in order to prejudice the question of whether we can find principles of universal justice in Mosaic statutes.[24]

We must also beware of relying too much on so-called "natural law," the natural sense of right and wrong impressed on our consciences. To do so is to misuse the personal perspective. It is true that even human beings without access to the written word of God have a sense of right and wrong (Romans 1:32). But Scripture nowhere indicates that they thereby know more ethical principles than those revealed in the Bible. In fact, the opposite is the case. The Bible indicates that the Jews by their access to the written law know God's will in a privileged way (Romans 2:17–22). We must recognize that human sin distorts our attitudes and our "natural" feelings. We must be ready to submit ourselves to Scripture over and over again as a remedy for sin.

We may show the effects of perspectives by examining the interpretation of Deuteronomy 4:6–8.

> Observe them carefully, for this will show your wisdom and your understanding to the nations, who will hear about all these decrees and say, "Surely this great nation is a wise and understanding people." What other nation is so great as to have their gods near them as the LORD our God is near us whenever we pray to him? And what other nation is so great as to have such righteous decrees and laws as this body of laws I am setting before you today?

Theonomists commonly appeal to this text to show that the Mosaic law has world-wide relevance.[25] It is obvious why theonomists should think that this text supports them. According to these verses the other nations and not only Israel can recognize the wisdom of these statutes and admit that they are "righteous" (4:8). The righteousness of Mosaic ordinances thus pertains not only to Israel but all other nations. When other nations have their eyes opened to the truth, the other nations want to have just such righteous laws and express admiration for Israel's wisdom. Mosaic laws thus express standards binding on all nations and not merely on Israel. Micah 4:2 picks up this same theme in the context of eschatological prophecy. "In the latter days" the house of the Lord will be established as the most prominent mountain, the nations will come to learn the law, and "the law will go out from Zion, and the word of the LORD from Jerusalem" (Micah 4:1–2). What the nations might potentially enjoy according to Deuteronomy 4 they actually do come to enjoy in the time of fulfillment.

This argument looks very convincing until we realize that the framework of assumptions of theonomy has had a large input in influencing what we notice in these texts.[26] To concentrate on the normative perspective is to concentrate on the norms, standards, or rules. By definition, norms or rules are the same in every situation. Hence, when we operate in this framework we are already predisposed to assume primarily continuity in space and time. Continuity in space implies that the same laws bind other places, that is, other nations besides Israel. Continuity in time implies that the same laws bind people at all times—past, present, and future.

But now suppose that we approach the same texts using the framework of intrusionists and the emphasis on the situational perspective. Immediately we have in the forefront of our minds the unique situation of Israel: Israel is the unique holy nation and a kingdom of priests with its shadowy typological institutions pointing forward to fulfillment. Within this hermeneutical framework, Deuteronomy 4:6–8 appears to mean something quite different. The other nations admire Israel not only for the righteousness of her laws (4:8) but for the God who is so near to Israel whenever they call on Him (4:7), for the wisdom expressed as God reveals His character and salvific purposes uniquely to Israel, and for the land that God gave Israel as a gift (4:5). That is to say, the nations do not notice the commandments merely as rules standing by themselves but as an expression of God's special communion with Israel. They understand the rules as what is wise for this special holy people, Israel. The nations are pictured not as saying, "We should have these same laws for ourselves," but "What a special God Israel has, what a special grace God has shown to Israel, and what wise statutes God has given them for their special situation. We would certainly want to have laws just like those if we were the special chosen nation. But, unfortunately, we are not the special chosen nation, so it is not immediately clear that we should exactly copy the laws of Israel in every case." A radical discontinuity in space exists between Israel and the other nations.

When the intrusionist framework comes to Micah 4:1–2 another difference is introduced. The "latter days" as the time of eschatological fulfillment means the revelation of the glory of God in a surpassing form (Isaiah 40:5). Shadows are superseded by realities, and whatever is shadowy in the Mosaic law finds fulfillment in transformed fashion. In the New Testament era the fulfillment comes, and the light of the revelation of the glory of God shines in the face of Jesus Christ (2 Corinthians 4:6). Now it is clear that the "word of the LORD" going forth from Jerusalem is preeminently the word of the gospel, the word concerning the life, death, and resurrection of Jesus Christ (Luke 24:44–49; Acts 1:8). The righteousness of the law is fulfilled in Christians as they live in union with Christ (Romans 8:4). The whole Old Testament including the Mosaic law is to be interpreted in the light of the Christocentric character of fulfillment (Luke 24:44–46). Thus a radical discontinuity arises in time through the coming of Christ. Taken together, the discontinuities in space and time prohibit us from carrying over Old Testament statutes directly to ourselves.

Thus the same two texts, Deuteronomy 4:6–8 and Micah 4:1–2, look very different depending on our hermeneutical framework. If our framework stresses norms and continuity, we see the implications of continuity. If our framework stresses the different redemptive-historical situations and therefore discontinuities arising from differences in situation, we see the implications of discontinuity. In my judgment, neither framework finds any difficulty with these particular texts. Neither framework forces an unnatural sense on the texts or is forced to overlook a phrase that is difficult to harmonize.[27]

In fact, if we are already thoroughly committed to one of the frameworks our interpretation of these and many other texts looks obvious. Our whole position is obviously right, and only someone insensitive to the obvious or sinfully resisting the clear teaching of Scripture could fail to agree with us. A certain dogmatism and harshness toward opponents can creep in unawares because we are not fully aware of how much the prechosen framework and its imperfections has influenced our conclusions. The arguments have more circularity in them than is commonly understood.

Of course, Deuteronomy 4:6–8 and Micah 4:1–2 still have relevance to the debate. We should not just throw up our hands and say that both positions are right or that no one can know which is right. We must look again at these passages and others to try faithfully to understand all their implications. But initial impressions are not enough. We must be patient in trying to understand the whole warp and woof of God's revelation and not merely quote passages like these in isolation because we can see how they support our position when interpreted against the background of that same position. It is too easy to read in what we afterwards read out.

The interpretation of Deuteronomy 17:2–13 may further illustrate the interaction of frameworks with texts. Deuteronomy 17:2–7 articulates principles for dealing judicially with false worship. Whereas Deuteronomy 4:6–8 superficially might appear to affirm the complete universality of all Mosaic law, Deuteronomy 17:2–13 superficially appears to affirm its special character. Intrusionists sensitive to the special status of Israel can immediately point out all the indications of ways in which the penalty for false worship is connected with the unique Israelite situation. The actions take place within the land given by God (17:2, 4). False worship involves transgression of God's covenant, that is, the covenant made especially with Israel in a unique historical event at Mount Sinai (17:2). Execution is by stoning (17:5), which may be analogous to the production of stone memorial altars testifying to God's history with Israel (cf. Joshua 22:10–34; Genesis 28:18).[28] The execution redemptively purifies the community (17:7). Difficult cases are to be referred to the priests in the place that God will choose (17:8).

But theonomists can also point out how this unique Israelite situation is a model embodying principles of universal application. The land of Palestine is a special holy land given by God, but it is thereby a symbol of the fact that all the earth is owned by God (Psalm 24:1) and given to human beings as He chooses (Acts 17:26). Israel is under special covenant with God, but this covenant is not only analogous to the covenant made with all human beings through Adam but also to the new covenant whose rule will extend to all nations (Matthew 28:18–20). Execution by stoning may have no special significance, since it is apparently the common method for capital crimes. Even if it has the significance of memorializing, it embodies the general principle of remembering the Lord's past dealings with us (Psalm 77:11). With regard to the note of purification (Deuteronomy 17:7), just acts of the civil government are among the means by which national well-being is maintained and enhanced and the wrath of God turned away (cf. God's judgment on nations in Amos 1–2). Thus Deuteronomy 17:7 embodies a general principle. The procedure for consulting with the priests in 17:8 expresses the general principle of having a system of appeals (cf. Ecclesiastes 5:8–9) and being able to consult people knowledgeable in the law.

As before, the real question is not whether Deuteronomy 17:2–13 is relevant to us or binding on us, but how is it binding? More precisely, what changes take place as we expand the application of the Mosaic law from Israel to the nonholy nations and as we expand its application in time through the changes introduced by fulfillment in Jesus Christ? What is permanent principle and what is adaptation to a unique situation in time and space?

Some verses of the Old Testament express a general principle pretty much as they stand (Leviticus 19:4). Other verses express a principle in the form of a foreshadowment (Leviticus 19:8). As a matter of degree we may therefore classify many of them as primarily "moral" or "ceremonial." But we oversimplify if we say merely that one verse is specific to Israel and another verse is universal. In fact, all the verses are God's personal covenantal communication to Israel first of all and are colored by their unique redemptive-historical context. At the same time all the verses express God's character and His abiding principles of justice. To put it another way, all the verses point forward to Christ. They point forward to the uniqueness of His incarnation, death, and resurrection once and for all, and hence have a unique redemptive-historical coloring. Simultaneously, they point forward to the universality of the principles of justice by which He reigns. They therefore express in some way God's character and are generalizable into rules with universal bearing.

Deuteronomy 17:8–20 is a particularly good illustration of this dual reality. If we read Deuteronomy 17:8–20 from a theonomist framework, we are on the lookout for unchanging principle. So we notice the practical wisdom of a system of appeals and the necessity and justice of dealing radically with a person who would destroy the very foundations of authority by contumacy (vv. 12–13). If we read Deuteronomy 17:8–20 from an intrusionist framework, we immediately recognize the typological status of the high priest, the judge, and the king as special officers foreshadowing Christ. Hence, we see the passage as speaking of the necessity of listening to the voice of God in Christ and the penalty for rebellion against Christ. In fact, both of these readings are true as far as they go. Israel is a nation among nations, and so of course God's political wisdom for Israel will embody lessons for all government. All governments are subject to God's rule. At the same time, Israel is a nation filled with typological symbols, and so of course there is a fruitful analogy between Israel's system of government and the government of Christ. But we are in danger of missing something if we consistently adopt only one of these frameworks. What we miss may sometimes be crucial to understanding the Old Testament in depth and therefore crucial to applying it rightly in changed circumstances. For example, if we rigidly applied a principle of continuity, with no understanding of the typological role of the high priest, we would be forced to set up a contemporary earthly high priest for ourselves. If we rigidly applied a principle of discontinuity, we would simply learn nothing about principles for organizing a modern state.

In the case of Deuteronomy 17 it is comparatively easy to see some of the basic insights to be derived from each of two perspectives. In such a case, a typical reader operating within one perspective might still notice complementary truths. But what happens when we come to more difficult cases? Then the reader is all the more tempted to stop short simply with the answers obtained from one perspective.

Old Testament Penalties

Old Testament penal laws, where some notorious disagreements arise, involve some of the same difficulties that we have just seen. Penal laws clearly involve a principle of justice and fit punishment, and hence embody permanent principle. Some penal laws just as clearly involve restoration (e.g., the thief repaying what he has stolen and the manslaughterer being free to return to his home after the death of the high priest, Numbers 35:9–28). Such restoration foreshadows the coming of Christ. If we have decided beforehand that a particular penal law (e.g., Exodus 21:14) is moral, its function is primarily to define sin and restrain evil. If we have decided beforehand that a particular penal law (e.g., Leviticus 20:2–3; Numbers 1:51; 3:10) is ceremonial and is based on the special holiness of Israel, its function is partly to assert the special holiness of Israel as a foreshadowing of the holiness of Christ, the holiness of the church, and the cleansing from sin by Christ's substitutionary penal death. But it is wiser not to impose our classification at all, lest we compress the richness of the passage or prejudge the limits of its implications. Instead we should patiently try to understand the function of the particular law in its broader context and on this basis discern how it applies—perhaps in a variety of respects—in the New Testament era.

Bahnsen and many other theonomists maintain as a general principle that the penal laws are all moral, that is, that they all express permanent, universal principles.[29] At a minimum, such an assertion may mean only that every law expresses universal principles by revealing God's justice. Such is in fact the case, as we can see from the uniform Biblical testimony to the holiness and goodness of the law (e.g., Psalm 119; Romans 7:14; 13:8–10), the unchangeable character of God, and the fact that God's word is always consistent with every aspect of His character, including His justice. The whole of this book functions to illustrate these truths.[30] But theonomists appear to be saying something more. At a maximum they are claiming that penal laws require no substantial adjustments because of the coming of Christ. Theonomy as popularly understood involves such a maximalist position, but it is more accurate to say that Bahnsen's general statements concerning penal law are qualified by the places where he says that we should presume continuity unless we have Biblical evidence to the contrary.[31]

Bahnsen and others have much to say in favor of this general principle concerning penal law. But their most powerful arguments and proof texts deal with the fact that universal principles of God's justice are embodied in all God's statutes whatsoever. If their arguments point to pure permanence for all laws whatsoever, they prove too much because food laws clearly do not fit. If their arguments allow (as in fact they do) for changes in the form of application due to advance in redemptive history, such changes may also affect some of the penology (such as Exodus 30:33, 38; Leviticus 20:10, 18; 23:29; and Numbers 35:28). Which parts are affected and how? That remains to be seen. But then we must look at the penal law statute by statute, context by context, and try to understand its functions. We do not merely assume that no changes can ever be entertained. Such is what I have endeavored to do in Part 2 of this book.

Bahnsen's advocacy of a presumption of continuity is understandable in a Christian atmosphere given to ignoring the Old Testament in general and its penology in particular. He is summoning the troops to awake from their slumber and their compromises with the evil world around, and to recognize the wisdom of the Old Testament. I am uncomfortable with his stance because I am attacking a different evil, namely, the presumption that we know what sort of literature we will find in the Old Testament before we read it. Theonomists run the danger of presuming that the Mosaic law consists in blueprints for modern economics and politics, while intrusionists run the danger of presuming that the Mosaic law consists in typological truths about spiritual redemption in Christ, truths necessarily unrelated to modern earthly governments. Both of these moves flatten Mosaic literature in one direction and so hinder the rich understanding that we need to do the job accurately in political ethics and in Christological understanding. Bahnsen himself shows sensitivity to this danger when he writes:

> We need to be sensitive to the fact that interpreting the Old Testament law, properly categorizing its details (for example, ceremonial, standing, cultural), and making modern day applications of the authoritative standards of the Old Testament is *not an easy or simple task*. It is not always readily apparent to us how to understand an Old Testament commandment or use it properly today. So the position taken here does not make everything in Christian ethics a simple matter of looking up obvious answers in a code-book. Much hard thinking—ex-

egetical and theological homework—is entailed by a commitment to the position advocated in these studies.[32]

We shall have to do our homework to understand the whole Bible in depth. Some theonomists' simple arguments to the effect that the Old Testament law is confirmed in the New Testament and therefore must be kept now in a literal and straightforward way are not adequate. Some intrusionists' simple arguments to the effect that many laws are not found outside of the Mosaic era and therefore may safely not be kept are equally inadequate. Both of these routes are the lazy way out in the sense that they do not come to grips with the full richness of Old Testament revelation. We shall have to work to understand what God is saying—and that means understanding in indissoluble and harmonious unity both how God dealt uniquely with Israel to foreshadow Christ and how God constantly revealed His eternal justice as an aspect of the wisdom that is found in Christ (Colossians 2:3). When we neglect to use both normative and situational perspectives (and for that matter the personal perspective) to supplement our understanding, we flatten out the depth of Old Testament revelation and eventually distort our understanding of God Himself.

The best representatives of both theonomy and intrusion are of course not so simplistic. But I think that even the best representatives might be able to learn by some more sensitive listening to the other side. And I would appeal to the followers not to be so swallowed by the persuasive rhetoric of an admittedly insightful framework that they are unable to see nuances that come readily to light only by adopting another point of view. It would be a shame if theonomists' commendable attempt to evaluate politics, economics, and civil government in the light of the standard of God's written word should fail to produce godly fruit. But our labors will be corrupted if Christian infighting takes over or if overconfidence in a hermeneutical framework makes us stop short of deep penetration into God's word. If we stop short, we may be in possession of unjust principles that we think just.

If we are largely ignorant of the Old Testament, we have a heavy responsibility to become familiar with it. As we become knowledgeable, our knowledge of the Old Testament gives us more weighty responsibility to apply it. But we also have a responsibility not to dishonor the name of God by putting forward inordinately dogmatic claims as God's justice what in some cases may turn out afterwards not to be so.

The Relation of This Book to Theonomy

In this book I disagree with theonomy on some significant matters of detail, but I affirm much of its principle concern regarding the value of the Old Testament.[33] Let us first be more specific about the disagreements. I repudiate the view that state penalties for false worship are ever just or appropriate within this age. But I do so on the basis of my understanding of the Mosaic law and of the penalties for false worship in Deuteronomy 13:1–18 and 17:2–7 in particular. Hence, I affirm what is often regarded as the essence of the theonomic view, i.e., the abiding value of the law. I affirm with great vigor the continuing value and relevance of the whole Old Testament, on the basis of the fact that it reveals our Lord Jesus Christ. Its law and its tabernacle imagery express the righteousness and holiness of Christ.

Thus the most significant disputes between myself and theonomy concern not the question of whether the law is binding but what the law means. The law is indeed binding on Christians. For example, we should obey the principles articulated in Deuteronomy 13 and 17 and other Old Testament passages. But to obey them properly we must understand what they mean and how they foreshadow the fullness of righteousness and holiness found in Jesus Christ. Once we have that understanding, we can see that keeping the law means following Christ.

We are thus saying what all Christians know in their hearts: Jesus is Lord. We are to follow Him, reflect His character, and praise His beauty and holiness. We are to know Him, to use the language of Philippians 3:10. Knowing Him in a full and deep way includes knowing "the power of His resurrection and the fellowship of sharing in his sufferings." The Old Testament law helps us in this process because it reveals Him (Luke 24:25–27, 44–48). The challenging task remaining for us is to appreciate just how the law reveals Christ.

When I phrase things in this way I may appear to differ from theonomists mainly in emphasis. But such differences may be far-reaching in practice. If the law is related in a comprehensive fashion to the death and resurrection of Christ, and if it is full of typological correspondences to Christ, we must expect radical transformation of the texture of the law and radical reinterpretation in the light of the accomplishments of Christ. Such transfiguration is just as significant as the truth that the deepest principles of God's righteousness are unchangeable. I would therefore urge readers to be just as much at home with Paul's affirmations about the passing away of the Mosaic law as they are at home with Matthew's affirmation about its continuing force (Ephesians 2:15; Galatians 3:25; 2 Corinthians 4:3–11; Romans 6:15–7:6).

One function of the law is to reveal general principles of justice, that is, universal standards of Christ's righteous character and His rule. But here also there is a difficulty: how do we find general principles of justice in the law? Some laws are adapted in obvious ways to unique cultural and redemptive-historical circumstances in Israel, as both Bahnsen and I would agree. Other laws, such as "Love the LORD your God with all your heart and with all your soul and with all your strength" (Deuteronomy 6:5) and "Love your neighbor as yourself" (Leviticus 19:18), are completely universal moral principles. But every law, even the most specialized adaptations to Israel, expresses God's character and reveals something of Christ; thus every law somehow expresses universal principles. In fact, every law illustrates the principles of loving God and loving neighbor. Obviously, the principles of loving God and loving neighbor are binding and applicable now. Jesus and the apostles affirm so. Hence, the whole law, as an illustration of these two principles, is applicable.

But other principles besides these two basic ones are also universal. How do we determine what they are? More precisely, how do we discern the universal principles in what is more specialized, and how do we discern in what is more universal a special focus on God's care for Israel? One major difficulty in interpreting the Old Testament and in applying it lies precisely here.[34]

Suppose that in our hermeneutics we want to "play it safe." We decide only to extract the most obviously universal principles from each particular law. Then we are left only with the two general principles of loving God and loving neighbor. Or perhaps we look for slightly less general principles than those and end up with the Ten Commandments as our summary of the law. Every law is seen as a particularization of one or more of the Ten Commandments. Such a result is valid enough as far as it goes, but it still does not go far enough. We miss the rich instruction from the details of the law.

On the other hand, suppose that we want to "play it safe" in the other direction. We fear that we will miss something by overgeneralizing. So we cling fanatically to each detail. We argue, perhaps, that we must follow all the details literally today, except those specifically abolished in the New Testament. The law regarding sowing with two kinds of seeds would have to be included, the law about making tassels on one's cloaks (Deuteronomy 22:12), and many other particulars. If we follow this route, we inevitably miss the true generalizations and carry over many unnecessary features of the Israelite situation. Worse, we run a risk of missing or underestimating the heart of the matter, namely, the Old Testament's revelation of Christ. We destroy the liberty of Christian people with unnecessary extra rules. We obscure the fact that Christians are betrothed to Christ, not to the law, and that their love of the law arises from its revelation of Christ, not from some innate property of self-sufficient rules.

In actual fact, the level of generality that we happen to find in a particular passage depends a great deal on our point of view. Inferring a very general principle from a passage is a little like looking at a meadow from the top of a mountain. We may not see the details very well, but we see one way in which the meadow fits into a whole mountain range. On the other hand, when we come down to the foot of the mountain and stand right in the meadow, we see many details. But these details may so overwhelm us that we have little idea how the meadow is related to the whole mountain range. Likewise, when we look at a passage, we may infer from it either a very general principle or a very specific teaching that may not have obvious broad implications. We can represent the general principle as the peak of a triangle and the specific details as the base of a triangle. In between are other, intermediate generalizations (see figure 2). Then the question remains, just how general do we have to become to obtain something directly binding on our situation? How far up the mountain do we have to go to "see our situation," as it were?

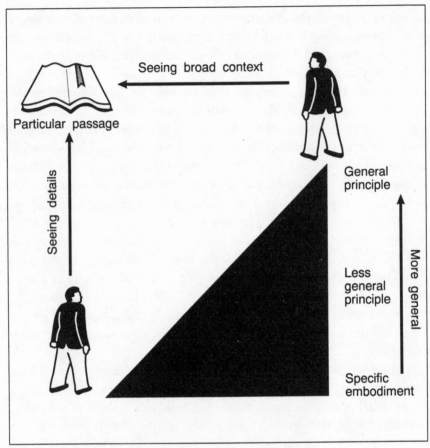

Figure 2: Triangle of Generality

We may illustrate these issues using the passage Deuteronomy 13:1–18. What general principles of morality and justice are expressed in this passage? Let us start at the most general level (the top of the triangle). The rejection of idolatry in Deuteronomy 13:1–18 expresses the principles of loving God. Loving your neighbor is expressed by preventing the false prophet from staying around to tempt other people. Hence, at the level of greatest generality, Deuteronomy 13:1–18 expresses the two general principles of morality, loving God and loving your neighbor.

Let us descend to a slightly lower level of generality. Deuteronomy 13:1–18 expresses the principles of some of the Ten Commandments, in particular the first commandment. Having no other gods before the Lord is expressed in rejecting temptations from a false prophet or seducer.

Other kinds of general principle are also illustrated and embodied in the text. The purity of the people of God and their separation from overt unbelief is expressed by the rejection of the false prophet. "Be holy because I, the LORD your God, am holy" is embodied. As I have argued in chapter 10, the retributive principle, "as you have done it will be done to you" is expressed, as is the principle of restoring what is damaged (in this case, restoring the damaged purity of Israel).

The instructions concerning holy war that are particular to Israel are also embodied in the language of "condemned things" (Deuteronomy 13:17). As we saw in chapter 10, the whole process of holy war contains principles of destruction of sin and purification through divine power and through divinely ordained sacrifice. Such principles are still operative in the New Testament, though the particulars of our spiritual holy war are transformed in a way suitable to the circumstances of the New Testament and the reign of the resurrected Christ.

At a lower level of generality the language of Deuteronomy 13 applies only to the circumstances of Israel while in the land. The formula, "physically kill proven false prophets and seducers to false worship," represents this level of generality. Most theonomists agree that this formula does not represent an absolutely general principle, since they would want to qualify it in the form, "Kill convicted false prophets and seducers to false worship in a nation that has become largely Christian and in which such laws have been adopted as the law of the land." (However, I do not agree with theonomists even when they make their special restriction.) We can also put forward even more particular formulas, such as "stone to death the seducer, the hand of the witness being first in throwing a stone, and all the people also doing the stoning." This formula is even closer than the others to the exact specifications of Deuteronomy 13:9–10. Are the new particulars that we have added here part of a general principle that we dare not ignore in any circumstance? Or are they specialized to Israel? Are they part of the "meadow" of Israel's specific circumstances, but not characteristic of the whole "mountain range" of universal moral principle? How do we tell? Must execution be by stoning? Must the witness throw the first stone? Must all the people participate in stoning?

We can raise similar questions concerning the passage in Deuteronomy 13:12–18 on an idolatrous town. We can compose a whole succession of formulas that include more and more detail.

1. Destroy any idolatrous town.
2. Destroy any idolatrous town proven to be idolatrous by further investigation.
3. Destroy any idolatrous town within a nation dedicated to God.
4. Destroy any idolatrous town within Israel.
5. Destroy any idolatrous town completely.
6. Destroy any idolatrous town completely, including animals.
7. Destroy any idolatrous town completely, including animals and all goods ("plunder" in Deuteronomy 13:16).
8. Destroy any idolatrous town completely, with the sword.
9. Burn it in addition to the above.
10. Gather the plunder into the public square and then burn it.
11. Never rebuild it in addition to the above.
12. Make the town a burnt offering in addition to the above.

Thus we can summarize the teaching and the implications of Deuteronomy 13 either with a very general summary ("love God") or with a very specific description including many of the details. All the details were relevant to the Israelites to whom the commandments were originally given. All the details are in a sense relevant to us, since we must try to understand what God spoke through Moses to the Israelites. But not all details are relevant in the same way. To learn lessons for our own situation and to apply the law to our own situation, we must have some grasp of its purpose. (We must see how the meadow is related to the whole mountain range.) Such a grasp is obtained in the light of the context.

Which contexts, then, throw light on the purpose? The context of the Mosaic law is certainly relevant, and so are the Ten Commandments as the heart of the law. The context of the tabernacle is also relevant because the tabernacle and the law are closely related. The context of the exodus from Egypt is relevant too, not only because it is mentioned in Deuteronomy 13:5, 10, and elsewhere, but because for Moses and the Israelites, the Exodus was the immediate background experience of the revelation of God that would have qualified everything that God said in the revelation at Mount Sinai and subsequent revelation through Moses. The context of the whole Bible is also important because the Bible is the whole story of which God's story in Deuteronomy 13 is a part. Finally, the context of Christ's life and death is important, because it is the preeminent revelation to which the whole Old Testament points forward. All in all, interpreting Deuteronomy 13:1–18 involves a large number of factors.

Let us return now from the particular example of Deuteronomy 13 to the general issues. Understanding the law involves discerning its general principles in order that it may be properly applied in changed circumstances.[35] Everyone must engage in this process, because everyone must decide when details of Israelite context are tangential to general principle and when they are part of it or influence it.

The advice that we should presume that the Old Testament law continues to bind us does not really help much. The advice really means that the *general principles* of the law bind us. But to say this much is a truism. By definition general principles continue to be the same, because to be general or to be principle is to be applicable to all times and places. Of course the principles continue! We do not need to *presume* that they continue; we *know* that they continue because it is so by definition of the word *principle*.

Do we need continuity of other things *besides* the general principles? The only other things besides principles are details that are not principial, that is, details that in themselves need not be continued.

The basic issue, then, is not whether there is continuity but what are the general principles embedded in each Old Testament law. At precisely what level of generality (what level in the triangle of generality) will we find a universal principle, either in Deuteronomy 13 or in some other passage? To answer that question is simultaneously to answer what carries over to today.

On this issue no simple formula will do. No formula will automatically guarantee that principles of just the right amount of generality will automatically pop out of each law of Moses. There is no substitute for careful study and meditation. Disagreements exist between Bahnsen and me, not over whether the Old Testament law applies but what are the general principles embodied in penal law. I think that there are such principles. Bahnsen thinks that there are such principles. Neither of us wants to abandon valid general principles, and neither wants blindly to carry over details whose significance has altered in our time.[36]

Bahnsen wrote as he did to encourage respect for the Old Testament and careful meditation on its precepts. The language in his books about presuming continuity between Old Testament and New was part of this effort. In this respect his work is valuable. But his language can be misused to prejudge the meaning of the Old Testament. Suppose that we have listed before us a whole series of increasingly particular formulations of a supposedly general principle, such as the formulations I have provided above for Deuteronomy 13. "Presuming continuity" can easily mean, "Stop at the lowest level of generality that you can, subject to not being too absurd, not carrying over what look to you like real trivia, and not coming into direct tension with any New Testament pronouncement." Such a recipe gives us *quick* answers, but there is no particular reason to believe that we will always obtain the *right* answers. In addition, the desire for quick answers short-circuits the process of meditating on the unfathomable wisdom of God in the riches of His word, riches that come to their fulfillment in the full treasure of wisdom and knowledge hidden in Christ (Colossians 2:3). Such a short-circuiting is the opposite of what Bahnsen and his books intend.

Moreover, when we look for general principles in the Bible, there is always a danger that we conceive of such principles as abstract, *impersonal* absolutes. But in the Bible all general moral principles are deeply *personal*. They are expressions of God's character, implications of who He is in His righteousness and holiness. The Bible never gives us naked principles, but reveals Jesus Christ, who in His righteousness, justice, and mercy is the same yesterday, today, and forever (Hebrews 13:8). Principles always exist "incarnated" in the particulars of Israel and the particulars of God's ways with His people, leading up to the great particular of the incarnation of Jesus Christ. Hence, in looking for principles in the Old Testament, we must never imagine that such principles constitute something different from or unrelated to the foreshadowing of the New Testament kingdom of God, which is summed up in Christ our King.

A dispute about state punishments can be settled only by studying the Bible as a whole, studying the Old Testament, studying its penology in particular, studying its fulfillment in Christ, and endeavoring ever more capably to discern principles expressed in the law. Our discernment grows only as we know Christ more and more deeply (Ephesians 3:17–19), for His law reflects His just character. Such is the purpose of my book. In my view, it represents an advance in our understanding of Old Testament law. Others may write books in turn that will advance our understanding still further. I hope that they do. But let us not unfairly understand Bahnsen's books. Comparatively speaking, his books are at the beginning of this process rather than at its end. If they are understood as dogmatically closing down our options for interpreting the Old Testament, they are understood in less than the best light.

Modifying the Theses of Theonomy

Because of my positive view of the Old Testament, I can affirm virtually all of Bahnsen's ten main theses concerning theonomy (listed above). But this apparent "agreement" can easily be misunderstood. Paradoxically, I can also agree with a good deal in Kline's intrusionist approach, the supposed antithesis of theonomy. Each of the approaches includes important qualifications, and if I allow myself to expand those qualifications with my own insights, I can adopt much for my own point of view.

I am uneasy over the theses that might appear to suggest a presumption in favor of straight-line, direct enforcement of a large class of Old Testament laws today (theses 4, 6, 9, 10). In the hands of lazy people presumption gets turned into superficiality and arrogance. As I observed above, presumption can easily become a recipe for finding principles at the lowest possible level of generality, and as such it would sanction an arbitrary stopping point.

But in principle I can interpret even these problematic theses in a favorable sense, because a "presumption" means only a preliminary judgment in the absence of definite evidence to the contrary. Thus presumption can always be overthrown by evidence of the type that I present in the body of this book.

In my own work I try not to presume a general system either of continuity or discontinuity, because I want to notice and understand both. When I study the law of Moses, I think I discover more and more what it means and then it becomes clearer how it applies. To discover in depth what the law means is to discover how it centers on the promise of Christ and His justice. By means of that center point we grasp how it bears on us as disciples of Christ. When we understand the law in its full richness and in its functions of foreshadowing Christ, we obtain simultaneously insights into how it applies to us now.

Consequently, a great deal of the differences between Bahnsen and me can be treated as differences of emphasis. But the differences in emphasis and in hermeneutical framework also lead me to prefer modified formulations of some of Bahnsen's theses. In order that people may see the differences more concretely, let me spell out some alternative formulations to theses 4, 6, 9, and 10.

Thesis 4

We should presume that Old Testament standing laws continue to be morally binding in the New Testament, unless they are rescinded or modified by further revelation.[37]

In an accompanying footnote Bahnsen adds this explanation:

"Standing law" is used here for *policy* directives applicable over time to classes of individuals (e.g., do not kill; magistrates, execute rapists), in contrast to particular directions for an individual (e.g., the order for Samuel to anoint David at a particular time and place) or positive commands for distinct incidents (e.g., God's order for Israel to exterminate certain Canaanite tribes at a certain point in history).[38]

I prefer the following alternative:

Modified thesis 4: All Old Testament laws foreshadow Jesus Christ, His work, and His righteousness. Since Jesus Christ is "the same yesterday and today and forever," the laws by testifying to Christ express principles binding in the New Testament era.

The stress on Jesus Christ I regard as very important. We are supposed to understand the Old Testament not as a mere statute book but as a testimony to Christ (see the discussion in chapter 17). The Old Testament does have indirect relevance for governmental practices today. But this relevance derives not from any abstract universality of its formulations, but rather from the universality of Christ's rule and His righteousness.

In my thesis I include all laws, not only standing laws. I might also have included narratives, songs, and other material from the Old Testament. Bahnsen conveniently restricts himself to "standing laws," but actually the scope of his favorite key text, Matthew 5:17–20, is broader. Not one jot or tittle of *any* of the Law or the Prophets fails to be fulfilled. Bahnsen, because of his interests, understandably chooses to focus on standing laws, since in their literal form they cover the largest number of particular cases. But other parts of the Old Testament also reveal God's justice.

Moreover, the distinction between standing law and positive law is in one respect a relative one. For example, the commandment to stone any person or animal that touches Mount Sinai (Exodus 19:12–13) directly applies not to only one time and one incident but to a period of time (the time at Mount Sinai) and to whole classes of individuals (anyone who touches the mountain). The commandments for conquering Canaan apply to the whole time period during which Canaan is conquered, however long that period may last. The time is open-ended. Commandments with respect to the tabernacle apply to the whole period during which the people live with the tabernacle. These time periods are relatively short in comparison with the whole of history, so we can easily think of them as a "particular case." But technically speaking they are not merely a single incident. Accordingly, we may classify these commandments as either "standing" or "positive" law, depending on how long a time period we use as a criterion.

Conversely, commandments that are normally considered as standing law can also be regarded as positive law. The commandments in Deuteronomy 13 and 17 regarding false worship are, in terms of technical details of their wording, restricted to a particular time and place. They are addressed to the people whom the Lord brought out of Egypt (Deuteronomy 13:5, 10) and are to be operative in their society and land, the land of promise (Deuteronomy 13:1, 12; 17:2, 7). Their principles of justice are generalizable beyond these immediate circumstances, but so are the principles of justice operative in all commandments whatsoever. The important issue is how this generalization takes place.

Hence, Bahnsen's choice to focus on standing law alone puts into the background some complexities. It does not mention the possible ambiguity in the distinction between standing law and positive law, for one thing. But more important, it discourages people from raising a very important question, namely, whether some of the supposed "standing laws" are standing laws for Israel that are not immediately generalizable to settings other than Israel, just as the law for stoning people at Mount Sinai (Exodus 19:12–13) and the laws for holy war are not immediately generalizable. On the average the standing laws are likely to be more obviously generalizable simply because their original literal form covers a wider range of occasions. But "on the average" cannot be completely equated with "presume in favor of complete independence of situation."

Thesis 6

God's revealed standing laws are a reflection of His immutable moral character and, as such, are absolute in the sense of being nonarbitrary, objective, universal, and established in advance of particular circumstances (thus applicable to general types of moral situation).[39]

I prefer the following:

> Modified thesis 6. God's revealed laws are a reflection of His immutable moral character, which is climactically revealed in Jesus Christ. As such, His laws are absolute in the sense of being nonarbitrary, objective, and expressive of general principles of justice. These principles of justice are thus applicable to general types of moral situation. God's revealed laws are also a revelation to particular peoples at particular times, looking forward to the particular once-for-all revelation of justice through the sacrifice and resurrection of Christ. Thus God's laws always express God's knowledge of the particular needs of the people for direction in their particular circumstances.

My uneasiness with Bahnsen's thesis 6 is very similar to my uneasiness with thesis 4. Both theses become better guides if they direct us more pointedly toward the Christocentric character of the Old Testament. Unless they are reformulated, both theses tend to push readers into presuming that every Old Testament law is completely general in form as it stands, or at worst is very easily generalizable. Bahnsen himself elsewhere distances himself from such naive generality,[40] but his followers may not always do so.

Thesis 9

The general continuity which we presume with respect to the moral standards of the Old Testament applies just as legitimately to matters of socio-political ethics as it does to personal, family, or ecclesiastical ethics.[41]

I prefer to say the following:

Modified thesis 9. The guidelines that we have suggested apply to laws commonly classified as moral, ceremonial, and civil. Old Testament law is useful first of all through its testimony to the coming of Jesus Christ. But secondarily it has instruction on socio-political ethics as well as on personal, family, and ecclesiastical ethics. But special care must be exercised in all applications to understand how it foreshadows Christ's work. In addition, special care must be exercised in socio-political and ecclesiastical ethics. Extra complexities in interpretation in the ecclesiastical area are introduced by the fact that the form of the people of God has changed through the coming of Christ, which led to the transition to the New Testament era. Socio-political ethics must take into account not only this redemptive-historical transition but the ways in which Mosaic law is adapted to the socio-political culture of Israel.

The same general principles of God's justice apply both to Israel and to us now. Jesus Christ is the same, and God's character is always the same. But the church of the New Testament is different from Israel in the Old Testament because of the differences introduced by the resurrection and ascension of Christ. Moreover, the changes from an agrarian society to a secularized postindustrial society and from tribal to monarchical to democratic forms of political power must be taken into account when we move toward modern social and political applications.

I imagine that Bahnsen agrees with me in large measure on this point, but I just wish that some of my concerns had been expressed in his thesis 9. Bahnsen's thesis as it stands tends to encourage people to assume that social and political ethics undergo no greater changes than personal ethics. The standards for such ethics, i.e., the general principles of morality and justice, always undergo no change at all, because by definition, standards are what remain the same. But it would have been helpful to note that the concrete forms of society and politics are more subject to alteration than the forms of individual and family life. Bahnsen's laudable concern for making us use the Bible as our standard for socio-political ethics has perhaps led to the formulation of this thesis in too unguarded a way.

Thesis 10

The civil precepts of the Old Testament (standing "judicial" laws) are a model of perfect social justice for all cultures, even in the punishment of criminals.[42]

I prefer the following statement:

> Modified thesis 10. The civil precepts of the Old Testament ("judicial" laws) are an earthly model of the perfect social justice in Christ's kingdom. The principles of justice embodied in these precepts foreshadow Christ's righteousness. Since Christ is Lord of all, His standards are applicable to all cultures, even in the punishment of criminals.

The word *model* can mean a concrete embodiment of general principles, and so might allow that Israel foreshadows the perfect justice of Christ and His kingdom. If the model is a concrete embodiment in one set of circumstances, the application of God's principles of justice to other circumstances and other states might in many respects take somewhat different form. But Bahnsen's original thesis 10 does appear to me to suggest that we may carry over all the standing civil laws in a straightforward, formulaic manner. Such a suggestion is similar to the presumption in favor of continuity that we find in some of the earlier theses.

Possible Objections

Let me now try to anticipate a few objections that may arise in the minds of theonomists and at the same time try to clarify my previous points.

Objection 1. Your position cannot possibly be right because Bahnsen has refuted it. In particular, he has shown that Mosaic penalties ought still to be used by magistrates today. Actually, the differences between Bahnsen and me are complex, so that it is not clear how far Bahnsen's previous arguments have a bearing on my position. Bahnsen's refutations are directed mostly towards people who reject the Old Testament in a wholesale fashion, which is not true of my position.

But let us concentrate on the most noteworthy unbridgeable difference. Bahnsen's books have taken the position that Deuteronomy 13 and 17:2–7 provide a Biblical basis for the death penalty for false worship today.[43] Such a view contradicts my position. But Bahnsen's key arguments regarding false worship do not in fact effectively challenge my findings. Bahnsen's key chapters[44] appeal primarily to the continuity of the moral law (i.e., the moral standards expressed in the Ten Commandments), principles of justice, and the obligation of magistrates to execute justice. With all these principles I agree, because they are all ways of talking about the consistency of God's character and the constancy of Christ's rule. Precisely on the basis of the Biblical texts to which Bahnsen appeals, I come to some of the same principial conclusions. That is to say, I believe that God's principles of justice are abiding and that magistrates have an obligation to execute justice. But I come to different conclusions in detail because of differences in hermeneutical framework and my different understanding of the Old Testament in detail.

In addition, especially in his book, *Theonomy*, Bahnsen appeals repeatedly to Matthew 5:17–20 to justify the continued use of Old Testament law in all its detail. I too would appeal to it, but I would raise the question as to what kind of fulfillment the Gospel of Matthew is talking about in Matthew 5:17. Is it "confirmation" as Bahnsen understands it, or climactic manifestation of righteousness in Jesus Christ and His kingdom? The fulfillments that I suggest in this book are consistent with Matthew 5:17.

Objection 2. Your position cannot be sustained because you rely on pictorial, imaginative, and inferential correspondences among the various laws, between the laws and the tabernacle, and between the laws and the work of Christ. Only direct, explicit deduction from explicit texts gives us a guarantee and moral certainty in our results. Actually we need to use both explicit deduction and artistic sensitivity to the influence of larger Biblical contexts. If we do not pay careful, detailed attention to explicit texts, we may be filling ourselves merely with our own ideas. If we do not use artistic sensitivity to explore carefully more remote connections, we may miss significant generalizations and Christological correspondences that help us immensely in seeing the broader implications of texts.

All of us, no doubt, have some biases and some tendencies to concentrate on what we are most gifted at or what comes most naturally to us. Some people are most at home in the world of strict deductions and tight, finely tuned analytical arguments. Other people are most at home with literary allusions, loose analogies and illustrations, and artistically harmonized pictures of a whole field. The texture of large pieces of literature and the allusive connections between different areas of thought fascinate them.

The strength of the analytical approach is in giving maximum weight to each individual passage or verse by exploring all the deductions that we can make. In addition, the rigorous explicitness of a tight analytical argument can uncover concealed assumptions and presuppositions and cause us to rethink whether such assumptions are truly Biblical.

The strength of the artistic approach is in giving maximum weight to context. Each individual passage or verse is seen as one paint stroke on a large canvas. The broader contribution and significance of the particular verse can be assessed properly only when we take into account the whole book (i.e., the literary whole in which it is embedded) and the multidimensional connections that the verse enjoys with various themes and structures, large and small. Both direct, obvious connections and more allusive but deep connections qualify the implications of the verse in subtle ways.

These two approaches are in fact complementary to one another. But one of the two approaches will often prove more useful with a particular type of literature. A mathematics textbook or a legal statute book calls primarily for tight deduction. A book of poetry, a love note, or a novel calls primarily for artistic sensitivity and literary criticism.

The books of the Bible in general and the five books of Moses in particular fall somewhere between the two extremes. But precisely because they are between extremes, people are likely to notice only that with which they are most comfortable. For example, the books of Moses contain enough statutory law to make analytical people think that they are dealing with mere statute books. But the statutes are embedded in a narrative context, making artistic people think that they are literature. Both law and narrative alike contain theological teaching and exemplify general truths about God. The presence of theology makes analytical people think that here are general truths to be subjected to deductive analysis. Both law and narrative express a personal covenant or treaty between God and Israel, making artistic people decide that both law and theology belong within the literary framework of ancient Hittite treaties or a father-son relation between God and His people. The personal relation to God is primary in their minds.

The analytical people tend to be more isolating and fragmentary in their approach. Their ideal is deduction, and deduction requires that truths be rigorously formulated in a manner isolated from any literary context. Hence, analytical people tend to assume that each verse or passage can be studied pretty effectively by itself. Conversely, artistic people tend to be more synthesizing and holistic in their approach. Because their ideal is a picture into which all parts fit, they tend to assume that only the large structures carry the true message. They may be content to have an artistically satisfying picture of the whole even if it is in tension with some details of the parts.

The five books of Moses point forward to Christ, as we have seen. Both analytical people and artistic people may acknowledge this truth, but they are likely to understand it in two different senses. Analytical people think first of all of the fact that the abstract principles that they have deduced continue to be valid and are confirmed by being more fully expressed in the time of Christ, the time of the New Testament. Artistic people think first of all of the fact that the pictures of Christ and redemption in the Old Testament are transformed into realization, and shadows are transformed into realities.

In my view, we understand the Old Testament best if we listen to one another and are ready to appropriate the insights of both analytical and artistic approaches. With this approach Greg Bahnsen expresses agreement in principle: "The artistic and pedagogical designs inherent in the Scriptures certainly must not be ignored or despised; however, neither must they be abused by trying to make them say something which Scripture itself does not say."[45] However, in my judgment Bahnsen too quickly dismissed the possibility that the typological meaning of holy war and of the holiness of Israel might result in extensive reassessment of the penal significance of Deuteronomy 13, Deuteronomy 17, and other passages.[46] Moreover, Bahnsen's violent rejection of Meredith G. Kline's view shortchanged some of the valuable holistic, analogical, and artistic insights available in Kline's approach, including his emphasis on typology and the unique holiness of Israel.[47] It is thus symptomatic of theonomists' tendency in practice one-sidedly to employ an analytical, deductive approach.

Objection 3. *Daniel 3:29, 6:26, and Ezra 7:25–27 show the propriety of state laws to promote true religion even outside the bounds of Palestine.* Let us first consider the passage Ezra 7:25–27.

> And you, Ezra, in accordance with the wisdom of your God, which you possess, appoint magistrates and judges to administer justice to all the people of Trans-Euphrates—all who know the laws of your God. And you are to teach any who do not know them. Whoever does not obey the law of your God and the law of the king must surely be punished by death, banishment, confiscation of property, or imprisonment.
>
> Praise be to the LORD, the God of our fathers, who has put it into the king's heart to bring honor to the house of the LORD in Jerusalem in this way.

Ezra is here commissioned by Artaxerxes to appoint magistrates and judges who will enforce "the law of your God and the law of the king" (v. 26). At first glance it might appear that Ezra's responsibility extends to the whole population in the Trans-Euphrates province. But elsewhere in Artaxerxes's decree his responsibility is focused on Judah and Jerusalem (v. 14). The most revealing limitation is found in verse 25 in the phrase "all who know the laws of your God." In Aramaic this phrase begins with the same opening preposition (*lě*) as does the preceding phrase, "all the people of Trans-Euphrates." The total grammatical structure of these two phrases forms what is called an "apposition," in which the second phrase more closely defines the first.[48] Thus Ezra's responsibility extends specifically to "all who know the laws of your God," that is, the Jews. Then the further remark is added, "And you are to teach any who do not know them," referring to the Jews who had become unfamiliar with the law. This extra remark is necessary as a realistic qualification, since the preceding phrase about "all who know the laws of your God" might otherwise have been understood as implying that there was no need for teaching.

Hence, Ezra's commission results not in the extending of the rule of the law to Gentiles but in its reapplication to the Jews, the people to whom it had originally been delivered. This result agrees with the Jewish-centered intentions of Ezra apparent in the rest of the book of Ezra. If the intention of Artaxerxes had been to give Ezra more sweeping authority over the total population of Trans-Euphrates, we would have expected a different wording, such as "administer justice to all the people of Trans-Euphrates, including teaching all those who do not yet know the law." The introduction of the extra phrase "all who know the laws of your God" is the key to the qualified form of Ezra's task. On this interpretation scholars agree.[49] Thus Ezra 7:25–27 is completely consistent with my views regarding the special relation of laws in Israel to the special holiness of Israel.

Next let us consider the two passages in Daniel. In Daniel 3:29, after the incident of the fiery furnace, Nebuchadnezzar issues a decree, "Therefore I decree that the people of any nation or language who say anything against the God of Shadrach, Meshach and Abednego be cut into pieces and their houses be turned into piles of rubble, for no other god can save in this way." Likewise in Daniel 6:26, after the incident of Daniel in the lions' den, Darius says, "I issue a decree that in every part of my kingdom people must fear and reverence the God of Daniel."

Superficially these verses might indeed appear to contradict my position that no state penalties are appropriate for false worship and blasphemy. But a closer analysis shows that they are no more difficult for me than for those holding the most common form of theonomy.

First, both decrees are issued in unbelieving kingdoms. The vast majority of those ruled by Nebuchadnezzar and by Darius were pagan idolaters and polytheists. Theonomists usually envision erecting prohibitions of false worship only in Christianized countries.[50] Hence, these verses pose some difficulty for theonomists as well as for me.

Second, the decree of Darius commands fear of the true God, which is not fully parallel to forbidding worship of false gods. In fact, in the polytheistic context of Darius's kingdom, this decree would be understood as fully compatible with worshipping many other gods. Neither theonomists nor I advocate that the state command that people worship or fear the true God; such is the task of evangelism rather than the state. Hence, this decree constitutes a difficulty for all of us.

Third, Nebuchadnezzar's decree in Daniel 3:29 requires punishment for people "who say anything against the God of Shadrach, Meshach and Abednego." The particular wording here appears to differ from Mosaic statutes on false worship and blasphemy. Mosaic law contains several statutes on worship of false gods (e.g., Exodus 22:20; Leviticus 20:2; Deuteronomy 13:1–18; 17:2–7). But Nebuchadnezzar within his polytheistic context is definitely *not* forbidding such false worship. The only statute relevant to blasphemy is found in Numbers 24:10–16, which involves cursing the name of God. "Saying anything against" is really much broader than cursing the name of God. Therefore, strictly speaking, Nebuchadnezzar's decree does not match Mosaic law. Because of the lack of match, it is a problem for the common theonomic position.

Thus the difficulties with these verses are really difficulties for both my position and the common position of theonomists. I believe that the difficulties can be best relieved through the following observations.

First, these two decrees are presented as part of a narrative in Daniel. The narrative itself does not explicitly approve or disapprove of these decrees. Narratives elsewhere in Scripture, as we know, sometimes include records of sins without any explicit mark of disapproval (e.g., Genesis 19:30–38). Sometimes in a narrative the basic purposes of a person may be good but the means chosen less than ideal (Genesis 25:29–34; 27:1–29).

Second, the narrative introduces the two decrees for a positive purpose. The narrative in Daniel has as one primary purpose the encouragement of oppressed and discouraged Jews. Daniel and his three friends are heroes and models for Jews to emulate. The narratives in Daniel 3 and 6 naturally end with a note of vindication by God and by the heathen king, because this final note effectively suggests to the readers God's more general promises to be with His people and vindicate them among the nations. In fact, in Daniel 2 and 7 God explicitly promises that His final messianic kingdom will come to supersede and destroy the bestial, earthly, idolatrous kingdoms of Nebuchadnezzar and his successors. Within this context, Nebuchadnezzar's and Darius's decrees already contain a hint of worldwide extension of the knowledge of God. What happens through these decrees in the earthly kingdom foreshadows the way in which through the coming of God's own divine kingdom peoples of all nations will give allegiance to God. Hence, there are some definite and firm narrative purposes for introducing Nebuchadnezzar's and Darius's decrees, quite apart from the question of whether the narrator completely approved of the exact form of the decrees.

Third, both Nebuchadnezzar and Darius probably issued the decrees partly to block attempts at sedition. In both cases the preceding narrative indicates that evil people directed their energies towards destroying officers of the state, in the one case Daniel's three friends and in the other case Daniel himself. In the latter case the motives of the plotters were clearly political rather than narrowly religious in nature (Daniel 6:1–5). But the distinctive religious commitments of Daniel and his friends could serve as a pretext or an entering wedge for disruption of their status and thereby disruption of the state. Nebuchadnezzar and Darius after learning their lessons would naturally want to block any future attempts to attack Daniel and his friends. The two kings saw the need, at least as a temporary measure, to protect their officers of the state against seditious action.

We cannot be sure of all the motives of Nebuchadnezzar and Darius. Certainly they were impressed with the power of God (Daniel 3:28; 6:26–27). Their decrees might be simply the result of a general overflow of zeal on behalf of the true God. But the specification of punishment in the one case (Daniel 3:29) might still be based partly on a subordinate motive of protecting the state. As we have seen in chapter 12 above, the state is justified in protecting itself and punishing usurpers and rebels. The state might even exercise some power of discretion in laying down temporary extra rules in a case where sedition is likely to take a particular form. Nebuchadnezzar's decree might still not be a perfect example of justice, but it begins to make sense. If it intends to punish the beginnings of sedition, it is at least roughly compatible with the principles of justice that we have seen in the Mosaic law.

Some Possible One-Sidedness in Theonomy

Up to this point I have tended to describe my differences with many theonomists primarily as differences in emphasis and differences in detail. We differ in emphasis because I prefer to emphasize more prominently the Christocentric character of Old Testament law. And we differ in detail over the interpretation of passages like Deuteronomy 13 and 17. But in another sense these differences in emphasis and in detail may be far-reaching in their consequences. The popular movement of theonomy is distinguishable theologically from most other Reformed Christianity mainly by its view that civil punishments in the Mosaic law ought to be exactly matched in form and in intensity by modern state punishments. Without this distinctive, it is not clear how theonomy as a whole differs decisively from the rest of Reformed thought. Since I do not agree with this distinctive myself, it is also not so clear whether theonomists would welcome my ideas.

The differences over Deuteronomy 13 and 17 have further consequences. Deuteronomy 13 and 17 give us a foreshadowing of the triumph of Christ's rule through the gospel. They also imply that the churches should excommunicate unrepentant false worshipers. But suppose that we were to believe incorrectly that Deuteronomy 13 and 17 gave warrant for inaugurating modern state punishment for false worship. Assuming, as I do, that the position is indeed incorrect, it has unfortunate effects.

. One possible effect is that the position might actually be put into practice in a modern state. A law might be enacted that would require the execution of false prophets and false worshipers. Then we would be guilty of a most monstrous injustice. Moreover, we would be claiming to do so in the name of Christ and the Bible, and so we would throw discredit on Him whom we love. The effects of making a mistake like this one are so bad that I need not elaborate. Fortunately, in the near future there is no likelihood that such a thing will happen. Hence, we may turn to examine subtle secondary effects among those who hold this position merely as a theory.

To begin with, the position requires contemporary evangelicals to make large-scale adjustments in their emotional reactions. Evangelical instincts are on the side of state toleration of false worship, not only out of love for the sinners but out of a feeling that the evangelistic task involves mingling with professing unbelievers and believers in other religions (see appendix A). Those who do adjust their emotional reactions are adjusting them in the wrong way. Thus they may be tempted to become less loving or less sympathetic to the evangelistic task in other ways. Because of the magnitude of the adjustment involved, they will also be tempted to become more suspicious of evangelical instincts on a broader basis. Their suspicions can easily become an occasion to stop listening to criticisms or ideas coming from circles outside their own. A certain polarization can take place in their minds between "we who have the truth and who have purified our emotions" and "the unwashed."

Second, when Deuteronomy 13 and Deuteronomy 17 are improperly applied, the holy war theology implicit in the practices of those passages begins to be carried over into our day inappropriately. Theonomists, to be sure, recognize that the conquest of Canaan was a unique holy war and is not to be directly imitated today.[51] But the carrying over of Deuteronomy 13 and 17 in a direct way nevertheless introduces a temptation for theonomists to think and to feel the same way that an Israelite was supposed to think and feel on the matter. When the state is understood as having an obligation to punish false worship, people may in an improper sense begin to view the state as a weapon of warfare against false worship. What is appropriate to New Testament spiritual warfare may begin to be confused with what is appropriate to Old Testament fleshly warfare. To some extent (though not totally) the value of fleshly weapons is confused with spiritual.

Thus the process of introducing practices from Deuteronomy 13 and 17 potentially produces wider confusion. People may invest undue hopes and energies in political warfare against unbelief. Moreover, they may partially lose sight of a decisive difference between Canaan and today, due to the resurrection of Christ. Canaanites were not called to repent. They were destroyed but not raised to new life. The resurrection of Christ introduces a new era whereby the gospel and discipleship people are both killed spiritually and raised to life (Romans 6:1–23). All are commanded to repent and believe (Acts 17:30). To be sure, even in Old Testament times there were exceptions like Rahab (Joshua 2) and the Gibeonites (Joshua 9). But in their exceptional character such incidents pointed forward to a future day of greater harvest from the Gentiles. If we lose sight of these distinctions, we think too much of fighting non-Christians rather than winning them over through words and deeds of love. Dominion is understood too readily as primarily earthly dominion over non-Christians rather than the heavenly dominion that has already been achieved for us and into which we have already entered in union with Christ (Ephesians 2:6). We think of dominating non-Christians politically and economically rather than praying for Christ to dominate them through renewing their hearts.

It would be grossly unfair to theonomy to say that the movement as a whole has succumbed to these temptations. Many people within the movement are conscious of such temptations and fight them.[52] But the tendency to create these temptations is there, and I suspect that some people have partially succumbed.

The confusions over Deuteronomy 13 and 17 create another unfortunate tendency, namely, a tendency toward weakness in love and humility. Temptations to weak love and humility confront almost any movement that claims to have fresh answers. But the temptations may perhaps be intensified if thoughts of domination and warfare, inadequately defined, make us push into the background the basic principle of Christian living through union with Christ in His sufferings as well as His resurrection (Philippians 3:10). There is a spiritual power in the humility and love of Christ as He surrendered Himself to the cross (Philippians 2:8). There is spiritual power also in the love and humility of Christians who reflect the image of Christ in themselves. Such power tends to be overlooked if we improperly appropriate the images of dominion and war in Deuteronomy 13 and 17.

Finally, though theonomists are zealous for Christ's kingdom, their interpretation in practice has underestimated the Christocentric character of Mosaic law. Law, tabernacle, priesthood, and holy land belong together as a many-sided promise of the coming of Christ and a channel of God's fellowship. When the law is interpreted in isolation from this purpose, the danger of producing a legalistic mood to Christian obedience is real. Legalism has sometimes taken the form of basing salvation in its entirety on good works. Theonomists repudiate such blatant legalism and affirm that our justification is by grace alone, through faith alone. But a subtler form of legalism can arise, with its attendant arrogance, unless obedience is thoroughly shaped by personal communion with Christ, and Old Testament instruction received as a word saturated with anticipations of His glory and His love (2 Corinthians 3:15–18).

Theonomic Stridency

A considerable number of Christians have received the impression that in practice theonomists are contentious and quarrelsome, a continuous source of aggravation, fights, wounds, and church splits. To be sure, such impressions can be one-sided and unfairly generalized. Sometimes the fault lies partly in the violent hostility and slanders of anti-theonomists. But theonomists are not wholly innocent either. Such faults should bother theonomists more than they apparently do. For one thing, the repeated recurrence of the difficulties suggests not merely that theonomists are still sinful like all other Christians, but that something within the movement itself somehow unleashes or encourages sin of this particular kind.[53]

The problems are compounded by the fact that theonomists are concerned with social and political issues. Feelings often run very high on such issues to begin with. But they run even higher when an informed Christian looks at the surrounding American society and sees it disintegrating into godlessness before his eyes. Naturally, Christians become indignant about aspects of mainstream American society: abortion, secularism in state schools, drugs, the criminal system, the welfare system, advertising, television programing, and so on. This legitimate indignation very easily injects emotional heat into discussions *with fel-*

low Christians. Indignation about the system gets transfigured into apparent indignation with Christian brothers and sisters. The tone used to denounce false ideas is unfortunately understood by hearers as a denunciation of *them personally*.

Moreover, theonomists are also vulnerable when they think that they have definite Biblical answers to social and political problems. Some of these putative answers, as we have seen, are wrong. Others may be simplistic. But some are genuinely helpful, and many are at least moving in profitable directions. Unfortunately, to have answers and to be convinced that they are Biblical, may very well tempt people to sound dogmatic when talking to others less informed. And such a tone of dogmatism signifies lack of love.

Ironically, such difficulties are innately opposed to the deepest desires of the theonomists themselves. Theonomists hope for the triumph of Christ's rule both in the lives of individuals and in society as a whole. All the leading theonomists stress that this triumph comes not through the force of arms, or even primarily through strident social and political action, but through the power of the gospel and the work of the Holy Spirit in the hearts of people. Evangelism and the empowering of the church must play a primary role at least until the time when the great majority of the population of a nation is Christian. Such is the official theonomic theory. But many theonomists appear to be far too impatient about the intervening time before the millennium. Theonomists too often do not invest enough energy in promoting evangelism and church vitality through love. In fact, by prematurely investing too much energy in more technical theological and political disputes, and by being intolerant of those who disagree, they may produce divisions among Christians that actually hinder the vitality needed for the most fervent prayer and evangelism.

In addition, theonomists may sometimes succumb to an impatience at odds with their postmillennial eschatology. According to postmillennialism, the reign of Christ over social and political institutions is established gradually, perhaps even over a period of many generations, as when leaven leavens the whole lump of dough. This triumph is first of all the work of Christ Himself, not the work of postmillennial zealots. The glory all goes to Christ, not to His followers, not even to those who have most accurately discerned Christ's triumph beforehand. Faithful saints still play a most significant role as instruments. They bring the gospel of Christ and the rule of Christ to bear on their lives and their environment as they faithfully serve Him day by day. But postmillennial confidence ought to give patience to people who do not see their ideas accepted immediately. If Christ must indeed triumph, they have no need to trample their Christian opponents violently. The working of the Holy Spirit over longer periods of time can bring remarkable change. They must not rend the church of Christ and thereby destroy the prime instrument of kingdom transformation, just because other people do not immediately adjust to their program.

A word needs also to be said to rabid antitheonomists. Remember the Bible's revelation of God's justice and the cry of the psalmist, "O how I love your law" (Psalm 119:97). Remember that Paul says that "The law is holy, and the commandment is holy, righteous and good." (Romans 7:12) Have you been able to learn something here? Then do not simply write off theonomists. You may continue to disagree with them, but try to reform them rather than simply slandering them. And ask yourself whether the deepest hurts have arisen from attitudes of zealotism among theonomists in their practice, rather than merely from theonomic theory. Can you decrease the contentiousness of theonomists to an acceptable level by reminding them, as I have above, of their own desires? And will you also be wary of falling into the same sin yourself?

I hope that my own reflections in this book, imperfect though they be, may promote both truth and peace in Christ's universal church, the pillar and foundation of the truth (1 Timothy 3:15).

DOES THE GREEK WORD *PLĒROŌ* SOMETIMES MEAN "CONFIRM"?

S ome interpreters have held that the Greek word *plēroō* occurring in Matthew 5:17 is to be translated "confirm," "validate," or "establish."[1] But this position is plausible only if it can be established that the Greek word *plēroō* sometimes does bear the sense "confirm."[2] I maintain that such a sense for *plēroō* is not well established, whereas the sense "fulfill" is well established.

The Nature of the Dispute

Bauer's lexicon, the standard lexicon for New Testament Greek, lists the following senses for *plēroō*:

1. *make full, fill (full)*

2. of time, *fill (up)*, *complete* a period of time, *reach its end.*

3. *bring* something, *to completion, finish* something, already begun.

4. *fulfill*, by deeds, a prophecy, an obligation, a promise, a law, a request, a purpose, a desire, a hope, a duty, a fate, a destiny, etc.

5. *complete, finish, bring to an end*

6. *complete* a number, pass. *have the number made complete.*[3]

The standard lexicon for classical Greek, the standard lexicon for patristic Greek, and the lexicon for papyri essentially agree with the picture offered by Bauer: they do not cite either "confirm" or "validate" as possible senses of the word.[4]

Such are the basic data concerning the possible meanings of *plēroō*. But since the meaning of Matthew 5:17 is debated, it is understandable that with regard to this particular text the scholarly opinion becomes more complicated. Bauer's lexicon therefore includes under meaningn number four a brief indication of the scholarly discussion on Matthew 5:17: "[D]epending on how one prefers to interpret the context, *plēroō* is understood here either as *fulfill* = do, carry out, or as *bring to full expression* = show it forth in its true [meaning], or as *fill up* = complete. [Bibliographic citations follow at this point.]"[5] Thus various scholars have chosen to interpret Matthew 5:17 as involving meaning four ("fulfill") or a subdivision of meaning 3 ("bring to full expression") or meaning one ("fill up"). Bauer's lexicon dutifully cites Dalman's work arguing for the sense "confirm," but does nothing to indicate agreement with it. It should be noted that Dalman's putative meaning would actually not belong to any of the established categories numbered one through six offered by Bauer.

But the meaning of Matthew 5:17 is not now our concern. We are concerned rather to investigate the range of meanings of *plēroō* within koine Greek. For our purposes, the disputes over Matthew 5:17 are best set aside, and the possibilities for meaning determined by a broad investigation of Greek literature.

For this purpose, Greg Bahnsen provides for us a large number of verses where *plēroō* might have the sense "confirm."[6] We shall have to examine these verses one by one. But before doing so, we must make clear in our own minds what sort of evidence would count in favor of postulating a distinct sense "confirm," and what sort of evidence would not.[7]

Let us start with some examples from English rather than Greek. In nearly all cases the theological idea of fulfillment implies confirmation. For example, when Jesus rode into Jerusalem on a donkey in Matthew 21:1–5, He fulfilled the prophecy of Zechariah 9:9. Simultaneously Jesus' action confirmed that Zechariah 9:9 is true. Since any fulfillment brings some Old Testament passage to realization, it thereby confirms its truthfulness.

Hence, we might say that the English word *fulfill* implies or connotes "confirm." But the words *fulfill* and *confirm* are not absolutely identical in meaning. The word *fulfill* includes more than confirmation, since, when taken together with the total context, it implies that a later event brings to realization something that was anticipated or foreshadowed in earlier Scripture. If we simply replace *fulfill* by *confirm* we lose the distinct nuances of realization, completion, and consummation. *Confirm* suggests a static maintenance of an existing rule, whereas *fulfill* suggests an advance towards realization. Accordingly, English dictionaries do not say that "confirm" is one of the senses of *fulfill* or that the two words can replace one another without loss. The theological and logical fact that *fulfill* implies "confirm" must not be confused with the linguistic question about the distinct senses of the English word *fulfill*.

Nevertheless, the distinction between *fulfill* and *confirm* in English is a subtle one. The two words are related in meaning. Texts using the word *fulfill* may therefore still make sense when the word *confirm* is substituted. For example, "This took place to fulfill what was spoken through the prophet" (Matthew 21:4) becomes, "This took place to confirm what was spoken through the prophet." With this alteration the passage still makes sense because Jesus did as a matter of fact confirm Zechariah 9:9. The effect of the substitution of one word for the other is to retain one of the implications of fulfillment, i.e., confirmation, but to leave out the other nuances associated with the word *fulfill*.

This phenomenon of implication without identity is a common occurrence in natural languages. For example, when more precise terms are used, they typically imply the ideas that might be expressed with less precise terms that are related in meaning. *To wound* implies "to hurt"; *to rub* implies "to come in contact with"; *to saunter* implies "to move." Inferences can also be of a more complex kind. *To obey* typically implies acknowledging the authority of the one you are obeying. *To persuade* typically implies belief that your listener is open to rational argument. To understand a text, one must have read it. *Understand*, in the context of texts, implies "has read." To sell an object, one must have owned it beforehand. Thus *sell* implies (or perhaps presupposes) "previously possessed." And so on. Such inferences are, in a loose sense, involved in the meaning of a word. But lexicologists are not satisfied merely with a random sample of this type of information. They want to state as precisely as possible the full force of a word. They may offer extended definitions to try to indicate as exactly as possible the distinctive characteristics of a word meaning. They also try to offer glosses or synonyms for the word, that is, other words that could be substituted without either loss or gain in the meaning of the whole sentence in which a word is embedded. *Wound* and *hurt* are not synonyms, because *wound* includes the additional idea of producing a laceration of the skin, whereas *hurt* is a broader term that could be used for many other kinds of damage.

We must therefore be careful. In English, *fulfill* in many contexts implies "confirm," but *fulfill* and *confirm* are not synonyms, nor are they equivalent in meaning. An English dictionary in listing *fulfill* does not offer "confirm" as a definition, but rather alternatives like "put into effect" and "convert into reality." *Roget's Thesaurus* lists "confirm" under the general category "Change" and the subcategory "Stability"; while "fulfill" falls under the general category "III. Quantity D. Wholeness" and the subcategory "Completeness."[8]

I maintain that the situation in Greek is similar to the situation in English. In Greek there are at least three words, *plēroō*, *bebaioō*, and *histēmi*, corresponding roughly to the English words "fulfill," "confirm," and "establish."[9] We know from the lexicons that the first word, *plēroō*, has as one possible sense the meaning "fulfill." Many of its uses will naturally imply the idea of confirmation. Moreover, in many of its uses we may find that we can substitute the translation "confirm" and still have the passage make sense. But these phenomena are quite compatible with the well-attested sense "fulfill." By themselves, they are not evidence for the existence of a distinct new sense ("confirm") for the word *plēroō*. Only if the additional nuances of "fulfill," such as realization, completion, and advance, are *absent* will we really have significant evidence in favor of a possible new sense, "confirm." Even then, we must be careful to do our work with as much data as possible, because it may often be hard to tell whether or not some additional nuances of "fulfill" are present in a particular case.

Next, we must exercise particular care when using evidence derived from the Septuagint, the ancient Greek translation of the Old Testament. Again, an example from English may help to clarify the problem. Suppose that a translator with imperfect command of Greek undertakes to translate the New Testament from Greek to English. The translator knows that *plēroō* has as one possible sense the meaning "fulfill." So whenever the translator encounters the Greek word, it gets translated "fulfill," even in those cases where "fill" or "complete" might be more appropriate. Now suppose that we were not native speakers of English but were trying to learn English using the translation. We would observe that the English word *fulfill* was used in some contexts where the meaning was apparently "fill" or "complete," and we would deduce that *fulfill* has the distinct senses "fill" and "complete." Our deduction would be plausible, but would have overlooked the possibility that the translator was simply following the Greek text woodenly or literalistically.

This example is not artificial, because similar phenomena occur in the Septuagint translation. For some books of the Bible the Septuagint translators proceeded rather woodenly. We must not too quickly assume that Greek words in the Septuagint are used in a manner completely consistent with their normal range of senses. But still another complication arises from the later use of the Septuagint. Since the Septuagint became the commonly used Bible of Greek-speaking Jews and Christians, its non-normal usage of Greek may in turn have influenced Jewish and Christian Greek at some points. Hence, we must not too quickly say that Septuagint use is irrelevant to the New Testament even if it is demonstrably non-normal.[10]

Does the Septuagint influence the New Testament use of *plēroō*? The Greek word *plēroō* occurs in the Septuagint almost exclusively as a translation of *ml'*. The range of senses of the Hebrew word matches fairly closely the range of *plēroō*,[11] so that such a consistent pattern of translation would not much affect the meaning of *plēroō* in New Testament use. But it should be noted that the lexicons list one instance of the sense "confirm" for *ml'*, namely, the passage 1 Kings 1:14.[12] The one instance, while not enough to affect New Testament usage, does perhaps indicate a difference between the range of meaning of the Hebrew word and the Greek word.

Finally, it is wise to establish a clear terminology for describing the various senses of a single word. Bauer's lexicon enumerates six distinct categories of meaning for *plēroō* (see the list above). For convenience, we may call these six senses. But several of the senses are virtually indistinguishable from one another. For example, sense three, "*bring* something *to completion, finish* something" is virtually identical with sense five, "*complete, finish*." Thus Bauer's entries three and five can be grouped together and regarded as a single meaning of the word, namely, the meaning "*bring* something *to completion, finish*." Bauer's sense six, "*complete* a number," appears to differ not by giving a new meaning to the word *plēroō* but by supplying a different kind of object for the completion, namely, a number. Similarly Bauer's sense two, "*complete* a period of time," differs from the other senses mainly by having a different object of completion, i.e., a period of time. The word *plēroō* seems in all these cases to retain the basic meaning "complete." Bauer's attempt to give special space to the cases of completing a time or completing a number is obviously useful, but it does not necessarily imply that the word *plēroō* has a distinct new meaning in each case.

If we want to express the fundamental unity among the different senses two, three, five, and six, we may say that they are all one "meaning" or one semantic value. In our own minds we may reorganize Bauer's classification if it seems revealing. In fact, we may argue that all six senses have a fundamental unity, perhaps best expressed in English with the word "complete." Sense one, "make full, fill (full)" represents instances where spatial or quasispatial items are in some sense brought to completion. Sense four, "fulfill," represents instances where the purpose or meaning of some plan or idea is brought to completion. Senses one and four are best still translated with the words "fill" and "fulfill" rather than with "complete," but they are very closely related to the instances in senses two, three, five, and six where we might translate using the word "complete."[13]

Because of the measure of unity in the different senses of *plēroō*, some lexicographers might prefer to describe the word as having only one "sense," namely, "bring something to completion." While some words have only one broad sense, other words, like the English word *cork,* have several distinct but related senses ("a stopper," or "a piece made of cork oak," or "to put a stopper in").

For the sake of clarity, I shall speak of six senses of the word *plēroō,* corresponding to the six main subdivisions in Bauer's lexicon. The sense "confirm," if it exists, is a seventh sense. But it should still be remembered that all six of Bauer's senses have an impressive measure of unity. All six contain an idea of completion or achievement of an end, whereas the sense "confirm" would connote only the reaffirmation of something already established or complete. Moreover, though "fulfill" implies "confirm," "fulfill" belongs to the general category or semantic domain of meanings having to do with wholeness, while "confirm" belongs to the semantic domain having to do with noetic matters such as strengthening of belief.[14]

Analysis of Possible Examples of the Sense "Confirm"

We are now ready to look at the examples that Bahnsen cites as possible instances of using *plēroō* with the sense "confirm."

Third Kings 1:14

Let us examine 3 Kings 1:14 (corresponding to 1 Kings 1:14 in Hebrew). In the context, Nathan discusses with Bathsheba what to do about Adonijah's plans. He proposes that Bathsheba go in to David to make a complaint. Then he says, "While you [Bathsheba] are still there talking to the king, I will come in and confirm what you have said."[15] The key word "confirm," *ml'* in Hebrew, is translated with the Greek term *plēroō.* There are two problems with this example. First, 1 Kings 1:14 is the one instance in the Hebrew Old Testament where the Hebrew word *ml'* does perhaps mean "confirm." Since *ml'* is normally translated with the word *plēroō,* the translator may have continued normal practice in this instance without asking whether an unusual use of the underlying Hebrew word was involved.

Second, it is not certain that the Hebrew text itself contains nothing beyond the idea of confirmation. Bathsheba was supposed to remind David of his promise to Solomon and report to David that Adonijah had already assumed the trappings of kingship. David may conceivably have forgotten his promise, and he was probably not aware of Adonijah's doings. Hence Nathan intended to come in and "confirm" matters in Bathsheba's report about which there might be doubt. But Bathsheba's report also has the nature of an argument. In verse 14 Nathan may have been saying that he would come in and *complete* the argument. Thus a nuance of "completion" and not mere confirmation may well be involved. As we have observed, only the absence of such a nuance would count as evidence in favor of postulating a distinct new sense for the Greek word *plēroō*. Moreover, even if such a nuance was not involved in the Hebrew original, the translator may have thought that the Hebrew intended the sense "complete" or may have chosen the customary equivalent for Hebrew *ml'* because of uncertainty about the exact nuance. All in all, 3 Kings 1:14 is weak evidence in favor of a distinct new sense.

First Maccabees 2:55

Though the Hebrew original of 1 Maccabees is no longer extant, it appears that the present Greek 1 Maccabees is a translation from a Hebrew original.[16] We must therefore introduce the same cautions appropriate for the rest of the Septuagint. The passage in question reads, "Phineas our father for being very zealous received the covenant of an everlasting priesthood. Joshua for fulfilling [*plērōsai*] the word was made a judge in Israel. Caleb for bearing witness before the congregation received the heritage of the land. David for being merciful inherited the throne of a kingdom forever" (1 Maccabees 2:54–57).[17] What does it mean that Joshua fulfilled the word? In view of the parallel with Caleb in the next verse, the faithfulness of Joshua and Caleb when they spied out the land of Canaan must be in view. The "word" in question may mean simply Moses's instructions to spy out the land and bring a report (Numbers 13:17–20). More likely, it is a comprehensive label for God's instructions concerning the Promised Land.

Bahnsen argues, "It is not that Joshua obeyed the word (for the word was one of promise, not a demand), but that he confirmed it by his testimony."[18] But Bahnsen's reading of the text is not the only possibility. For one thing, the promises of God do imply demands, namely, that we should believe them. Joshua is commended precisely because he, unlike the rest of the congregation, responded properly to God's word. Of course any proper response to God's word is in a broad sense a "confirmation." Even obedience to a direct command confirms the force and validity of the command, since it is a testimony that the command is valid and is worth obeying. But Joshua's faithfulness to God's word, not the fact of confirmation, seems to be preeminent. Hence, this use of the word *plēroō* may well match one of the normal senses of the word, namely, "fulfill" an obligation (sense four in Bauer's lexicon). Moreover, in Numbers 14:6–9, the only place where the original narrative of the spies contains Joshua's testimony, Joshua is recorded as saying, "Only do not rebel against the LORD." Thus Joshua construes his own response as a question of loyalty in contrast to rebellion. "Fulfilling the word" in 1 Maccabees 2:55 may mean, "fulfilling God's word calling for loyalty to himself."

In addition, we should note that Joshua's speech in Numbers 14:6–9 confirms God's words of promise only in a rather loose sense. Joshua does not anywhere directly refer to God's promises, though he does use language concerning "a land flowing with milk and honey" and concerning the fact that "God will lead us into that land" (v. 8). He appeals explicitly to the question of whether "the LORD is pleased with us" and the fact that "the LORD is with us" (v.v. 8, 9). Thus his language connects up with other teachings besides the promise of the land, and these other teachings involve corresponding obligations (as the "if" of v. 8 hints).

Next, observe that the context of 1 Maccabees contains a list of faithful Israelites together with the rewards that they received for their faithfulness. If the context contained a discussion of the validity of God's word, we might expect something to be said about confirmations of it. But instead the context contains a discussion of human faithfulness. In such a context, the meaning "fulfill the command implied in God's word" is more natural than "confirm the truth of God's word." Human faithfulness implies in a secondary sense a kind of confirmation of God's word, as we have just observed. But as long as something more is involved than mere confirmation, the example of 1 Maccabees 2:55 does not convincingly exhibit a distinct new linguistic sense "confirm."

Fourth Maccabees 12:14

In a passage concerning seven Jewish brothers undergoing martyrdom, 4
Maccabees 12:14 runs, "But they [the previous six martyrs], nobly dying,
fulfilled their piety toward God."[19] The use of *plēroō* here matches sense
five given in Bauer's lexicon, "complete, finish, bring to an end." Completion certainly implies confirmation, but the logical implication of a
known sense of a word must not be confused with the establishment of
a new sense for the word.[20]

First Kings 20:3

Let us look at 1 Kings 20:3 (corresponding to 1 Samuel 20:3 in Hebrew). In this instance the word *plēroō* in the Septuagint does not correspond directly to any underlying Hebrew word. The Septuagint runs,
"As the Lord lives and as my soul lives, as I have said, it [the time or
perhaps space] has been filled up [*empeplēstai*] between me and death."[21]
Bahnsen claims that *plēroō* here means "establish, set" but gives no argument for it. Perhaps he thinks that the word here has a sense "fix,
ordain." Such a sense fits the context. But it is otherwise an unknown
sense of the word *plēroō*, and it is not quite the same as the sense "confirm" that Bahnsen needs. "The time has been confirmed between me
and death" does not make good sense. Moreover, the text makes perfectly good sense if we retain the normal sense of *plēroō*, "fill (up)"
(Bauer's senses one and two).

Song of Solomon 5:14

"His hands are turned gold set with beryl."[22] The underlying Hebrew
has the word *ml'* in the semitechnical sense, "*fill in*, i.e. *set* precious
stones," amply attested in the lexicons and illustrated with several other
verses (Exodus 28:17; 31:5; 35:33; 39:10).[23] The Septuagint translates
this semitechnical sense with the ordinary word *plēroō*, perhaps merely
out of habit, perhaps because the idea of "filling in" is still present in
the semitechnical use of the Hebrew word *ml'* (fill in the area around
the stones, so that they will not fall out of their setting). Bahnsen simply overlooks this usage when he claims that Song of Solomon 5:14
contains the sense "establish, set."[24]

Numbers 7:88; Judges 17:5, 12; 3 Kings 13:33; 2 Chronicles 13:9; and Sirach 45:15. These verses all have a Greek phrase roughly equivalent to "fill the hand(s) [of someone]," using the word *plēroō*. This Greek phrase represents a literal translation of the Hebrew phrase *millē' yad*, an idiom used to describe the consecration of priests.[25] Possibly this idiom evolved because "filling the hand(s)" connoted authorizing and empowering the hands to perform some function. Whatever may be the history of the idiom, the Septuagint translators have in many cases chosen to translate it word for word. Such a mechanical translation almost surely did not result in producing a familiar idiom in Greek, since idioms are almost never preserved by word-for-word translation. The translators sometimes chose to render the phrase in other ways (e.g., Exodus 29:9, 29, 33, 35; Leviticus 8:33), confirming the fact that no fixed idiom existed in Greek. Moreover, even if the idiom had existed in Greek, the meaning "consecrate" would belong to the idiom as a whole rather than to the word *plēroō* by itself. Bahnsen needs several questionable steps to move from these verses back to his postulated meaning "confirm." Those steps are as follows: (1) establish that the meaning "ordain" is a natural meaning of the phrase in Greek and not merely an effect of mechanical, word-for-word translation from Hebrew; (2) move from the meaning "ordain" attached to the whole phrase "fill the hands" to the same meaning attached to the word "fill" (*plēroō*) by itself; (3) move from the meaning "ordain" or "consecrate (as a priest)" to the general meaning "establish (in any office)"; and (4) move from the meaning "establish (in office)" to "confirm (the validity)."

Bahnsen's book next discusses a whole series of passages that involve a connotation of confirmation. "Viewed theologically, even when *plēroō* is used for the actualization of a prophecy (as it often is) the word has the unmistakable connotation of 'confirmation.' "[26] This factor of "connotation" is exactly what we dealt with above in distinguishing between the theological implications of the established sense "fulfill" and the idea of a new, distinct sense "confirm." Bahnsen's statement just quoted is reasonably accurate. The Greek word *plēroō* often implies confirmation in the same way as the English word *fulfill* does. But such an observation is no evidence at all in favor of postulating "confirm" as a distinct new sense of the word. Thus the verses that Bahnsen cites[27] are evidence only for the established sense, "fulfill," not for a new sense "confirm."

James 2:23

"The scripture was fulfilled saying, Abraham believed God, and it was imputed to him for righteousness."[28] James asserts that in the incident recorded in Genesis 22, when Abraham offered up Isaac, the earlier scripture in Genesis 15:6 was "fulfilled." It seems best, in agreement with Bauer's judgment, to take the word *plēroō* in sense four, "fulfill."[29] Since Genesis 15:6 is not a prophecy but a statement, the "fulfillment" of Genesis 15:6 takes the form of fulfilling the purpose of God that is expressed in the verse. As Bauer indicates in defining sense four, the sense "fulfill" includes not only fulfilling prophecy but fulfilling "an obligation, a promise, a law, a request, a purpose, a desire, a hope, a duty, a fate, a destiny, etc."

As usual, "fulfill" implies confirmation but its primary thrust is in another direction. James 2:14–26 as a whole argues that true faith is always manifested in and demonstrated by good deeds. The good deeds certainly do confirm that the person has faith, but more is involved. The preceding verse, James 2:22, says, "You see that his faith and his actions were working together, and his faith was made complete by what he did." Thus Abraham's action *completed* as well as confirmed his faith. The idea of completion carries over naturally to the next verse. The statement of God in Genesis 15:6 enunciated that Abraham believed, and therefore in James's reckoning necessarily involved the implication of a subsequent life of faith for Abraham. Such a purpose and destiny enunciated in the verse were "fulfilled" in Abraham's later action.[30]

Second Corinthians 10:6

"And we will be ready to punish every act of disobedience, once your obedience is complete."[31] Bauer's sense three is used here, "*bring* something *to completion*."[32] Bahnsen virtually agrees with this interpretation in his comments: "Punishment will be restrained until it is not needed, that is, when the obedience of his readers is a standing fact. Obedience

is not established as such until it is completed; to 'fill up' obedience is
equivalent to confirming or establishing obedience."[33]

In his last sentence, however, where he speaks of two meanings as
"equivalent," he goes too far. Completion of obedience may imply confirmation and establishing of obedience. But the two nevertheless are
not semantically equivalent, as if "confirm" were an exact synonym for
"complete." Evidence for an implication must be distinguished from evidence for a new sense of the word.

Revelation 3:2

"For I have not found your deeds complete in the sight of my God."[34]
Once again sense three, "complete," is involved, as Bauer agrees.[35] If
the people of Sardis did succeed in completing their deeds, it would
doubtless confirm that they were obedient. But the word *confirm* does
not work very well as a substitute. "For I have not found your deeds
confirmed in the sight of my God" makes much less sense than the
alternative with "complete."

Romans 15:19

"So from Jerusalem all the way around to Illyricum, I have fully proclaimed the gospel of Christ."[36] The New International Version translates the underlying word *plēroō* with "fully proclaimed." Sense three,
"bring something to completion," is appropriate, as Bauer agrees.[37] Paul
has brought to completion a plan to proclaim the gospel throughout the
region of the Roman world from Jerusalem to Illyricum. In the next
verse (v. 20) Paul gives further indications of the general nature of his
ambitions for preaching the gospel. He wants to spread the gospel to
places that have not yet heard it. Up to the present, that plan has
confined him to the region from Jerusalem to Illyricum (v. 22), but now
that he has completed his work in these regions, he is ready to go on to
Rome (v. 23) and beyond to Spain (v. 24). The idea of completing
work throughout a region is in view throughout verses 19–24.

Though the Greek of verse 19 presents us with an unusual expression, commentators have a reasonable measure of agreement that some
such meaning is involved. Consider two examples. Murray remarks,

"Paul had discharged his commission and fulfilled the design of his ministry within the wide area specified."[38] Cranfield agrees with Murray's understanding: "We understand [Paul's] claim to have completed the gospel of Christ to be a claim to have completed that trail-blazing, pioneer preaching of it, which he believed it was his own special apostolic mission to accomplish."[39]

Colossians 1:25

Paul mentions "to fulfill the word of God."[40] With Bauer I understand this verse as an instance of the sense three, "bring something to completion."[41] Paul brings the word of God to completion either by preaching it "in its fullness," as the New International Version translates, or by spreading it throughout the world, as in Romans 15:19. In view of the parallel expression in Romans 15:19 and the fact that the context of Colossians 1:25 mentions the spread of the gospel to the Gentiles (1:27), the idea of completing the purpose of God to spread the gospel is probably the right one.

Though confirmation is an implication of Paul's work, a conjecture that *plēroō* here has the distinct new sense "confirm" does not seem to fit the context very well. Paul's preaching is not primarily functioning merely to confirm the truth of the gospel but to fulfill God's plan that the gospel should be communicated and spread to the Gentiles (1:27).

Conclusion

In summary, none of the texts that Bahnsen puts forward offers substantial evidence in favor of a distinct new sense "confirm" for the Greek word *plēroō*. The texts can all be understood on the basis of already well-established senses of the word *plēroō*. In only one case, namely, 3 Kings 1:14, is the use of a sense "confirm" really plausible, and even here we have seen that there are weighty reasons for preferring another explanation. In the case of several other texts, Bahnsen apparently confuses evidence concerning the implications of a verse with evidence for a semantically new sense of the word *plēroō*.

The testimony of the standard lexicons must be allowed to carry great weight in cases like this one. A massive amount of literature exists in ancient Greek, and the lexicons have endeavored to summarize it. Of course the lexicons are not always as accurate as they could be, but even when they are guilty of minor inaccuracies the problems usually do not arise from theological bias. Many known instances exist for the established senses of the word *plēroō*. We ought to have firm evidence for some hypothetical new sense, if we are to believe that such a sense is not merely a queer, unexplainable exception, but was firmly established in the minds of Greek speakers through repeated usage. Hence, it is safe to say that *plēroō* does not have the sense "confirm" in Greek.

NOTES

Chapter 1—The Challenge of the Law of Moses: Interpreting Moses in the Light of Christ

1. I owe much to Edmund P. Clowney and Richard B. Gaffin, Jr., for their endeavors to help to make clear the implications of this passage from Luke. See in particular Edmund P. Clowney, *Preaching and Biblical Theology* (Grand Rapids: Eerdmans, 1961), and Richard B. Gaffin, Jr., *The Centrality of the Resurrection: A Study in Paul's Soteriology* (Grand Rapids: Baker, 1978).

2. Further discussion of principles of interpretation will follow at the end of the next chapter and in appendix B. Note also the further reading suggested in the notes in the next chapter.

Chapter 2—The Tabernacle of Moses: Prefiguring God's Presence Through Christ

1. See the discussion in Menahem Haran, *Temples and Temple-Service in Ancient Israel: An Inquiry into the Character of Cult Phenomena and the Historical Setting of the Priestly School* (Oxford: Oxford University Press, 1978), 246–59.

2. More precisely, saints in the Old Testament were saved through Christ, but only through the anticipatory working of the benefits of Christ's sacrifice, which was still to be accomplished in the future. There is much mystery here.

3. Serious distortions can be introduced by the adoption of the antisupernaturalist framework of the historical-critical method. Under the influence of this method many modern scholars have come to believe that the books of Moses derive not from Mosaic times but from much later periods, and that they contain various layers of tradition in tension with one another. Often they then lose sight of the way in which the books of Moses are meant to be read as a larger unity, each part being interpreted in the light of the whole rather than set at variance with other parts.

   A full discussion of the arguments of modern Old Testament scholarship is outside the scope of this book, but it is worthwhile making some basic methodological points. We should repudiate the antisupernaturalist biases associated with the historical-critical method. Various strands of evidence both from the Old Testament books themselves and from the New Testament (see John 5:45–47) confirm the Mosaic origin of the bulk of the material in Exodus through Deuteronomy. Genesis does not directly indicate its author or its sources, but it seems to me likely that it was written by Moses. Later inspired writers with divine authorization may have added the account of Moses's death in Deuteronomy 34:1–12 and perhaps other notes enabling Israelites better to apply the teaching of Moses to their own circumstances. However, scholars cannot validly deduce the date of origin of material merely from observations about its relevance to later situations, since God knows the end from the beginning and what He writes is always relevant to later situations. Stylistic differences between hypothetical sources are also unreliable, since Moses himself may have used sources in some cases. While writing under inspiration he like any other writer had the liberty of shifting style in accordance with subject matter.

Scholars used to regard a position like mine as obscurantist, but a shift within scholarship itself is now making it more obvious that the books of the Bible are works with a unity, integrity, and literary artistry of their own, and that they deserve to be interpreted as wholes.

4. See the very helpful discussion in Geerhardus Vos, "Revelation in the Period of Moses," in *Biblical Theology: Old and New Testaments* (Grand Rapids: Eerdmans, 1948), 115–200. People interested in the further ramifications of my own position should consult a number of my articles and books. Note especially Vern S. Poythress, "Divine Meaning of Scripture," *Westminster Theological Journal* 48 (1986): 241–79, concerning the relation of the meaning of parts of the Bible to the meaning of the whole; idem, "God's Lordship in Interpretation," *Westminster Theological Journal* 50 (1988): 27–64, concerning the basic presuppositions of interpretation; idem, *Symphonic Theology: The Validity of Multiple Perspectives in Theology* (Grand Rapids: Zondervan, 1987), concerning the value of judicious use of the imagination and metaphor; and idem, *Science and Hermeneutics: Implications of Scientific Method for Biblical Interpretation* (Grand Rapids: Zondervan, 1988), concerning the importance of breaking out of modern Western biases.

Chapter 3—The Sacrifices: Prefiguring the Final Sacrifice of Christ

1. Leviticus 22:23 represents an exception.

2. Vos, *Biblical Theology*, 179–86; Patrick Fairbairn, *The Typology of Scripture*, 2 vols. (reprint; Grand Rapids: Baker Book House, 1975), 2:265–77.

3. Cf. the discussion in Gordon J. Wenham, *The Book of Leviticus: The New International Commentary on the Old Testament* (Grand Rapids: Eerdmans, 1979), 51–66; Fairbairn, *Typology*, 2:302–5.

4. Wenham, *Leviticus*, 57.

Chapter 4—The Priests and the People: Prefiguring Christ's Relation to His People

1. Christopher J. H. Wright, *An Eye for an Eye: The Place of Old Testament Ethics Today* (Downers Grove, IL: InterVarsity, 1983), 88–102. Of course, if we use the term "church" to designate broadly the people of God throughout all ages, Israel was the Old Testament phase of the church, as well as having typological relations to the New Testament phase of the church.

Chapter 5—General Principles for God's Dwelling with Human Beings: Prefiguring Union with Christ

1. *The International Standard Bible Encyclopedia*, 2d ed., s.v. "Ark of the Covenant."

2. Meredith G. Kline, *Treaty of the Great King: The Covenant Structure of Deuteronomy: Studies and Commentary* (Grand Rapids: Eerdmans, 1963); idem, *The Structure of Biblical Authority* (Grand Rapids: Eerdmans, 1972); idem, *By Oath Consigned* (Grand Rapids: Eerdmans, 1968); George E. Mendenhall, *Law and Covenant in Israel and the Ancient Near East* (Pittsburgh: Biblical Colloquium, 1955); Viktor Korosec, *Hethitische Staatsverträge: Ein Beitrag zu ihrer juristischen Wertung* (Leipzig: Theodor Weicher, 1931); Delbert R. Hillers, *Covenant: The History of a Biblical Idea* (Baltimore: Johns Hopkins, 1969); Dennis J. McCarthy, *Treaty and Covenant: A Study in the Ancient Oriental Documents and in the Old Testament* (Rome: Pontifical Biblical Institute, 1963); idem, *Old Testament Covenant: A Survey of Current Opinions* (Oxford: Blackwell, 1972).

3. Mendenhall, *Law and Covenant*; Korosec, *Staatsverträge*, 12–14.

4. But note that heaven and earth are called as witnesses in Deuteronomy 31:28, probably in analogy with that part of the Hittite god list that mentions heaven and earth. Compare the words of the Hittite treaty between Mursilis and Duppi-Tessub of Amurru:

> all the olden gods, Naras, Napsaras, Minki, Tuhusi, Ammunki, Ammizadu, Allalu, Anu, Antu, Apantu, Ellil, Ninlil, the mountains, the rivers, the springs, the great Sea, *heaven and earth*, the winds (and) the clouds—let these be witnesses to this treaty and to the oath.

> Consider also the text of the Hittite treaty between Suppiluliumas and Mattiwaza:

> Ammizadu, Alalu, Anu, Antu, Ellil, Ninlil, Belat-Ekalli, the mountains, the rivers, the Tigris (and) the Euphrates, *heaven and earth*, the winds (and) the clouds; Tessub, the lord of heaven and earth, Kusuh and Simigi, . . . at the conclusion of the words of this treaty let them be present, let them listen and let them serve as witnesses.

See James B. Pritchard, ed., *Ancient Near Eastern Texts Relating to the Old Testament* (Princeton, NJ: Princeton University Press, 1950), 201, 205, 206 (emphasis mine).

5. Ibid., 203.

Chapter 6—The Land of Palestine, the Promised Land: Prefiguring Christ's Renewal of and Dominion over the Earth

1. Kline, *Structure*, 31–34; M. Weinfeld, "The Covenant of Grant in the Old Testament and in the Ancient Near East," *Journal of the American Oriental Society* 90 (1970), 184–203.

2. William D. Davies, *The Gospel and the Land* (Berkeley: University of California Press, 1974), 368.

3. Wright, *An Eye for an Eye*, 88–102.

Chapter 7—The Law and Its Order: Prefiguring the Righteousness of Christ

1. See Kline, *Structure*, 35–36.

2. For further development of these ideas, see Wenham, *Leviticus*, 18–25; and Mary Douglas, *Purity and Danger: An Analysis of Concepts of Pollution and Taboo* (London: Routledge and Kegan Paul, 1978).

3. I am indebted to James Jordan for this line of thinking.

4. The KJV describes these diseases as "leprosy." It is clear from the descriptions of disease in Leviticus 13 that a number of types of skin disease fall within the classification in Leviticus. What we know of as "leprosy" or Hansen's disease attacks the nervous system first and spreads very slowly, so that it does not really correspond to the descriptions in Leviticus 13. Accordingly, newer translations like the NIV more accurately translate the Hebrew word as "infectious skin disease" or "mildew" (in the case of a spreading infection in a garment or a house).

5. Wenham, *Leviticus*, 21.

6. For fuller argumentation, see Vos, *Biblical Theology*, 148–50.

Chapter 8—The Purposes of the Tabernacle, the Law, and the Promised Land: Pointing Forward to Christ

1. See Bruce K. Waltke, "Theonomy in Relation to Dispensational and Covenant Theologies," in *Theonomy: A Reformed Critique*, ed. William S. Barker and W. Robert Godfrey (Grand Rapids: Zondervan, 1990), 70–73.

2. For fuller discussion, see Wright, *An Eye for an Eye*, 158–59.

Chapter 9—The Punishments and Penalties of the Law: Prefiguring the Destruction of Sin and Guilt Through Christ

1. C. S. Lewis, *The Problem of Pain* (reprint; New York: Macmillan, 1962), 93.

2. Cf. John I. Durham, *Exodus*, Word Biblical Commentary, vol. 2 (Waco, TX: Word Books, 1987), 325.

3. A more secularized discussion of the restorative element in *lex talionis* is found in David Daube, *Studies in Biblical Law* (New York: Ktav, 1969), 102–153.

4. In confirmation of the idea of singlefold punishment, see Meredith G. Kline, "Double Trouble," *Journal of the Evangelical Theological Society*, 32 (1989): 171–79.

5. For a list, see James B. Jordan, *The Law of the Covenant* (Tyler, TX: Institute for Christian Economics, 1984), 261–63.

6. Jordan in his book *The Law of the Covenant*, 263–71, proposes an ingenious symbolical explanation based on inferences from symbolic associations of the numbers four and five and symbolic associations of cattle and sheep. But the distant and doubtful character of the associations make me think that his solution is no less speculative than mine or those solutions based on general speculations concerning what practical differences Israelites might see between cattle and sheep. More recently, in an unpublished communication, he has pointed out that Deuteronomy 12:15–25 includes special provisions governing the slaughter of these animals, and that such indicates that "God had a proprietary interest in ox and sheep." Perhaps so. And perhaps this circumstance makes appropriate the more severe penalty when a thief slaughters or sells such an animal. But the focus of Deuteronomy 12 seems to be on what people are supposed to do with the blood and with firstborn or vowed animals. The procedures with respect to blood apply equally to wild and domestic clean animals. The procedures with respect to firstborn or vowed animals do not apply to all animals of their class. Thus neither of these provisions says anything directly about the class of all oxen or all sheep. It is not clear that oxen and sheep are being treated in a special way principally because all animals of this kind are potentially sacrificial animals.

One crucial fact to weigh is that Exodus 22:4 appears to classify donkeys in the same class with oxen and sheep. "If the stolen animal is found alive in his possession—whether ox or donkey or sheep—he must pay back double." Does this verse assert merely that twofold restitution is appropriate for all cases of live animals? Or does it also indirectly suggest that a more severe penalty is appropriate for all cases when the stolen animal is no longer alive, including donkeys? If we ignore the context, the verse merely states what is true for living animals, and need not warrant any implications for dead ones. But when the entire passage, Exodus 22:1–15, is taken into account, implications do seem to follow.

Verses 1–15 specify restitution in cases involving various stolen, borrowed, or otherwise misplaced or destroyed items. Introductory "if" clauses in each major division specify the type of case in view. Verses 2–3 are rightly seen as parenthetical, in that they specify how one disposes of other matters of concern relating to theft.

Hence, the operative contrasts are found in the "if" clauses of verses 1 and 4. When the two verses are compared, the fundamental contrast appears to be between animals that have already been disposed of and animals that are still alive in the thief's possession. In verse 4, not only the general phrase "the stolen animal" (Hebrew *haggenēbâ*, "the stolen thing") but the explicit inclusion of donkeys pushes us towards understanding the fundamental distinction as disposed-of versus still-alive. Jordan's interpretation, on the other hand, makes sense only on the assumption that the operative contrast is between ox-and-sheep and all-other-animals, or perhaps between animals-offered-in-sacrifice and all-other-animals. But if such were the operative contrast, we would expect a different type of wording, such as, "if another kind of animal is stolen, whether found in the thief's possession or slaughtered, the thief must restore double." The main plausibility for Jordan's reading arises from the mention of oxen and sheep in verse 1, apparently with no other animals included. But the Hebrew word for "ox" is a general name for cattle, both male and female, and the Hebrew word for "sheep" is general enough to include both sheep and goats. Together these two terms included the entire range of the most common livestock animals in Israel. Hence, a perfectly general principle concerning disposed-of animals might naturally be formulated in this way. Cases of stolen camels, horses, and donkeys would be less common and might easily be left as a matter of inference from the more common case.

Granted this understanding of the relation of verse 1 and verse 4, it follows that stolen donkeys are handled with double payment *only* when the animal is found still alive. A bigger payment (four or five?) is appropriate if the animal is killed or sold. Since Jordan's type of symbolic explanation does not apply to donkeys, it presumably does not offer the correct explanation of the penalty for oxen or sheep either.

However, it is still possible that my explanation is wrong and that Jordan's is right. Why are donkeys and horses not mentioned in verse 1? In the absence of more explicit information, we should be cautious. Despite the disagreements, Jordan agrees with me concerning the general rule of double payment and its motivation, and that is enough for us to build on (see ibid., 134–35).

7. Ibid., 134.

8. James Jordan, *The Law of the Covenant*, 135, acknowledges the possibility of my interpretation, but prefers a literal interpretation of "sevenfold." So I should set forth reasons for my preference.

(1) The book of Proverbs sets forth wise advice about life similar to the advice that a father would give to his son (cf. Proverbs 1:8, 10; 2:1). The mention of Solomon (1:1; 10:1) hints that the advice is most pertinent to a future king. But it is not exclusively advice to judges, much less legal, statutory additions to the law code. Proverbs 6:30–31 is therefore most naturally interpreted as an observation about the realities of actual life, not a legal statute specifying what ought to be done. In particular, verse 30 does not match the character of a case law, since the language about not despising appears to be a description of actual life ("men do not despise") or possibly a prohibition to any arbitrary listener ("do not despise"), but is

technically irrelevant to the judicial decision of the judge. The form of language does not suggest that this verse is formally introducing a new case law. But if such a case law is not introduced here, where is it introduced?

(2) Jordan justifies the severity of the penalty by arguing that the poor man is despising God's mercy as expressed in the laws about gleaning and the tithe (Deuteronomy 14:28–29). But (a) the argument has greatest force only if the rich and prosperous consistently observed their obligations with regard to the poor, which was far from being the case in Israel. (b) The argument shows only that the poor man has offended God grievously, not that he has offended more grievously the person from whom he has stolen. As we shall see, the severity of offense against God has no direct role in the reckoning of debt to other human beings.

(3) It is impossible to deduce sevenfold repayment from the principles of justice enunciated in the time of Moses. During Mosaic times, judges would have acted on the basis of the principle of double payment or possibly fourfold payment in the case of items that had already been consumed or sold by the thief. Thus Jordan's interpretation implies that Proverbs 6:30–31 introduces a change in penalty in comparison with Mosaic times. It is difficult to supply a motivation for such a change.

In an unpublished personal communication Jordan has informed me he has changed his mind and now agrees with my interpretation.

9. Greg Bahnsen comes close to this position by speaking of the social nature of crime, *Theonomy in Christian Ethics*, expanded ed. (Phillipsburg, NJ: Presbyterian and Reformed, 1984), 436, 438, 440, Bahnsen's emphasis:

> While all crime is sinful, not every sin is a crime. An offense against God's law is a crime when it is a *social* misdeed punishable by the governing authorities; sin, on the other hand, is always judged and punished by God. The magistrate cannot presume to punish a man's sin, but he is obligated to enforce penal sanctions against a man's crime. Thus a crime bears two punishments: one before the magistrate (as a social misdeed), one before God Himself (as a sin). . . .

> The penalties imposed upon social crime are just as appropriate, equitable, and just with respect to their sphere of reference (civil society) as the eternal punishment for that crime (considered now as sin) is just with respect to its sphere of reference (the God-man relation with respect to eternity). . . .

> The *civic* punishment upon a man's crime could not be eliminated even though he was required to make atonement and find God's ultimate forgiveness by means of sacrifice for sin (cf. Leviticus 4–6). Social restitution (the penal sanction) was not incompatible with being forgiven by the trespass offering (6:4–7; Numbers 5:5–8). Therefore, the *civil* punishment was required to be executed upon every criminal unconditionally—without consideration of his status, without mercy, without cancellation through atoning sacrifice. Such are the demands of justice in the realm of civil judgment; a crime always receives what it, with respect to the context of social life, deserves as equitable for the nature of the offense.

Chapter 10—False Worship, Holy War, and Penal Substitution: Prefiguring the Spiritual Warfare of Christ and His Church

1. Cf. the discussion in Meredith G. Kline, *By Oath Consigned: A Reinterpretation of the Covenant Signs of Circumcision and Baptism* (Grand Rapids: Eerdmans, 1968), 16–17.

2. Of course, the New Testament still uses symbols and sacraments of its own, baptism and the Lord's Supper.

3. Not all Christians agree with me concerning the modern application of Deuteronomy 13. In particular, some advocates of a position called "theonomy" have understood Deuteronomy 13 as a basis for modern capital punishment of idolaters. But such a conclusion misunderstands the true implications of the Old Testament. For further discussion on this matter, see appendix A.

Chapter 11—Principles of Justice for the Modern State

1. See appendix A. Compare also Bahnsen, *Theonomy*, 436, 438, 440.

2. See Greg L. Bahnsen, *By This Standard: The Authority of God's Law Today* (Tyler, TX: Institute for Christian Economics, 1985), 11; Gary North, *Dominion Covenant: Genesis*, 2d ed. (Tyler, TX: Institute for Christian Economics, 1987), appendix E.

3. Wenham, *Leviticus*, 285.

4. Walter C. Kaiser, Jr. (*Toward Old Testament Ethics* [Grand Rapids: Zondervan, 1983], 73) argues that Numbers 35:31 "apparently permitted" a monetary substitute in *every* capital case except premeditated murder. Numbers 35:31 does indeed imply that a ransom was possible in *some* other cases, and Exodus 21:30 supplies an example of one such case. But Numbers 35:31 offers no direct grounds for generalizing from "some cases" to a sweeping rule involving "every case except murder." For such questions we must rely on the wording of other statutes and on the general principles of justice.

  On the basis of general principles of equity, it would seem that a ransom would be appropriate in all cases of diminished responsibility, such as is contemplated in the context of Exodus 21:30. In cases of full responsibility, the offender can settle with the victim for whatever penalty the two agree on, but if the victim is not satisfied with what the offender offers, the formally specified penalty is the only option left. In the case of murder the victim as well as the polluted land (Numbers 35:33–34) cannot commute the sentence, and hence it must be carried out without alternation. In cases of crimes that profane the holy community, the community cannot by its own mere fiat alter its profanation or the profanation of the land, so once again, I would argue, a ransom is not permitted.

5. For actual examples of such a process, see Daniel W. Van Ness, *Crime and Its Victims* (Downers Grove, IL: InterVarsity, 1986), 157–75.

6. C. S. Lewis, "The Humanitarian Theory of Punishment," in *God in the Dock: Essays on Theology and Ethics*, ed. Walter Hooper (Grand Rapids: Eerdmans, 1970),

287–300. Lewis contends that "this doctrine, merciful though it appears, really means that each one of us, from the moment he breaks the law, is deprived of the rights of a human being" (ibid., 288). For a more general discussion of how the present criminal system developed, see Van Ness, *Crime and Its Victims*, 61–99.

Chapter 12—Just Penalties for Many Crimes

1. The case where a thief steals money and then spends the money is difficult. Has he destroyed the property in a way analogous to eating or selling a stolen sheep? Since money by nature consists of fully interchangeable units of exchange, a thief's restoration of the same *amount* rather than the precise bills or coins that have been stolen would appear to me to constitute full restoration. Hence, I would argue for double repayment rather than fourfold repayment in this case.

2. We should note that a policy of having an additional penalty for items that are destroyed or sold would focus in practice mostly on professional thieves and wanton destroyers (e.g., vandals) rather than on people who might steal once out of envy or covetousness. Thus the additional penalty may have practical wisdom, though it should not be followed for this reason alone.

3. Cf. Van Ness, *Crime and Its Victims*, 174.

4. Jordan, *The Law of the Covenant*, 136.

5. For examples of modern attempts to work out a schedule of repayment, see Van Ness, *Crime and Its Victims*, 157–75.

6. But one advantage of the Israelite system is that taxpayers are not required to support the bureaucracy involved in parole.

7. In confirmation, see Jacob Milgrom, *Cult and Conscience: The Asham and the Priestly Doctrine of Repentance* (Leiden: Brill, 1976), 104–124.

8. See Milgrom, *Cult and Conscience*, 84–104.

9. Wenham, *Leviticus*, 285. In cases of premeditated murder and other heinous crimes, however, no alteration of the penalty was permitted (see Numbers 35:31–32).

10. Genesis 9:6 is universal in character, and Numbers 35:31 explicitly disallows exceptions in the case of murder. Nevertheless, Van Ness (*Crime and Its Victims*, 184–91), argues with some plausibility for using capital punishment only in a few unusually intractable cases. He points out that in the U.S. justice system at present, offenders who are poor or black are statistically more likely to receive a capital sentence. But the proper remedy for such inequity is a consistent, just system of punishments, not the mere abolition of any one particular type of punishment.

Van Ness also points to cases in the Bible where the death penalty was not executed: Cain's murder of Abel, David's murder of Uriah, David's adultery with Bathsheba, the woman taken in adultery in John 7:53–8:11, and Onesimus the runaway slave. But in appealing to these cases, Van Ness fails to distinguish the obligations of witnesses, accusers, and judges. In the cases of Cain and David, the witnesses necessary for legal process were lacking. People would presumably have guessed who was guilty, and of course God knew infallibly, but human witnesses were still necessary for human courts. Moreover, in the context of ancient Israel a case would only come to court if there were a human accuser. Nathan the prophet accused David, but he did so only in his capacity of being a prophet of God, not because he was a legal witness. In the case of Cain, the mark mentioned in Genesis 4:15 protected Cain against any attempt at vigilante "justice," to which people are tempted to resort when a presumed offender cannot be convicted by due process of law.

In the case of Onesimus, Philemon would have had a legal case. But Philemon as a victim was under no legal or moral obligation to prosecute a case when the offender was repentant. In addition, the Roman law specifying the death penalty for runaways slaves was unjustly harsh (see Deuteronomy 23:15), and Philemon was well advised not to invoke it.

In the case of the woman caught in adultery, some ancient manuscripts omit the entire passage or place it at another location in Luke or John. It almost certainly did not belong to the original manuscript of John, but it is an ancient tradition and probably represents a real incident from the life of Jesus. It appears that Jesus' opponents, desiring to trap him, deliberately set up the whole situation. Probably they connived to have some special circumstance in which people could be caught in adultery with the necessary witnesses. But if so, they were themselves guilty of having tacitly consented to the adultery rather than stopping it beforehand. Because of their complicity in the act, their status as witnesses was forfeited. Without the necessary witnesses, the legal case collapsed. Hence, the passage gives us no clear basis for drawing broad conclusions about penology. In addition, we will see that it is not so clear whether adultery merits the death penalty outside of the context of the special holiness of Israel.

11. Bahnsen, *By This Standard*, 6.

12. Another factor in the consideration might be that if the owner has ignored repeated warnings from the authorities, he is guilty of incorrigibility. See the discussion below on incorrigibility.

13. In conformity with Reformed theology I believe that the Bible teaches the perseverance of the saints. But I am now considering matters in terms of participation in the visible community of faith (see 1 John 2:19). As Hebrews indicates, membership in the church and public commitment to Christ involves a most serious responsibility to Christ. Apostasy therefore incurs special guilt (Hebrews 10:26–31).

14. See Wenham, *Leviticus*, 285–86; idem, "Law and the Legal System in the Old Testament," in *Law, Morality, and the Bible*, ed. Bruce Kaye and Gordon Wenham (Downers Grove, IL: InterVarsity, 1978), 43.

15. Leviticus 18:21 and 20:1–5 involve murder as well as false worship, and so they are not merely a ceremonial violation. The laws on sexual crimes will be discussed in chapter 13.

16. The same reasonings apply to the unusual penalty falling on the violation of sexual separation in Deuteronomy 25:11–12.

17. See also Jordan, *The Law of the Covenant*, 93–94, 104; and Gary North, *Tools of Dominion: The Case Laws of Exodus* (Tyler, TX: Institute for Christian Economics, 1990), chapter 4.

18. Adoption of a child outside family lines would still be necessary when a whole family line was corrupted by abusive practices.

19. But it should be noted that modern states tend to regard all children as belonging to the state rather than to parents and to overreach themselves. They impose ungodly standards on parents and may actually remove children to a foster home merely because the parents have spanked their children! Such tyrannous actions are bound to occur so long as the state recognizes no God-given boundaries to its authority.

20. But in the village setting of Israelite society, such a son would have become a notorious pest to the whole community, and the citation of witnesses would be a mere formality.

21. I do not intend to exclude the possibility of delegating authority, as when parents give permission for a school teacher to use corporal punishment.

22. James B. Jordan, "Slavery in Biblical Perspective" (Th.M. thesis, Westminster Theological Seminary, 1980); North, *Tools of Dominion*, chapters 1–2.

Chapter 13—Just Penalties for Sexual Crimes

1. Note, for example, the differences between John Murray, *Divorce* (Philadelphia: Presbyterian and Reformed, 1961); and Jay Adams, *Marriage, Divorce and Remarriage* (Phillipsburg, NJ: Presbyterian and Reformed, 1980).

2. Ibid.

3. See also Roland de Vaux, *Ancient Israel*, 2 vols. (New York: McGraw-Hill, 1965), 1:26.

4. Ibid., 1:29.

5. Ibid., 1:30.

6. Ibid., 1:27.

7. Ibid.

8. Cf. ibid., 1:26.

9. In 1 Samuel 18:23–25 Saul did not honor his earlier commitment to accept the death of Goliath as the equivalent of a marriage present (1 Samuel 17:25). In spite of this additional complexity, 1 Samuel 18:23–25 reveals some of the social expectations for marriage to a king's daughter.

10. Jordan, *The Law of the Covenant*, 149.

11. The verb "lay hold of, seize" (*tps*) in verse 28 is used elsewhere in the Old Testament in a number of cases where definite use of force is in view (e.g., 1 Samuel 23:26; 1 Kings 13:4; 18:40; 20:18; 2 Kings 10:14; 14:13; Jeremiah 34:3). The verb in verse 25, namely, "take hold of, seize" (*hzq* in the hiphil plus the preposition *bĕ*),

has a quite similar range of meaning. It can be used in contexts where exertion of some force is in view (e.g., 1 Samuel 17:35; 2 Samuel 2:16; Jeremiah 50:33). It can also be used for taking hold of someone's hand in a gentle manner (Judges 16:26; Isaiah 51:18; Jeremiah 31:32; cf. 2 Samuel 15:5). Like the word in verse 28, it can be used for holding a weapon (Nehemiah 4:16–17; Psalm 35:2; Jeremiah 6:23). Even in a sexual context, it can be used simply of seizing in a general way (Proverbs 7:13). Even in Judges 19:25 and 2 Samuel 13:11, where the context speaks of rape, the key word is used only to describe holding the girl, presumably by the wrist or arm. (The word is also used in 2 Samuel 13:14, but in another stem and with another sense in order to assert that Amnon was physically stronger than Tamar.) Hence, its use even in these cases does not differ at all from the supposed meaning of *tps* in verse 28, namely, "take hold of." Thus a survey of the evidence shows no notable difference in meaning between the two verbs. They would surely be understood as basically synonymous in Deuteronomy 22:25 and 22:28, because of the otherwise notable parallels between the two verses.

12. Thus, to classify rape of an unengaged woman under verses 25–27 rather than under verses 28–29 would be to ignore the obvious distinction between the two passages as well as to postulate a second type of distinction that the passages do not support.

13. Such a situation would be comparable in some respects to the situation that Joseph mistakenly thought that he was in according to Matthew 1:19.

14. The case of an engaged servant, such as in Leviticus 19:20, is exceptional. But the servant girl is still under the authority of her master until she is actually married. Hence, the nature of the situation does lead to a salient difference between this case and other cases of engaged women.

15. The question of how the church (in distinction from the state) should deal with potential or actual divorces between professing Christians is a matter that cannot be discussed in this book.

16. It must be remembered that we are here focusing on the horizontal relations between human beings. The absence of fixed *horizontal* penalties to rectify offenses against other human beings in no way mitigates the seriousness of a sin before God.

17. Theoretically, it is possible to advocate castration as the penalty for adultery. But such a position is certainly wrong. Adultery involves deep guilt on the part of both the man and the woman involved. Both man and woman should receive basically the same punishment. The equivalent of castration for a woman is now medically possible, but because of its dependence on medical procedures it could not be the penalty implied by truly universal principles of justice.

18. The case of rape initiated by women might perhaps be left undiscussed because it is so rare. Moreover, I do not wish to speak unnecessarily of topics whose shameful details are better left unspoken. But for the benefit of readers who desire to follow my reasoning to the end, I will venture to be more specific.

Rape by a gang of women or rape by one woman using a weapon is of course conceivable. Israelite statutes do not deal directly with the issue, so reasoning using general principles of justice is our only resource. In modern times a penalty equivalent to castration has become medically possible. But it is exceedingly doubtful whether such a penalty is appropriate to general justice in all times and places, that is, in situations other than those associated with the special holiness of Israel. It seems to me much more in line with God's justice to treat such cases as cases tantamount to kidnapping and the violence in its wake.

Gang rape or rape with a weapon involves domination with several sides. The offenders threaten bodily injury through a weapon or through gang violence; they abuse sexually; they have power and some intention to compel detailed obedience from the victim; and there is no obvious limit to the time during which the victim will be held and forced into perhaps a whole series of indignities. Taken together, these multiple dominations are tantamount to kidnapping, even though their goals may differ in detail from other cases of kidnapping. Thus it seems just to inflict the penalty for kidnapping, whether the offenders are men or women.

19. I am grateful to James B. Jordan for calling my attention to some of the complexities of this issue.

20. I have here assumed that homosexual practice is sinful. I am aware that this view is disputed by a portion of evangelicals. Moreover, much of the time loathing of homosexuals among evangelicals has created an atmosphere contrary to the Christian obligations to seek out the lost and to help Christians struggling with temptation. I cannot discuss the issues at length within the scope of this book. I therefore confine myself to the following observations:

(1) In this whole book I assume that we cannot dismiss uncomfortable Old Testament teaching by saying that it is merely the word of human beings. The Old Testament is God's word, and Mosaic laws were God's word to the Israelites. Of course, we are not supposed to apply the Old Testament directly to ourselves, as if there were no changes with the coming of Christ. But neither are we supposed to ignore it or dismiss it.

(2) In Leviticus 20:10–21 homosexual practice is grouped together with other sexual irregularities, not with idolatrous and occult practices. The claim that homosexual practice was banned merely because of idolatrous associations is not plausible.

(3) The penalty in Leviticus 20:13 attaches to homosexual acts whatever their motivation and background. In particular, it does not distinguish between acts by people with heterosexual, homosexual, or bisexual emotional orientation. One cannot reasonably claim that homosexual orientation was an exception.

(4) The normative pattern enunciated in Genesis 2:18–25 is part of the background of Levitical law. In the light of this norm, the homosexual practice of Leviticus 20:13 should be seen as a deviation from the creational purpose of God for the sexes, rather than a temporary ceremonial prohibition of a mere symbolic disorder.

(5) If homosexual practice were wholly a matter of psychic disease rather than a sin, one would have expected it to be treated at worst like leprosy. But admittedly the importance of passing on inheritance in Israel may also have an influence on

penalties for homosexual practice. This fact makes it difficult to assess what reasons may be involved in the statutes.

(6) Romans 1:26–27 condemns homosexual practice. It is sometimes claimed that the condemnation is directed only against abuses like paederasty, that is, abuses conducted by those with a dominantly heterosexual orientation. The "exchange" of natural relations that Paul mentions is thought to indicate a previous underlying heterosexual orientation. But such an interpretation misunderstands the focus of Paul's analysis in the whole of Romans 1:18–32.

Paul is not conducting a psychological analysis or setting forth a series of psychological stages that unbelievers must pass through in succession. Rather, he is conducting a theological analysis. He asserts that all unbelief, whatever psychological forms it may take and whatever may be its historical development in a particular culture, is always a reaction against pervasive general revelation of the character of God (vv. 19–20) and equally pervasive revelation of moral standards (v. 32). In particular, in verse 25 the exchange of the truth of God for a lie does not imply that at some earlier point in their childhood people were psychologically conscious of being in full possession of the truth. Rather, this exchange repeatedly goes on as people repeatedly suppress the truth and repeatedly distort and replace it with lies. Similarly, the exchange in verse 26 describes a repeatable process of replacement of good for evil, not a one-time psychological personal history of two stages. Paul is not in fact describing anyone's psychological history. Hence, Paul's statements about the evil of homosexual behavior are quite general and do not restrict themselves as would some modern views to people with heterosexual or bisexual orientation.

(7) Modern social and sexual research showing the difficulty of changing sexual orientation should give us caution, sympathy, and circumspection in drawing conclusions. But such research can never prove that homosexual practice is not a sin. The sinfulness of sin is not determined by how difficult it is to resist or whether its temptations can be easily eliminated. Whatever their circumstances and sins, all people are called on to repent of sin and turn toward Jesus Christ for healing (Acts 17:30–31).

(8) God is all-powerful, and may choose if He wishes to reverse homosexual desires and orientation in a moment. However, we ought not to promise newly repentant Christians instant freedom from this or any other temptation. God nowhere promises that there will be no temptation. Rather, He promises that temptations can always be resisted (1 Corinthians 10:13). Often times Christians must resist temptations that continue to beset them over a long period. We are obliged to serve God even if it means torture, loss of family, or our own death. Loss of the short-range possibility of a permanent, exclusive bond of social and sexual intimacy is no worse. But if repentant Christians with homosexual orientation cannot immediately change their orientation and must suffer this loss, they deserve the special support and warmth of the community of Christians in the struggle.

(9) In the West the current cultural pacesetters put a very high value on tolerance of alternative lifestyles. This general stance has tended to skew the technical

psychological literature and its popularizations in favor of mere acceptance of homosexual lifestyles. Those whose research has led them to other conclusions have to stand against the tide. In spite of this bias, it is noteworthy that the technical literature regarding homosexuality does not speak with a single voice. Some specialists do indeed maintain that homosexuality is abnormal, stemming primarily from self-pity or inadequate parent-child relations, and that with patience, love, and commitment exercised intelligently over a long period of time it can be remedied. I would direct readers' attention to Elizabeth R. Moberly, *Homosexuality: A New Christian Ethic* (Greenwood, SC: Attic Press, 1983); Gerard van den Aardweg, *Homosexuality and Hope: A Psychologist Talks about Treatment and Change* (Ann Arbor, MI: Servant Books, 1985); idem, *On the Origins and Treatment of Homosexuality: A Psychoanalytic Reinterpretation* (New York: Praeger, 1986). A brief theological analysis is found in John R. W. Stott, *Homosexual Partnerships? Why Same-Sex Relationships Are Not a Christian Option* (Downers Grove, IL: InterVarsity, 1985).

21. Mature theonomists clearly make such distinctions, and so they repudiate a blind, mechanical attempt to reproduce Israelite society point by point in modern times. See Bahnsen, *By This Standard*, 5–7.

Chapter 14—Deterrence and Rehabilitation

1. Van Ness *Crime and Its Victims*, 190 says, "Imprisoning murderers for life under appropriate security and surveillance also prevents them from killing." But on the next page Van Ness envisions the possibility that "a prisoner already serving a life sentence kills a guard." Nothing short of draconian measures (solitary confinement for life? in an Alcatraz from which escape is all but impossible?) can provide a high degree of security, especially because masters of martial arts can kill people using their hands or feet. See chapter 15 for my critique of imprisonment.

2. Van Ness, *Crime and Its Victims*, 143–75.

Chapter 15—A Critique of Prisons

1. For an introductory discussion, see Charles Colson, "Towards an Understanding of Imprisonment and Rehabilitation," in *Crime and the Responsible Community*, ed. John Stott and Nicholas Miller (Grand Rapids: Eerdmans, 1980), 152–180.

Chapter 16—Our Responsibilities Toward Imperfect States

1. John Calvin, *Institutes of the Christian Religion* (reprint, Grand Rapids: Eerdmans, 1970), 4.20.22–32.

2. Ibid., 4.20.31.

3. Ibid., 4.20.16.

Chapter 17—Fulfillment of the Law in the Gospel According to Matthew

1. Richard T. France, *The Gospel According to Matthew*, Tyndale New Testament Commentaries (Grand Rapids: Eerdmans, 1985), 40–41.

2. For a fuller discussion of these matters, see, e.g., Geerhardus Vos, *The Teaching of Jesus Concerning the Kingdom of God and the Church* (reprint; Nutley, NJ: Presbyterian and Reformed, 1972); and Herman Ridderbos, *The Coming of the Kingdom* (Philadelphia: Presbyterian and Reformed, 1969). On the equivalence of "kingdom of heaven" and "kingdom of God," see Ridderbos, *Kingdom*, 8–13, 18–19. In view of the reasonable consensus about "inaugurated" or "semirealized" eschatology, I have bypassed the scholarly disputes on such questions.

3. Douglas J. Moo, "Jesus and the Authority of the Mosaic Law," *Journal for the Study of the New Testament* 20 (1984), 14.

4. E.g., David Hill, *The Gospel of Matthew*, New Century Bible (Greenwood, SC: Attic Press, 1972), 117; Gustaf Dalman, *Jesus-Jeshua: Studies in the Gospels* (New York: Macmillan, 1929), 56–61; see other examples in Bahnsen, *Theonomy* (see chapter 10, n. 8), 70–72.

5. John Calvin, *Commentary on a Harmony of the Evangelists, Matthew, Mark, and Luke*, 3 vols. (reprint; Grand Rapids: Eerdmans, n.d.), 1:277.

6. John Murray, *Principles of Conduct* (Grand Rapids: Eerdmans, 1957), 150.

7. Donald A. Carson, "Matthew," in *The Expositor's Bible Commentary*, ed. Frank E. Gaebelein (Grand Rapids: Zondervan, 1984), 8:143–44. See also France, *Matthew*, 114, 117.

8. Since this point is disputed, I have included in appendix C a more technical discussion of the possible meanings of the Greek word.

9. See Carson, "Matthew," 142–43.

10. Ibid., 142, 154.

11. Ibid., 142.

12. Bahnsen, *Theonomy*, 71–72, argues that *plēroō* is preferred because the Pharisaic corruption of the law had reduced the meaning of the law to externals. A richer word than *histēmi* is supposedly used in order to indicate that Jesus restores the law from its corruptions. This argument has some weight, but other words would be appropriate for the meaning "restore," namely *apokathistēmi*, *katartizō*, or *anorthoō*. There is no real danger that any of the words in question would be misunderstood as implying the meaning "establish for the first time," since everyone knew that the law had already been established by Moses.

13. Suppose, for the sake of argument, that the sense "confirm" is the linguistically correct interpretation of verse 17. The overall theology implied in Matthew's conception of fulfillment might still lead to the same conclusions regarding the use of the Mosaic law now. For one thing, the language of confirmation could mean either of two things. If "confirm" connotes "confirm as rules binding on all," Mosaic law becomes a rule for our obedience. But if "confirm" connotes "confirm the

validity or truthfulness of," Jesus may be simply asserting that the Old Testament law remains the authoritative word of God, as part of the canon. Such an assertion would be compatible with abolishing or radically altering its role as a rule for obedience. Verse 18 easily harmonizes with the latter sense, while verse 19 tends to suggest that the former sense is in view. Even if verse 19 has in view straightforward, plain obedience, rather than obedience transformed by the new circumstances, it is still possible to interpret it as a saying that Jesus intended to apply only during His earthly life, and not to the situation subsequent to His resurrection. If, on the other hand, verse 19 is viewed as applying to the church age in an untransformed way, it contradicts undeniable changes in the observance of the law, as understood both in Matthew and the other New Testament documents.

14. Carson, "Matthew," 145–46. See also France, *Matthew*, 115.

15. Ibid., 146.

16. Hermann L. Strack and Paul Billerbeck, *Kommentar zum Neuen Testament aus Talmud und Midrasch* (München: C. H. Beck, 1922–28), 1:608–610.

17. On this whole issue, see also Moo, "Jesus and the Authority of the Mosaic Law."

18. Bahnsen, *Theonomy*, 84–85. To be fair to Bahnsen, one should note that he elsewhere introduces complex qualifications to his key chapter title, "the abiding validity of the law in exhaustive detail." But his qualifications create tension with his exegesis of Matthew. In his exegesis, the interpretation of *fulfill* as "confirm" and the strong affirmations concerning "jot and tittle" appear to leave no room for any qualifications whatsoever.

19. See also France, *Matthew*, 18–19, 50–56.

20. See Fairbairn, *Typology* (see chapter 3, n. 2), 2:175, who represents many others. Fairbairn introduces noteworthy qualifications on the role of the law because of the prominence given to the Spirit in the New Testament (2:164–75). But even these qualifications do not quite free him from the problems arising from a too-sharp initial dichotomy.

Appendix A—False Worship in the Modern State

1. The basic theses of theonomy are ably set forth by Bahnsen in his books *Theonomy* and *By This Standard*. The former of the two works specifically advocates the death penalty for false worship on the basis of Deuteronomy 13 and 17 (*Theonomy*, 445–46). It should be noted that in his works Bahnsen discusses mainly foundational issues concerning God's law. He specifically mentions the difficulty of understanding the law properly and the possibility of disagreements over the applications in detail (e.g., *By This Standard*, 7, 9). Hence his principial arguments leave open in principle the possibility of an alternative interpretation of Deuteronomy 13 like my own. At present, Bahnsen is uncertain about the question of civil penalties for false worship (see note 2 below).

   In 1987, in an open question and answer session, the question was posed, "Should we execute idolaters?" Bahnsen responds:

The *prima facie* understanding of the biblical texts would seem to support the justice of punishing idolarty, even today. But I have not done sufficient homework and reflection on this question. (Gary Scott Smith, ed., *God and Politics: Four Views on the Reformation of Civil Government: Theonomy, Principled Pluralism, Christian America, National Confessionalism* [Phillipsburg, NJ: Presbyterian and Reformed, 1989], 268).

In private conversation with Bahnsen in 1988, I also learned, without knowledge of the above quote, that he was uncertain about modern punishments for idolatry.

2. In my judgment the phrase "cut off from one's people" refers to covenant curse, often taking the form of death. When no instructions are given indicating a human executioner, God is assumed to be the executioner.

3. On the basis of such observations, Jacob Milgrom reaches conclusions similar to mine: "sins against God are punishable only by God . . . one's offense to the Deity is a private affair except when it jeopardizes the immediate welfare of the community." (*Studies in Levitical Terminology, I: The Encroacher and the Levite: The Term 'Aboda* [Berkeley: University of California Press, 1970], 56–57). Milgrom also observes that in the case of an unauthorized usurper of priestly duties, the death penalty is executed by human beings. As in the case of false worship and false prophecy, usurpation threatens to profane the priesthood as a whole (Numbers 18:1–7).

4. Note that if I am correct in my assessment of Israelite punishments, the punishments for false worship were never intended to be extended to nations outside the land of Palestine. Consequently, in their own day they could never have posed the same perceived threat to other nations as would a modern universal program.

5. I am aware of the arguments by the theonomist Greg L. Bahnsen, to the effect that the death penalty for false worship is compatible with evangelism (see his article, "M. G. Kline on Theonomic Politics: An Evaluation of His Reply," *The Journal of Christian Reconstruction* 6 no. 2 [1979-80]: 212–15). Some parts of these arguments are technically valid, but they are by no means sufficient to answer my concerns. For example, even in the case of state punishment and exile that I envision in this chapter, evangelism could still be carried on with non-Christians who decide not to go into exile. Some forms of evangelism might also be carried on in non-Christian nations, to the degree that evangelism is not suppressed. My claim is not that evangelism would become impossible but merely that it would become more difficult.

One more factor is worth consideration. Bahnsen correctly observes that evangelistic opportunities for a murderer are terminated when the murderer is executed (ibid., 212–13). But at least with respect to my difficulties this case is not a helpful parallel. Those who desire to murder are not significantly tempted to choose exile in order to murder with impunity. Virtually all societies have penalties against violations of commandments 5–9 of the Ten Commandments. Only with respect to commandments 1–4 will there be significant motivation for choosing exile, because violations of these commandments are not punished in non-Christian nations. It is interesting to note that my arguments on the basis of principles of God's justice result in placing penalties on violations of commandments 5–9 but not on violations of commandments 1–4, precisely the set of commandments that would create possible difficulties for evangelism. My conclusions are compatible with the general character of God's purposes for His kingdom during this age, which is exactly what we should expect.

6. Bahnsen, *By This Standard*, 322–23. But Bahnsen does not mention the possibility that we might generalize from the principles embodied in the holy war against the Canaanites.

Appendix B—Evaluating Theonomy

1. James B. Jordan in particular has written critically of theonomy in "Reconsidering the Mosaic Law: Some Reflections—1988," Biblical Horizons Occasional Paper No. 4, Tyler, TX. See also Ray R. Sutton, "A Redemptive Historical View of Theonomy," *The Geneva Review* 29 (June, 1986): 6–7 and 30 (July, 1986): 6–7.

2. A sample of other literature concerning theonomy and Christian reconstruction is included in the bibliography.

3. Bahnsen, *By This Standard*, 345–47. The same theses appear also in the preface to the second, expanded edition of *Theonomy*, xvi-xvii.

4. Bahnsen, *By This Standard*, 348–49.

5. Ibid., 8.

6. Rousas J. Rushdoony, forward to *Theonomy in Christian Ethics*, by Greg L. Bahnsen, xi; Gary North, *Dominion and Common Grace: The Biblical Basis of Progress* (Tyler, TX: Institute for Christian Economics, 1987), 139.

7. This section is a slightly altered version of my essay, "Effects of Interpretive Frameworks on the Application of Old Testament Law," in *Theonomy: A Reformed Critique*, ed. William S. Barker and W. Robert Godfrey (Grand Rapids: Zondervan, 1990), 101–123.

8. Some of the sharpest opposition to theonomy is represented by Meredith G. Kline, "Comments on an Old-New Error," *Westminster Theological Journal* 41 (1978–79), 172–89; and idem, *Structure* (see chapter 5, n. 2). Bahnsen's reply to Kline is found in "M. G. Kline on Theonomic Politics."

9. See Douglas A. Oss, "The Influence of Hermeneutical Frameworks in the Theonomy Debate," *Westminster Theological Journal* 51 (1989), 227–58.

10. See Kline, *Structure*, especially 154–71.

11. Bahnsen, *Theonomy*, 207–232; *By This Standard*, 7, 345–47.

12. Kline, *Structure*, 101–102, 160.

13. See Bahnsen, *Theonomy*, 204–216.

14. However, in a context discussing *modern* Christian obedience, Rousas J. Rushdoony asserts that "hybrids are clearly a violation of this law" (*The Institutes of Biblical Law* [Phillipsburg, NJ: Craig, 1973], 255).

15. Bahnsen, *By This Standard*, 345–46.

16. Ibid., 346.

17. Bahnsen, *Theonomy*, 445–46. For many people the theonomic position is associated with the definite-sounding position enunciated in this earlier book. However, note the qualifications in Appendix A, note 2.

18. Ibid., 214.

19. Ibid., 215.

20. Ibid., 214.

21. In my judgment, the apostles presuppose the divine authority of the Old Testament. Hence, they are able to draw from it many kinds of conclusions in both doctrinal and ethical areas. But their hermeneutical approach to the Old Testament is typological and Christocentric, not woodenly literal. Thus their own examples are in line with the type of approach that I am advocating.

22. See John M. Frame, *The Doctrine of the Knowledge of God* (Phillipsburg, NJ: Presbyterian and Reformed, 1987), 15–18.

23. See John M. Frame, "The Doctrine of the Christian Life" (Westminster Theological Seminary, Philadelphia, 1979, Mimeographed); Vern S. Poythress, *Symphonic Theology* (see chapter 2, n. 4), 34–36.

24. I should make it clear that I regard the outstanding representatives of the positions, Greg L. Bahnsen and Meredith G. Kline, as intelligent and sophisticated interpreters of the Old Testament. A close reading of their positions shows that they are well aware of both continuity and discontinuity between the two Testaments. They are aware of the relevance of both norms and situations. But tendencies at work in their positions get exaggerated by their followers.

25. See, e.g., Bahnsen, *Theonomy*, 356.

26. For further discussion of hermeneutical frameworks, see Poythress, *Science and Hermeneutics* (see chapter 2, n. 4).

27. Some people might reject as "unnatural" the intrusionist interpretation of Micah 4:1–2. But to undermine such an interpretation one must reject the intrusionist's global hermeneutical theory about shadows and fulfillment and the possibility of Old Testament prophetic literature expressing itself in the symbolic language of shadow appropriate to an audience living under Mosaic structures. See the discussion of this issue in Vern S. Poythress, *Understanding Dispensationalists* (Grand Rapids: Zondervan, 1987).

28. In my opinion it also looks forward to Christ, who is the final "stone" crushing rebellion against God (Daniel 2:34–35, 44–45; Matthew 21:44; Luke 20:18; 1 Peter 2:8).

29. See Bahnsen, *By This Standard*, 3–4, and 347, thesis #10.

30. The *Westminster Confession of Faith* gives confessional status to this principle when it affirms the following: "To them [Israel] also, as a body politic, He gave sundry judicial laws, which expired together with the State of that people; not obliging any other now, further than the general equity thereof may require" (chapter 19, par. 4). The phrase "general equity" implies recognition of permanent principles of justice.

31. Bahnsen, *By This Standard*, 6, 345–46.

32. Ibid., 7.

33. My expressions of sympathy for theonomy must not, however, be understood as disagreements with the major competing position, that of Meredith G. Kline. I have learned much from Kline and it is arguable that my approach owes even more to him than to the theonomists.

34. See, for example, Michael Schluter and Roy Clements, *Reactivating the Extended Family* (Cambridge, England: Jubilee Center Publications, 1986), 31–32; idem, "Jubilee Institutional Norms: A Middle Way between Creation Ethics and Kingdom Ethics as the Basis for Christian Political Action," *Evangelical Quarterly* 62 (1990), 48–50.

35. Bahnsen and I are in formal agreement over this point. See Bahnsen, *By This Standard*, 5–7, 137–38.

36. Ibid.

37. Ibid., 345–46.

38. Ibid., 346, n. 1.

39. Ibid., 346.

40. Ibid., 5–7.

41. Ibid., 347.

42. Ibid.

43. Bahnsen, *Theonomy*, 445–46.

44. See Ibid., 435–68; and idem, *By This Standard*, 270–84.

45. Bahnsen, *Theonomy*, 456.

46. Ibid, 455–58.

47. Ibid., 571–84; idem, "M. G. Kline on Theonomic Politics" (see appendix A, n. 6).

48. See the discussion in Emil Kautzsch, ed., *Gesenius' Hebrew Grammar*, 2d Eng. ed., trans. A. E. Cowley (Oxford: Oxford University Press, 1910), section 131h, and the example from Genesis 47:29; likewise, Theodor Nöldeke, *Compendious Syriac Grammar* (London: Williams and Norgate, 1904), section 213, with an example from *The Homilies of Aphraates*, ed. W. Wright, 161.12. Hebrew and Aramaic are similar at this point of grammar.

49. See, for example, F. Charles Fensham, *The Books of Ezra and Nehemiah*, The New International Commentary on the Old Testament (Grand Rapids: Eerdmans, 1982), 107–8.

50. Bahnsen, *By This Standard*, 322, says, "We are not advocating the forcible 'imposition' of God's law on an unwilling society." Despite the explicitness of Bahnsen's statement, some ambiguity on this matter still remains. Do theonomists mean that imposing laws on an unwilling society is merely infeasible or that it is unjust in principle? If it is unjust in principle, then Nebuchadnezzar's and Darius's decrees would appear to be unjust. If, however, the imposing of such laws is just, it would appear that in monarchical countries or countries ruled by a small minority the imposition might also sometimes be feasible. Even in countries with democratic voting processes a small minority might theoretically impose its will if the percentage of people participating in elections were small, or if the voters were poorly informed about the positions of candidates, or if the available candidates offered little to choose between.

Bahnsen's explicit statement above appears to assert the injustice of imposition. On this basis, I have addressed my discussion in this book to a nonimposition viewpoint. However, as far as I can see the arguments in Bahnsen's books all reinforce the idea that the principles concerning what is a crime and what is its just punishment are *completely* universal and that legislators are divinely obligated to bring laws into conformity with these principles whenever and wherever they legally can. Bahnsen presents no arguments at all as to *why* it would be unjust to impose laws, provided the laws do indeed agree with God's standards and provided legal processes are followed in introducing the new laws. In addition, Bahnsen cites Ezra 7:25–27 as a passage confirming the propriety of extending the rule of God's law over non-Jewish nations (*By This Standard*, 243–44, 333; *Theonomy*, 358–59). His interpretation of Ezra 7:25–27 is incorrect, as we have seen. But if it were correct, it would present us with a Biblically approved instance of imposition of laws. Pagans within the Trans-Euphrates would hardly have welcomed the imposition of the death penalty for false worship. Altogether, Bahnsen's principial arguments plus the use of the text from Ezra create grave tension with what Bahnsen says theonomists advocate.

Suppose, then, that theonomy actually does imply the legitimacy of imposing laws against false worship whenever legally possible. Such a position would strengthen my arguments in appendix A concerning the tensions with the evangelistic mandate, and my arguments near the end of this appendix concerning the dangers of granting inordinate significance to political weapons.

51. For example, Bahnsen, *By This Standard*, 5, 322.

52. For example, see the distinctions introduced by Bahnsen, *Theonomy*, 414–24.

53. In the immediately preceding section, I have given one suggestion about a possible source encouraging the sin of contentiousness.

Appendix C—Does the Greek Word Plēroō Sometimes Mean "Confirm"?

1. E.g., Hill, *Matthew* (see chapter 17, n. 4), 117; Gerhard Barth, "Matthew's Understanding of the Law," in *Tradition and Interpretation in Matthew*, ed. Günther Bornkamm, Gerhard Barth, and Heinz Joachim Held (Philadelphia: Westminster,

1963), 69; Dalman, *Jesus-Jeshua* (see chapter 17, no.4), 56–61. Bahnsen provides a longer list in *Theonomy*, 66–72. (However, not all the people that Bahnsen cites in his favor hold a position identical with his. Some are merely observing that fulfillment implies confirmation of the law, without thereby committing themselves to a special position with regard to the semantic value of the word *plēroō*. Moreover, though Hill and Barth both argue for the meaning "establish," the context of their discussions shows that they have in view an "actualization" of the will of God, going beyond the idea of simple confirmation.)

2. I will ignore discussions like Dalman's (*Jesus-Jeshua*, 56–61) that rely on constructing an underlying Aramaic or some earlier stage of tradition. The problems in Aramaic are not entirely dissimilar to those in Greek, since Aramaic possesses two words, *ml'* and *qym*, corresponding to the Greek words *plēroō* and *bebaioō* and to the English words *fulfill* and *confirm*. In any case the Greek text of Matthew, not the postulated underlying Aramaic, is our authoritative Scripture. Even if the underlying Aramaic could be confidently reconstructed, we could not know whether Matthew in his translation of the Aramaic brought out an additional implication of Jesus' words that was implied by the context of Jesus' ministry rather than by the words in isolation. In establishing theological doctrine we must not evade the force of the text by retreating behind it to an earlier stage of revelation, even if hypothetically that earlier stage can be accurately reconstructed.

3. Walter Bauer, *A Greek-English Lexicon of the New Testament and Other Early Christian Literature*, trans., William F. Arndt, F. Wilbur Gingrich, and Frederick W. Danker (Chicago: University of Chicago Press, 1979), 670–72.

4. Henry G. Liddell and Robert Scott, *A Greek-English Lexicon*, rev. ed. (Oxford: Oxford University Press, 1968), 1,420; G. W. H. Lampe, *A Patristic Greek Lexicon* (Oxford: Oxford University Press, 1961), 1,093–94; James H. Moulton and George Milligan, *The Vocabulary of the Greek Testament Illustrated from the Papyri and Other Non-Literary Sources* (Grand Rapids: Eerdmans, 1930), 520. Both Liddell-Scott and Lampe add certain other senses to the list given by Bauer, but none of the additions substantially alter the general picture.

The earlier lexicon by Joseph H. Thayer, *A Greek-English Lexicon of the New Testament* (New York/Cincinnati/Chicago: American Book Company, 1886), 517–18, substantially agrees with Bauer. But in subheading 2.c.ß Thayer says, "of sayings, promises, prophecies, *to bring to pass, ratify, accomplish.*" The word *ratify* comes close to the sense "confirm" or "establish" that we are interested in. However, the passages cited by Thayer indicate that he has in view the sense "fulfill," going beyond mere confirmation. The English word *ratify* is less adequate than the other alternatives, "bring to pass" and "accomplish."

5. Bauer, *Lexicon*, 672.

6. Bahnsen, *Theonomy*, 67–70.

7. Readers desiring further guidance on issues of meaning should consult the excellent works of Moisés Silva, *Biblical Words and Their Meaning: An Introduction to Lexical Semantics* (Grand Rapids: Zondervan, 1983); and Peter Cotterell and Max Turner,

Linguistics and Biblical Interpretation (Downers Grove, IL: InterVarsity, 1989), 106–187.

8. *Roget's International Thesaurus*, 3d ed. (New York: Crowell, 1962). Further references to "confirm" and "fulfill" occur under other headings, but nowhere do they ever come under the same general category, let alone subcategory. Thus, despite the relation of implication between the two words, the differences between them are still wide. A claim that the two are synonymous or that "confirm" is one sense of "fulfill" is patently false.

9. Cf. the more complex analysis in Johannes P. Louw and Eugene A. Nida, et al., eds., *Greek-English Lexicon of the New Testament Based on Semantic Domains*, 2 vols. (New York: United Bible Societies, 1988). As in English, so in Greek *plēroō* and *bebaioō* are regarded as belonging under different general categories rather than as belonging to a common semantic domain. *plēroō* is listed primarily under the general categories "59. Quantity" and "13. Be, Become, Exist, Happen" (the sense "fulfill"). *bebaioō* is listed under the categories "28. Know" and "31. Hold a View, Believe, Trust." The verb *plēroō* has to do with arrival at wholeness, while *bebaioō* deals with the noetic sphere. These two are surely not the same, though arrival at wholeness may in many cases have noetic implications.

10. For a more thorough discussion see Silva, *Biblical Words*, 53–73.

11. The main exception is in some specialized uses of the word *ml'*, such as "satisfy," "take a handful of," "grasp," etc. The specialized uses are listed in Francis Brown, S. R. Driver, and Charles A. Briggs, *A Hebrew and English Lexicon of the Old Testament* (Oxford: Oxford University Press, 1907), 570, *pi'el* meaning #2.

12. Brown, Driver, and Briggs, *Lexicon*, 570; Ludwig Koehler and Walter Baumgartner, *Lexicon in veteris testamenti libros* (Leiden: Brill, 1953).

13. One should also take note of the fresh analysis of *plēroō* in Louw and Nida, *Greek-English Lexicon*, 2:199. Seven distinct senses are listed, namely, "fill," "make complete," "finish," "provide fully," "proclaim completely," "give true meaning," and "cause to happen." The first three correspond well with Bauer's meanings, but let us consider the other four more closely.

"Provide fully" is the meaning assigned to Philippians 4:18, "I have been fully provided for." Perhaps this instance deserves a separate listing, though it may be only a metaphorical extension of the meaning "fill full." In any case, the idea of filling a need is present, which means that this meaning is still closely related to the meaning "fill."

"Proclaim completely" is the meaning assigned to Romans 15:19 and probably Colossians 1:25. As our discussion below will show, these passages are almost certainly an extension of the sense "complete (a purpose)," and hence are closely related to Bauer's meaning #3.

"Give true meaning" is assigned to Galatians 5:14 and Matthew 5:17. Perhaps these instances do indeed deserve to be classified separately. But if we translate "give full expression," the relation of this use to Bauer's meaning #3 is clear.

For "cause to happen," the alternate gloss "fulfill" is provided, showing that this sense is virtually identical with Bauer's meaning #4.

14. Note the treatment of these terms in *Roget's Thesaurus* and of *plēroō* and *bebaioō* in Louw, *Greek-English Lexicon*.

15. *kai idou eti lalousēs sou ekei meta tou basileōs kai egō eiseleusomai opisō sou kai plērōsō tous logous sou.*

16. Otto Eissfeldt, *The Old Testament: An Introduction* (New York: Harper and Row, 1965), 578; Jonathan A. Goldstein, *1 Maccabees*, The Anchor Bible, vol. 41 (Garden City, NY: Doubleday, 1976), 14.

17. 1 Maccabees 2:55 in Greek reads, *Iēsous en tōi plērōsai logon egeneto kritēs en Israēl.*

18. Bahnsen, *Theonomy*, 68.

19. *all hoi men eugenōs apothanontes eplērōsan tēn eis ton theon eusebeian.*

20. Moses Hadas, ed. and trans., *The Third and Fourth Books of Maccabees* (New York: Harper and Row, 1953), 209, confirms my view with the translation, "They, indeed, have died nobly, and so fulfilled their piety to God."

21. *zēi kurios kai zēi hē psychē mou, hoti, kathōs eipon, empeplēstai ana meson mou kai tou thanatou.* There is some textual variation, but it is does not affect the point at issue.

22. *cheires autou toreutai chrysai peplērōmenai tharsis.*

23. Brown, Driver, and Briggs, *Lexicon*, 570; Koehler and Baumgartner, *Lexicon*, 524.

24. Bahnsen, *Theonomy*, 68.

25. Brown, Driver, and Briggs, *Lexicon*, 570.

26. Bahnsen, *Theonomy*, 68.

27. 1 Kings 2:27; 8:15, 24; 2 Chronicles 6:4, 15; 36:21–22; Matthew 1:22; 2:15, 17, 23; 8:17; 12:17; 13:35; 21:4; 26:54, 56; 27:9; Mark 14:49; 15:28; Luke 1:20; 4:21; 24:44; John 12:38; 13:18; 15:25; 17:12; 18:9, 32; 19:24, 36; Acts 1:16; 3:18; 13:27.

28. *kai eplērōthē hē graphē hē legousa, Episteusen de Abraam tōi theōi, kai elogisthē autōi eis dikaiosunēn.*

29. Bauer, *Lexicon*, 671.

30. See also Douglas J. Moo, *The Letter of James* (Grand Rapids: Eerdmans, 1985), 133:

> It [*plēroō*] is used to designate the 'filling up' or 'culmination' of the Old Testament through the advent of Jesus. This can take the form of a 'fulfilment' of a prophecy, the bringing out of the ultimate significance of a historical event (Matthew 2:15) or the climactic interpretation and application of the Old Testament law (Matthew 5:17). There is no need, then, to think that James views Genesis 15:6 as a prophecy that was 'fulfilled' later in Abraham's career. What he is suggesting, rather, is that this verse found its ultimate significance and meaning in Abraham's life of obedience.

31. *kai en hetoimōi echontes ekdikēsai pasan parakoēn, hotan plērōthēi hymōn hē hypakoē.*

32. Bauer, *Lexicon*, 671.

33. Bahnsen, *Theonomy*, 69.

34. *ou gar heurēka sou ta erga peplērōmena enōpion tou theou mou.*

35. Bauer, *Lexicon*, 671.

36. *hōste me apo Ierousalēm kai kyklō mechri tou Illyrikou peplērōkenai to euaggelion tou Christou.*

37. Bauer, *Lexicon*, 671.

38. John Murray, *The Epistle to the Romans*, Thε New International Commentary on the New Testament, 2 vols. (Grand Rapids Eerdmans, 1959, 1965), 2:214.

39. C. E. B. Cranfield, *A Critical and Exegetiᵃl Commentary on the Epistle to the Romans*, 2 vols. (Edinburgh: T. and T. Clark, 1ᶜ 75, 1979), 2:762.

40. *plērōsai ton logon tou theou.*

41. Bauer, *Lexicon*, 671.

BIBLIOGRAPHY

orks representing some form of the Christian Reconstruction
W movement are labeled "Reconstruction." Other works are listed
here because I cited them and not necessarily because I approve of or
recommend them in every respect. Readers who desire to understand
the law better will find much help from Gordon Wenham, *Leviticus*;
Geerhardus Vos, *Biblical Theology*, chapter 8 ("Revelation in the Period
of Moses"); Meredith G. Kline, Images of the Spirit; and Walter Kaiser,
Toward Old Testament Ethics. The older work of Patrick Fairbairn, *The
Typology of Scripture*, while not in harmony in every respect with my
own point of view, still contains much useful and valuable instruction.

Adams, Jay. *Marriage, Divorce and Remarriage*. Phillipsburg, NJ: Presbyterian
    and Reformed, 1980.

Bahnsen, Greg L. *By This Standard: The Authority of God's Law Today*. Tyler,
    TX.: Institute for Christian Economics, 1985. Reconstruction.

————. "M. G. Kline on Theonomic Politics: An Evaluation of His Reply."
    The Journal of Christian Reconstruction 6 no. 2 (1979–80):195–221. Recon-
    struction.

————. *Theonomy in Christian Ethics*. Expanded edition. Phillipsburg, NJ: Pres-
    byterian and Reformed, 1984. Reconstruction.

Barker, William S., and Robert W. Godfrey, eds. *Theonomy: A Reformed Cri-
    tique*. Grand Rapids: Zondervan, 1990.

Barth, Gerhard. "Matthew's Understanding of the Law." In *Tradition and Inter-
    pretation in Matthew*, edited by Günther Bornkamm, Gerhard Barth, and
    Heinz Joachim Held, 58–64. Philadelphia: Westminster, 1963.

Bauer, Walter. A Greek-English Lexicon of the New Testament and Other Early Christian Literature. 2d ed. Translated by William F. Arndt, F. Wilbur Gingrich, and Frederick W. Danker. Chicago: University of Chicago Press, 1979.

Brown, Francis, S. R. Driver, and Charles A. Briggs. A Hebrew and English Lexicon of the Old Testament. Oxford: Oxford University Press, 1907.

Burgess, Edward Earl. Christ, the Crown of the Torah. Grand Rapids: Zondervan, 1986.

Calvin, John. Commentary on a Harmony of the Evangelists, Matthew, Mark, and Luke. 3 vols. Reprint. Grand Rapids: Eerdmans, n.d.

————. Institutes of the Christian Religion. Reprint. Grand Rapids: Eerdmans, 1970.

Carson, Donald A. "Matthew." In The Expositor's Bible Commentary, edited by Frank E. Gaebelein, vol. 8, 1–600. Grand Rapids: Zondervan, 1984.

Clowney, Edmund P. Preaching and Biblical Theology. Grand Rapids: Eerdmans, 1961.

————. The Unfolding Mystery: Discovering Christ in the Old Testament. Colorado Springs, CO: NavPress, 1988.

Cranfield, C. E. B. A Critical and Exegetical Commentary on the Epistle to the Romans. The International Critical Commentary. 2 vols. Edinburgh: T. and T. Clark, 1975.

Dalman, Gustaf. Jesus-Jeshua: Studies in the Gospels. New York: Macmillan, 1929.

Daube, David. Studies in Biblical Law. New York: Ktav, 1969.

de Vaux, Roland. Ancient Israel. 2 vols. New York: McGraw-Hill, 1965.

Douglas, Mary. Purity and Danger: An Analysis of Concepts of Pollution and Taboo. London: Routledge and Kegan Paul, 1978.

Durham, John I. Exodus. Word Biblical Commentary, vol. 3. Waco, TX.: Word, 1987.

Eissfeldt, Otto. The Old Testament: An Introduction. New York: Harper and Row, 1965.

Fairbairn, Patrick. The Typology of Scripture. 2 vols. Reprint. Grand Rapids: Baker, 1975.

Fensham, F. Charles. The Books of Ezra and Nehemiah. The New International Commentary on the Old Testament. Grand Rapids: Eerdmans, 1982.

Frame, John M. "The Doctrine of the Christian Life." Westminster Theological Seminary, Philadelphia, 1979. Mimeographed.

———. *The Doctrine of the Knowledge of God.* Phillipsburg, NJ: Presbyterian and Reformed, 1987.

———. "Toward a Theology of the State." *Westminster Theological Journal* 51 (1989):199–226.

France, Richard T. *The Gospel According to Matthew.* Tyndale New Testament Commentaries. Grand Rapids: Eerdmans, 1985.

Gaffin, Richard B., Jr. *The Centrality of the Resurrection: A Study in Paul's Soteriology.* Grand Rapids: Baker, 1978.

Goldstein, Jonathan A. *1 Maccabees.* The Anchor Bible, vol. 41. Garden City, NY: Doubleday, 1976.

Hadas, Moses, ed. and trans. *The Third and Fourth Books of Maccabees.* New York: Harper and Row, 1953.

Haran, Menahem Haran. *Temples and Temple-Service in Ancient Israel: An Inquiry into the Character of Cult Phenomena and the Historical Setting of the Priestly School.* Oxford: Oxford University Press, 1978.

Hill, David. *The Gospel of Matthew.* New Century Bible. Greenwood, SC: Attic Press, 1972.

Hillers, Delbert R. *Covenant: The History of a Biblical Idea.* Baltimore: Johns Hopkins, 1969.

Jordan, James B. *The Law of the Covenant.* Tyler, TX: Institute for Christian Economics, 1984. Nonstandard Reconstruction.

———. "Reconsidering the Mosaic Law: Some Reflections—1988." Biblical Horizons Occasional Paper No. 4, Tyler, TX

———. *Sabbath Breaking and the Death Penalty: A Theological Investigation.* Tyler, TX: Geneva Ministries, 1986. Nonstandard Reconstruction.

———. "Slavery in Biblical Perspective." Th.M. thesis, Westminster Theological Seminary, 1980. Reconstruction.

———. *The Sociology of the Church: Essays in Reconstruction.* Tyler, TX: Geneva Ministries, 1986. Nonstandard Reconstruction.

Kaiser, Walter C., Jr. *Toward Old Testament Ethics.* Grand Rapids: Zondervan, 1983.

Kautzsch, Emil, ed. *Genesius' Hebrew Grammar.* 2d English edition. Translated by A. E. Cowley. Oxford: Oxford University Press, 1910.

Kline, Meredith G. *By Oath Consigned: A Reinterpretation of the Covenant Signs of Circumcision and Baptism.* Grand Rapids: Eerdmans, 1968.

―――. "Comments on an Old-New Error." *Westminster Theological Journal* 41 (1978–79):172–89.

―――. "Double Trouble." *Journal of the Evangelical Theological Society* 32 (1989), 171–79.

―――. *Images of the Spirit.* Grand Rapids: Baker, 1980.

―――. *The Structure of Biblical Authority.* Grand Rapids: Eerdmans, 1972.

―――. *Treaty of the Great King: The Covenant Structure of Deuteronomy.* Grand Rapids: Eerdmans, 1963.

Koehler, Ludwig, and Walter Baumgartner. *Lexicon in veteris testamenti libros.* Leiden: Brill, 1953.

Korosec, Viktor. *Hethitische Staatsverträge: Ein Beitrag zu ihrer juristischen Wertung.* Leipzig: Theodor Weicher, 1931.

Lampe, G. W. H. *A Patristic Greek Lexicon.* Oxford: Oxford University Press, 1961.

Lewis, C. S. "The Humanitarian Theory of Punishment." Qouted in *God in the Dock: Essays on Theology and Ethics,* edited by Walter Hooper, 287–300. Grand Rapids: Eerdmans, 1970.

Liddell, Henry G., and Robert Scott. *A Greek-English Lexicon.* Rev. ed. Oxford: Oxford University Press, 1968.

Louw, Johannes P., and Eugene A. Nida, eds. *Greek-English Lexicon of the New Testament Based on Semantic Domains.* 2 vols. New York: United Bible Societies, 1988.

McCarthy, Dennis J. *Old Testament Covenant: A Survey of Current Opinions.* Oxford: Blackwell, 1972.

―――. *Treaty and Covenant: A Study in the Ancient Oriental Documents and in the Old Testament.* Rome: Pontifical Biblical Institute, 1963.

Mendenhall, George E. *Law and Covenant in Israel and the Ancient Near East.* Pittsburgh: Biblical Colloquium, 1955.

Milgrom, Jacob. *Cult and Conscience: The Asham and the Priestly Doctrine of Repentance.* Leiden: Brill, 1976.

―――. *Studies in Levitical Terminology, I: The Encroacher and the Levite: The Term 'Aboda.* Berkeley: University of California Press, 1970.

Moo, Douglas J. "Jesus and the Authority of the Mosaic Law." *Journal for the Study of the New Testament* 20 (1984):14–49.

————. *The Letter of James*. Grand Rapids: Eerdmans, 1985.

Moulton, James H., and George Milligan. *The Vocabulary of the Greek Testament Illustrated from the Papyri and Other Non-Literary Sources*. Grand Rapids: Eerdmans, 1930.

Murray, John. *Divorce*. Philadelphia: Presbyterian and Reformed, 1961.

————. *The Epistle to the Romans*. New International Commentary on the New Testament. 2 vols. Grand Rapids: Eerdmans, 1959.

————. *Principles of Conduct*. Grand Rapids: Eerdmans, 1957.

Nöldeke, Theodor. *Compendious Syriac Grammar*. London: Williams and Norgate, 1904.

North, Gary. *Backward, Christian Soldiers? An Action Manual for Christian Reconstruction*. Tyler, TX: Institute for Christian Economics, 1984. Reconstruction.

————. *Dominion and Common Grace: The Biblical Basis of Progress*. Tyler, TX: Institute for Christian Economics, 1987. Reconstruction.

————. *The Dominion Covenant: Genesis*. 2d ed. Tyler, TX: Institute for Christian Economics, 1987. Reconstruction.

————. *An Introduction to Christian Economics*. Nutley, NJ: Craig, 1973. Reconstruction.

————. *Tools of Dominion: The Case Laws of Exodus*. Tyler, TX: Institute for Christian Economics, 1990. Reconstruction.

————. *Unconditional Surrender: God's Program for Victory*. Tyler, TX: Geneva Press, 1981. Reconstruction.

Oss, Douglas A. "The Influence of Hermeneutical Frameworks in the Theonomy Debate." *Westminster Theological Journal* 51 (1989):227–58.

Phillips, Anthony. *Ancient Israel's Criminal Law: A New Approach to the Decalogue*. Oxford: Blackwell, 1970.

Poythress, Vern S. "Divine Meaning of Scripture." *Westminster Theological Journal* 48 (1986):241–79.

————. "God's Lordship in Interpretation." *Westminster Theological Journal* 50 (1988):27–64.

————. *Science and Hermeneutics: Implications of Scientific Method for Biblical Interpretation*. Grand Rapids: Zondervan, 1988.

————. *Symphonic Theology: The Validity of Multiple Perspectives in Theology*. Grand Rapids: Zondervan, 1987.

Pritchard, James B., ed. *Ancient Near Eastern Texts Relating to the Old Testament*. Princeton, NJ: Princeton University Press, 1950.

Ridderbos, Herman. *The Coming of the Kingdom*. Philadelphia: Presbyterian and Reformed, 1969.

Rushdoony, Rousas J. *The Institutes of Biblical Law*. Nutley, NJ: Craig, 1973. Reconstruction.

————. *Law and Society: Volume II of the Institutes of Biblical Law*. Vallecito, CA: Ross House, 1982. Reconstruction.

————. *Politics of Guilt and Pity*. Nutley, NJ: Craig, 1970. Reconstruction.

————. *This Independent Republic: Studies in the Nature and Meaning of American History*. Nutley, NJ: Craig, 1964. Reconstruction.

Schluter, Michael, and Roy Clements. *Reactivating the Extended Family*. Cambridge, England: Jubilee Center Publications, 1986.

————. "Jubilee Institutional Norms: A Middle Way between Creation Ethics and Kingdom Ethics as the Basis for Christian Political Action." *Evangelical Quarterly* 62 (1990):48–50.

Shearer, John B. *Hebrew Institutions, Social and Civil*. Richmond: Presbyterian Committee of Publication, 1910.

Silva, Moisés. *Biblical Words and Their Meaning: An Introduction to Lexical Semantics*. Grand Rapids: Zondervan, 1983.

Smith, Gary Scott, ed. *God and Politics: Four Views on the Reformation of Civil Government: Theonomy, Principled Pluralism, Christian America, National Confessionalism*. Phillipsburg, NJ: Presbyterian and Reformed, 1989.

Stott, John R. W., and Nicholas Miller, eds. *Crime and the Responsible Community*. Grand Rapids: Eerdmans, 1980.

Strack, Hermann L., and Paul Billerbeck. *Kommentar zum Neuen Testament aus Talmud und Midrasch*. München: C. H. Beck, 1922–28.

Sutton, Ray R. "A Redemptive Historical View of Theonomy." Parts 1, 2. *The Geneva Review* 29 (June 1986): 6–7; 30 (July 1986): 6–7.

————. *That You May Prosper: Dominion by Covenant*. Tyler, TX: Institute for Christian Economics, 1987. Reconstruction.

Thayer, Joseph H. *A Greek-English Lexicon of the New Testament*. New York/Cincinnati/Chicago: American Book Company, 1886.

Van Ness, Daniel W. *Crime and Its Victims*. Downers Grove, IL: InterVarsity, 1986.

Vos, Geerhardus. *Biblical Theology: Old and New Testaments.* Grand Rapids: Eerdmans, 1948.

————. *The Teaching of Jesus Concerning the Kingdom of God and the Church.* Reprint. Nutley, NJ: Presbyterian and Reformed, 1972.

Weinfeld, M. "The Covenant of Grant in the Old Testament and in the Ancient Near East." *Journal of the American Oriental Society* 90 (1970): 184–203.

Wenham, Gordon J. *The Book of Leviticus.* The New International Commentary on the Old Testament, vol. 3. Grand Rapids: Eerdmans, 1979.

————. "Law and the Legal System in the Old Testament." In *Law, Morality, and the Bible,* edited by Bruce Kaye and Gordon Wenham, 24–52. Downers Grove, IL: InterVarsity, 1978.

Wright, Christopher J. H. *An Eye for an Eye: The Place of Old Testament Ethics Today.* Downers Grove, IL: InterVarsity, 1983.

SUBJECT INDEX

SCRIPTURE INDEX

The typeface for the text of this book is *Goudy Old Style*. Its creator, Frederic W. Goudy, was commissioned by American Type Founders Company to design a new Roman type face. Completed in 1915 and named Goudy Old Style, it was an instant bestseller. However, its designer had sold the design outright to the foundry, so when it became evident that additional versions would be needed to complete the family, the work was done by the foundry's own designer, Morris Benton. From the original design came seven additional weights and variants, all of which sold in great quantity. However, Goudy himself received no additional compensation for them. He later recounted a visit to the foundry with a group of printers, during which the guide stopped at one of the busy casting machines and stated, "Here's where Goudy goes down to posterity, while American Type Founders Company goes down to prosperity."